THE HISTORY OF ANTHROPOLOGY

Critical Studies in the History of Anthropology

SERIES EDITORS

Regna Darnell
Robert Oppenheim

THE HISTORY OF ANTHROPOLOGY

A Critical Window on the Discipline in North America

REGNA DARNELL

University of Nebraska Press
LINCOLN

Acknowledgments for the use of previously published or
copyrighted material appear in each chapter's notes, which
constitute an extension of the copyright page.

Publication of this work was assisted by the Murray-Hong
Family Trust, to honor and sustain the distinguished legacy
of Stephen O. Murray in the History of Anthropology at the
University of Nebraska Press.

Library of Congress Cataloging-in-Publication Data
Names: Darnell, Regna, author.
Title: The history of anthropology: a critical window on the
discipline in North America / Regna Darnell.
Description: Lincoln: University of Nebraska Press, 2021. |
Series: Critical studies in the history of anthropology |
Includes bibliographical references and index.
Identifiers: LCCN 2021015793
ISBN 9781496224170 (hardback)
ISBN 9781496228147 (paperback)
ISBN 9781496228734 (epub)
ISBN 9781496228741 (pdf)
Subjects: LCSH: Anthropology—North America—History. |
Indians of North America—Research—History. | BISAC:
SOCIAL SCIENCE / Anthropology / Cultural & Social |
SOCIAL SCIENCE / Anthropology / Physical
Classification: LCC GN17.3.N7 D369 2021 |
DDC 301.097—dc23
LC record available at https://lccn.loc.gov/2021015793

Set in New Baskerville ITC Pro by Mikala R. Kolander

CONTENTS

ILLUSTRATIONS

TABLES

ACKNOWLEDGMENTS

Chapter 1

Although the surface content of this chapter introduces a reprint edition of my biography of Edward Sapir twenty years after its original publication, it also stands as a theoretical summary of what I mean by the history of anthropology and how I propose to study it. All acknowledgments of twenty years ago remain in force, but many more are now due. The University of Nebraska Press, under the leadership of Matt Bokovoy and his predecessor, Gary Dunham, has developed a unique list that encompasses "American Indian" ethnology and linguistics, Native American writing, the history of anthropology, and reprints of classic works in these fields. The late Stephen O. Murray, my coeditor in the Critical Studies in History of Anthropology series, and Frederic W. Gleach, my coeditor in Histories of Anthropology Annual, remain co-conspirators in these and other enterprises. I worked closely with Judith T. Irvine in editing the culture and ethnology volumes of Sapir's collected works, and we shared complementary insights from our very different sites of practice. As chairs of the centennial commission of the American Anthropological Association, Fred and I worked with the University of Nebraska Press on multiple publications (Darnell and Gleach 2002a, 2002b; see also Darnell 2002). The American Philosophical Society (APS) has long been my intellectual home away from home. I thank particularly Martin Levitt, Anthony F. C. Wallace, Eleanor Roach, and Linda Musumeci. I also acknowledge Michael Asch, Tim Bisha, Robert L. A. Hancock, Marc Pinkoski and the rest of the Crabgrass Collective, Jane Hill, H. C. Wolfart, Andrew and Harriet Lyons.

Chapter 2

This chapter reproduces a paper read at the Sociology Session of the World Congress of Sociology in Varna, Bulgaria, in September 1970. The paper was summarized from a more detailed discussion in my dissertation and draws on other documents cited there (Darnell 1969). To my knowledge, this was the first doctorate granted within a North American department of anthropology for work in history of cultural anthropology. I am grateful to Dell Hymes, A. Irving Hallowell, and George W. Stocking Jr. for their long-standing aid and encouragement. A number of revisions were suggested by Kurt Wolfe, who invited me to present in this session.

Chapter 3

This chapter draws on my dissertation (Darnell 1969) and Darnell 1971 (chapter 2, this volume). Dan Ben-Amos encouraged me to pursue the history of anthropology into the history of folklore and commented on earlier drafts. The University of Pennsylvania during my graduate studies from 1965 to 1969 was a disciplinary melding pot, a seething cauldron of ideas in which some faculty from anthropology (Dell Hymes, J. David Sapir), folklore (Dan Ben-Amos, Ken Goldstein), linguistics (Bill Labov), American studies (Charles Rosenberg), sociology (Erving Goffman), and the Annenberg School of Communication (Sol Worth) came together with graduate students regularly to share ideas. The Center for Urban Ethnography (John Swzed) was established after I left, though I remained in contact; by that time Hymes had moved first to folklore then to the Graduate School of Education as its dean, giving a public dimension to pedagogy within the academy. I took or audited courses with many of these adventurous faculty and am grateful for the freedom Penn granted to graduate students to take courses that fit their interests across the university. Anthony F. C. Wallace and Ward Goodenough in anthropology shared much of this meaning-based perspective, but their interdisciplinary ties were forged in other directions, and what I learned from them lacked the synergy of interactive discourse.

Chapter 4

A preliminary version of this chapter was presented in a session organized by George W. Stocking Jr. on "Continuity and Change in American Anthropology, 1880–1920" at the American Anthropological Association Meetings in New Orleans in November 1968 when I was job hunting. I express my appreciation to Dell Hymes, George W. Stocking Jr., and John Witthoft in the course of its preparation. The chapter draws on material from my MA thesis on Daniel Garrison Brinton (Darnell 1967, published much later as Darnell 1988) and my PhD dissertation then in progress (Darnell 1969, also published much later as Darnell 1998). The chapter included here deals exclusively with Brinton's institutional role in the history of anthropology; more problematic areas of the tension between the evolutionary perspective of his scientific racism and the psychic unity of mankind (somewhat more palatable to contemporary tastes) are treated in Darnell (1967) and Lee D. Baker (2010).

Chapter 5

This paper was read at a COPAR (Council for the Preservation of Anthropological Records) conference hosted by Don Fowler at the University of Nevada, Reno. I was delighted that mine was among the papers selected for the second edition of this volume with its incumbent invitation to contest the idea of many participants that preservation of anthropological documents is exclusively about the fieldnotes ["fieldnotes" as opposed to "field notes" is now consistent throughout unless in quotes, as in title of article by Rainier Hatoum] that provide verisimilitude alongside their published reports. I am grateful to Sydel Silverman for sponsoring the initial initiative through the Wenner-Gren Foundation for Anthropological Research, and to Nancy Parezo and Don Fowler for their unflagging energy in maintaining the COPAR momentum over many years, for their friendship, and for their myriad contributions to the history of anthropology alongside linguistic, museological, and archaeological specializations that entailed historical contextualization.

Chapter 6

This chapter is based on a paper read to the annual meeting of the American Philosophical Society in Philadelphia in April 2013. Due to the long delay in publication, I have updated some references but for the most part left the description of the *Franz Boas Papers: Documentary Edition* as it appeared at that time. As is inevitable in a research project that spans a decade, there have been changes in the personnel and scope of particular volumes. The structure of the project, however, remains intact. None of this would have been possible without the generous support of the Social Sciences and Humanities Research Council of Canada Partnership Grant #895-2012-1001. In addition to acknowledgments of APS support cited in the text, I thank Ann Westcott, Linda Musumeci, Charles Griefenstein, Adriana Link, Pat McPherson, M. Sam Cronk, and the late Michael Silverstein.

Chapter 7

I am grateful to Jill Cherneff and Eve Hochwald for the invitation to participate in this project to assess the role anthropology has played in the emergence of an activist pedagogy. It forced me out of my comfort zone in the documents on Boas's work within anthropology and its history. In order to meet the educational focus of their volume, I relied more than usual on secondary sources that turned out to provide a lens for examining how our predecessors come down to us through the standpoints of their various historians and how important it is as a consequence that there be multiple historians. I realized that I knew more than I thought I did about Boas as educator and activist on a broader stage; this portion of his career has received less attention, perhaps because it evades closure in the tendrils of its spread across disciplines and publics. Histories of anthropology written by anthropologists, including my own early career work, have not ventured far beyond the familiar territory of my home discipline. I would change very little despite additional detail from more recent work by myself and others (Darnell 2015, 2017).

Chapter 8

I draw here on material from my biography of Sapir (Darnell 1990). I thank Michael Foster, Dell Hymes, Konrad Koerner, and the late

Stephen O. Murray for comments on an earlier draft. I initially referred to a Boasian text tradition, but as I began to generalize the paradigmatic status of this tradition beyond its personal formulation by Franz Boas, I came to appreciate the solidarity, intense interaction, and collective achievement of the group that coalesced around him. Accordingly, I prefer the label "Americanist" text tradition and use it in later writing (see chapter 9, this volume). With rare exceptions, I have retained the "American Indian" usage rather than "Native American" because it is pervasive in the linguistic literature (see also chapter 10, this volume).

Chapter 9

This chapter was presented as the final substantive paper at the Edward Sapir Centenary Conference in Ottawa in 1984 during preparation of my biography (Darnell 1990). I have updated some references and elaborated context unfamiliar to Canadian readers. I have consulted the personal papers of Sapir, Diamond Jenness, Marius Barbeau, Thomas F. McIlwraith, Clyde Kluckhohn, Benjamin Lee Whorf, Ruth Benedict, Margaret Mead, John Alden Mason, Frank Speck, Franz Boas, Robert H. Lowie, Alfred L. Kroeber, Fay-Cooper Cole, Robert Redfield, and Berthold Laufer. Sapir's five children—Michael, Helen (Larson), Philip, Paul, and David—shared personal recollections and retrospective evaluations. My interaction with them was extensive during the years Judith T. Irvine and I worked on the Sapir Collected Works project with Mouton de Gruyter. I draw on discussions with Annette McFadyen Clark, Helen Codere, Fred Eggan, William Fenton, Raymond D. Fogelson, Michael Foster, John Fought, Catherine and Don Fowler, David French, Ives Goddard, Mary Haas, A. Irving Hallowell, Dell Hymes, Judith T. Irvine, Luis Kemnitzer, Theodora Kroeber, Michael Krauss, Frederica de Laguna, Stanley S. Newman, Cornelius Osgood, Joel Sherzer, Michael Silverstein, William Sturtevant, Elisabeth Tooker, and Anthony F. C. Wallace. The following shared research material and insights: Robert Allen, William Cowan, Richard Handler, Wendy Leeds-Hurwitz, Konrad Koerner, Judith Modell, Stephen O. Murray, James M. Nyce, Richard Preston, Mary Sacharoff, and George W. Stocking Jr. [A number of these individuals are now deceased so I have not added "the late" for Murray in this chapter; his death is much more recent and he appears here as my partner in sponsoring this series and at the time the paper was written.] Support was provided by the General Research Fund of the University of Alberta, the Phillips Fund of the American Philosophical Society, and a sabbatical fellowship from the Social Sciences and Humanities Research Council of Canada. I gratefully acknowledge all of the above, although responsibility for the resulting interpretation remains my own.

Chapter 10

This chapter begins with a leisurely description of its provenience in terms of how my personal experience situated me to ask particular historical questions and cultivate the social networks that provide occasions to explore disciplinary intersections and share the results with larger audiences in published form. The ideas of an author do not arise full-blown in a vacuum, and reflexivity is a crucial method of the intellectual historian. I explore here how Sapir's insistence on open-ended problems rather than tidily packaged conclusions, and his presentation of unassailable sound correspondences alongside suggestive ones, negatively impacted the credibility of his reconstructions among linguists. I will admit to a certain mischievousness in disrupting the tidy interpretation of the relationships of Edward Sapir, Leonard Bloomfield, and Franz Boas for an expected audience heavily weighted toward such a position because of its close association with Konrad's tenacious and wide-ranging editorial scope at John Benjamins. I am grateful to the editors for the opportunity to honor Konrad.

Chapter 11

I was invited by the editors Barbara and Dennis Tedlock, fellow travelers in our sense of what the discipline should be doing, to submit this chapter to the flagship *American Anthropologist* where it drew an audience across subdisciplines and reinforced my sense that such intersections are still important to many of my disciplinary colleagues. Now, as at the time of writing, I am grateful especially to the late Harold Conklin, whose interest in the persistence of Sapirian anthropology at Yale encouraged me to pursue the story beyond Sapir's lifetime. The biography (Darnell 1990) was too long, and considerable material had to be omitted, some of which is incorporated here. The Yale Department of Anthropology offered its hospitality during a visiting professorship in 1985 that enabled me to examine documents and come to know the institutional culture at more leisure than is usually provided by archival forays. I drew on interviews and conversations with Bingham Dai, Leonard Doob, Fred Eggan, William Fenton, Mary Haas, Charles Hockett, G. Evelyn Hutchinson, Weston La Barre, Stanley Newman, Floyd Lounsbury, Cornelius Osgood, Kenneth Pike, David Mandelbaum, Irving Rouse, Edgar Siskin, and Carl Voegelin, all now deceased. None are responsible for my readings of their words or of the documents. I draw on my collaboration with Judith T. Irvine on two volumes of Sapir collected works (Darnell and Irvine 1994; Darnell, Irvine, and Handler, 1999) on her masterful editing of multiple students' lecture notes from Sapir's psychology of culture course in each year it was given (Irvine 1994) and on Darnell 1990 [2010]. Raymond DeMallie, Dell Hymes, Stephen O. Murray, Douglas Parks, and Barbara and Dennis Tedlock sustained my conviction that Americanist anthropology as Sapir conceived it would continue alive and well into the twenty-first century.

Chapter 12

When I was invited to deliver the *JAR* (*Journal of Anthropological Research*) lecture on which chapter 12 is based, I chose to speak about the importance of the intersection of Ruth Benedict's southwestern fieldwork and gender research for the history of anthropology as topics relevant to the location of *JAR* at the University of New Mexico Department of Anthropology and to students and colleagues there. I thank Lawrence Strauss and Ann Braswell for organizing my visit and Char Peery and Sean Bruna for technical support. Louise Lamphere, David Dinwoodie, and Suzanne Oakdale provided feedback and hospitality. Special thanks to Xiomara Perez-Betances, academic departmental adviser, and Marilyn Astwood, student academic administrator, Department of Anthropology, Columbia University, for their assistance in obtaining the photograph. The chapter focuses less on primary documents than on subsequent debates over their interpretation. Benedict appeared frequently in my writing about both Sapir and Boas, but this invitation allowed me to approach Benedict's world from her standpoint and to problematize how her legacy has come to us via Margaret Mead.

Chapter 13

I am grateful to Christine Jourdan and Kevin Tuite for the invitation to participate in a review of the state of the ethnolinguistic art. Chapter 13 had its genesis at a meeting of the Canadian Anthropology Society where I contested Roger Keesing's view of Whorf's legacy; Roger's sudden death on that very occasion precluded further debate that might have produced common ground between our positions. I have been interested in Whorf from a number of standpoints (Darnell 1974, 1990, 1998a, 1998b, 2001). My thinking about his career and place in Americanist anthropology owes much to Ray DeMallie, Peter Denny, Ray Fogelson, Dell Hymes, John Joseph, Konrad Koerner, Stephen Leavitt, Penny Lee, Stephen O. Murray, Doug Parks, Jay Powell, and Samar Zebian.

Chapter 14

My reflections on Mary Haas's role in the first Yale school of linguistics owe much to Steve Murray's interview with her in 1976 (published as Murray 1997), which was invaluable in supplementing my own conversations with her, especially at the Sapir Centenary Conference in Ottawa in 1984 (Darnell 1986, see chapter 9, this volume) and in the preparation of my biography then in progress (Darnell 1990). I also thank Dell Hymes. The Yale departmental archives, during my visiting semester there in 1985, were stuffed in a box on a bottom shelf in the office of a faculty member who casually suggested in the course of conversation about something else that I might find something interesting in them. Disciplinary history was not a departmental priority. I am grateful to all of the above. These materials have since been deposited in the Yale University archives.

Chapter 15

The discussion in this chapter draws from my Sapir biography then in press (Darnell 1990). To my regret, I never met Stanley Newman, although we exchanged extensive correspondence. Our plan to meet at an upcoming conference was derailed by his death the preceding summer. I came to appreciate both his personal kindness and the scope of his intellect. More than any other Sapir student, he appreciated the irrelevance of disciplinary boundaries, in his own thinking and in Sapir's. This chapter pays tribute to him. I have profited from discussions of Newman's language psychology work with Judith T. Irvine, Stephen O. Murray, James M. Nyce, Robert Allen, Richard Preston, Philip Sapir, and Michael Silverstein. Murray (1986, chapter 9, this volume) is the best discussion of this work in relation to Chicago sociology. None of these colleagues are responsible for my interpretations.

Chapter 16

This chapter began as a paper in a memorial session for A. Irving "Pete" Hallowell at the American Anthropological Association meetings, only a year after his death in 1974; it was hard to write, and the first draft was handwritten on the plane en route to the conference. I have learned that deadlines produce miracles because they eliminate writer's block. Pete was a teacher, mentor, and friend from my final undergraduate year through my difficult transition from a small liberal arts college to the more regimented and impersonal graduate program at Penn where he retained an emeritus office, and we stayed in close regular touch to the end of his life. He wrote both about disciplinary history and his own experience of the discipline but did not attempt to integrate the academic and the personal voice (and that is another story). My thanks go to Dennison Nash, Ray Fogelson, and especially Maude F. Hallowell for their aid in preparation and revision for publication. I reflect here on the continuity of a scholar's oeuvre despite old preoccupations seemingly left behind. For Hallowell, as for the fledgling discipline, the trait distribution studies that seem so arid in a contemporary perspective set a baseline in their own era for getting at what Boas called "the native point of view."

Chapter 17

The Canadian Association of Physical Anthropologists met in Toronto in 1978 when I was in Toronto on behalf of the Canadian Sociology and Anthropology Association, making it imperative that I attend and desirable, at least in my own eyes, that I present a paper. I particularly enjoyed the double take of a physical anthropology colleague who blurted out, "What are you doing here?" I replied blandly, "Giving a paper," thereby demonstrating my conviction that a historian of anthropology is not restricted to investigating what they already know and that it's okay to step outside those boxes. At the time I knew almost nothing about Boas's physical anthropology except that the subject seemed to round out his contributions to the other subdisciplines I did know more about. Chapter 17 serves the same function in the present volume. It reflects the limitations of an initial foray into an otherwise new focus of documentary exploration, resulting in a descriptive rather than interpretive bent while simultaneously situating Boas's physical anthropology alongside his ethnology, linguistics, and archaeology (in the sense of time depth) for present-day readers. I have omitted bilingual French terminology, British spellings, and specifically Canadian references because the stated topic is explicitly North American and Canadian only incidentally by virtue of the location of its delivery. I have not attempted to incorporate my own later archival analyses (Darnell 2015, 2017). Given these constraints, the chapter seems to me to fill its purpose here, and I choose to retain the flavor of the original with very light editing.

EDITORIAL METHOD

The chapters in this volume have been edited for style, consistency, and relationship to the volume's overall story of methodology in the history of anthropology across the subdisciplines of Americanist anthropology as it has evolved to its present structure over the five decades of the author's career. The narrative emphasizes the institutional context in which this anthropology developed. I minimize the inevitable repetition across chapters covering similar background material by paraphrase, adding context, and occasionally telescoping parenthetical detail specific to its repeated citation presented elsewhere.

Short quotes are set off in the text as they were in the original (except in chapter 17), and I have not added additional ones. I retain the sentence structure, sequence, footnotes, and subheads of the original, while at the same time smoothing the flow of the prose and adding enough updates, clearly identified as such, to ensure that the chapters as they were first published remain in continuing dialogue with the contemporary field. References to subsequent scholarship, most often my own, reflect developments beyond the time frame of the reprinted chapter.

Some changes are stylistic: for example, papers written in the 1970s could not have used gender-inclusive language that did not yet exist, although today its absence is offensive. When the early Boasians wrote in the late nineteenth and early twentieth centuries, terms such as "primitive" were common and are retained in quotes; quotation marks, [*sic*], and bracketed updates such as man[kind] call the reader's attention to these changes in the conventions of discourse. Conventions of academic writing have evolved. I follow an informal rhetorical style, for example, substituting "that" for "which" and inserting myself into the text by use of the first person and personal commentary. Passive constructions are minimized and active verbs substituted for less effective ones.

Overuse of "of course," "however," and other hedges is common in the early writing of most scholars. Some infelicities are due to pragmatic constraints on authorial ability to edit multiple drafts. Editorial revision was more onerous before I acquired my first computer in 1985.

In expectation of an audience including students in interrelated disciplines who will be familiar with some but not all parts of the material, I have added brief parenthetical expansions to orient readers unfamiliar with particular contexts, such as linguistics or physical anthropology.

The chapters are arranged thematically rather than chronologically to emphasize their approach to similar subject matter from more than one standpoint. Readers are encouraged by this approach to track the intertextual construction of academic arguments over time.

INTRODUCTION

The volume is structured as a palimpsest to facilitate tracing how ideas arise and develop over time in the work of a single author. Readers who choose to skip this section will still learn much about the development of anthropology's institutional framework, sub-discipline structure, and key actors. But they will lose the layers of overlying repetition with nonrandom variation. For anyone who is interested in the construction of scholarly work, these chapters provide signposts along the way that are more revealing than a finished product that glosses over the hiccups of pulling it all together.

Writing a book is very different from writing a journal article or book chapter. Books come together in a variety of ways. First books based on a revised dissertation often come to fruition by gradual accretion. My MA thesis and PhD dissertation (Darnell 1967, 1969) reflect this kind of process; both appeared in print only after many years delay (Darnell 1988, 1998) in which their contents were incorporated into articles or conference papers (chapters 2, 3, 4, this volume). The original versions remain important because they document my priority in making arguments later reinvented by others who read only the published versions. Readers who only cite the most recent published version or edition muddle the chronology in which ideas develop, miss the continuity of a scholar's work, and fail to assign priority accurately.

Consolidation into book form, including late career reflections on the underlying integration of a lifetime oeuvre like this one, may follow the same trajectory, which is far more complex than simply juxtaposing a series of chapters. For many anthropologists as writers, the process goes something like this:

(1) The germ of an idea surfaces in casual conversation with colleagues, either locally or through conferences and networks established by participation in professional associations—especially important in opening up interdisciplinary relevance and expanded audiences.

(2) The incipient idea is more formally articulated in teaching, in either lecture or seminar format, and incorporates the ideas of interlocutors.

(3) The idea then becomes a conference paper that produces feedback on the occasion of its delivery and through follow-up connections thereafter—again especially important for interdisciplinary topics. The ideas feed into the next conference paper, with the content and rhetoric perhaps adjusted to address a different audience.

(4) A book results when the pieces cohere into a more general integration. *Invisible Genealogies* (Darnell 2001) followed this trajectory. Both the title and the concept it encapsulates emerged over the course of a decade of consolidation and integration. Chapters 6–11 (this volume) reflect the emergence of a coherent explication of the life and work of Edward Sapir and its relationship to that of Franz Boas. Darnell (1990 [2010]) makes it sound simpler than it was. Reprinting the work twenty years later (chapter 1, this volume) allowed me to reflect on what I think I was up to all along.

(5) Professional practice brings access to unpublished material, such as invitations to review manuscripts and books or when colleagues request feedback on work in progress. Reviewing unpublished books and articles allows feedback before things find their way into print and opens the path to putting scholars in touch during the revision process.

I have devoted considerable time and energy to editorial work, often with coeditors as a way to maintain dialogue and interdisciplinary connections. Coeditors do not always agree with me, but they do stave off complacency. University of Nebraska Press acquisitions editor Matt Bokovoy is a third voice both in his institutional role and as historian of the American West. The resulting negotiations demand reflexivity to produce collegial consensus on how to move forward. Critical Studies in History of Anthropology began in 2001 with coeditor and self-identified "gay sociologist" but also historian of anthropology and linguistic anthropologist Stephen O. Murray and, since his death in 2019, continues with his chosen successor, Robert Oppenheim, who combines Asian studies and anthropology. *Histories of Anthropology Annual* began in 2005 with coeditor Americanist archaeologist, ethnohistorian, and museum curator Frederic W. Gleach and moved to the book division with volume 8. The collaboration continues to sustain both of us in the belief that anthropology matters in the contemporary world. Our editorial policy is deliberately open-ended and inclusive. Volume titles and themes emerge only after the contents are decided; they have coalesced in ways that continue to surprise us at the culmination of a rhizomatic process that seemed more random at the time. Another kind of editorial collaboration results when conference organizers have edited revised papers (e.g., with medical anthropologists Janice Graham and Christina Holmes, Australian legal scholar Fiona MacDonald, and Darnell [2021]; feminist and cultural studies anthropologist Julia Harrison and Darnell [2006]; linguistic anthropologist Lisa Philips Valentine and Darnell [1995]; Darnell, historian Michelle Hamilton, Métis historian and educator Robert L. A. Hancock, and action anthropologist Joshua Smith [2015]).

Some scholars prefer to publish less and only when they feel that their work is neatly polished and imposes closure on its subject matter. The professional socialization of historians tends to this position whereas many anthropologists are inclined to a more contingent and open-ended approach, perhaps because their fieldwork does not lend itself to closure. My personal preference is to throw out ideas that reflect the present state of my thinking to elicit feedback and invite collaboration; this approach is conditioned but not determined by my disciplinary training. I accept that I will sometimes be wrong, that my analysis is necessarily incomplete, and that it will be superseded in due course. I have been known to change my mind.

Making this process public as I do in this volume, both for chosen actors and in my own work, rarely brings simple or singular answers. This strategy is better suited for reaching out to general public audiences. History is located in time and emerges into the present without its actors having access to foresight to reveal the outcome. Real-world decisions must weigh unhappy choices against even less happy ones; such choice is the essence of morality or ethics. That in retrospect a different course might have been preferable does not invalidate the integrity of the evaluation underlying the original decision.

As a fledgling scholar, I had to define my position in relation to that of historian George W. Stocking Jr., the founding guru of the HOA (history of anthropology) specialization, a meticulous gatekeeper, editor, and reviewer of the work of others. *Race, Culture and Evolution: Essays in the History of Anthropology* (1968) collected roughly a decade of his essays polished to elegant closure. There has been no serious challenge to his hegemonic stature over the five decades since, although two of my other mentors, A. Irving "Pete" Hallowell and Dell Hymes, pointed at the time to more anthropologically grounded alternatives. Several generations of anthropologists who took Stocking's courses at the University of Chicago tend to see themselves more as custodians of his legacy than as ideally situated to reassess its continuing impact. I consider it a marker of respect to reexamine Stocking's oeuvre in a contemporary world that has changed considerably over half a century. Both the method and substance of HOA have changed in the interim, and Stocking's body of work merits updating and reframing.

My own work carved out three pillars of divergence from the Stocking position:

(1) I chose to take HOA as an anthropological problem (Hallowell 1965) and to apply ethnographic methods to disciplinary history (Hymes 1962, 1983). I wanted to write for an audience in my own discipline about how anthropology might speak effectively to a larger audience. This entailed seeking what Franz Boas called "the native point of view," whether ethnographic or disciplinary. I introduced a hermeneutic distinction between the terms used in the original work and the ones accepted in contemporary discourse, the urgency of the distinction increasing with temporal distance. The advent of gender-inclusive language is a paramount example. The case is stated elegantly by Charles King, a professor of international relations who "gets" the anthropological standpoint and presents it effectively for a general public audience.

Honest writing means trying to use words the way they were used when they were originally spoken or written down even if those meanings might be obsolete or wrongheaded now. . . . I sometimes use the word "primitive" to describe what we would today call traditional or premodern societies since that was the term usually used by Boas and his contemporaries. They in turn meant it somewhat differently from what their predecessors meant by it. Other words and phrases—*native, Negro, Indian,* and *feeble-minded,* for example—appear in their own appropriate contexts. . . . [examples of changing references for Native American tribal entities] . . . The distance between this word and that one, between now and then, is history. (King 2019:349–50)

My own response has been to coin the phrase "assassination by anachronism" as a critique of attacking a straw target based solely on contemporary agendas that are themselves legitimate without such a gratuitous break with the past.

(2) I argued that scientific revolutions do not happen in a vacuum, despite the customary rhetoric of discontinuity and revolution that major figures employ in their more programmatic statements. I have focused on continuity, the process of overlap and negotiation by which things change, often accumulating imperceptibly until they flip into a new paradigm. Analytic models change with the era in which they are dominant: Einstein spoke of relativity, Darwin of natural selection; anthropologist Gregory Bateson in the language of cybernetics. A decade ago, I found the terminology of chaos and complexity congenial, but I now prefer a vocabulary of emergent resonance, rhizomes, and intersectionality. My dissertation examined the purported revolution from the Bureau of (American) Ethnology to Boas. The case for continuity still cannot be taken for granted. The publisher of *And Along Came Boas* (Darnell 1998) urged me to invert the order of terms in the subtitle to "revolution and continuity," thereby missing the analytic point. Anyway, Boas did come along, and, after a while, things really were different.

(3) The model of the day in the late 1960s was Thomas Kuhn's *The Structure of Scientific Revolutions* (1962); the first edition envisioned paradigms as autonomous circles fully replacing one another

and invalidating their predecessors. I adopted the concept of paradigm but redefined it so that paradigms could fade in and out of one another in variable ongoing relations other than substitution and annihilation—for example, coexisting (materialism and idealism) or nested within new larger fields (Newton's laws of gravity within Einstein's theory of relativity). I identified "professionalization" as the linear, cumulative, and irreversible mechanism of continuity across paradigms. Of course, I didn't articulate it that way in 1969, and I was surprised to find that chapters 2, 3, and 4 (this volume) use the term "professionalism" in most instances. I have resisted the temptation to impose more elegant paradigmatic conclusions retrospectively.

My understanding of "history" is deeply colored by fieldwork, beginning the year of my dissertation, among the Plains Cree of northern Alberta, later enriched by work with other Indigenous communities across Canada. They taught me to see history as a palimpsest, a product of relationship that changes over time as generations succeed one another, shifting the entire network of seven generations in each direction from the speaker into new alignment. Indigenous history emerges from oral tradition maintained by narrators who pass on accumulated knowledge from generations of their elders and add their own experience to its interpretation, leaving the hearer to decide what to make out of it all in relation to their life experience over time; combining narratives that reflect the overlapping experience of multiple narrators lends depth and credibility while maintaining the integrity of each standpoint. Indigenous children hear a traditional story for its plot and humor and through successive retellings gradually come to understand it as a template for making sense of their own unique life experience. Meaning is to be pondered over a lifetime.

Knowledge is transportable from one context to another—for example, in considering the grounds of discrimination in response to standpoint-based disciplines that sometimes cling to single-issue activisms. Black lives matter; so do Indigenous lives; and women's lives; and so on. Homelessness, poverty, disability, ethnicity, religion, nationality, and more, teach us how to move from one context to others and apply the resulting insights to the problem at hand. This generalization motivates the best output of both grass-roots activism and academic theorizing. Social problems are multi-variate, a term I don't like but came to use because demographers in my own institution understood what it meant, and we could discuss why I wanted it to mean something different, to move beyond their restriction of explanation to the correlations established by their numbers. We need quantitative research, but we also need qualitative analysis that draws on the world outside the numbers to contextualize them. Our ethical and moral responsibility is to the latter. Only public pressure can keep political and policy implications on track when their own momentum favors slapping on a Band-Aid and moving to the next crisis—which brings its own unintended consequences in an increasingly unsustainable global order.

What does all this have to do with the history of anthropology? The chapters in this volume talk a lot about Franz Boas and Edward Sapir and the "circles" or "schools" that formed around them. I do not fully distinguish between anthropology and the history of anthropology.

My initial plan for this volume divided the chapters into discrete sections.

Part 1, comprising chapter 1, defines the history of anthropology.

Part 2, comprising chapters 2 through 4, provides the Boasian baseline grounded in my early scholarship.

An interlude containing chapter 5 discusses archival method and audience.

Part 3, comprising chapters 6 through 11, deals with Boas and Sapir in the context of language, languages, and linguistics; but chapter 6 stands apart because it fast-forwards the Boasian narrative on race in the context of the Franz Boas Documentary Edition.

Part 4, comprising chapters 12 through 16, describes how various Boas students and former students responded to the Boas-Sapir paradigm. There is repetition across their experiences; each take on the "same" events and ideas enriches the overall picture. The first generation Boasians were not interchangeable and did not so perceive themselves. These papers counter the external stereotype of outsiders observing the solidarity and commonality of the early Boasians.

The "parts" that seemed so plausible on first consideration

kept cross-referencing one another; comparative dimensions arose across time frame, institutional setting, and actors. Chapter 17 was added as the subdiscipline focus of the volume crystallized. Chapter 6 briefly outlines what I know about the inextricable relationship of biology and culture in Boas's thinking about race almost forty years later, thereby updating chapter 17.

Actors whose standpoint is elaborated from their own point of view include Sapir, Boas, Daniel Garrison Brinton, George Byron Gordon, Frank Speck, William Wells Newell, WJ McGee, John Wesley Powell, Benjamin Lee Whorf, Ruth Fulton Benedict, Stanley Newman, Mary Haas, and A. Irving Hallowell. I do not explore the motives and standpoints of other, equally important, actors from their point of view, such as William Pepper, Sara Stevenson, A. L. Kroeber, Frederic Ward Putnam, W. E. B. Du Bois, Leonard Bloomfield, Mark May, John Dollard, George Peter Murdock, Leslie Spier, and Margaret Mead. Several appear in more than one chapter and context: Spier in chapters 11 and 16; Kroeber in chapters 9, 10, and 14; Bloomfield in chapters 8–11 and 13–14.

Institutions were confronted with similar dichotomies and factions: Pennsylvania, Yale, and Columbia struggled to balance museum and university, reflecting a more abstract debate between positivist natural science and interpretivist social science discourses.

Organization of the same material chronologically rather than thematically would obscure these patterns. I include this material to counter those who might be tempted to equate year of publication with development of a scholar's oeuvre.[1] Chapters 2 through 4 form a clear set in the 1970s, but Hallowell (chapter 16) is anomalous. The three chapters from the 1980s have nothing in common beyond the decade: chapter 9 provides context for the emergence of Darnell (1990); chapter 15 was related to the conference described in chapter 9 by venue but not substance; the dating of chapter 17 was fortuitous, dependent only on the year of the invitation to present; chapter 7 in 2006 also required me to scramble to meet a new research focus. The 1990s returned to Sapir (chapter 1 stands somewhat apart as a definition of HOA); chapter 8 in the same year is unrelated. Chapters 5, 7, 10, and 12 in 2008, chapter 13 in 2006, and chapter 15 are products of when invitations were issued and do not reflect a change in my scholarship. The dramatic expansion of such invitations reflects my move from Alberta to Ontario in 1990. In many of these cases, I did not present new archival or interview material but deployed that background to address the relevant topic.

My trusted assessors not represented directly in the work here (others are thanked in the appropriate acknowledgments) ground me in the audience of my writing beyond the scope of this volume: Danielle Alcock, Michael Asch, Kaylee Armstrong, Lee D. Baker, Eva Cupchik, Nathan Dawthorne, Frederico Delagado Rosa, Joel Faflak, Janice Graham, Neyooxet Greymorning, Tracey Hetherington, Keelung Hong, Dean Jacobs, Alice Kehoe, Wendy Leeds-Hurwitz, Won Jeon, Christine Laurière, Kate Lawless, Herb Lewis, Andy and Harriet Lyons, Dolleen Manning, Maureen Matthews, Gerald McKinley, Călin-Andrei Mihăilescu, Sarah Moritz, James M. Nyce, Driton Nushaj, Rob Oppenheim, Wade Paul, Bernie Perley, Alex Pershai, Alan Pero, Bimadoshka Anya Pucan, Carolyn Poduchny, Ian Puppe, Dan and Mary Lou Smoke, Heather Stauffer, Amardeep Thind, and Charles Trick.

Notes

1. Chapters by decade:

1970s	2—1971, 3—1974, 4—1970, 16—1977
1980s	9—986, 15—1989, 17—1982
1990s	1 and 8—1990, 5—1995, 10—1999, 11 and 13—1998
2000s	7 and 13—2006, 12—2008
2010s	6—2018

References

Baker, Lee D. 2010. *Anthropology and the Racial Politics of Culture.* Durham NC: Duke University Press.

Darnell, Regna. 1967. "Daniel Garrison Brinton: An Intellectual Biography." Master's thesis, University of Pennsylvania.

———. 1969. "The Development of American Anthropology, 1880–1920: From the Bureau of American Ethnology to Franz Boas." PhD diss., University of Pennsylvania.

———. 1971. "The Revision of the Powell Classification." *Papers in Linguistics* 4:234–57.

———. 1986. "The Emergence of Edward Sapir's Mature Thought." In Cowan et al., eds, 1–26.

———. 1974. "Rationalist Aspects of the Whorf Hypothesis." *Papers in Linguistics* 4:41–50.

———. 1988. *Daniel Garrison Brinton: The "Fearless Critic" of Philadelphia.* Philadelphia: University of Pennsylvania Museum Monograph Series 3.

———. 1990 [2010]. *Edward Sapir: Linguist, Anthropologist, Humanist.* Berkeley: University of California Press. Reprint, Lincoln: University of Nebraska Press.

———. 1998a. *And Along Came Boas: Continuity and Revolution in Americanist Anthropology.* Amsterdam: John Benjamins.

———. 1998b. "Camelot at Yale: The Construction and Dismantling of the Sapirian Synthesis, 1931–1939." *American Anthropologist* 100:361–72.

———. 2001. *Invisible Genealogies: A History of Americanist Anthropology.* Lincoln: University of Nebraska Press.

———, ed. 2002. *Presidential Portraits: Celebrating a Century of the American Anthropological Association.* Lincoln: University of Nebraska Press.

———. 2015. "Mind, Body and the Native Point of View: Boasian Theory at the Centennial of *The Mind of Primitive Man*." In Darnell et al. 2015, 3–18.

———. 2017. "Franz Boas as Theorist: A Mentalist Paradigm for the Study of Mind, Body, Environment and Culture." In *Historicizing Theories, Identities, and Nations*, edited by Regna Darnell and Frederic W. Gleach, 1–26. Vol. 11 of Histories of Anthropology Annual. Lincoln: University of Nebraska Press.

Darnell, Regna, and Frederic W. Gleach, eds. 2002a. *American Anthropology, 1971–1995: Selected Papers from the American Anthropologist.* Washington DC: American Anthropological Association and Lincoln: University of Nebraska Press.

———. 2002b. "Special Centennial Issue." *American Anthropologist* 204:417–564.

Darnell, Regna, Michelle Hamilton, Robert L. A. Hancock, and Joshua Smith, eds. 2015. *The Franz Boas Papers, Volume 1: Franz Boas as Public Intellectual—Theory, Ethnography, Activism.* Franz Boas Papers Documentary Edition Series. Lincoln: University of Nebraska Press.

Darnell, Regna, and Judith T. Irvine, eds. 1994. *Ethnology. Volume 4. Collected Works of Edward Sapir.* Berlin: Mouton de Gruyter.

Darnell, Regna, Judith T. Irvine, and Richard Handler, eds. 1999. *Culture. Volume 3. Collected Works of Edward Sapir.* Berlin: Mouton de Gruyter.

Graham, Janice, Christina Holmes, Fiona McDonald, and Regna Darnell, eds. 2021. *The Social Life of Standards: Ethnographic Methods for Local Engagement.* Vancouver: University of British Columbia Press.

Hallowell, A. Irving. 1965. "The History of Anthropology as an Anthropological Problem." *Journal of the History of the Behavioral Sciences* 1:24–38.

Harrison, Julia, and Regna Darnell, eds. 2006. *Historicizing Canadian Anthropology.* Vancouver: University of British Columbia Press.

Hymes, Dell H. 1962. "On Studying the History of Anthropology." *Kroeber Anthropological Society Papers* 26:81–86.

———. 1983. *Essays in the History of Linguistic Anthropology.* Amsterdam: John Benjamins.

Irvine, Judith T., ed. 1994. *The Psychology of Culture: A Course of Lectures.* [Reconstructed from class notes of Edward Sapir.] Berlin: Mouton de Gruyter.

King, Charles. 2019. *Gods of the Upper Air: How a Circle of Renegade Anthropologists Reinvented Race, Sex, and Gender in the Twentieth Century.* New York: Doubleday.

Kuhn, Thomas S. 1962. *The Structure of Scientific Revolutions.* Chicago: Phoenix.

Murray, Stephen O. 1986. "Edward Sapir and the Chicago School of Sociology." In *New Perspectives in Language, Culture and Personality*, edited by William Cowan, Michael K. Foster, and Konrad Koerner, 241–92. Amsterdam: John Benjamins.

———. 1997. "A 1978 Interview with Mary R. Haas." *Anthropological Linguistics* 39:695–713.

Stocking, George W., Jr. 1968. *Race, Culture and Evolution: Essays in the History of Anthropology.* New York: Free Press.

Valentine, Lisa Philips, and Regna Darnell, eds. 1995. *Theorizing the Americanist Tradition.* Toronto: University of Toronto Press.

ABBREVIATIONS

Archival Documents

ALK	Alfred Louis Kroeber Papers, University of California, Berkeley
ANSP	Academy of Natural Sciences of Philadelphia
APS	American Philosophical Society
NAA	National Anthropological Archives, Smithsonian
NMM	National Museum of Man, Ottawa
NRC	National Research Council
RHL	Robert H. Lowie Papers, University of California, Berkeley
UC	University of Chicago, Regenstein Library
UMA	University (of Pennsylvania) Museum Archives
UPA	University of Pennsylvania Archives
UPM	University of Pennsylvania Museum
YU	Yale University Archives
YUDA	Yale University Department Archives

Institutional Abbreviations

AAA	American Anthropological Association
AAAS	American Association for the Advancement of Science
ACLS	American Council of Learned Societies
AFS	American Folklore Society
APS	American Philosophical Society
ASW	Anthropological Society of Washington
BAE	Bureau of [American] Ethnology

CNAIR	Center for Native American and Indigenous Languages
DKS	Digital Knowledge Sharing
FBP	Franz Boas Papers
IAC	Indigenous advisory council
IHR	Institute of Human Relations, Yale
LSA	Linguistic Society of America
NAAHOLS	North American Association for the History of the Language Sciences
NRC	National Research Council
SSHRC	Social Sciences and Humanities Research Council of Canada

Journal Abbreviation

HOAA	*Histories of Anthropology Annual*

THE HISTORY OF ANTHROPOLOGY

1

....

Edward Sapir

Linguist, Anthropologist, Humanist

This introduction revisits my reading of the life and times of Edward Sapir two decades after the original publication of my biography with some combination of vertigo and nostalgia.[1] Sufficient time has elapsed for defamiliarization to impose its characteristic methodological distance. A startling sense of rediscovering in Sapir an old friend evoked the ongoing relationship of myself and my career to the personhood and career of a scholar I have admired since I first met his work as an undergraduate. In the double retrospective of 1990 and 2010, I savored the complexity of the man and the context in which he wrote. On the one hand, I retraced in memory my access to and interaction with the documents and commentaries through which Sapir continues to engage today's disciplines. On the other, I mused about alternative readings of Sapir in the rapidly changing context of contemporary social sciences and humanities scholarship.

On the surface, biography would seem to be a genre amenable to closure. Lives, after all, come to an end. In the absence of dramatic change in the relevant documentary record, the facts of the subject's life ought to retain an inalienable facticity and materiality. Although there is a grain of truth to this view, this notion of history is thoroughly old-fashioned. The intellectual grounding of historiography has shifted tectonically during my professional lifetime. When I was a graduate student in the late 1960s, George W. Stocking Jr., already the dean of an emergent history of anthropology, distinguished quite didactically between historicism as the side of the angels and presentism as the ubiquitous pitfall of anthropologists trying to be historians (Stocking 1968:1–12). Even

Fig. 1. Edward Sapir, ca. 1910.

then, however, there were alternative voices. Another of my early mentors, A. Irving "Pete" Hallowell, maintained that anthropologists should tell their own story because they are the ones with a stake in it; therefore, he defined the history of anthropology as an anthropological problem (Hallowell 1965) and claimed a disciplinary capacity to tell it well. He asserted that anthropologists trained for ethnographic fieldwork were already well prepared to exercise historicist judgment in the documentary archive. Later anthropologists have extended and even reversed his dictum by elaborating the momentum and implicit ethnographic agency of the archive and its bureaucratic foundation (e.g., Stoler 2009; Dawdy 2008). In the more contemporary language of Hayden White on history as narrative, genuine history only exists when its primary materials are subjected to interpretation—which by definition entails at least one interpretative road not taken. My own career-long position has been one of standpoint-based archival ethnography. Accordingly, I have argued strongly for the commensurability of historicism and presentism.

It is perhaps not surprising that Edward Sapir has refused to stand still and remain the Sapir of my prior engagement with him. My biography took form alongside the intense interpretive collaboration of anthropologists and linguists surrounding the centennial of Sapir's birth in 1984. There were sessions and conferences and conversations, commentaries and reprintings, all dutifully cited in my original text. Sapir scholarship and scholarly interest have continued apace in the interim. Judith T. Irvine's edited version of Sapir's class notes in the psychology of culture (Irvine 1994) and multiple volumes of Sapir's collected works (e.g., Darnell 2002; Darnell and Gleach 2002a, 2002b; Darnell and Irvine 1994; Darnell, Irvine, and Handler 1999) postdate the biography, although I was able to incorporate many of the then unpublished materials on which they were based. Konrad Koerner's three volumes of commentaries on Sapir's linguistics (2008) facilitate further cross-reference.

Evidence has a mind of its own. Through most of the 1980s I was immersed in Sapiriana. Sapir's five children shared memories of the family man. Many of his students were still living, and none of them refused to talk to me. The memories these elders failed to share at the time have been, for the most part, lost with their passing. The fragility of personally transmitted knowledge mitigates against leisurely abstraction; relatively recent history cannot be confined to an archive as though that rendered it inert. The urgency of recording memories and asking questions is not differ-ent in kind from the urgent ethnology that is purported to have driven Sapir from Germanic to Amerindian [sic] linguistics. Much of the raw material for scholarly biography, like the accumulated knowledge of Indigenous cultures, is passed on directly through oral tradition. Each source, whether oral or written, immediate or recalled from dormant records, calls for a (re)interpretation in relation to the whole field of what was and could be known. Much that I did twenty years ago to link the insights of archive and oral history could no longer be done now. I am thus delighted at the opportunity to update my contribution to this scholarly lineage.

What initially fascinated me about him is that there has never been a single Sapir. Moreover, his multiplicity expands yet again in this revisiting. The book's subtitle, descriptive as those of anthropol-ogists often are, singled out three distinct disciplinary personae—the linguist, the anthropologist, the humanist—and framed each within the anthropological and linguistic study of Native North Americans. In those heady late nineteenth- and early twentieth-century years of professionalization in his two formal disciplines, perennially leavened by his inextricable ties to the world of let-ters, Sapir challenged what he considered artificial barriers across and within the life of the mind. Although several colleagues joined forces to dissuade me from the provisional subtitle "architect of ideas," I still think this image captures the essence of Sapir when happy, of his capacity to be caught up in thinking and speaking, preferably with others, about whatever captured his attention at a given moment. I concede that his architecture was not of a for-mal structuralist kind but rather it was organic. His much-touted "genius" in the eyes of his contemporaries had a thoroughly rhi-zomatic character. Sapir loved and responded to beauty of pattern-ing, whether in language, music, mathematics, or, more elusively, in the impact of culture on individual creativity or personality. Particularly in his interdisciplinary work of the interwar years, he attempted to construct an inclusive collaborative edifice designed to capture the very essence of human existence. The architectural metaphor does not seem to me far-fetched.

Sapir's intellectual style made him the ideal mediator across dis-ciplines as the newly professional American social sciences, aided and abetted by the Rockefeller Foundation and other philanthropic institutions, attempted to test their collective insights in the public sphere. This interdisciplinary work was deeply embedded in the American pragmatism of John Dewey and George Herbert Mead. Sapir's was an intense enthusiasm that carried colleagues with him. Every new idea or new disciplinary perspective provided an opportunity to add collateral branches, not unlike those of distantly related linguistic families, to the enterprise that Sapir increasingly located at the intersection of culture and the individual. He drew in psychologists and psychiatrists, still only ambiguously discrete in their professional identities and credentiary requirements in the 1920s and 1930s, to talk to them about personality and learn from their clinical methods. Sapir's favorite metaphor, which has become a methodological principle in my own work, is the inseparability of the two sides of a given coin. His interdisciplinary colleagues, in turn, milked Sapir's ethnographic approach for its presumed exotica, a process that he doggedly undermined by choosing his examples from everyday North American life. They also sought from him a culturally nuanced sense of how to move toward the elusive universals of human psychodynamics based on the characteristic anthropological stance of cultural relativism.

I do not believe that Sapir clearly distinguished, or considered it important to distinguish, his colleagues in Chicago sociology from the anthropologists. Psychologist Harry Stack Sullivan, sociologist William Fielding Ogburn, and political scientist Harold Lasswell were often more congenial to Sapir than disciplinary colleagues who failed to share his expansive enthusiasms. He was, perhaps, a prophet outside his own country. His sociologist allies were also ethnographers, albeit their laboratory was the city of Chicago rather than the distant Indian [*sic*] reservation. The parallel was accentuated because Sapir himself refused to exoticize ethnographic data and focused his writing and teaching on the meaning underlying familiar social practices. He shared with sociology colleagues a commitment to what he called "culture" and they called "society." Darnell and Irvine (1994) argue that Sapir increasingly adopted the sociologists' usage of "society" as a third term in his own work. The goal was to integrate levels of analysis in order to reframe the particularistic insights of the various social science disciplines.

Anthropology played a far greater role in the interdisciplinary synthesis than the size or general prestige of the discipline would have predicted—by sheer force of Sapir's personality and intellect. No one else had his breadth. No one else could link the outliers into broader conversations. If Sapir were describing his own career, I suspect he would foreground these years of intense collaboration with the intellectual superstars of his generation. The jet setters of the mid-1920s to mid-1930s interdisciplinary conferences were confident that they were constructing a new scientific paradigm (see Koestler 1972 for a description of the peripatetic conference circuit at its most compelling for the core participants). Sapir and his colleagues found it a wonderful time to be alive—to participate in a scientific revolution in the making (Darnell 1998).

I retrace this interdisciplinary enthusiasm here because the story as I originally told it perhaps overemphasized the impasses that ultimately refracted the synthetic impulses so engaging to Sapir back to their constitutive disciplines. There were political contortions at Yale's Institute of Human Relations (IHR); there was anti-Semitism. The great philanthropic foundations drew back from social science funding, and the encroaching Nazi threat in Europe stalled scientific projects. Sapir died in 1939 at the cusp of even more dramatic change. Postwar American social science largely failed to acknowledge its roots in the intellectual maelstrom of its immediate ancestors. Margaret Mead, Ruth Benedict, and their neo-Freudian collaborators moved toward national character studies and psychoanalysis rather than following up on Sapir's meaning-based teasing out of the sociological implications of living in a particular ethnographic context for the creative individual.

Despite the apparent lack of continuity in mainstream American social science, however, Sapir's essays in culture and psychology have remained in print and have leavened diverse ensuing perspectives. "Culture, Genuine and Spurious" (1924) exemplifies his synthetic intentions. It has been much misread and little appreciated. His Chicago colleague Ogburn, for example, could make neither sociological head nor tail of the argument. Yet it encapsulates Sapir's thinking, and its lyrical defense of anthropological relativism as coeval dialogue and respect across cultural boundaries has endured. There is something prescient and remarkably postmodern about Sapir's essay.

The Indians [*sic*] of the Northwest Coast seemed to Sapir to live more comfortably in their own skins than his contemporary urban academic colleagues. World War I left behind a profound distaste for the technology, corporate mentality, and mendacity of North American society. Sapir labeled this culture "spurious." He wanted to equate culture and civilization, to draw the wisdom of the "primitive" into the moral discourse of the larger society. It was an impulse shared by Paul Radin and Alexander Goldenweiser among his Boasian cohort (Darnell 2001). Sapir did not romanticize the Indians [*sic*] he knew and did not want to "go native." But he did want the philosophers and poets of the societies he studied to have the same right to creative self-expression that he claimed for himself when he wrote poetry, composed music, or penned literary reviews.

The ethnoscience and cognitive anthropology that emerged in the 1960s was more Sapirian than Benedictine (Darnell 2008c, chapter 12, this volume). His book, *Language* (1921), continues to provide a sensible yet inspiring introduction to what the linguist can say about language and how that relates to the everyday speech surrounding each human individual. His process grammars of American Indian [*sic*] languages remain widely emulated models of how the world is organized within the categories available to the members of a given speech community. His musings, and those of his protégé Benjamin Lee Whorf, on the relation of language, thought, and reality inform contemporary debates in ways that the intervening behaviorism of structural linguistics does not. Sapir remains a hero to young scholars in disciplines ranging from linguistics and anthropology to psychology to education to literary studies and philosophy. His legacy does not lie entirely in the particular projects he pursued. Rather, he teaches us how to think about things and how to situate ideas in relation to one another.

From an author's point of view, critical response to a text matters. Biography is a widespread genre in the study of the history of anthropology, perhaps because it draws on the already familiar insights that life history methodology brings to ethnographic research. Nearly half of the volumes in the critical studies in history of anthropology series at the time of this writing were biographies, and more have been added since. Their cumulative weight exceeds the sum of the parts because so many biographical subjects engaged the same colleagues and disciplinary contexts from their own unique angles; their points of view are mutually enriching in juxtaposition. I want to share several observations of potential relevance to colleagues with biographical aspirations.

First, I wrote from the standpoint that Sapir is interesting because of the unparalleled range of subjects he took up during his career. I wondered how they hung together for him. Wonder is good starting point. Because his work defied chronological organization, I followed each train of Sapir's thought in its own integrity as well as in relationship to the others. Colleagues who congratulated me on the scope of the biography, however, often added with no apparent trace of irony that they only read the chapters about Athabascan linguistics or linguistic classification, or culture and personality, or the literary forays, or whatever. "I skipped all the linguistic stuff" was my particular favorite—and that from a distinguished Sapir scholar in other realms of the oeuvre. I was saddened but simultaneously reinforced in my conviction that Sapir still has no peer for tying things together and animating ideas in relation to one another. I wish readers might come to care as much as I do about the integrity of Sapir's thought as a whole.

Second, I realized that my own career has shadowed Sapir's in ways that have made his experience edifying for evaluating my own. I too have moved between anthropology and linguistics, albeit my linguistics is grounded in discourse and semantics rather than the older mantra of grammar, dictionary, and texts. I have remained in Canada whereas Sapir did not, although his fifteen-year sojourn left an indelible imprint on Canadian anthropology (Harrison and Darnell 2006). I moved in midcareer, as he did, to a position that enabled dialogue and collaboration beyond my prior imaginings. Yet the biography was a product of the years I spent thinking about Plains Cree language and culture in northern Alberta, talking to Cree people, and trying to establish a conversation in which the cultural credentials of my friends and consultants "in the field" would be recognized in the academy on a par with my own. Sapir would have enjoyed the experimental ethnographies of recent decades. Like him, I went on to develop anthropological and linguistic perspectives alongside new interdisciplinary colleagues: in science studies, in history and ethnohistory, in First Nations and Native American studies, in women's studies, and in the relationship of ecosystem health to Indigenous knowledge. For a scholar of broadly interdisciplinary bent, peers often see only one side. It may take a village of anthropological historians to characterize a complex career, each approaching it from a different angle.

Third, biography can be a thankless task on intellectual grounds. As scholarship, it has no closure. The tendrils of any biographical subject's interests and contacts meander beyond the possibility of full retrieval. I misspoke if there seemed a single story, told in the only or even best possible way. I made many conscious decisions about how to tell the story of Edward Sapir. I situated him at the center of a complex web of ideas, social networks, and institutional contexts. Like the peeling of an onion in reverse, I built outward, using his own words and those of his peers as evidence to uncover how his life and work articulated with the history of Americanist anthropology and the America in which it emerged and grew to maturity. Sapir's cohort was an incredible group that clustered around Franz Boas and accepted his challenge to record American Indian [*sic*] languages and cultures that seemed to be dying out. Native North Americans are, of course, patently still with us. Change has been rapid and often traumatic. Despite inherent inequities and downright failures of collaboration in the anthropological study of Native American communities, the data collected by early Boasians has now become a valued resource for cultural and linguistic revitalization in many communities. Collaborative research is now de rigeur.

Sapir's professional cohort came alive for me as I read their correspondence from his standpoint; long before feminist standpoint epistemology, "standpoint" was a key term for him. Immersion in how the world looked to Sapir as a particular individual enabled me to organize *Invisible Genealogies* (2001) around the identification and elaboration of the core ideas that drove Sapir and his contemporaries (Franz Boas, Alfred L. Kroeber, Paul Radin, Benjamin Lee Whorf, Ruth Benedict, Elsie Clews Parsons, A. Irving Hallowell), both in their own times and in our own. I implicitly framed

each of these scholars biographically and highlighted their relationships within a network of peers poking at pieces of the same
puzzle and sharing their insights.

The book was widely reviewed and was nominated in Canada for
the governor general's award for nonfiction. Most reviewers talked
a great deal about Edward Sapir and very little about the strategy
of the biography, as genre or product. I was discouraged to find
a decade of my own scholarship virtually invisible and went on to
do rather more self-conscious theoretical work at the juncture of
history of anthropology and Amerindian [*sic*] ethnography. I am
disappointed that no one else has attempted a biography of Sapir,
whereas there are multiple biographies of Boas, Kroeber, Mead,
Benedict, and Julian Steward, among others. Alternative analyses
that highlight my reading of various aspects of Sapir's work as one
possible interpretation are rampant in the current reassessment
of Americanist anthropology's roots, but they are rarely biographical or archival in emphasis.

What would I do differently today? I have talked about Sapir in
various subsequent publications, but the story I told twenty years
ago still rings true for me. I now think the greatest opportunity
missed was to accept propinquity as the standard of intellectual
exchange in the cluster of Sapir, Diamond Jenness, and Marius
Barbeau in Ottawa anthropology. Much more is now known about
both of these British-trained colleagues (e.g., Hancock 2006; Nowry
1995; Jessup, Nurse, and Smith 2008). My sense of who were Sapir's
peers has changed. I now see the fellow Boasians he hired during
the heady Ottawa years from 1910 to 1916 as the remarkable cohort
that established the baseline for Sapir's own extraordinary productivity during this period. This group, including Paul Radin, Alexander Goldenweiser, Wilson Wallis, Harlan Smith, and sometimes
Frank Speck, shared a particularly Americanist vision. They formed
the largest cluster of Boasians outside New York City in this seminal period that lasted until Canadian anthropological research
was crippled by World War I cutbacks.

I never intended to emphasize Sapir's failures and impasses.
Two decades ago, however, I was cautious about the ubiquitous
danger of overidentifying with a biographical subject. A woman
writing about a male subject is particularly vulnerable to such cri-

tique. I never thought of him as Eddie or even Edward, and my assessment of his work and personality includes both kudos and distastes. I have tried, in these brief pages, to make clear my continuing optimism about the value of Sapir's ongoing legacy.

Notes

1. This chapter was originally published as the introduction to the reprint edition of *Edward Sapir: Linguist, Anthropologist, Humanist* (Lincoln: University of Nebraska Press, 2010), v–xiv.

References

Darnell, Regna. [1990] 2010. *Edward Sapir: Linguist, Anthropologist, Humanist.* Berkeley: University of California Press. Reprint, Lincoln: University of Nebraska Press.

———. 1998. "Camelot at Yale: The Construction and Dismantling of the Sapirian Synthesis, 1931–1939." *American Anthropologist* 100:361–72.

———. 2001. *Invisible Genealogies: A History of Americanist Anthropology.* Lincoln: University of Nebraska Press.

———, ed. 2002. *American Anthropology, 1971–1995: Selected Papers from the American Anthropologist.* Washington DC: American Anthropological Association; and Lincoln: University of Nebraska Press.

———. 2008. "Benedictine Revisionings of Southwestern Cultural Diversity: Beyond Relativism." *Journal of Anthropological Research* 64:469–82.

Darnell, Regna, and Frederic W. Gleach, eds. 2002a. *Celebrating a Century of the American Anthropological Association: Presidential Portraits.* Lincoln: University of Nebraska Press.

———. 2002b. "Special Centennial Issue." *American Anthropologist* 204:417–564.

Darnell, Regna, and Judith T. Irvine, eds. 1994. *Ethnology. Volume 4. Collected Works of Edward Sapir.* Berlin: Mouton de Gruyter.

Darnell, Regna, Judith T. Irvine, and Richard Handler, eds. 1999. *Culture. Volume 3. Collected Works of Edward Sapir.* Berlin: Mouton de Gruyter.

Dawdy, Shannon Lee. 2008. *Building the Devil's Empire: French Colonial New Orleans.* Chicago: University of Chicago Press.

Hallowell, A. Irving. 1965. "The History of Anthropology as an Anthropological Problem." *Journal of the History of the Behavioral Sciences* 1:24–38.

Hancock, Robert L. A. 2006. "Diamond Jenness's Arctic Ethnography and the Potential for a Canadian Anthropology." *Histories of Anthropology Annual* 2:155–211.

Harrison, Julia, and Regna Darnell, eds. 2006. *Historicizing Canadian Anthropology.* Vancouver: University of British Columbia Press.

Irvine, Judith T., ed. 1994. *The Psychology of Culture: A Course of Lectures.* [Reconstructed from class notes of Edward Sapir.] Berlin: Mouton de Gruyter.

Jessup, Lynda, Andrew Nurse, and Gordon E. Smith, eds. 2008. *Around and about Marius Barbeau: Modelling Twentieth Century Culture*. Mercury Series, Cultural Studies Paper 83. Ottawa: Canadian Museum of Civilization.

Koerner, Konrad, ed. 2008. *Edward Sapir: Critical Assessments of Leading Linguists*. 3 vols. Berlin: Mouton de Gruyter.

Koestler, Arthur. 1972. *The Call Girls*. London: Hutchinson.

Nowry, Lawrence. 1995. *Marius Barbeau: Man of Mana*. Toronto: University of Toronto Press.

Sapir, Edward. 1921. *Language: An Introduction to the Study of Speech*. New York: Harcourt, Brace.

———. 1924. "Culture, Genuine and Spurious." *American Journal of Sociology* 29:401–29.

Stocking, George W., Jr. 1968. "On the Limits of Presentism and Historicism in the Historiography of the Behavioral Sciences." In *Race, Culture and Evolution: Essays in the History of Anthropology*, 1–12. New York: Free Press.

Stoler, Ann. 2009. *Along the Archival Grain: Epistemic Anxieties and Colonial Common Sense*. Princeton: Princeton University Press.

2

The Professionalization of American Anthropology

A Case Study in the Sociology of Knowledge

Science and the History of Science

The history of particular sciences developing in interaction with one another in a general social and intellectual milieu as a result of the actions of a group of practitioners is one of the most intriguing problems in the relationship between consciousness and society.[1] It is an increasingly commonplace assumption that science does not exist in the abstract and scientists are both molded by and molders of the world around. A scholar is trained to accept the basic premises of their own society and may do so for many years before reaching scientific maturity. Yet scientists are judged on the basis of the science they produce, often interpreted more literally by the general public than ever intended, in ways that shape the social theory of their time.

In anthropology, the idea of cultural relativism has become part of the general Western culture and is no longer exclusively a conceptual tool of the discipline of anthropology. The idea of culture as the transmitted body of custom that characterizes each human society also has a limited origin within anthropology. These are anthropological contributions whose point, in a sense, has already been made. The anthropologist is no longer the only social scientist interested in exotic societies; interdisciplinary social science is becoming the rule rather than the exception. Questions about the interaction of society and science are crucial for the sociology of knowledge. The conceptual apparatus of a science develops historically within a particular discipline but cannot be completely separated from the society in which that science has developed.

In approaching the historical development of concepts in a science, in this case anthropology, we must pose the more proximate question of who should write the history and from what point of view. Until quite recently, the history of particular social sciences has been written from within, with an aim of providing historical context of problems and ideas for students being socialized into a profession. Because such history has been guided by the present needs and concerns of a discipline as perceived by particular practitioners, development of ideas has been dissociated from its historical roots. The result is too often a chronology of founding fathers [*sic*] suspended in an unmotivated social and historical vacuum. Organized around isolated anecdotes, such history rarely becomes "relevant" for the students who constitute its major audience.

Conventional histories have almost invariably restricted themselves to discussion of theoretical developments influential in the version of the discipline currently practiced by the author. Existing teaching materials for the history of anthropology confirm this diagnosis: the long-time classic work *The History of Ethnological Theory* by Robert H. Lowie records the development of Boasian anthropology as he came to understand it during a distinguished career. A more recent but already classic treatment is Marvin Harris's *The Rise of Anthropological Theory*, which explicitly aims to clarify the present theoretical priorities of American anthropology; for Harris, this involves a critique of Boasian anthropology as understood by Lowie (Lowie 1937; Harris 1968). This gives the reader a choice but still does not go beyond the perspective of the practitioner trying to come to terms with whatever they consider relevant from the past history of the discipline.

The work of historian George Stocking (by far the best scholarship on the history of anthropology) avoids the pitfalls of theoretical commitment but evades the problem of identification with an ongoing tradition (or traditions) of anthropology by seeking standards for anthropological history in the separate discipline of history. Since his reasons for writing such history differ from those of an anthropological audience for reading it, Stocking's success in recording and interpreting his material does not resolve the epistemological question. Indeed, the nature of the historian's own training precludes access to the detailed knowledge of the particular discipline that enables meaningful assessment of their interpretations for the scientists who continue to constitute the major portion of their audience. This approach further fails to raise the questions about the nature of historical perception from within that are most interesting for the sociology of knowledge.

Despite the difficulties of this position, social scientists have a contribution to make to the writing of their own history. In striving for objectivity about this history, they cannot avoid analyzing the results of their own methodology. In dealing with the relevant past, the manner of procedure as a social scientist becomes itself an object of awareness. This does not mean that every social scientist must become a historian of their discipline. Rather, those few scientists who turn historian as a significant part of their professional task can learn the portion of historical method that is crucial to their enterprise, especially the historicist ideal of presenting past events in something resembling their original context and use of the unpublished materials that are the historian's traditional sources. By extracting themselves from current controversy and framing the development of their own discipline in terms of its members' actions, writers of history, regardless of professional training or affiliation, can free themselves from some of the obvious biases of their own historically situated view of the world.[2]

From a perspective such as the sociology of knowledge, the legitimacy of such a view requires exploration. In the struggles of the various social science disciplines for autonomy and professional unity, the process of being such a scientist has been relegated to a minor place as an object of scientific attention. To argue for the importance of understanding oneself at work is both to strengthen each discipline internally and to assert the need for communication across existing disciplinary boundaries.

From a more traditional perspective, the outcome of the history of a science is cut-and-dried, known in advance; had the results been different, the present discipline would also have been different. Yet from the point of view of participants, the development of a science is always in process, with details of the outcome uncertain. In part, this is a matter of historicism (Stocking 1968), in the sense of seeing events in their own context. At the end of an individual's career (when they are most likely to inherit the required graduate course in the history of the discipline), such gradual development may appear to have had a consistent pattern or direction. Knowing the outcome encourages ignoring or glossing over the ups and downs of the actual process. But the honored heroes of the present generation were not born with an aura of fame and respectability; their careers were not built overnight. The "Great Man" [*sic*] theory of history postulates that such individuals not only develop revolutionary ideas over long years; they also convince others of the validity of these ideas and develop an institutional and social structure for their implementation. Most often, they do so self-consciously, fully aware of the possibility of failure. Ideas, even what may seem in retrospect to be good ideas, do not automatically come to fruition in the history of a discipline.

An example may be taken from the history of sociology as it developed at the University of Chicago. Chicago during the 1920s and 1930s was the self-conscious and to some extent self-appointed center of American sociology. Robert Park and Ernest Burgess, in a textbook that summarized past developments and set the tone for at least the next decade, maintained that sociology was the pinnacle and synthesis of all other social sciences: anthropology, ethnology, folklore, and archaeology were concrete or *merely* historical sciences while politics, education, economics, and social services constituted simple, almost mechanical applications of sociological laws (Park and Burgess 1921:43).

In context, this seems to have been as much an attempt to legislate new goals for the developing science of sociology as a report on reality. A recent history of sociology at Chicago, however, has accepted the optimistic statement of goal (which *preceded* the empirical studies now associated with the Chicago school) as literal truth: "Almost none of this work was solely descriptive in the tradition of the folk anthropology of the time. Instead, it was analytical and concentrated on exploring the behavior patterns and processes of adjustment and change as the immigrant adapted to the new economic environment" (Faris 1967:36). Robert Faris correctly emphasizes that social studies in the city of Chicago gave the "school" its empirical character. The situation at the time was, however, more complex. In an earlier review of sociology from its inception at Chicago, Albion Small (1916:321) commented that the earliest empirical studies led to a "jungle of uncontrolled facts" and that "in spite of our brave efforts to the contrary, most of our work resulted, not in explanations, not even to a great extent in making out secondary causes and effects, but chiefly in exhibiting a miscellany of societary forms."

A revised view preserves the magnitude of the Chicago school's achievement, but it is of a different sort, making sense out of something that at first did not seem amenable to scientific explanation. Developments in sociology can now be compared to those in anthropology under Boas and his students. At about the same period, the presence of cross-cultural diversity seemed so overwhelming as to virtually preclude the search for general laws holding for all cases. The empirical orientation, paralleling that in sociology, responded to a previous period of over-facile theorizing on the basis of limited data.

In the social sciences, the methods of the historian are part of or at least consistent with the training of most practitioners. Moreover, the analytical tools of a discipline can be used to describe its history in terms intelligible to members of the profession. To take anthropology as an example, a persistent problem of fieldwork among "primitive" peoples has been the effect of the observer upon the people studied. For example, Franz Boas, throughout his long career, defined the ultimate problems of anthropology as psychological. His successive interests in physics, geography, and ethnology were integrated by his persistent concern with the nature of perception and its implications for successful scientific experimentation. Every anthropologist is concerned with how to evaluate "informants'" actions and judgments. Standards applied to historical documents are not thus different in kind from those that structure an adequate ethnographic description of a so-called primitive community. For a serious, albeit whimsical comparison of the outside historian of anthropology to the anthropological fieldworker studying their own tribe, see Dell Hymes (1962). Although a historian or even historian of another social science might not choose these particular terms to explicate their enterprise, they resonate for an audience of anthropologists because they place the history of the field alongside its ongoing practice and justify the position of history of anthropology as a special area within the discipline.

What makes the role of scientists qua historians interesting is the nature of consensus within the scientific community itself. Science is a "group product" in which the "reasonable agreement" (Kuhn 1962) necessary to ratify a scientific truth must come from the community of practitioners. The scientific audience is primarily concerned with this ongoing process of evaluation so that new research can be built on the old. Science, past or present, can be studied from multiple points of view: it is simultaneously a body of knowledge, a series of activities of persons recognized by themselves and by the general public as scientists, and a social institution (Zieman 1968:11). In each of these functions, the existence of the science depends on the recognition of its reality. To this extent, disciplinary history does not exist until its view of the past is ratified by members of the discipline.

Professionalism in Science

History of science written by practitioners presupposes the existence of a science and of scientists conscious of their own identity as such. In the history of human societies, such a self-concept has been fairly recent. Many of the features necessary to such self-consciousness may be summarized under the rubric of professionalism. Professionalism involves at least the following factors: setting of disciplinary boundaries as particular social sciences become differentiated; establishment of institutions for scientific research, such that a scientist could expect to earn a living by their inquiries; emergence of a community of scholars in contact with one another; standards for membership in that community through formal training or research results. In North America, these things began to coalesce during the mid-nineteenth century and have continued to develop to the present time. Rates of scientific discovery and dissemination of its results have been greatly accelerated. Given that science is always done within a social context, science becomes a new kind of enterprise as a result.

The most widely known attempt to interpret the history of science is that of Thomas S. Kuhn (1962), who argues that "normal science," the sequential development and refinement of general theories that define solvable research problems, leads to gradual changes in the perception of anomalies in theory by practitioners.

This results in a "scientific revolution" that creates a new "paradigm" of normal science, which in turn sets guidelines for the scientific community for a time. In Kuhn's view (modified somewhat in the second edition in 1970), social sciences are "pre-paradigmatic" because their content permits alternative but simultaneous and overlapping theoretical formulations. Such a picture is useful insofar as it stresses the shared culture of scientists at a given period and avoids the impression that science is purely cumulative and chronological.

The notion of "paradigm" requires some reformulation if it is to be applied successfully to the history of social sciences. There is, indeed, a stage in the development of American anthropology (hereafter the major focus of attention) before which it is unilluminating to rely on a concept of "paradigm." There was a tradition of anthropological study but not yet a *profession* of anthropology. The difference is a crucial one because of its implications for the identity and interaction of anthropologists. In attempting to recognize professionalization and specify its importance, the major criterion will be the change brought about in the nature of the scientific community and its effect on the kind of science that could be done. Professionalism is much more than the content of a science. It requires a group of people in contact with one another who share certain concepts and methods for the practice of their common profession. Such a social organization presupposes an institutional framework that can provide full-time employment for a number of these scholars. A "paradigm" is possible when such a stage has been reached, not when all practitioners have agreed on the exact nature of the task at hand, as Kuhn seems to require.

There was no single moment at which American anthropology became professional. Rather, there was a long period during which a number of individuals worked to create as reality their idea of what the profession should be. There were frequent setbacks— for example, when personnel or institutional resources were not available. Franz Boas's history of American anthropology written for *Science* in 1904 discussed work leading in the direction he envisioned for the entire discipline; even a decade later he would have been able to cite work by his own colleagues and students that actually met his rigorous standards. The article was written prior to the implementation of its new perspective in order to influence development of the discipline in a direction that was already in progress. By singling out what was valid in the past, Boas attempted to define both anthropology's present and future.

In one sense, the professionalization of American anthropology has proceeded chronologically. The process has been irreversible in that the development of personnel and resources tends to produce further developments of the same nature. Each change in the social and institutional structure of the discipline has been gradual as anthropologists moved toward an idea of anthropology that changed in response to their movement toward it. Such a view at least partially contradicts that of a series of successive paradigms replacing one another. The research that produces a new paradigm takes place within the old one, and it is the established practitioners who must be won over to alternative perspectives and methods. Thus, continuity in the social organization of the scientific community is virtually inevitable.

Two Paradigms in American Anthropology

The rest of this paper delineates the transition between two periods in American anthropology that might be classified as distinct "paradigms." According to the criteria outlined above, the first paradigm of professional American anthropology crystallized around the Bureau of [American] Ethnology (BAE) founded by John Wesley Powell, then head of a government geological survey, in 1879. The bureau was one of a number of government research institutions established in the aftermath of the American Civil War, a period of geographical expansion and optimism about the results of science. Most of the new bureaus were intended to provide practical information. Geologists mapped the river and mountain systems of the West. Coastal waterways were developed. The Army Corps of Engineers worked hand in hand with pure research teams. Political opportunism, graft, and overlap of projects were common. There was no correlation of the labors of the proliferating institutions for government research.

Ethnologists were expected, in this framework, to study the "aborigines" whose presence made development of the West so difficult. The Bureau of Indian Affairs was established in 1819 but remained within the War Department until 1849, an accurate indication of America's attitude toward its native peoples. Powell was expected to provide solutions to these pressing political problems and received limited congressional appropriations to do so. The full-time scientific staff never exceeded fifteen, but Powell had an implicit mandate to collect information from whoever would provide it. This meant drawing on the time, energy, and accumulated data of America's nonprofessional students of the Indians [*sic*]—members of local societies, traders, missionaries, soldiers, and other government officials.

The founding of the bureau has been taken by historians of anthropology as the beginning of professional anthropology in America. Indeed, it provided a new kind of institutional framework for studies that had been building for some time already by 1879. Powell and several members of his staff had been studying "aboriginal" languages and customs for a number of years as part of their geological survey work. Boas's innovation was less in the institution of new research areas than in the addition of a new institutional resource for the study of anthropology. This role was crucial to later developments, although the bureau itself did not long remain at the forefront of anthropological science in America.

The importance of the bureau waned in the early twentieth century, partially because of conflicts internal to its own institutional structure. Powell accepted the limitation to potentially practical researches and pursued more theoretical lines of research indirectly when time and funds permitted. But the precedent for professional anthropology as a subject of scientific inquiry for its own sake had already been set, opening up an institutional gap that the bureau could not meet. Franz Boas, the most outstanding figure of twentieth-century American anthropology, stepped into this gap. Previous histories have stressed the discontinuity of Boas's relationship to the bureau tradition. In fact, the time was ripe for the innovations he proposed, and the bureau gave him an initial means for doing so.

In writing the history of anthropology, the very magnitude of Boas's stature has forced his intellectual heirs to focus on defining their relationship to the Boasian tradition. Earlier developments have been read primarily if not exclusively in this perspective. Commentaries from American anthropologists have ranged from eulogy to depreciation, usually with the urgency of present concerns taking precedence over historicism as understood by the historian. A number of Boas's early students, especially Alfred L. Kroeber and Robert H. Lowie, attempted to "set the record straight" about their teacher's contribution to the substance of anthropology and the training of anthropologists. The American Anthropological Association (AAA) devoted two memoirs to evaluation of Boas's contribution; Melville Herskovits wrote a biography. All of these works reasserted the unity of the discipline and the shared culture of its practitioners. More specifically, they were characterized by a nostalgia for the unity or consensus that they perceived the discipline to have had under the leadership of Boas.

For other American anthropologists, however, the previous consensus was restrictive; criticism of Boas became a strategy to protest the lack of disciplinary interest in certain topics. Boas was criticized for his lack of interest in evolution and resultant focus on limited aspects of culture theory. As long as the major concern was to legitimize neo-evolutionary approaches, the state of the discipline that motivated Boas's emphasis on the history of particular cultures was lost from view.

Each of these internal views of the role of Boas and the consequent nature of the American anthropological tradition is somewhat myopic. Each is part of the discipline, but the integrating historical perspective that might have brought alive the issues that structured Boas's own career and work is missing. Several possible reasons for the simplification emerge: the students who wrote their recollections did not know Boas during the early years of his career when the direction anthropology would develop was more problematical; by the time Boas died at the age of eighty-four, his position was virtually unassailable, and the history he had made was a matter of legend; those who had worked toward a unity of the discipline of anthropology did not want to stress the disruption and conflict by which its autonomy was won. Boas's early struggles to refine the theoretical and methodological emphases of evolutionary anthropology and his problems earning a living at his profession are recorded primarily in archival materials rarely consulted by contemporary anthropologists.

In the light of such documents, it is clear that Boas built on the work of his predecessors in the BAE and that much of his success in changing the kind of anthropology practiced in America in the 1880s depended on his ability to leverage available personnel and resources as a means to implement his vision of the science of man[kind]. The influence of the Boasian tradition solidified gradually between Boas's appointment at Columbia just before the turn of the century until about the First World War, when Boas's personal power could no longer be effectively challenged. Up to this point, the Boasian tradition retained clear continuity with the bureau tradition by virtue of the common concern with professionalization—both in theories and in development of organizational resources. In some ways this meant that similarities between the two traditions were greater than their differences. After about 1920, although the date is arbitrary, anthropology held a reasonably secure position among American sciences, and new concerns, commonly associated with the Boasian tradition today, began to emerge.

The Bureau of American Ethnology

The changes initiated by Powell's BAE cannot be understood without first examining the anthropological tradition upon which its researches were built (see Hallowell [1960] for a summary of this period). Study of the American Indian [sic] was a political necessity in the New World. Long before anthropology existed as a science, its methods and subject matter were important to the political and social history of the nation. Thomas Jefferson was perhaps America's first anthropologist; his instructions to the Lewis and Clark Expedition established a tradition of government inquiry into Indigenous customs. Missionaries, traders, and settlers had similar urgent motivations to understand the "Indians" for their own practical purposes as the frontier moved westward.

Early American Indian [sic] scholars were divided between those who recorded their observations and those who prepared scholarly treatises using these reports as primary data. Jefferson himself had no firsthand experience with the western frontier. Even so, the presence of the American Indian [sic] was crucial in lending early scholarly identity and self-consciousness to those concerned with anthropological subjects. The American Philosophical Society (APS), founded by Benjamin Franklin in 1743, established a committee on American Indian [sic] languages in its early years. This practical necessity predetermined that the history of anthropology in America would be somewhat different from that of the other social sciences. Whereas the scholarly disciplines of history, psychology, and political philosophy took their guidelines from Europe and consequently had to declare their independence from European scholarship during the late nineteenth century (Herbst 1965), scholars located in the New World were established as the major authorities on the American Indian [sic] because of their geographic proximity.

It would be inaccurate to call this early tradition of American Indian [sic] studies a professional science. Practical students were not interested in accumulation and dissemination of knowledge; learned society members did not restrict their inquiries to anthropological topics; the science was not practiced for its own sake. Partly this was due to lack of institutional resources. The idea of being an anthropologist had not yet been born. The learned societies only supported "gentleman scholars" and were localized to a point that made communication difficult among those interested in the same subjects. There was no accepted definition of a qualified student of the American Indian [sic]. Since there was no anthropological training, anyone could be an expert, and there was no channel for evaluation by a scientific community at the national level.

Of necessity, the BAE built on such a foundation. When Powell received authorization for a new institution to formalize the long-standing government interest in information about the Indians [sic] that would permit intelligent pacification and administration, he built on earlier although less systematic attempts. Powell was a self-made man with firsthand experience of the West through his geology, a veteran of the Civil War, a man of action, and a devotee of serious but amateur natural science. Unlike many of his contemporaries, he also had a vision of professional science, in which men [sic] of knowledge could enable rational social action. His idealism in politics and devotion to the American destiny of expansion showed up nowhere more clearly than in his faith in the rational study of aboriginal [sic] culture as a necessary path to the fulfillment of the American dream.

Even before the founding of the bureau, there were individuals who shared Powell's vision. Like him, of necessity they were trained in non-anthropological fields. Many progressed through several careers before settling on ethnology. Several worked for Powell in the Geological Survey of the Rocky Mountain Region (which turned gradually from the study of physical features to human, including aboriginal [*sic*], use of the environment in order to secure a unique niche among the multiple such surveys). That they followed him into ethnology does not mean their loyalties were entirely personal; for their generation the divisions between the sciences of geology and anthropology did not exist. Powell's commitment was to science, which he considered overarching and unitary regardless of the phenomena studied, and to the American West, whose development he believed must proceed by rational planning. He was willing, indeed eager, to make the bureau a project in what we would now call applied anthropology. Practical politicians were not segregated from scientists because science was expected to serve as a practical tool to achieve social ends. The chronological development of Powell's interests from exploration to geology and from political action to ethnology contains no obvious discontinuities. No Powell biographer to date has done justice to the consistency with which he contributed to what are today rather diverse fields. Despite his contribution to the development of professionalism in science, Powell himself remained part of the older philosophical tradition of the local societies in which such boundaries were irrelevant.

The professionalism of the bureau cannot be considered entirely apart from the history of the Anthropological Society of Washington (ASW) with which it was associated. Like Powell's new professional staff, its members were self-educated, many were veterans, most had lived in the West; they were natural scientists before they were anthropologists. Scientists from other government bureaus appeared frequently. Most significantly, the members were not young men seeking a professional career. Anyone with an interest in Indians [*sic*] was welcome. Powell refused to isolate his bureau from its roots in such a scientific community.

Anthropology was not unique in the directions of its development toward professionalism during the late nineteenth century

(Daniels 1967; Dupree 1957). By this time the United States government was a major world supporter of scientific research and operated with a concept of science not far from Powell's own. Science was envisioned as a major tool toward the progress of the nation, and scientists were viewed as public servants. Science for its own sake, indeed, would have been considered incompatible with American democracy. It was the end of the century before scientists in any discipline were sufficiently secure in their professionalism to argue for the necessity of pure research, with problems chosen by a scientific community not accountable to the general public.

There were, however, different kinds of government science. The choice farthest from Powell's was that of the Smithsonian Institution, founded in 1846 for the "increase and diffusion of knowledge." The first director, physicist Joseph Henry, devoted the rest of his life to the development of an apolitical clearinghouse for scientific research that would increase communication within the scientific community and systematize research results in a manner impossible for the isolated scholar. Henry's vision of American science operated within the utilitarian view prevalent in the earlier part of the century, but his efforts also provided a major stimulus to the development of autonomous, professional scholarship. The Smithsonian helped unify the American sciences because it contributed to the entire range of the nation's scientific endeavors.

Other government institutions for scientific research were more dependent on the vicissitudes of financial doles from Congress, which prevented them from making long-range research plans. When the post–Civil War boom in science subsided in government circles not long after the founding of the Smithsonian, Henry's institution was one of the few to feel little pressure. Because of Henry's wisdom in avoiding political ties, Powell was able to retreat from the Geological Survey, which was much curtailed after 1890, into the relative quietude of the Smithsonian. Other federal agencies were not so fortunate. The affiliation was doubly appropriate since it was Henry who had first encouraged Powell to collect Indian [sic] vocabularies and eventually study human utilization of land resources. Although many programs were cut back around 1890, Powell was able to continue his basic tasks of collecting information about the "aborigines," while avoiding the political controversy sparked by his arid lands work, which had posed a threat to western business interests.

The theoretical perspective by which Powell held the bureau staff together integrated the wide scope of anthropology as now understood in the United States within an overall evolutionary view of human society. Lewis Henry Morgan's *Ancient Society* was the explicit model for Powell's own *Wyandot Society* and John Owen Dorsey's *Omaha Sociology*. The entire staff was expected to have read and assimilated Morgan's synthetic work. Powell was not interested in Morgan's data on social organization, but he used Morgan's evolutionary philosophy to integrate the diverse projects and specialized interests of his staff.

Powell's view of the scope of the discipline has generally prevailed in North America, in sharp contrast to the European development of cultural and physical anthropology as largely separate endeavors. In part this is because the presence of the American Indian [*sic*] required diverse methods. Archaeological researches were imposed on the bureau by Congress because of their popular appeal. Powell quickly incorporated the problem of continuity between archaeological and ethnological cultures within his view of the scope of anthropology. A synthetic evolutionary theory could integrate such distinct subject matters in a way that later bureau archaeology, stressing details of sequence and the autonomy of archaeology, could not. Powell's evolutionary history of mankind permitted a broad definition of relevance. Because there was no established content for the science in 1879, the individual staff members largely followed inclination and previous experience. Special interests included such narrow topics as sign language and mortuary customs that were worldwide in scope with a broadly evolutionary tenor. Others followed more traditional subdivisions of anthropology: social organization, religion, language, mythology. A few were areal specialists within North America.

In practice, however, a professionalism was not yet possible in which everyone did their independent research in isolation from the overall aims of the institution. Every staff member was expected to contribute to the broad tasks by which Powell hoped to "organize anthropologic research in America." The staggering task of systematizing and supplementing records of the Indians [*sic*] inspired

Powell to seek a new institutional basis for anthropological studies and led him to encourage a new kind of professionalism. The proof of his foresight is the bureau's ability to complete cooperative research projects beyond the scope of traditional scholars working alone.

Individual researches were, to a certain extent, subordinated to the collective projects, which continued throughout Powell's term as director. Nonprofessional collaborators were encouraged. The staff designed and circulated questionnaires, particularly linguistic ones, collated the results, pored over the Smithsonian manuscripts they had inherited, and supplemented existing knowledge with selective field work by the small staff. The best known of these broadly conceived and imaginatively executed projects was the 1891 classification of American Indian (in the terminology of the period) languages, which still remains the conservative baseline for Native American linguistics (Darnell 1971). The general commitment to overall goals often makes authorship difficult to establish, and it was not a matter of concern. For example, Powell designed the linguistic classification project; Henry W. Henshaw, a biologist, applied the nomenclatural principles; Albert S. Gatschet was primarily responsible for the linguistic field work. Each, in a sense, was the author and considered himself to be so. The point is not that they were confused about the nature of their mutual roles, but that each saw the goal of the bureau as the "mapping" of North America (Darnell 1969), the collection of basic information as a foundation for effective administration and later more detailed studies.

Powell's implementation of this program was self-consciously designed to change the professional standards obtaining in North American anthropology. Although the actual size of the bureau staff always remained small, its influence was augmented by the national circulation of its publications and its role as arbitrator of the contributions of independent scholars. Because the bureau did not reject the inclusive concept of science out of which it had developed, research standards of amateur enthusiasts could be remediated gradually. Powell himself believed that the bureau constituted the nation's first truly professional and scientific anthropology, and most of his staff felt a similar ideological commitment.

This vision of professional science inspired them to develop institutional resources for its implementation.

Part of the bureau's strategy was imposed by its potentially restrictive status as a government institution. Publications had to be deployed to justify the program to Congress, and disagreement had to be masked for the staff to preserve their status as experts. Congress expected the research to terminate when the American Indian [*sic*] stopped being the major foreign policy problem of the government. Powell himself had encouraged such practical justification of bureau researches. His first annual report had stressed the bureau's potential function in the rational categorization of Indians [*sic*] for reservation settlement.

By the end of Powell's life, the role of the United States as a world power was changing radically. The bureau tried unsuccessfully to justify extending its researches geographically so that it could continue to serve as policy adviser to Congress. After Powell's death in 1902, the evolutionary synthesis fell apart; the bureau drifted into fact-collecting projects, which, to Powell, had been only the means to the larger task of elucidating the history of mankind. In sum, the decline of the bureau as the leader of professional anthropology in America was an inevitable consequence of the changing role of the government in science and the progressively more rigorous character of what would qualify as meaningful scientific results. The Boasian critique of evolutionary method and theory further highlighted the bureau's failure to develop a new and viable manner of integrating its researches. Boas's early success owed much to his ability to exploit institutional tensions already plaguing the bureau.

Projects begun by Powell were continued at least nominally by his successors, but new ones were rarely initiated. Boas, who had cooperated with the bureau and found support for his initial Northwest Coast fieldwork available in no other American institution at that time, opposed restriction of the bureau's research function but could not stem the trend toward retrenchment. He was forced to seek alternatives to the very support that had enabled him to begin establishing a professional anthropology infused by standards of German scholarship. In the late 1880s, only the bureau had had the prestige, funds, and freedom of research to further his ambitions. Powell had been delighted to cooperate with the young German scholar who shared his commitment to professional science and empirical research; he needed Boas's help to secure the bureau's position at the forefront of American anthropology. After Powell's death, however, Boas's competence was perceived as arrogance and his finagling for research funds as dishonesty. The bureau could no longer support changing standards of professionalism in anthropology. Boas and a few colleagues knew what they needed and could not find it in the bureau.

Professionalism in Museum and University

Meanwhile, as the bureau was illustrating the feasibility of a new kind of support for scientific research, more localized institutions faced similar problems in their efforts to develop a professional science of anthropology. At first, these institutions were museums with strong ties to the local scientific societies. Later, increasingly, the most attractive resource was university affiliation, because academic training programs were designed to produce new professionals. Training specific to anthropology was the obvious next step in professionalization. Just as the revolution to produce professional sciences grew out of the previous organization of these sciences, another revolution was needed to develop academic institutions to train and credential scientists.

The traditional American university had stressed moral philosophy rather than training in practical skills. Toward the end of the nineteenth century, however, students became progressively more distressed by the sterility of these programs and migrated to Germany in increasing numbers for their advanced training. American graduate education blossomed after the founding of Johns Hopkins University in 1876 when the excitement of the German university system combined with national pride to produce a series of rapid changes in curriculum and educational goals, even at the undergraduate level. Although there were protests, particularly from administrators and financial patrons, the tide could not be diverted from the new scholarship, from academic study for its own sake. Changes already in process as American science moved away from being a gentleman's [*sic*] pastime increased the likelihood of effective acceptance of the German educational system.

It was perhaps inevitable that anthropology would become involved in these changes. For the most part, anthropologists sought training in the traditional natural and social sciences; these subjects were an innovation in the classics and liberal arts curriculum of the American colleges. It seemed, at least to anthropologists, logical to include anthropology along with other new disciplines. Indeed, anthropology had substantial affinities of method and subject matter to German history, sociology and psychology. Anthropologists urging teaching programs found it expedient to stress such affinities. Boas's German background was an important ingredient of his enthusiasm for academic anthropology. His own scholarly standards had developed in such a tradition rather than in the utilitarian vein of the bureau philosophy. Boas wanted a freedom *from* politics and *for* research, which was most easily found in the academic world. University affiliation would become an increasingly important marker of public recognition for anthropology as a science and for the professional status and later for the disciplinary autonomy of anthropologists. Boas was the model, again perhaps because of his German background, wherein a single professor dominated the research of a generation of scholars whose aim was to replace them by doing the same kind of painstaking research (Zieman 1968). This was a long way from the cooperative research ethic of the bureau but could not have developed without that institution's illustration that professionalism could answer the growing need to study the American Indians [*sic*].

Despite the enthusiasm of many anthropologists for the new academic developments, early attempts to teach anthropology were abortive. The first professor was Daniel Garrison Brinton, appointed without salary at the University of Pennsylvania in 1886 (Darnell 1970, chapter 4, this volume). Brinton attracted no students, and his position depended primarily on the ambitions of the university provost to develop a popular museum of archaeology and ethnology in Philadelphia. Brinton's primary scientific affiliation remained with the American Philosophical Society, and he quarreled with the museum because its commitment to popularization contradicted his idea of scholarship. Brinton was, however, fully committed to the idea of academic anthropology. In 1892 he prepared a proposal, never seriously considered by his superiors, for the teaching of anthropology at the University of Pennsylvania. Since only the cover letter dealt explicitly with the situation at Philadelphia, it seems clear that Brinton intended a theoretical statement of institutional possibilities for the future of anthropology and did not foresee local implementation.

Anthropology was established in two of the new graduate universities. The University of Chicago opened with Frederick Starr teaching anthropology in conjunction with sociology. Because Starr refused to abandon evolutionary theory and to cooperate with other scholars or disciplines, the program was a great disappointment, particularly to Boas. The other early effort was at Clark University, where Boas produced the first American PhD in anthropology in 1892. The university's founder was unenthusiastic about additions, among which anthropology was conspicuous, to the traditional curriculum, and Boas was among the dissatisfied faculty who resigned en masse a few years later. At Clark, Boas's work was associated with psychology based on the German model—which was not incompatible with his own aims. His problems there were mired in the growing pains of the American graduate school rather than internal to the discipline of anthropology.

These failures were discouraging, but Boas continued to search for any possible institutional support and to insist on the autonomy and professionalism of anthropology. The most successful alternative, especially before 1900, was the museum, despite its dependence on popular support. Indeed, the first successful teaching of anthropology was at Harvard University, where Frederic W. Putnam of the Peabody Museum took on the additional task of teaching and promoting the academic future of anthropology. His teaching was the result of a long career in archaeology and museum curatorship. Although committed to academic teaching in principle, he never became primarily an educator and viewed teaching as a way of training and ensuring professional competence of his younger associates. Amateur recruitment was incompatible with the professional self-image he considered crucial.

Putnam did not concern himself with the theoretical development of the discipline. His major contribution was to develop institutional bases for professionalization. He was influential in establishing the major archaeological and ethnological museums of the country—successively at Chicago, New York, and Berkeley. Perhaps predictably, his associate in the first two of these endeavors was Franz Boas, the young German scholar who believed in the future of professional anthropology. This was the transitional period for Boas in which he turned first to the bureau, later to museums and research foundations, and ultimately to academic standing in the university. Boas's goals, however, went beyond Putnam's: he *preferred* training new students as a professor. He accepted a joint appointment with the American Museum and Columbia University, where he developed his vision of the science of anthropology. His initial optimism for the position was primarily due to institutional potential for things he had long wanted to do:

> I am trying to develop the collections of this Museum in such a way that they will ultimately form the basis of university instruction in all lines of anthropological research. This aim of course must be combined with the general educational aims of the museum, but I find that both are very easily harmonized. I am endeavoring to develop each department to such a point that within a very short time it will demand the care of a specialist, and this will be the opportune moment for introducing instruction in each particular line in Columbia University. (Boas to Zelia Nuttall, May 16, 1901: APS)

Although the optimism was, in retrospect, somewhat premature, Boas continued to recognize that the necessity of institutional resources for the implementation of an idea, particularly so complex an idea as professional, scholarly science. When he had a chance to escape the conflict of museum and university in favor of Putnam's third institutional experiment in California, Boas declined. By that time, Putnam could hire instead his first Columbia PhD, Alfred L. Kroeber in California. The results of the Columbia academic program were already bearing fruit.

In the early twentieth century, Columbia became the model for academic anthropology. Over the next two decades, departments chaired and staffed by Boas's students were established in most of the nation's major universities. Each of these had its unique flavor, but Boas consciously created a social network encompassing the entire profession in America. Although many of his former students remained personally ambivalent toward Boas throughout their careers, in outline they were loyal to their professor; Boas's view of the task at hand prevailed until the Second World War. At Columbia he hoped to make the academic program independent of the museum, to train archaeologists to ensure a program of holistic anthropology, and to extend the department's geographical focus beyond North America. For many years these were unrealized but unforgotten dreams. Through it all, Columbia remained the center of Boasian anthropology, with exchange and movement of like-minded faculty and students sustaining the momentum of anthropology.

Academic teaching of anthropology grew rapidly. By 1902 thirty-one institutions offered courses, usually in association with sociology or psychology (MacCurdy 1902). Boas himself grew progressively more vocal about the importance of academic anthropology in response to restrictions on his own research freedom at the American Museum. In 1916 he organized a symposium for the American Association for the Advancement of Science (AAAS) to summarize the role of academic teaching in anthropology. The place of the museum and the need for trained academic personnel to teach were the two overriding themes. The symposium was both assessment and propaganda. Boas and his students were convinced and determined to persuade others.

In these years, independently of Boas's struggles in anthropology, all American scientists were developing organizations and communication media to enforce their sense of common professionalism. Most of the present academic disciplines founded journals and societies around the end of the nineteenth century. The national journal of anthropology was established in 1898 and the professional association in 1902. Thereafter, academic discipline rather than occupation as teacher or museum curator would become the primary identification of scholars. Scientists, as a result, were less dependent on local exigencies and more subject to standards imposed by their discipline as a whole.

In anthropology, the struggle for professionalism also meant a struggle for dominance by Boas and his students. Much was continuous with the past: Powell's "mapping" of North America was incomplete; Boas and his students were influential in completing several bureau projects. Powell agreed with them that increased institutional support and professional communication were crucial to the development of anthropology. However, in practice, as Boas gained strength, partially through the prominence of his students, he came into increasing conflict with the bureau, now on the defensive. He turned away from the Washington-dominated *American Anthropologist* toward the American Folklore Society (AFS), where he could control editorial policy more effectively (Darnell 1974, chapter 3, this volume). This led to an occasional direct confrontation until around the First World War, when Boas was too firmly established and academia too clearly the direction of anthropology's future to sustain further effective challenge.

We have dealt thus far with the gradual task of building the resources for a profession of anthropology in America, arguing that these developed out of a basic tradition of Native American research, which had existed in a professional context at least since the founding of the bureau in 1879. Although subsequent anthropologists, primarily Boasian, have seen the process as beginning much later, this is an oversimplification. Most treatments have taken the emergence of professionalization for granted because it exists now and have stressed the *theoretical* discontinuities between Boas and his predecessors. This is inadequate because theories could not be implemented through the empirical work now associated with the Boas school until institutional resources existed and professional recognition of anthropologists was assured. Ideas do not exist in a vacuum, and practitioners work to bring ideas into reality. Boas was such a man, and it is the measure of his stature that his view of professional anthropology so entirely prevailed that the struggle for it could be forgotten.

The remaining crucial question is of the unity of the Boasian "school." Particularly in the early years when conflicts with the earlier establishment were frequent, the solidarity of Boas's students was considerable (Stocking 1968). The early successes were negative. Boas reacted against evolutionary ethnology by taking as problematical the diverse historical development of particular historical cultures. He insisted on the analytical discreteness of race, language, and culture and stressed synchronic pattern within a single culture or geographical area. Each of his students took a particular subject matter or point of view to attack the theoretical apparatus of evolutionary anthropology. Often this procedure was self-conscious. Sapir referred to the "body of historical critiques that anthropology owes to Boas," and Lowie noted "methodological principles which are becoming the common property of all the active younger American students of ethnology." Anthropology under Boas was deliberately conservative in response to the excesses of previous theorizing. Laws of human nature would come later when the facts had been assembled and evaluated.

Two examples suffice to illustrate the increasing unity and consciousness of common purpose among Boasian anthropologists in the years just before the First World War. In 1914 a series of summary papers prepared for the International Congress of Americanists defined the scope of the discipline as practiced by Boas. Invited contributors were carefully selected to represent work in process. At about the same time, a number of "paradigm statements" articulated both methods and tentative results. These works summarized the state of current factual knowledge and lent aesthetic unity to the social group of "Boasians." It was a stocktaking by young scholars, mostly men, who had won their right to professional status as anthropologists and felt they had the methods to attack remaining problems effectively. For the first time, there were textbooks in anthropology, the best known being Kroeber's *Anthropology* (1923), Sapir's *Language* (1921), Lowie's *Primitive Society* (1920), and Wissler's *The American Indian* (1917). By this point, the professionalization of American anthropology was essentially complete. A paradigm had been defined and, with considerable collective effort, had won acceptance.

Summary

In many ways, the views set forth here may not seem to differ drastically from those described initially as coming from the oral history of American anthropology. The great heroes, Powell and particularly Boas, retain their greatness. Discussion has proceeded more or less chronologically, because events occur in time, and participants are constrained by it in their choice of actions. Yet disciplinary histories have rarely stressed purposeful human behavior, intended to bring about specific kinds of changes in the nature of a discipline and the status of its practitioners. The "paradigms" that guide the development of a science have proved to be a composite of theories, men who believed in them, institutions that supported their research, and, perhaps above all, scientific consensus within a community of scholars—a process heavily dependent upon the social context in which individual ideas vie for paradigmatic status. This is perhaps the most important bequest of Powell, Boas, and their colleagues in other American (social) sciences to their intellectual heirs: the concept of professionalism in science. Its irreversibility makes it inevitably part of present and future paradigms, since all anthropologists are now committed to its implementation.

Notes

1. Originally published as "The Professionalization of American Anthropology: A Case Study in the Sociology of Knowledge." *Social Science Information* 10 (1971): 83–103.

2. Some problems in the history of science can only be solved by scholars with multidisciplinary interests, if not training. For example, the histories of the various social sciences merge as one moves backward in time. Philosophy, history, sociology, economics, political science, and anthropology all have their roots in the expansion of the medieval worldview that began with the age of discovery. Each of these disciplines has a stake in writing the history of this period.

References

Daniels, Glynn H. 1967. "The Pure Science Ideal and Democratic Culture." *Science* 156:1699–702.

Darnell, Regna. 1969. "The Development of American Anthropology, 1879–1920: From the Bureau of American Ethnology to Franz Boas." PhD diss., University of Pennsylvania.

———. 1970. "The Emergence of Academic Anthropology at the University of Pennsylvania." *Journal of the History of Behavioral Sciences* 6:80–92.

———. 1971. "The Revision of the Powell Classification: A Chapter in the History of American Indian Linguistics." *Papers in Linguistics* 4:70–110.

———. 1974. "American Anthropology and the Development of American Folklore Scholarship, 1880–1920." *Journal of the American Folklore Institute* 10:23–39.

Dupree, A. Hunter. 1957. *Science in the Federal Government: A History of Policies and Activities to 1940.* New York: Harper.

Faris, Robert. 1967. *Chicago Sociology, 1920–1932.* San Francisco: Chandler.

Hallowell, A. Irving. 1960. "The Beginnings of Anthropology in America." In *Selected Readings from the American Anthropologist, 1888–1920,* edited by Frederica de Laguna, 1–99. Evanston IL: Row, Peterson.

Harris, Marvin. 1968. *The Rise of Anthropological Theory.* New York: Thomas Crowell.

Herbst, Jurgen. 1965. *The German Historical School in American Scholarship.* Ithaca NY: Cornell University Press.

Hymes, Dell. 1962. "On Studying the History of Anthropology." *Kroeber Anthropological Society Papers* 26:81–86.

Kroeber, Alfred L. 1923. *Anthropology.* New York: Harcourt, Brace.

Kuhn, Thomas S. 1962. *The Structure of Scientific Revolutions.* Chicago: Phoenix.

Lowie, Robert H. 1920. *Primitive Society.* New York: Harper.

———. 1937. *The History of Ethnological Theory.* New York: Farrar and Rinehart.

MacCurdy, Grant. 1902. "The Teaching of Anthropology in the United States." *Science* 15:211–16.

Park, Robert, and Ernest Burgess. 1921. *Introduction to the Science of Sociology.* Chicago: University of Chicago Press.

Sapir, Edward. 1921. *Language: An Introduction to the Study of Speech.* New York: Harcourt, Brace.

Small, Albion. 1916. "Fifty Years of Sociology in the United States: 1865–1915." *American Journal of Sociology* 21:177–269.

Stocking, George W., Jr. 1968. *Race, Culture and Evolution: Essays in the History of Anthropology.* New York: Free Press of Glencoe.

Wissler, Clark. 1917. *The American Indian.* New York: McMurtrie.

Zieman, John. 1968. *Public Knowledge: The Social Dimension of Science.* Cambridge MA: Cambridge University Press.

3

The Development of American Folklore Scholarship, 1880–1920

It has long been a matter of folk knowledge within the discipline of folklore that anthropologists contributed significantly to the early development of the American Folklore Society.[1] More rarely, however, do anthropologists or folklorists cross their habitual disciplinary boundaries to note interaction of individuals and institutions or cross-disciplinary fertilization of ideas. On the one hand, much of the character of the AFS from its establishment in 1888 to about 1925 was shaped by the activities of Franz Boas, the major figure of twentieth-century American anthropology, and his students. On the other hand, this Boasian participation in the AFS affected the character and substance of American anthropology at a time when it was itself becoming a full-fledged discipline centering in universities. Members of either discipline, examining these claims, might be inclined to wonder "why folklore?" or "why anthropology?" The answers to these questions are to be found in the state of both of those subjects of inquiry in late nineteenth-century America.

Much of nineteenth-century American science centered in learned societies supported by gentlemen [*sic*]scholars who were interested in diverse areas of knowledge. Among the most important were the American Philosophical Society and the Academy of Natural Sciences of Philadelphia, the American Antiquarian Society and Peabody Museum in Boston, the American Oriental Society and Connecticut Historical Society in New Haven, the American Geographical Society and American Museum of Natural History in New York, and the Anthropological Society of Washington (ASW) and Smithsonian Institution in Washington. The only body situated to break the isolation of scholars in their local societies on a national basis was the American Association for the Advancement of Science founded in 1848.

The line between professional and amateur science was not yet firm. The AAAS was technically run by professional scientists; many of its members were self-trained scholars who never made their living through practice of their discipline. Members included amateurs of all sorts, and their participation in annual meetings was encouraged as a means to boost the growth of a critical mass for professional science. Many of the foremost figures of nineteenth-century American folklore and anthropology came from such backgrounds, among them William Wells Newell in folklore and Daniel Garrison Brinton in anthropology. Although comparable transformational figures were responsible for the founding of journals and professional societies in a number of disciplines during the last two decades of the nineteenth century, the success of their efforts to develop institutions and professional standards rendered them anachronistic. Professionalization occurred differently in different disciplines, but its overall direction remained constant.

Anthropology preceded folklore in developing a professional institutional framework. Nineteenth-century American anthropology centered in the BAE founded by John Wesley Powell in 1879 for the practical study of the "aborigines" of North America; "American" was added to the name in 1892. The U.S. Congress was willing to support such research because the "Indians" were the major foreign policy problem of the nation, and their prompt and peaceful settlement on reservations was essential to the American manifest destiny of national security and growth. The bureau funded a great deal of ethnographic research, much of which falls within the scope of what would come to be known as folklore studies. Popular support for the bureau came from the Anthropological Society of Washington, composed largely of amateurs except for the bureau staff.

The other established institutional framework for late nineteenth-century anthropological study was the museum. Museums attracted popular support because of their exotic collections of antiquities. Ethnology was never as important in museum programs as archaeology, but considerable study of the languages and cultures of North American Indians [*sic*] took place under museum auspices. Particularly important here was the Peabody Museum associated with Harvard University, under the direction of Frederic W. Putnam. The most successful collaboration between a museum and a university department was the program he developed at Harvard.

This was the context in which Franz Boas, a German-born immigrant who had gradually modified his interests from physics to geography to ethnology, took up a position at Columbia University in 1895 to develop an academic program in anthropology. A hoped-for collaboration with the American Museum of Natural History did not work out, and Boas was forced to seek fieldwork funds and publication outlets for himself and his students elsewhere. In his early efforts to do so, he came up against the Washington establishment on the one hand and the Cambridge establishment on the other.

At this juncture, the development of folklore as an independent field of study became important to the history of American anthropology. Folklore was a subject that had traditionally been recognized within anthropology as a broadly defined science of man[kind]. As early as 1883, the bureau assigned Jeremiah Curtin, who was primarily a diplomat and literary translator, to collect American Indian [*sic*] myths that were expected to reveal the psychological system of the various tribes. Such information was considered crucial for the evolutionary theories propounded by the bureau under Powell's leadership. According to Curtin (quoted in Shafer 1940:36):

> Mythology and philology taken together form a science bearing the same relation to the history of the human mind that geology does to the history of the earth . . . so in mythology, folklore, and languages of nations we find stereotype impresses of the mental conditions of these nations at successive periods. [Each language] has a system of thought, an entire philosophy of things.

Curtin's indexed collection of the myths of the world was never completed, but it would have found a natural place within the bureau's description of the Indigenous cultures of North America.

Boas agreed that folklore was part of anthropology. As early as 1890, he suggested to the bureau that the new folklore society could collaborate with it in publishing material on the mythology of major American Indian [*sic*] tribes (Boas to William Henry Henshaw, December 6, 1890: BAE). Boas proposed to include work by John Murdoch, Garrick Mallery, Daniel Brinton, Reverend McLean, Horatio Hale, James Mooney, Albert Gatschet, J. Owen Dorsey, John Wesley Powell, Jesse Walter Fewkes, Washington Matthews, John Bourke, Curtin, and Alice Fletcher. This list reflects the state of the discipline of anthropology at the time. The majority of these individuals were members of the bureau staff. Of the others, some were missionaries who reported on the peoples among whom they worked, others were independent scholars interested in the American Indian [*sic*]. A professional position in anthropology was too stringent a qualification at that time to prepare a general work on American Indian [*sic*] mythology. Only for the Northwest Coast could Boas depend on the results of his own fieldwork. He had not yet trained a group of students on whose work he could draw. Therefore, he turned to the bureau and the best of the amateurs for personnel and data. The plan was abortive for a combination of reasons, particularly lack of funds for publication through either the folklorists or the bureau, and the difficulty of getting would-be contributors to submit appropriate material.

The AFS, on which Boas had hoped to draw for this material, was not originally intended to be an anthropological organization, although anthropology fell within its scope. The society would focus on the study of the vanishing folklores of the Old English, Negro [*sic*], American Indian [*sic*], French-Canadian, and Mexican cultures as "an important and essential part of history"; the record of human civilization necessarily included "a complete representation of the savage [*sic*] mind" even when its products might appear cruel or immoral. Newell believed that American folklore legitimately drew its problems from the European science of folklore. Accurate collection of materials for later study was a greater priority than immediate comparison of inadequate materials (Newell 1888a:5–7). The AFS, then, intended to study all of the cultures and traditions that had gone into forming the American way of life, among them the "aboriginal."

Although not himself an anthropologist, Newell nonetheless appreciated the rigor of Boas's methods and believed that fieldwork was the key to accurate collection of folklore materials:

> What is needed is to examine that psychology; to study the mythology of native races not as curious fancies or absurd superstitions but as living beliefs having a relation to the intelligence and imagination, the motives and conduct, of men [*sic*] who hold them to be an explanation of the world. (Newell 1888b:162)

With specific reference to Boas, he stated:

> While most English and French folklorists have been amusing themselves with comparing the merits of explanations offered by the "anthropological" and "philological" schools of mythic interpretations, Dr. Boas, belonging to no school, but being both anthropologist and linguist, has put these theories to the only practical test of more extended comparison. (Newell 1896:76)

Boas, in his turn, had great personal respect for Newell, partially due to his lack of personal ambition and his devotion to the progress of folklore as a field of study:

> He always seemed to me in a way like a representation of a time of greater devotion to ideals and a greater unselfishness than we are accustomed to find at the present time. (Boas to Roland B. Dixon, February 1, 1907: APS)

Newell was a graduate of Harvard Divinity School and not professionally trained in folklore or anthropology, but at the Newell Memorial Meeting (March 10, 1907: APS), Boas expressed appreciation for his contributions to the development of professionalism:

> [He pointed out] the analogy between primitive [*sic*] lore and that of Europe, the need of application of the well-grounded principles developed in literary research, the necessity of viewing many expressions of primitive [*sic*] thought as the artistic or philosophic expression of popular ideas formulated by artists or thinkers of high rank. . . . Thus it came to pass that he set anthropologists to thinking in new lines, that he added new recruits to our ranks and that he pressed one after another of

us into his service, and thus led in the work of making room in anthropology for a broad historical viewpoint.

Newell's management of the AFS was congenial to Boas because it permitted considerable emphasis on anthropological publications. Although the members of the AFS were no more professional than those of the ASW, Newell's editorial policy gave Boas virtually a free hand in publishing his own materials and those of his early students. Newell was not entirely partisan, however, and tried to steer a neutral course when he could do so without compromising the scientific usefulness of the society vis-à-vis folklore studies. He realized that local amateurs would continue to contribute to the society for the immediate future (Newell to Boas, May 9, 1890: APS) but doggedly encouraged increasingly rigorous standards of scholarship among the membership.

Newell was also concerned to define a viable niche for himself within the developing discipline of folklore (Bell 1974). His insistence on a scope that included anthropology helped to differentiate him from the society's semiprofessional collectors of folklore materials. Newell hoped that anthropological materials would strengthen the scholarly output of the *Journal of American Folklore*. Moreover, his alliance with Boas, and with anthropology more generally, aligned the weight of Boasian insistence on professional science along German academic lines behind Newell's own efforts to professionalize his fellow folklorists. The relationship of Newell and Boas proved mutually beneficial for a number of years.

Within anthropology itself, there were at least two strong factions in partial opposition to Boas: one in the bureau and the other in Cambridge. Folklore was not a central concern for either of these groups, and Boas's collaboration with Newell and his society did not threaten the autonomy of their work. Boas's progress in remolding the face of American anthropology went less smoothly within his own discipline. The earliest efforts at professionalization occurred under the auspices of the AAAS, within which anthropology gradually separated itself out from other fields of study. Ethnography and geography appeared in the subject headings as early as 1851;

after the Civil War, ethnology was listed separately. The name was changed to anthropology in 1873, and a separate subsection was established in 1876. Anthropology became Section H in 1882.

In 1896 an informal committee of Section H met at the instigation of WJ McGee (whose particular idiosyncrasy was to omit the periods in his initials) to consider the proper role of American anthropology within the larger organization. The committee consisted of Daniel Brinton (primarily affiliated with the APS), James McKeen Cattell (a psychologist), and Franz Boas representing the revitalized American Ethnological Society. Upon urging from Boas, the committee concluded that the time was not yet ripe for an independent professional society and that the immediate goal should be to increase cohesiveness among those interested in anthropology.

In 1897, again at the meetings of the AAAS, the same committee adopted the temporary expedient of changing the scope of the *American Anthropologist*, founded in 1888 as the journal of the ASW to make it truly national. The newly organized journal would stand in relation to Section H and "all other anthropologic institutions" as the then existing journal had stood to the Anthropological Society of Washington (Minutes of Section H Committee, February 19, 1898: APS). The Washington society, however, aspired to retain considerable control over their journal in its expanded national function.

The AAAS committee assumed that an independent professional organization would be founded at a future date. The journal committee elected by that organization was carefully structured to represent the full range of American anthropology in 1898; it included Boas, McGee (from the bureau), Brinton (an independent scholar), Putnam (the permanent secretary of the AAAS and head of the archaeology/anthropology program at Harvard), and Frank Baker (of the ASW). Mostly through the administrative efforts of McGee, a circular (September 30, 1898: NAA) publicized "a policy of devoting the journal in the fullest manner possible to the needs of working anthropologists in America." In practice, however, the arrangements involved considerable jockeying of position among the major factions—BAE, Cambridge, and Boasian, with a strong but more amorphous component of independent scholars.

McGee was willing to leave the scientific organization of the journal to Boas in return for its administrative focus remaining in Washington. McGee guaranteed the contribution of the Anthropological Society of Washington in number of subscriptions. The ASW board was extremely parochial at this time and considered their organization the center of American anthropology (McGee to Brinton, November 19, 1898: NAA). McGee was faced with the formidable task of minimizing the conservative dominance of his own faction in order to ensure cooperation of non-Washingtonians, particularly Boas. The compromise—that the journal became the joint organ of the ASW and the AES in New York—was satisfactory to Boas since it increased his eventual potential control.

The major resistance came from Brinton, who was adamant that the ASW, with which he had long been at odds, should not control the editorial board and choose the managing editor. Brinton was prepared to offer a minority report until McGee and Boas jointly persuaded him that the good of the majority required a positive and unanimous report to the AAAS (McGee to Boas, June 10, 1898: NAA; see also Boas to McGee, August 13, 1898: NAA). Both Boas and McGee felt it necessary to obtain Brinton's support. He was an established figure in anthropology and represented the conservative faction clustered primarily in the learned societies. Both Boas and the bureau in the person of McGee had much to lose if this semiprofessional source of support were antagonized.

The journal's original executive board was designed to project the semblance of representing the geographical and institutional diversity of American anthropology. Four were Washingtonians, including the managing editor, one from Cambridge, one from Chicago, one from the Geological Survey of Canada, plus Brinton as the independent, and Boas. McGee realized that the Washington group would be suspected of "having ulterior motives" (McGee to Boas, June 7, 1898: NAA) and was eager to minimize any possible charge of control from Washington. This disciplinary factionalism enabled Boas to maximize his own position by placing the AES and New York on a par with the BAE.

The establishment of the *American Anthropologist* as a national journal did little to lessen the pressure toward establishment of a professional organization. Boas approached Putnam at the AAAS meetings arguing that the proposed relationship was inappropriate because the Washington contingent was inactive in the larger society (Boas to Putnam, January 27, 1903: APS) and insisted that geographical balance was as important as professionalism to the developing science of anthropology. McGee supported the establishment of an independent society in light of "the magnificent distances of America" (McGee 1901:280) and stressed the revival of the AES in New York under Boas as evidence of the need for a more formal institutional framework. He was most concerned that the scope be national, to promote the science of anthropology; to stimulate the efforts of American anthropologists; to coordinate anthropology with other sciences; to foster local and other societies devoted to anthropology; to serve as a bond of union among American anthropologists and American anthropological organizations, both present and prospective; and to publish and encourage the publication of matter pertaining to anthropology (McGee 1903:187).

Despite these rather grandiose statements, McGee still thought primarily in terms of a professional association dominated by Washingtonians. For Boas, the issues were rather different; his primary concern was to eliminate the amateur base of the AAAS. Because McGee was not trained in anthropology, he had less commitment to its increasing professionalism. Moreover, McGee's power base in Washington anthropology declined sharply after the death of Powell in 1902. Boas thereafter had fewer allies in Washington anthropology and was predictably less enthusiastic about the establishment of a professional society in danger of being dominated from that direction.

At the time of the founding of the American Anthropological Association, Boas claimed that "a conservative estimate of the number of anthropologists who can lay claim to a fairly symmetrical training, and who contribute to the advance of anthropology, would hardly exceed thirty" (Boas 1902:808). Thirty individuals, at that time, would include most of those with firsthand field experience within the older traditions. Boas asserted that the new programs at Harvard and Columbia were rapidly producing the personnel for a higher-caliber professional society. He tried to argue the wisdom of remaining within the AAAS with its distinction between members at large and professionals within each discipline until a truly exclusive professional society could be maintained. This delay would, of course, increase his own prestige within the eventual organization since his students would form much of the new contingent.

McGee, again seeking to forge compromise, prepared a list of sixty-eight individuals who might found a society, mostly fellows of the AAAS. Boas reduced the list of sixty names approved by the committee of thirteen incorporators to only forty. "From the character of the final list it is obvious that Boas emphasized employment in anthropological work and formal graduate training as criteria of inclusion"; most of the founders were government, museum, and university staff; twenty held an MD or PhD degree, eighteen were members of the ASW, and twelve of the AES (Stocking 1960:16, 13). Boas's power in this group was maximized by the emphasis on academic credentials and by the proportionately large New York contingent. Numerically, a large group of Washingtonians remained who were opposed in principle to Boas's plans to remake the discipline as an increasingly academic one. Boas's major victory, therefore, was the elimination of the least professional sector of the ASW. Amateurs were permitted to join the AAA, but the governing council would be a much smaller group who were professionals in Boas's sense.

The board remained dominated by Washingtonians, and Boas still had to look elsewhere for publication outlets and recognition of his students. He turned to the American Folklore Society, where anthropologists were prominent among the officers from the beginning. Of the twelve men to hold the presidency before Boas in 1900, eight were anthropologists; of these, three were independent, one was from Cambridge, and the remaining four were Washingtonians.

From 1900, when Boas broke the Washington power bloc in the presidency of the AFS, anthropologists from Cambridge still challenged Boasian dominance of the anthropological portion of the society. But by 1906 Kroeber held the office, and by 1909 John Swanton; both were students of Boas and part of the gener-

TABLE 1. Presidents of the American Folklore Society and the American Anthropological Association

Year	AFS	Profession	AAA	Affiliation
1888	James Francis Child	folklorist		
1889	Daniel Brinton	anthropologist, independent		
1890	F. W. Putnam	anthropologist, Cambridge		
1891	Otis T. Mason	anthropologist, Washington		
1892	John Wesley Powell	anthropologist, Washington		
1893	Horatio Hale	anthropologist, independent		
1894	Alcée Fortier	folklorist		
1895	Washington Matthews	anthropologist, Washington		
1896	John Bourke	anthropologist, Washington		
1897	Stewart Culin	anthropologist, independent		
1898	Will Wood	folklorist		
1899	Charles Edwards	folklorist		
1900	Franz Boas	anthropologist, Boasian		
1901	Frank Russell	anthropologist, Cambridge		
1902	George Dorsey	anthropologist, Boasian	WJ McGee	Washington
1903	Livingston Farrand	anthropologist, Boasian	WJ McGee	Washington
1904	G. Lyman Kittredge	folklorist	WJ McGee	Washington
1905	Alice Fletcher	anthropologist, Cambridge	F. W. Putnam	Cambridge

1906	A. L. Kroeber	anthropologist, Boasian	F. W. Putnam	Cambridge
1907	Roland Dixon	anthropologist, Cambridge	Franz Boas	Boasian
1908	Roland Dixon	anthropologist, Cambridge	Franz Boas	Boasian
1909	John Swanton	anthropologist, Boasian	W. H. Holmes	Washington
1910	H. M. Belden	folklorist	W. H. Holmes	Washington
1911	H. M. Belden	folklorist	J. W. Fewkes	Washington
1912	John Lomax	folklorist	J. W. Fewkes	Washington
1913	Pliny Goddard	anthropologist, Boasian	R. B. Dixon	Cambridge
1914	Pliny Goddard	anthropologist, Boasian	R. B. Dixon	Cambridge
1915	Pliny Goddard	anthropologist, Boasian	F. W. Hodge	Washington
1916	Pliny Goddard	anthropologist, Boasian	F. W. Hodge	Washington
1917	Robert Lowie	anthropologist, Boasian	A. L. Kroeber	Boasian
1918	Marius Barbeau	anthropologist, Boasian	A. L. Kroeber	Boasian
1919	Elsie Clews Parsons	anthropologist, Boasian	Clark Wissler	Boasian
1920	Elsie Clews Parsons	anthropologist, Boasian	Clark Wissler	Boasian
1921	Frank Speck	anthropologist, Boasian	W. C. Farabee	Cambridge
1922	Frank Speck	anthropologist, Boasian	W. C. Farabee	Cambridge
1923	Aurelio Espinoza	anthropologist, Boasian	Walter Hough	Washington
1924	Aurelio Espinoza	anthropologist, Boasian	Walter Hough	Washington
1925	Louise Pound	folklorist	Aleš Hrdlička	Washington

ation he had hoped would establish a national professional association of anthropologists.

In contrast, the American Anthropological Association presidency remained an exclusive matter. McGee served three terms, Putnam two, and Boas two. Washingtonians and archaeologists then held office until Kroeber became president in 1917. He was succeeded by Boas's somewhat estranged student, Clark Wissler, a museum anthropologist. Through the 1920s, the other presidents were archaeologists from Washington or Cambridge. While American anthropology was becoming increasingly Boasian during these years, the formal structure of the national professional association remained more conservative.

The *American Anthropologist* provided the focal point for the silent battle between Boas and the Washingtonians over control of the AAA. By the time Kroeber became president in 1917, most officers of the association had received academic degrees since 1900. The original council of twenty-four had increased gradually to about sixty by 1920, and most of the new members were Boas's students (Stocking 1960:13). In 1910 Pliny Earl Goddard became journal editor and moved the *American Anthropologist* to New York. In 1920 Goddard was forced to resign in a final effort to return control to Washington, but open conflict was avoided by the choice of John Swanton, trained by Boas but employed by the bureau. Swanton was succeeded by Robert Lowie, and the journal was thereafter predominantly Boasian in focus.

During these years, the struggle for power in the American Anthropological Association was largely political. Boas and his students needed an alternative outlet for their publications and found it in the American Folklore Society. The earliest anthropological contributions to the *Journal of American Folklore* were in the characteristic Washingtonian style of descriptive collecting on a natural history analogy. Many bureau contributions were incidental to work on other topics; rarely did any of the Washingtonians venture into folklore theory. In the words of Otis T. Mason of the U.S. National Museum:

> The work is done by men [*sic*] who insist on hearing a narrative over and over again until there is no mistake about accuracy; no

physicist or mineralogist is more careful than Dr. Dorsey and his colleagues at this point. No attempt has yet been made to combine this material, to atomize it, as yet there need not be. In all sciences, the period of accurate instrumental, multiplied observation must succeed that by the mere senses, preparatory to higher generalization. . . . For my own part, I have found it better to work the other way, to make collections in the smallest possible classes of folklore, just as our museum collectors gather specimens, waiting for those to group themselves as occasion may depend. (Mason 1891:100–104)

The pre–World War I *Journal of American Folklore* contained a much heavier concentration of Boasian work than the *American Anthropologist*. Of the bureau staff, seventeen were primarily contributors to the *Anthropologist*, with only John Bourke, Frank Cushing, and Washington Matthews contributing nearly as much to the folklore journal. Dorsey published more articles in the folklore journal, but the number is misleading; his publications for the bureau were major studies, and most of the folklore publications were brief notes. Of Boas's students, at least half divided their contribution between the two journals.

Such tabulations reinforce the impression of the strong Washington orientation of the Anthropological Association and its journal. The *American Anthropologist* also had a much greater proportion of contributions from independent (semiprofessional or avocational) anthropologists, such as Brinton, J. Dyneley Prince, E. I. Bushnell, and George Bird Grinnell. That journal, of course, also included archaeology, while the *Journal of American Folklore* stressed British and European folklore, a better fit with Boas's notions of the need for theory in cultural anthropology.

After Newell's death, he was succeeded as editor of the folklore journal by Boas's former student Alexander F. Chamberlain, a Canadian, who was succeeded by Alfred Tozzer, an ally of Boas but located in Cambridge, where much AFS activity was already centered. Tozzer thought the journal should expand its anthropological work in a literary direction to distinguish it in function from the *American Anthropologist*, but Boas protested that overlap between the two provided more scope for individual research (Tozzer to Boas,

January 28, 1907: APS). Tozzer's policy was designed to avoid factionalism and Boas's to provide publication outlets independent of Washington. During Boas's editorship of the *Journal of American Folklore* from 1908 to 1924, the problem was not so much to fill the pages of the journal but to accommodate bulky text publications on American Indian [*sic*] languages and folklore (Boas to Kroeber, July 24, 1917: ALK). Boas also stressed the need for firsthand materials and professional standards. Specialized and theoretically oriented contributions were strongly encouraged. Entire numbers were devoted to Canadian folklore, American Indian [*sic*] folklore, and similar topics. Boas continued to see a significant function for the Washington-dominated journal, insisting that "general anthropological matter" should be reserved for the *Anthropologist.* He even favored cooperation between the two journals in sponsoring reviews of periodicals.

Boas was quite self-consciously developing a viable alternative to rather than a substitute for the bureau-dominated organization of anthropologists:

> My only reasons for preferring the Folklore Society are that there the author is in a better position to control the form of the publication, and the publication will be so much more prompt than in the Bureau. (Boas to Kroeber, December 15, 1902: ALK)

In the *Journal of American Folklore,* the "longer articles of greater weight" (Boas to Kroeber, April 27, 1908: APS) were primarily by Boas's own students. Kroeber, although Boas's former student, continued to insist on the value of purely descriptive contributions (Kroeber to Boas, May 5, 1908: APS). Boas had little sympathy with Kroeber's self-interested efforts to appease the semiprofessional membership of the California branch of the AFS and continued his editorial policy of rigorously professional anthropology centered at Columbia.

In 1905, after Boas had established a firm commitment from the AFS to support his version of American anthropology, he returned to the idea of a collection of Indian [*sic*] myths, which had failed to materialize through the bureau in 1890. In 1905 there was already a group of Boas's students with data from their own fieldwork who were willing to produce a myth concordance under his supervision, much along the lines of the bureau's collaborative projects a generation earlier. Both Boas and his students realized that the task was theoretical as well as descriptive:

> In any case I hope the project will not be turned over to anyone who is a mere compiler or summarizer and has not had occasion, through having done productive works, to understand the problems and requirements of the subject. (Kroeber to Boas, December 15, 1905: ALK)

Boas chaired an Anthropological Association committee on myth concordance that also included Dorsey, Kroeber, and Swanton. Swanton was appointed by Boas to chair the Folklore Society committee, which also included Roland Dixon. Swanton began his task by asking Boas how to proceed (Swanton to Boas, August 3, 1907: APS).

Boas, who was much more interested in folklore theory than he had been fifteen years before, suggested listing folklore material by "catch-words" referring to incidents (Boas to Dixon, May 21, 1907: APS). Each committee member was expected to collect these from the area of his (they were all men) specialization (Boas to Kroeber, May 21, 1907: APS). Boas defined the problem in relation to his own studies of myth element diffusion on the Northwest Coast and wanted to extend the comparative database on grounds of verification for theoretical generalizations. His students were less sanguine. Kroeber sent a list but didn't know how to generalize from "this mass of material" (Kroeber to Boas, September 8, 1907: APS). Swanton asked for an example of a catchword (Swanton to Boas, August 3, 1907: APS). Both worked hard to convince themselves that the project could produce a new level of generalization for folklore elements. Swanton thought that myths could be distinguished that were directly related, probably related, or merely similar (Swanton to Kroeber, September 9, 1910: ALK). For them, the overall goal was more elusive, both conceptually and in the implementation:

> If we take an extreme Humanistic position we can not prove connection between more than a thousandth part of our myths, but even if we should do so the resemblance between many more

than that is sufficient for some sort of classification that is vastly better than our present chaos. (Swanton to Kroeber, September 23, 1910: ALK)

As a result of the initial studies, in 1907 the *Journal of American Folklore* published Swanton's theoretical article suggesting a method to bring together similarities of "genuine" American myths by means of "mythic formulae" or separate episodes and ideas. In 1908 and 1909 Robert Lowie contributed lists of "suitable tags" for North American myths. Sapir's introduction to *Washo Texts* in 1907 stressed the need for a myth concordance. Kroeber wanted a system that would deal with concrete ideas and episodes as well as the more inclusive groups that organized them. In 1912, after the complexities of the problem had become apparent to all, Kroeber's student Thomas T. Waterman decided to tackle the matter in earnest. Kroeber was cautious:

Your plans for a handbook on mythology interest me greatly, but I fear you will find it a bigger undertaking than you imagine. I have played around the fringe of the problem enough to be impressed by it. (Kroeber to Waterman, June 17, 1913: ALK)

Waterman approached the bureau to produce a concordance for the occurrence and diffusion of every tale, apparently believing that the bureau was already engaged in such a compilation. Hodge, then the director, immediately referred him to Boas (Hodge to Waterman, June 10, 1912: ALK). Waterman had apparently hoped to approach Boas only when he had a "matured" scheme (Waterman to Hodge, May 29: ALK). Waterman's dissertation, under Boas at Columbia, was considerably more limited in scope, dealing only with the "explanatory elements" in American mythology. Boas's interest in Waterman's project was primarily theoretical:

Towards the end of your dissertation you make the remark rather incidentally that there is no reason to suppose that the psychological conditions in early times were different from what they are now among primitive [*sic*] people. It seems to me that this thought ought to be expressed very much more emphatically . . . because it is really the raison d'être of your whole thesis. (Boas to Waterman, February 12, 1913: APS)

That is, Boas was concerned with the general implications of myth themes, their diffusion, psychological reality, and functional integration within cultures—all of these being questions not raised by the earlier, Washington-dominated efforts toward myth concordance.

After this time there was no further Boasian attention to the idea of a complete myth concordance. Boas's failure to muster the necessary cooperative effort for a concordance through the resources of the AFS and the research of his students and former students signaled the end of the effort from anthropology per se. The first comprehensive concordance was Stith Thompson's *Tales of North American Indians* in 1929. Thompson's dissertation under George Lyman Kittredge at Harvard analyzed European borrowings in American Indian [*sic*] folktales. He had inquired about the progress of Boas's concordance as early as 1913 (Thomson to Boas, May 29, 1913: APS). His work drew inspiration from the Boasian folklorists but came to fruition within that portion of the growing discipline of folklore that was independent of anthropology.

By the time Thompson began his serious work, therefore, Boas and with him the emphasis of American anthropology had turned in different directions. The important role of the AES in consolidating Boas's position in American anthropology was no longer necessary. The AFS, however, has continued to maintain a scope that facilitates inclusion of the work of anthropologists—a development that might not have taken place as easily without the struggles for institutional recognition that both folklore and anthropology were undergoing in the years between 1890 and 1920.

Notes

1. Originally published as "The Development of American Folklore Scholarship, 1880–1920," *Journal of the Folklore Institute* 10 (1974): 23–39.

References

Bell, Michael J. 1974. "William Wells Newell and the Foundation of American Folklore Scholarship." *Journal of the Folklore Institute* 10:14–22.
Boas, Franz. 1902. "The Foundation of a National Anthropological Society." *Science* 15:808.
McGee, WJ. 1901. "An American Senate of Science." *Science* 14:277–80.

———. 1903. "The American Anthropological Association: Antecedent Conditions." *American Anthropologist* 5:178–92.

Mason, Otis T. 1891. "The Natural History of Folklore." *Journal of American Folklore* 4:100–104.

Newell, William Wells. 1888a. Editorial. *Journal of American Folklore* 1:1–11.

———. 1888b. "The Necessity of Collecting Information of the Native Races." *Journal of American Folklore* 1:162–63.

———. 1896. Review of Franz Boas's *Indianische Sagan von der Nord-Pasifischen Küste Amerikas, 1891–1895*. *Journal of American Folklore* 11:328–30.

Shafer, Joseph, ed. 1940. *Memoirs of Jeremiah Curtin*. Madison: State Historical Society of Wisconsin.

Stocking, George W., Jr. 1960. "Franz Boas and the Founding of the American Anthropological Association." *American Anthropologist* 62:1–17.

4

·········

The Emergence of Academic Anthropology
at the University of Pennsylvania

The University of Pennsylvania has played a significant role in
the institutional development of modern American anthropology at several periods.[1] Taken as a whole, the growth of the University Museum and an academic department of anthropology at
Penn illustrates a major cross-section of the general history of this
period.[2] Nineteenth-century American anthropology was centered
in regional scientific societies, among which the American Philosophical Society (APS) and Academy of Natural Sciences of Philadelphia were representative of more general trends.[3] The University
of Pennsylvania, with the honorary appointment of Daniel Garrison Brinton as professor of archaeology and linguistics in 1886,
was technically the first American university to hold a professorship in anthropology, although effective teaching programs were
established earlier at Harvard under Frederic W. Putnam and at
Clark under Franz Boas (Freeman 1965). Brinton bridges the transition from the scholarly society to the specifically anthropological institution in which full-time professional employment was
possible. Until after 1900, however, the museum showed greater
viability than the academic department; only in the twentieth century did the University of Pennsylvania become important as an
outpost of Boasian academic anthropology. Simultaneously, the
Penn Museum moved further from the broad-based anthropological scholarship that would have facilitated cooperation with the
academic program. The confrontation between university and
museum as alternative institutional frameworks for anthropological
activity was resolved in a particularly dramatic way at Penn, high-

lighting the nature of the innovations introduced by Boas in the early twentieth century (see Darnell 1998 for comparative cases).

The Museum

Philadelphia's first professional anthropological activity developed in the context of a museum loosely affiliated with the University of Pennsylvania, where Provost William Pepper developed a major graduate program during the 1880s (Cheyney 1940). Ethnology and archaeology were disciplines that received Pepper's special attention in both the graduate school and museum. In 1886 he hired on the university faculty Near Eastern philologist Morris Jastrow, Babylonian archaeologist Hermann Hilprecht, and anthropologist Daniel Brinton. These appointments were meant to facilitate the establishment of a museum. The Museum of Archaeology and Paleontology was founded at the university in 1889.[4] Pepper conceived of the two institutions as inseparable; although this was never the case, he referred to the Penn Museum as the name of the institution in order to gloss over the administrative duality. Jastrow spent most of his time as university librarian, Brinton's scholarship remained relatively independent of both museum and university, and the expeditions of Hilprecht and others were financed by private patrons having little connection with the university. Under Pepper's successor as provost, the museum moved even further from the university (Sara Stevenson to Bitter, June 30, 1897: UMA).

The "archaeology" of the museum's original title was understood as the past history of human civilization from an evolutionary perspective. Pepper's circular (1890: UMA) referred to "a great ethnological museum," indicating that the study of living peoples was also part of "archaeology" as a holistic science of man[-kind]. Evolution was the concept that integrated Pepper's goals of "instruction in archaeology, ethnology, and paleontology." Within this inclusive program, the study of primitive [*sic*] peoples had its place alongside if not equal to investigations of the history of Western civilization. Pepper regarded public instruction as the primary function of a museum. The 1890 circular envisioned "a vast means of instruction in anthropology and not a mere collection of curiosities." Popular lectures at the museum constituted "a movement of the first importance, not only in the interest of the museum, but of the entire subject of archaeology in this community" (Pepper to Brinton, April 25, 1892: UMA). Although the museum existed in a university context, Pepper's vision was oriented to the Philadelphia scientific and intellectual community at large. His educational intent was the popular diffusion of archaeological knowledge, not the training, theoretical definition, or technical study of anthropology.

In practice, the early museum focused on classical and Near Eastern archaeology, subjects that excited great public interest and readily attracted funds to support expeditions. The local amateur archaeologists and museum patrons were led by Dr. Pepper's close friend Sara Stevenson, Egyptian archaeologist, feminist, philanthropist, museum curator, board member, and volunteer secretary until 1905.[5] Mrs. Stevenson was not interested in a definition of archaeology sufficiently broad to include ethnology or provide employment for professional archaeologists. The narrowness of museum policy confronted with such constraints induced conflict on several fronts. Stewart Culin, Charles C. Abbott, and Brinton each tried unsuccessfully at different times to defend the place of anthropology in the museum in terms of their own distinct priorities for the growing professionalism of American archaeology.

Paradoxically, the only paid curator on the original museum staff was the Americanist, Abbott, who had been associated for some years with Putnam at the Peabody Museum (Madeira 1964:20). Pepper's inclusion of such an individual on his early staff signifies the importance he attached to having at least one person with professional experience. He assumed that Abbott would have imbibed some of Putnam's philosophy of scientific research in a museum context during his time at Harvard.

Unfortunately for the professional caliber and Americanist focus of the museum's scientific work, Abbott's career in Philadelphia was not entirely happy. He was insulted by the precedence of the museum sections controlled by Mrs. Stevenson over his own work and complained that his salary was unreasonably low and his scientific reports not published. These are the priorities of a professional archaeologist with clear standards for his work and a network of ties to other institutions. Abbott resigned in 1894. The animosity of his bitter dispute with the trustees is reflected in his correspondence with Brinton over presumed but unspecified charges:

> My annual report was ready in season and never called for. Why indeed are there no facilities for my work? . . . I was even deprived of my office. . . . What is the secret of all this fault-finding? And why have I never had a word from the Managers, if they—collectively—are dissatisfied? You say that it has been with difficulty that you have defended me. Good Lord, why have I not been permitted to defend myself? Where is it that all this discussion goes on? (June 13, 1892; June 18, 1892: UMA)

Similar conflicts arose when Stewart Culin became curator of the general ethnology and American sections in 1892. Although Culin held the title of director, his authority did not extend to Mrs. Stevenson's Babylonian, Egyptian, and Mediterranean sections (Madeira 1964:20). Culin's efforts to act as director of the whole museum sparked bitter conflicts over administrative authority. His goals diverged from those of Mrs. Stevenson, who was supported in her policies by the board, a group of interested but nonprofessional Philadelphia businessmen. In 1894 a prominent board member resigned because he felt that the "scope of the British Museum" was unwarranted in Philadelphia (C. Howard Colket to Culin, March 6, 1894: UMA). The tone of the ongoing dispute is illustrated by the following exchange between two board members:

> The repeated attacks of Mr. Culin, Currator of the American Section of the Anthropological Museum, upon Mrs. Stevenson, more especially culminating in the open attack upon her at the recent annual meeting, must, I think, convince everyone interested in the welfare of the Museum that his connection with it should be terminated with the least practicable delay. Mrs. Stevenson has given her time to the Museum both as curator of the Egyptian and Mediterranean Section and also as Secretary of the Board, without compensation, for many years and is admittedly mainly responsible for the very existence and present prosperity of the Museum itself. It would therefore be the height of injustice and ingratitude that she should be subject to the malignant and insidious attacks that have been made upon her

by an employee of the Museum, for several years past. (Wells to Strawbridge, January 14, 1903: UMA)

The affair degenerated to personal attacks, nearly culminating in a defamation of character suit by Culin against Mrs. Stevenson and the museum. Culin's dismissal in 1903 was virtually inevitable in light of Mrs. Stevenson's political power within the museum. Culin moved to the Brooklyn Institute of Arts and Sciences, where his goals for museum research and administration could be pursued more effectively.

The divergence between scholarly and popular goals is once again exemplified by the role of Brinton in the development of the museum. Brinton, Philadelphia's internationally acclaimed linguist and ethnologist, was committed to the *idea* of academic anthropology and to the importance of research in the *role* of a museum.[6] Brinton shared with Pepper a holistic concept of the study of man integrated by the concept of evolution. But while Brinton's scholarly work focused on linguistics and mythology, which could be pursued as well in a library as in a museum, Pepper turned to archaeology and popular education. Pepper chose to become involved in the politics of museum administration while most of his associates, including Mrs. Stevenson, were more interested in the material artifacts of exotic cultures than in the broad panorama of human history. Thus, Brinton failed to receive the support of the museum administration in his attempts to organize ethnological fieldwork in North America (Brinton to Abbott, February 21, 1890; Bandelier to Leidy, March 11, 1890: UMA). In 1894 Brinton withdrew from active participation in the museum, emphasizing his fundamental disagreement with Mrs. Stevenson's conception of a museum:

> Moreover, I am in certain main points, a valueless antiquary; I have no money to give, and no capacity for raising any . . . as I pursue my scientific studies only for the pleasure they give me. I will not antagonize others, or tacitly give consent to what I do not like. (July 8, 1894: UMA)

The limited policies enforced during Mrs. Stevenson's regime, which lasted until 1905, were hardly unique to the museum at

Penn. Franz Boas was appointed jointly to the staffs of the American Museum of Natural History and Columbia University in 1896 on the assumption that the anthropological research of the two institutions would be connected. However, administrative conflicts soon developed over the relationship of scholarly research to public instruction and the need for scientific publications to supplement the collection of specimens. By the time he resigned from the museum, Boas was convinced that, in practice at least, museum and university duties were incompatible (Boas to Clark Wissler, June 22, 1905: APS). In an article on museum administration, Boas pointed out that the United States National Museum and the Field Museum in Chicago had suffered similar restrictions of anthropological research due to administrative policies (1907:925). The problems were systemic. Only at the Peabody Museum had the potentially productive cooperation of museum and research been realized:

> I believe that among American museum administrators Professor F. W. Putnam deserves the highest credit for having been the first to recognize the limitations of the activity of the museum if restricted entirely by the desire for the acquisition of specimens, and for having courageously set to the museum scientific problems selected in accordance with their scientific importance rather than with the probability of yielding many specimens. (Boas 1907:931)

It was precisely this broad concept of scientific research in a museum context that was lacking at Penn and that had sparked the conflict between trained and salaried archaeologists and their administrative superiors.

The University

Although at the beginning of the twentieth century the museum at Penn had demonstrated its institutional viability, its development had been attained largely independently of collaboration with the affiliated university. Moreover, it had not provided a satisfactory basis for the development of a professional discipline of anthropology. In the interim, the latter had remained a solitary crusade by Daniel Brinton with consistently disappointing results (Darnell 1967, 1988). Although he was one of only four nineteenth-century ethnologists to serve as president of the American Association for the Advancement of Science and despite his international reputation, Brinton was preeminently a Philadelphian, trained as a medical doctor but choosing to devote himself to scholarly pursuits. Almost one third of his more than two hundred publications appeared in the journals and proceedings of Philadelphia intellectual societies, among them the American Philosophical Society, the Academy of Natural Sciences, the Museum of Archaeology and Paleontology, the Numismatic and Antiquarian Society, and the Philadelphia Oriental Society. None of these were exclusively ethnological; in each, Brinton was the major if not the only practicing ethnologist. Prior to the founding of the Penn museum, Brinton constituted Philadelphia's claim to fame in anthropology, and Philadelphia provided him with a conduit of communication to wider audiences.

Brinton's teaching appointment at the University of Pennsylvania was preceded by one at the Academy of Natural Sciences of Philadelphia in 1884. There is more evidence regarding the nature of his position there. A professorship of ethnology and linguistics was created for him as part of the academy's program of public instruction, which drew mostly on the scientific pursuits of its members. When Brinton died in 1899 the appointment was permitted to lapse, suggesting that he had been the major stimulus to its ethnological interests and that the position would not have existed without the inducement of his presence in Philadelphia.

The academy distinguished two types of educational series: popular lectures on assorted topics and full courses on specialized topics. In the second series, Brinton presented his scholarship in progress; *Races and Peoples* (1890) and *The American Race* (1891) both originated in such lectures. This feedback from lectures into professional output indicates that Brinton valued his teaching and the implied popularization of his subject. Brinton's description of his teaching makes it clear, however, that he distinguished between a professional or potentially professional audience and the one he in fact addressed (Brinton to Educational Committee, April 24, 1884: ANSP):

Upon more mature reflection (after one semester of teaching) . . . I do not believe it (my lecture synopsis) represents precisely the most attractive form in which the science can be presented from the platform. Few people understand what ethnology is, or why it should be studied—surprisingly few: They must first be taught this.

In this context, Brinton found a university appointment attractive.

Brinton appears to have been a peripheral figure at the university. His role must be surmised from lists of committees, boards, and faculties. Documents give the overwhelming impression that Brinton did not actually *teach*. In the catalogs, his courses were almost alone in being listed without hours, and his listings changed only in response to the reorganization of the graduate school. Their content, however, remained constant: introductory work in American archaeology and linguistics, with advanced work in linguistic classification and in five American Indian [*sic*] languages. After 1894, when the system of majors and minor was introduced, the catalog commented that "The instruction in this group (Archaeology and Linguistics) will be in large measure based upon the unusually rich collections of the University Museum and will be arranged with reference to the preparation and aims of applicants." But as we have seen, Brinton's relations to the museum were already somewhat strained.

Nor does Brinton appear to have had students. This can be documented for the years between 1894 and 1899: The annual report of the Provost for 1899–1900 indicates that during these five years, no students elected American languages as a major or minor for the MA or PhD. The one special student, a nondegree candidate who registered in 1894–95, cannot be identified. Brinton's professorship was not contingent on his making a contribution to the academic program of the university. Whatever influence he had on younger men [*sic*] in anthropology was personal, not institutional. Hilborne Cresson, Stewart Culin, and Frank Cushing all note him as a source of personal inspiration, but none were students at the University of Pennsylvania.

In short, Brinton's professorial appointment at Penn was a formality resulting from the growth of the university during the late nineteenth century and the interest of Provost Pepper in ethnology and archaeology. No serious attempt was made to replace him after his death in 1899, highlighting the impression that his teaching was of little concern to anyone except Brinton. A proposed memorial chair failed to materialize. Provost Harrison's annual report for 1899–1900 recorded the formation of a graduate group in ethnology and archaeology under the chairship of Hilprecht. It included Babylonian, Greek, Roman, and American archaeology, separating the first three from their respective language departments, with the language professors responsible for these courses also serving as curators for related collections in the museum. Within the new group, Culin was to offer courses in American archaeology and ethnology analogous to those listed by Brinton, although his proposed courses omitted linguistics. Culin's primary interest, unlike Brinton's, was in the museum, not in the development of an academic program; professional anthropology to him meant professional museum work. When Culin left Philadelphia in 1903, American ethnology disappeared altogether from the nominal program. Anthropology was no longer part of the Penn curriculum even in theory. The ease of its disappearance confirms its marginality during Brinton's tenure.

If Brinton's professorship was simply a false start, the limited effects of his efforts also emerge in the context of his conception of what professional training would entail and his personal commitment to promoting it. Brinton's *Anthropology as a Science and as a Branch of University Education in the United States* in 1892 was ostensibly a practical prospectus for a teaching program at Penn. Although rejected summarily by the university, Brinton's suggested program clarifies his prescience about the growing tide of professionalism and the changing institutional structure of anthropology.

Brinton began his prospectus with a lengthy defense of the need for anthropologists to receive specialized training, citing in some detail both European and American precedents for anthropological instruction. He devoted the body of the essay to the proper scope and content of a holistic science of anthropology. Although the content of his program was inclusive, stressing the need for work in classroom, library, laboratory, and field to produce well-rounded anthropologists, Brinton concerned himself primarily with semantic definitions of the subdisciplines of anthropology rather than with his own personal areas of research.

Brinton intended the document to be programmatic. The text deals with anthropology as a discipline; only in the cover letter to Pepper (June 2, 1892: UPA) did he discuss the specific situation at Pennsylvania. At Penn, Brinton noted the presence of faculty willing to teach in the various subdisciplines of anthropology included in his outline (physical anthropology, archaeology, and ethnology). Drawing on the existing staff of the university, the museum, and Wistar Institute, his program contrasts sharply with the limited archaeological perspective of the graduate group set up after his death. Brinton was not sufficiently influential in the university to be able to organize these resources into the program he envisioned, nor was the university prepared to sponsor it on his behalf. Brinton realized that the museum was equally unlikely to concern itself with the training of anthropologists. His presidential address to the American Association for the Advancement of Science (1895:5) stated:

> We erect stately museums, we send out costly expeditions; but where are the universities, the institutions of higher learning, who train young men [*sic*] how to observe, how to collect and explore in this branch?

These are the bitter words of a man who has watched the growth of a museum without corresponding growth in educational facilities or professional consciousness.

During the period of Brinton's failure, successful teaching programs in anthropology were initiated at Harvard and Clark Universities (Freeman 1965). At Harvard, Putnam had trained archaeologists (among them Abbott) in the Peabody Museum for some years before he became a member of the university faculty in 1887; the department of anthropology was empowered to grant academic degrees in 1890. The addition of an academic program did not substantially modify the priority of the museum; the advanced coursework consisted of a three-year program tailored to ongoing research and personal interests. In contrast, the Penn Museum was not oriented toward anthropological research, and Brinton could not muster sufficient unanimity of purpose to permit cooperation of museum and university programs, or to provide fieldwork for potential students.

At Clark University, Franz Boas developed a viable though short-lived graduate program that awarded the first American PhD in anthropology in 1892. Although Boas's program became fully effective only after he moved to Columbia in 1896, his view of the scope of anthropology, the need for rigorous training, and the emphasis on empirical research in the field were already clear in his abortive efforts at Clark: There, Boas's students initiated an anthropometric survey of schoolchildren in Worcester, Massachusetts, and he continued his own American Indian [*sic*] fieldwork for the British Association for the Advancement of Science and the World's Columbian Exposition. After Boas relocated in New York, the organizational resources of Columbia, the American Museum, and the American Ethnological Society united to underwrite a more elaborate program of empirical research. In addition to these institutional factors, Boas's understanding of the growth of anthropology across America and his perception of his own formative role in it formed a sharp contrast to Brinton's programmatic statement. Boas's was clearly the voice of the future.

The University within the Museum

In 1903 Philadelphia anthropology faced a turning point. The university program was by then virtually defunct, and the museum was faced with the problem of replacing Culin as curator of general ethnology and American archaeology. There were already eleven American PhDs in anthropology, and viable academic departments had been established at Columbia, Harvard, and Berkeley. Given the orientation of the museum, however, the choice was effectively limited to Harvard, which held a virtual monopoly on the training of archaeologists. Putnam first suggested William Curtis Farabee but then found himself able to retain Farabee at Harvard as an instructor (Putnam to Stevenson, July 3, 1903: UMA). The only other available candidate was George Gordon, leader of the Peabody Museum Honduras Expedition. Although Putnam recommended Gordon less enthusiastically than Farabee, he appeared to fit the museum's specification of an academically trained archaeologist with museum and field experience. Gordon also meshed well with Boas's suggestions to Mrs. Stevenson (January 23, 1903; May 12, 1903: UMA) that Culin should be replaced by a man who could develop the connection between museum and university to train a new generation of anthropologists in this dual context.

Gordon took for granted that both university and museum were necessary to the development of anthropology; in accordance with his own training, he saw academic courses as a means to produce competent archaeologists for museum work. Affiliation with the university program provided a way to solidify his position in the museum, which, as we have seen, was inclined to factional politics.

One of Gordon's first acts in 1903 was to present Provost Harrison with a proposal for "the needs and outlook for instruction in Anthropology in the University of Pennsylvania" (UMA). Gordon's proposal echoed Brinton's a decade earlier in emphasizing existing precedents in Philadelphia for anthropological teaching and existing facilities to support such a program. He stressed the rapid growth of anthropology during the past ten years without mentioning Brinton or his nominal teaching program. Gordon's proposal suggested nine specific courses, four designed especially for graduate students and covering archaeology, ethnology, and somatology—any or all of which he offered to give himself. As a result of this ambitious proposal, Gordon was authorized to offer an introduction to archaeology and general ethnology in 1904–5. Anthropology became Section C under archaeology and ethnology, the nominal graduate group formed after Brinton's death and still headed by Hilprecht. During the early years of his appointment, Gordon's efforts to build up the academic program often involved considerable personal sacrifice; for example, when the university refused to appropriate funds for teaching American archaeology, he voluntarily offered a course to arouse interest in the subject (Gordon to Bowditch, October 31, 1905: UMA).

In 1907 Gordon presented a second proposal to the graduate school, this time requesting permission to teach anthropology as a full major and to add courses in anatomy and laboratory work. He pointed out that since 1903 courses and enrollments had been increasing, and little more was needed to achieve "a large and flourishing department of anthropology." In 1908 Gordon began his struggle for the recognition of anthropology as an independent department (Gordon to Dean Ames, September 22, 1908: UPA). Classical and Semitic archaeology would be relegated to their respective language departments; the prehistoric archaeology that remained within the new anthropology division was held to be quite distinct.

This growth of the academic program required new staff. By strategic use of museum resources to pay salaries, Gordon was able to hire Frank Speck in 1907 and Edward Sapir in 1908. Speck, who had received his MA under Boas and had come to Penn to accept a newly established fellowship in anthropology, taught some courses in 1907–8 and was listed on the university faculty. The next year, after receiving his PhD from Penn, Speck became an instructor in the university, teaching courses within the broad definition of anthropology established by Gordon (archaeology, ethnology, and somatology), while working as a museum assistant to justify the payment of his salary by a museum patron as a personal favor to Gordon. In 1911 Speck was promoted to assistant professor in the university and withdrew from active work in the museum.

Edward Sapir became a teaching fellow in 1908 and an instructor and museum assistant the following year. Only during these two years was linguistics part of the curriculum, and thus part of the effective scope of anthropology. Although Gordon wanted to continue the work, he could find no suitable instructor when Sapir left after two years to accept a position to develop anthropology under the auspices of the Geological Survey of Canada. Although both Speck and Sapir had been offered the inducement of an assured certain teaching position in the university after a few years, Sapir became convinced that Gordon was overly optimistic about what he would be able to provide and that in any case, "He doesn't know enough about the necessary work in ethnology and linguistics to know just what he wants, though he may mean well" (Sapir to Kroeber, May 7, 1909: ALK). Sapir believed, probably correctly, that Gordon's major financial backers were not enthusiastic about ethnological research or academic anthropology, and therefore he happily accepted employment elsewhere.

Although the new graduate department had a number of students, professional training was subordinated to interdisciplinary work. Graduates and undergraduates took the same courses since neither had any background in the discipline (Gordon to Dean Ames, May 8, 1911: UPA). Between 1904 and 1915, nine students listed anthropology as their *only* field of study (this tabulation counts the same student once for each year in which they did so); twelve elected anthropology as a *major* field of study. Sociology was the most frequently allied field, with that department offering an introductory course that covered "primitive" society in some detail. Political science, psychology, economics, biology, and philosophy also appeared often enough to indicate connection between the departments. Eighteen students from the new history of religion department elected anthropology courses in the first five years after its founding in 1910. Both Gordon and Speck were listed on the initial faculty of the religion department, although Gordon dropped out within a year. Speck, however, took this responsibility quite seriously, feeling an obligation to train missionaries in the scientific study of other cultures. This affiliation also gave Speck a place in the university independent of the museum-centered anthropology department.

Conflicting Goals

From his arrival in 1907, Gordon attempted to behave as director of the museum, although he was formally granted the title only in 1910. In the same year, the title Museum of Archaeology was changed to University Museum, reflecting the gradual transformation under Gordon's administration toward strengthening and cooperating with the academic program. Ironically, from 1910 on, Gordon's duties in the museum left less and less time for the graduate program he had worked so hard to initiate. Both the board of managers and the scientific staff of the museum were gradually modified in accordance with Gordon's policies of popular education, with a somewhat narrower concept of archaeology than had been characteristic of his own training under Putnam. An early student in the department, J. Alden Mason, recalled in 1964 that Gordon never enjoyed teaching; the official history of the museum (Madeira 1964:58) reports that Gordon came to believe museum work was inherently incompatible with university teaching. The academic department, like American anthropology generally under the influence of Boas, was moving further away from museum concerns. Sapir and Speck were interested in linguistic and ethnological fieldwork and in instruction that emphasized non-material culture. Gordon's retrenchment policy after 1910 further widened the gap between the museum and academic traditions.

In this context, a struggle developed between Gordon and Speck for control of the academic department of anthropology, and the situation became so tense that individuals were forced to take sides. The students were firmly with Speck and the purely academic orientation. By 1913 Speck and Wilson Wallis, then an instructor, complained to Dean Quinn (February 11 and 13, 1913, respectively: UPA) that they were not welcome in the museum and that public lectures were scheduled for the hours their classes were supposed to meet. Specimens were locked up, and graduate students had no more privileges in the museum than the general public. The situation became so awkward that courses were held across the campus from the museum, which Speck (to Dean Quinn, February 13, 1913: UPA) described as a "decided detriment to the interests of this department." He complained, "My work this year has not developed any man [*sic*] who can be expected to become a serious and permanent candidate for the advanced research or field work in Anthropology which it is my aim to require." By this time, such a goal was no longer compatible with Gordon's policy in the museum.

Although in this instance the provost intervened, and the availability of the museum lecture hall for courses was politely though formally confirmed through the dean (Quinn to Speck, March 18, 1913: UPA), the episode had considerable repercussions for the organization of the academic program. Beginning in 1913–14, Speck replaced Gordon as group adviser for the department and in 1914–15 became its chair. In the same year, Wilson Wallis taught Gordon's physical anthropology course, and in the next year Robert Aitken, the graduate assistant, taught Gordon's prehistoric archaeology of Europe and ethnology courses. By 1917 Gordon's courses had been eliminated from the roster entirely. Letters in Quinn's files indicate that the initiative for the changes came from Speck (May 16, 1913; March 23, 1914; May 27, 1916: UPA).

The detailed politics are difficult to reconstruct from the incomplete archives of the museum and university, but the personal papers of Speck and Boas provide glimpses of what was involved.

Aiken reported to Boas as a former student (August 5, 1916: APS) accounts that Gordon's name was "dropped from the roll by action of the faculty at the instigation of Deans Ames and Quinn with the full knowledge and approval of the Provost." Wallis (Waterman to Kroeber, November 7, 1915: ALK) even went so far as to publicly charge Gordon with drunkenness in the presence of university officials. Speck's papers include a three-page handwritten list of grievances, apparently notes for an otherwise unrecorded committee meeting late in 1913. Speck stated that Gordon had attempted to make his personal research difficult or impossible, tampering with manuscripts, excluding him from his office, and withdrawing support for field research. He also interfered with Speck's teaching, arbitrarily devising course rosters, imposing work for the museum, preventing use of museum specimens for classes, appearing in Speck's courses, and contradicting his authority. A brief quotation illustrates the animosity of the dispute:

> When I suggested some changes in course announcements and other improvements in Dept. of Instruction, after 4 or 5 years of experience with the work [Gordon] told me I was a boy and he would condescend to give me advice. Then he wrote announcements to courses and intended me to give them in accordance with the announcement. He had never given some of the courses under question. I had for some years, and so far as I know he had never had such courses in his career at Harvard.

In these circumstances, Speck preferred the predictability despite the inconvenience of meeting his classes outside the museum.

The battle between Speck and Gordon for control of the academic program extended beyond Penn. Speck and his allies staged a widespread effort to discredit Gordon's abilities both as a teacher and as a scientist. Former Penn students were loyal to Speck but often hesitated to become involved in personal accusations (Hawkes to Speck, November 25, 1913: APS). Speck had considerably more success outside the university. His obvious allies were Boasians. Robert Lowie, who remembered the decade as one in which every student of Boas had to stand firmly behind his version of anthropology (Stocking 1968:276), expressed his willingness to state publicly that Gordon was in his opinion nothing but a promoter, although he admitted to not knowing Gordon personally (November 28, 1913: APS). Lowie also assumed that Pliny Goddard of the American Museum and Roland Dixon of the Peabody were likely to agree. Alfred Tozzer of the Peabody was sympathetic, but he hesitated to become involved in a local dispute (July 12, 1915: APS) and requested the return of a previous more "bellicose" letter.

The composition of this group is interesting. Lowie and Speck were direct students of Boas; Goddard was an ardent admirer; and Tozzer served as the communication link between Boas and the Archaeological Institute of America. When Boas was censured by the American Anthropological Association over political issues in 1919, all of them were among his defenders. Gordon, on the other hand, voted *for* censure, as did William Farabee, who was by then a member of the museum staff. Indeed, in 1919, probably in protest over Boas's political and anthropological activities, Gordon dropped his membership in the American Anthropological Association and in the Folklore Society (Tozzer to Boas, March 28, 1919: APS).

Events at the University of Pennsylvania had thus foreshadowed the confrontation of Boasian anthropology with the rest of the discipline. At least three of the five factors in the division over Boas's censure at the Cambridge meeting of the Association (Stocking 1968:276–77) appear to have operated at Penn also: cultural anthropologists were opposed, for the most part, to archaeologists; the students of Franz Boas acted cooperatively; and the position of Philadelphia as part of the Boasian camp was clearly at stake. At the cost of the association with a major museum, the academic department at Penn went with Boas.

The Aftermath

Anthropology was not a strong department within the university and encountered severe financial problems during the First World War when the university dropped all its instructors. Predictably, Gordon did not respond to Boas's appeal (June 7, 1918: APS) to offer them museum positions in the interim. Only after the war did the department begin to grow again, this time fully under the direction of Speck and fully independently of the museum.

The separation of museum and academic department at Penn remained virtually inviolate until well after Gordon's death in 1927.

The matter remained in abeyance until personal ties were gradually reforged under the museum directorships of George Vaillant from 1941 to 1945 and Froelich Rainey from 1945 to 1977. The physical reincorporation of the department within the museum was not accomplished until some years after Speck's death in 1950.

Conclusion

The period from the founding of the Penn Museum in 1889 to the decisive split between university and museum in 1913 spans much of the development of anthropology as a professional discipline. In 1889 institutional support of any kind for anthropology was at best problematic. Outside the BAE, the alternatives were museums or universities. In several major centers of anthropological activity—New York, Boston, Chicago, and Berkeley, in addition to Philadelphia—both a museum and a university department emerged, and these interacted in various ways. After 1900 the existence of anthropology as a profession was taken more for granted and *either* a museum *or* a university department could provide sufficient institutional backing for anthropological research. Prior to Putnam's retirement in 1909, his broad concept of archaeological research helped keep the Peabody Museum and the other museums he was connected with close to the developing academic programs in anthropology. Under the leadership of Boas, however, American anthropology came to be associated more and more with universities. The department at Berkeley, although founded by Putnam, developed in a Boasian direction under Kroeber. There, at Columbia, and at Penn, academic anthropology moved away from material culture and the training of museum archaeologists toward ethnographic and linguistic fieldwork and the training of cultural anthropologists. Although the development varied in important ways in each geographical location, its major themes have been illustrated by the detailed discussion of events at the University of Pennsylvania.

Notes

1. Originally published as "The Emergence of Academic Anthropology at the University of Pennsylvania," *Journal of the History of the Behavioral Sciences* 6 (1970): 80–92.

2. Darnell (1969) discusses the changing institutional structure of American anthropology between 1880 and 1920 in which several other cases of museum and university development are discussed in detail.

3. The American Philosophical Society tradition of studying American Indians [*sic*] went back to Thomas Jefferson and Peter Stephen Duponceau. In the mid-nineteenth century, scholars such as Samuel Morton were affiliated with local scientific societies. Specifically anthropological institutions and professional employment for anthropologists were lacking in all cases.

4. Paleontology was quickly relegated to the Academy of Natural Sciences and the Wistar Institute (founded in 1892 with Pepper as its first president and Harrison Allen of the academy as its first director). The "archaeology" in the title of Brinton's professorship accurately reflects the major interests of the museum's founders and the patrons who supported them. Philadelphia's cultural institutions were supported by interlocking boards of movers and shakers.

5. Until 1901 the plans of Pepper and Mrs. Stevenson were supported by Phoebe Apperson Hearst. After Pepper's death in 1908, however, Mrs. Hearst transferred her attention to the plans for a museum at the University of California, Berkeley, under the direction of Putnam of Harvard. Mrs. Stevenson, who was firmly committed to Philadelphia and Pepper's ambitions for the museum there, unsuccessfully attempted to ignore her efforts to resign (Hearst to Stevenson, January 24, 1901: UMA).

6. Brinton used the term "anthropology" in a wide sense analogous to Pepper's "archaeology" to refer to the whole range of human culture (although Brinton did not restrict himself to material culture).

References

Boas, Franz. 1907. "Some Principles of Museum Administration." *Science* 25:921–33.

Brinton, Daniel. 1892. *Anthropology as a Science and as a Branch of University Education in the United States.* Philadelphia: Privately printed.

———. 1895. "The Aims of Anthropology." *Proceedings of the American Association for Advancement of Science* 44:1–17.

Cheyney, Edward. 1940. *A History of the University of Pennsylvania, 1740–1940.* Philadelphia: University of Pennsylvania Press.

Darnell, Regna. 1967. "Daniel Garrison Brinton: An Intellectual Biography." Master's thesis, University of Pennsylvania.

———. 1969. "The Development of American Anthropology, 1880–1920: From the Bureau of American Ethnology to Franz Boas." PhD diss., University of Pennsylvania.

———. 1988. *Daniel Garrison Brinton: The "Fearless Critic" of Philadelphia.* University of Pennsylvania Publications in Anthropology No. 3.

———. 1998. *And Along Came Boas: Continuity and Revolution in the History of Americanist Anthropology.* Amsterdam: John Benjamins.

Freeman, John. 1965. "University Anthropology: Early Departments in the United States." *Kroeber Anthropological Society Papers* 32:78–90.

Madeira, Percy. 1964. *Man in Search of Man: The First 75 Years of the University Museum of the University of Pennsylvania.* Philadelphia: University of Pennsylvania Press.

Mason, J. Alden. 1964. "Anthropology at the University of Pennsylvania." *Bulletin of the Philadelphia Anthropological Society*: 17–23.

Stocking, George W., Jr. 1968. "The Scientific Reaction against Cultural Anthropology." In *Race, Culture and Evolution: Essays in the History of Anthropology,* 270–307. New York: Free Press.

5

....

Documenting Disciplinary History

Most anthropologists probably identify "the anthropological record" primarily as the documentation of what anthropologists do in their research.[1] The first conference on the subject of its preservation (Silverman and Parezo 1992) arose from a Wenner-Gren conference with limited participation, whereas the second edition evolved from a workshop hosted by Don Fowler in Reno, Nevada, and selected papers were revised on the basis of input from COPAR (Conference on Preserving the Anthropological Record) for which I was invited to present this paper (Fowler and Parezo 1995). I structured it to persuade archivists that history of anthropology was an essential resource for the needed preservation of records. The professional socialization of anthropologists valorizes data collected during fieldwork but may also induce blinders to other important resources. The history of anthropology contextualizes the shared goal of recording the diversity of human cultures through time and space and enabling comparison of their empirically attested variabilities to arrive at human universals or cross-cultural regularities.

Few anthropologists would dispute the need to preserve the primary documents from fieldwork as crucial potential evidence for readers to assess the validity and reliability of theoretical writing based upon them. Ethnographic writing is a genre, and it assumes that readers cannot literally share the experience of the anthropologist who "was there" in the field; the claim to authority incumbent upon that experience has to be made, however, in one way or another. Clifford Geertz (1988) suggested that the basis of this claim is a characteristic rhetorical strategy that operates at considerable distance from the substance of the ethnographic experience. But professional readers, among them fellow fieldworkers, can and do require that particular evidence be adduced for particular claims. Such evidence both adds verisimilitude to "having been there" and attests to the rigor and scientific character of the relationship between evidence and interpretation, method and theory, experience and inference.

Fieldnotes are our primary data, and they have an almost mystical reality. The identity of the anthropologist, as well as that of the people studied, is encoded in them. Jean Jackson (1980) approached the question of the role of fieldnotes in the social construction of anthropology as a discipline by asking seventy colleagues, chosen without systematic sampling, how they felt about their fieldnotes. Her interviews revealed two common themes: first, most of the anthropologists queried felt very strongly about their fieldnotes; and second, this feeling was often highly ambivalent. To expose one's fieldnotes to public scrutiny was widely perceived as creating vulnerability, an implicit challenge to professional competence, perhaps even personal veracity. A theoretical paper that might be received critically lacked this emotional valence.

The intensity of the association between the fieldwork experience, the personal biography of the anthropologist, the fieldnotes, and the published ethnographic report calls into serious question the idea that anthropologists' documentation of their fieldwork is somehow "objective," a "mirror" of what goes on in the real world. Defensiveness about fieldnotes is itself evidence of the need for documentary fieldwork of a different kind, that is, among the "tribe" of anthropologists. Most of us know deep down how problematic and contingent our cherished understandings are, how indirectly and tenuously they are based in "facts" and observations. The turn toward such reflexivity in anthropological theory that arose in the 1980s is at the core of the "experimental moment" then hailed by James Clifford, George Marcus, and others. Many anthropologists who do not embrace the strong form of this critique nevertheless share the conviction that the relationship between theory and evidence, including the firsthand experience underlying it, is a necessary part of interpreting any anthropological argument. The revolutionary character of that "moment" seems overblown in retrospect, but the issues it raised have settled into a more tempered integration within the mainstreams of both anthropology and cultural studies.

Epistemological paradox is inherent in our disciplinary practice, with the most striking example being the seemingly opposed stances of participant and observer in our hybrid fieldwork method of "participant-observation." Dramatically different modes of interpretation and writing often alternate in the corpus of a single anthropologist and may even be combined in a given work.

Although it is hardly surprising that the initial efforts toward preserving the anthropological record documented in this volume assign primacy to field notes, the second challenge is to record systematically the "history of anthropology for anthropological purposes" as Sydel Silverman (1992) puts it in her introduction. These tasks are interdependent. Anthropologists' reflections on fieldwork and fieldnotes should persuade us that data provided about "other" cultures are never fully separable from what the researcher brings to the fieldwork in the form of both professional training and biographical experience.

If whatever we learn or say about another society is necessarily arbitrary in relation to the totality of which it is a part, then it becomes essential to specify the context of observations and interpretations. This means treating the history of anthropology as a problem in anthropology, a problem of ethnographic context that can be documented by fieldwork among ourselves. Such an effort is feasible because most anthropologists are already familiar with the methods of archival research and have conducted interviews within an orally transmitted culture, be it professional or tribal.

Anthropology as a social science is committed to the premise that there is something out there in the world ("culture" or "society") that can be described and interpreted in various ways. Although few would claim today that any given interpretation remains "true" for all time, to the preclusion of alternative interpretations, most of us remain convinced that it is possible to evaluate better or worse interpretations, at least in relation to particular purposes. Despite the necessarily limited snapshot of a particular anthropologist's time in the field, these purposes and the utility of our interpretations at any given moment change over time in relation to changes in the discipline and the larger society in which it is embedded.

A generation after the original research was carried out, the interpretative context of the original work, easily available and so self-evident as to be trivial to contemporaries, will require reconstruction. Such reconstruction is only possible if documents about the anthropologist, their research, and the professional milieu of the time have been preserved. Therefore, records usually considered part of the history of anthropology are simultaneously fundamental to the interpretation of primary documents from fieldwork.

Much of the reevaluation of "writing culture" (Clifford and Marcus 1986) revolved around rereading the disciplinary canon, perhaps an indication that anthropology was becoming more introspective. There are not enough "traditional" cultures to go around these days; a single anthropologist can no longer expect to remain the sole interpreter of a culture to the larger world. Moreover, members of so-called traditional societies increasingly claim the right to speak for themselves and see no need for an anthropologist as mediator. Even more importantly, anthropological self-interrogation often proceeds most comfortably at a distance. To assess the work of a Malinowski or a Boas or a Lévi-Strauss is less personal or threatening than to confront the basis of one's own ethnography. Many questions being asked in today's introspective rereading of the disciplinary canon have been previously posed by students of the history of anthropology. They require teasing out of interpersonal networks, professional trainings, institutional frameworks, theoretical perspectives, and personal experiences brought to fieldwork and other disciplinary interpretive practices.

To take a single example, the fieldnotes and, above all, the diaries of Bronislaw Malinowski have laid bare invaluable traces of how the mystique of fieldwork entered professional anthropology as a rite of passage and how British functionalism rather than any home-grown American anthropology came to be seen as its backbone. Publication of the diaries demonstrated that the anthropologist as hero had feet of clay, with moments of personal despair and distaste for their fieldwork, and that the diaries—by the standards of our time rather than his own—were replete with expressions of racism, sexism, and ethnocentrism. Regardless, Clifford

Geertz (1988) chose Malinowski's diaries rather than the ethnographies to represent his reportative strategy. Malinowski's reputation among anthropologists as the master of firsthand fieldwork and empathetic evocation of cultural difference dramatically altered the confidence in his authority of many anthropologists who struggled to incorporate the insights his diaries brought to his ethnographies. The fieldwork and the fieldworker proved inseparable.

It is fashionable these days to read earlier works, and some contemporary ones as well, "against the grain." Geertz claimed that his book about several major anthropologists contributed to the theory of anthropology rather than to its history, implicitly rejecting any critique of his interpretation based on what Malinowski (or any of his contemporaries) thought he was up to. This is a blatantly ahistoricist stance.

Nonetheless, Malinowski left behind sufficient documentation of his life and his fieldwork to allow reevaluation of both his career as an anthropologist at a particular point in the history of the discipline and the adequacy with which he represented the culture of the Trobriand Islanders at the time of his fieldwork. To use this available information within the canons of responsible historicism does not invalidate present-day revisionism; rather, it distinguishes the context of the original life and work from the one within which it is interpreted anew. It contends that existing documents of fieldwork and personal experience are relevant to contemporary interpretation of Malinowski's life and work.

These theoretical debates demonstrate a clear interest in and need for documentation of our disciplinary history. Our theory should tell us that knowing the context of our practice is just as crucial to understanding how we do our work in the field, the library, and the classroom as it is to understanding the classic work on which the discipline is based. Reflexivity has become part of anthropological practice. The observers are observed and observe themselves.

Who Writes Disciplinary History?

Taking seriously what can be learned from documents in the history of anthropology is not entirely new. We have an honorable disciplinary tradition of doing so, beginning with the question of

Fig. 2. Staff of the Department of Anthropology, U.S. National Museum in 1904. Standing (*left to right*): Edwin H. Hawley, George Maynard, Aleš Hrdlička, Thomas W. Sweeny, Walter Hough, Henry W. Henshaw, Richard A. Allen, Edwin P. Upham, Paul Beckwith, Immanuel M. Casanowicz, and Joseph Palmer. Seated (*left to right*): Miss Malone and Miss L. A. Rosenbusch. National Anthropological Archives, Smithsonian Institution [NAA-42012].

whether that history should be written by historians or anthropologists. A. Irving Hallowell (1965) pioneered in this endeavor, insisting that the history of anthropology should be approached by anthropologists using the same standards of evidence and argument that they bring to their work as ethnographers of other cultures. Hallowell wrote both personal reminiscences of the discipline and document-based histories of the early Americanist tradition. For him, the history of anthropology was, in the first instance, "an anthropological problem." The archival skills of historians were necessary to all anthropologists, whether they were writing disciplinary history or ethnohistory or contemporary ethnography. The history of anthropology was interesting primarily insofar as it drew on the reflexivity of participants assessing their own traditions and ongoing practices. Taking up Hallowell's challenge, Darnell (1974) privileged readings on "history from within the discipline," a series of reflexive papers by anthropologists for anthropologists.

Although historians and historians of science certainly have legitimate interests in anthropology and other social sciences, this is a far different problem than the relationship between data and observer that arises from within the reflexivity of anthropologists. For one thing, historians who turn to the history of anthropology are more likely to distance themselves from their subjects than anthropologists reflecting on the accumulated wisdom and beliefs of their own "tribe" (Hymes 1962).

Indeed, many anthropologists are still uncomfortable being subjects of study rather than students of others. We prefer to speak for ourselves about what it is we do. The epistemological position of the anthropologist as fieldworker has not generally been considered reciprocal. To paraphrase Johannes Fabian (1983), we deny coevalness to the peoples we study when we assume that "we" are analysts and "they" are not. A genuinely reflexive history of anthropology would have to make room for alternative readings of the documents preserved in the anthropological record, by insiders and by various kinds of outsiders (not only historians, but even more importantly by the peoples anthropologists have traditionally studied).

Anthropologists writing about their own history have also differed from historians by privileging the data of the discipline. Historians rarely have the enthusiasm for the minutiae of ethnographic description that fascinates most anthropologists, both as historians and as readers. When anthropologists define their responsibilities to preserve the record, their deeply ingrained respect for ethnographic documentation colors the way the task is set. Fieldnotes get first attention, and only as a kind of afterthought do they turn to the papers of the anthropologist in their full professional and personal capacity.

Anthropologists of the Americanist tradition tend to emphasize the importance of the individual in the emergence of culture. The historicism of the early generations of North American anthropologists lent itself to the collection of life histories, including personal memoirs of their own lives as anthropologists (e.g.,

Lowie 1959; Kroeber 1950, 1956, 1959; Mead 1972). The methods of studying other cultures were transposed to studying the culture of anthropology itself; personal experiences were significant because they assumed that culture was to be understood in relation to the individual. British social anthropology, in contrast, tended to emphasize synchronic social structure over the role of the individual within it. This view produced an intellectualized structural approach to the history of British social anthropology that did not encourage interest in reflexive continuities to contemporary practice. The simple dichotomy has proved far more complex in practice, however, with the intersection of perspectives and peripatetic careers in both directions across the Atlantic.

Linguists in North America, having come of age with close historical ties to anthropologists, also established a tradition of autobiography and personal documentation (e.g., Sebeok 1963; Davis and O'Cain 1980; Koerner 1991). Linguistic fieldwork with a few fluent speakers of endangered Native American languages may have drawn linguists even more intimately than cultural anthropologists toward the personal dimensions of disciplinary history. At least in the case of Edward Sapir (Darnell 1990a), this created an awareness of the unique integration of culture in the mind of each speaker that led Sapir to move theoretically between grammar, life history, and what he called "the impact of culture on personality."

In contrast, our disciplinary neighbors in another direction, the sociologists, have been socialized professionally to study impersonal social forces. Autobiography is minimal and, when it does occur, rarely personal. The proper role of the sociologist is to bear witness to forces of sociological concern. The enormous literature on the history of the Chicago School of Sociology contains little biography and almost no informative "gossip" in the sense so beloved of anthropologists (Darnell 1990b, chapter 8, this volume).

The Documentation of Americanist Anthropology

North American anthropology is relatively well documented in part because anthropologists are socialized to value the role of individuals in creating and transmitting culture over time. Working in disciplinary history has not been perceived as utterly different in

Fig. 3. Group portrait of Oxford anthropologists, 1910. Standing: Wilson William Wallis, Diamond Jenness, and Charles Marius Barbeau, all students at Oxford. Seated: Henry Balfour of the Pitt Rivers Museum; Arthur Thomson, professor of anatomy and physical anthropologist; and Robert R. Marett, who was appointed about this time to a chair in social anthropology. Pitt Rivers Museum [1998.271.11].

kind from work in other cultures, leading many to a commitment to preserve personal papers as well as fieldnotes.

A few major institutions have established extensive collections of anthropological papers. As described by Mary Elizabeth Ruwell (1995), the National Anthropological Archives holds both the records of the BAE and the personal papers of anthropologists associated with it from the 1870s on, such as John P. Harrington and John Napoleon Brinton Hewitt. The American Philosophical Society holds a significant collection of documents on American Indian [*sic*] linguistics, ethnology, and ethnohistory, including the papers of Frank Boas, Edward Sapir, A. Irving Hallowell, Frank Speck, William Fenton, and Elsie Clews Parsons. The collections continue to grow with additional donations.

Several other institutions maintain substantial archival resources for disciplinary history. North American anthropology through the end of the Second World War was centered in a few cities and concentrated in collaborations between universities and museums (Darnell 1969, 1998). The University of California, Berkeley has the Kroeber and Lowie papers. The University of Chicago holds the records of Robert Redfield, Fay-Cooper Cole, Fred Eggan, and Sol Tax, with additional documents located at Chicago's Field Museum. Clyde Kluckhohn's papers are at Harvard University, but documents important to archaeology are at the associated Peabody Museum. The University of Pennsylvania Museum maintains a substantial archive. The Library of Congress has the papers of Margaret Mead. Yale University has extensive documentation on Edward Sapir, Bronislaw Malinowski, George Peter Murdock, and others affiliated with the IHR. In New York, the American Museum of Natural History and Columbia University maintain significant collections of anthropologists' personal records. The Canadian Museum of Civilization (formerly the National Museum of Man and currently the Canadian Museum of History) in Ottawa has the administrative papers of Edward Sapir, Diamond Jenness, and Marius Barbeau.

Some anthropologists have chosen to leave their papers to institutions closely tied to their personal careers. Ruth Benedict's materials are at her alma mater, Vassar College, while Leslie White's are at the University of Michigan, Ann Arbor. Alexander Golden-

Fig. 4. Officers of American Association for the Advancement of Science at the Ann Arbor, Michigan, meeting in 1885. The Rev. James Owen Dorsey (1848–95), vice-president of the section on anthropology, is standing third from the right. Erminnie A. Smith is seated in front. National Anthropological Archives, Smithsonian Institution [33-02872300].

weiser left some papers at Reed College (copies are now available in the William Fenton papers at the American Philosophical Society), while Edward Spicer's papers are at the University of Arizona.

For some individuals, there are gaps in the record. Edward Sapir, for all the quantity of materials in his administrative files and among the personal papers of his contemporaries, did not leave his own archive of personal correspondence. Disciplinary oral tradition accepted as fact, without need for a specific source, that Sapir burned his papers at the end of his life. For Paul Radin, Alexander Goldenweiser, and Morris Swadesh, no single major collection offers an easy starting point for the potential biographer. Their activities must be reconstructed, partly through what has been preserved in the papers of other individuals and institutions.

Archived documentation for the history of anthropology has become much more systematic, careful, and accessible over the last two or three decades, the same period during which anthropologists have become more interested in their history in relation to their practice. As a researcher in the history of anthropology in the 1960s, I was frequently pointed to a file cabinet in a corner or handed several cardboard cartons of unsorted papers and asked to report on the contents if I found anything interesting. I admit a certain nostalgia for the euphoric rush of discovery that accompanies finding a treasure no one would ever have thought to search for. More recently, I have returned to the same collections to find professional archivists eager to demonstrate new systems of cataloging and retrieval. It makes our archival lives much simpler but perhaps not as much fun. Technological developments have made cooperation among archives more accessible and documents easier to locate, although desire for cooperation may conflict with institutional autonomy for many institutions.

Much of the information that goes into our histories remains available only by word of mouth. A history of anthropology newsletter produced by George Stocking and recently revitalized by historians of science at the University of Pennsylvania is joined by a history of archaeology bulletin published by the Society for American Archaeology, and both are beginning to publish notifications of the location and composition of anthropological record sets, including the papers of individual practitioners. There is still no centralized on-line or published location finding aid.

The wealth of documents available to write the history of anthropology in North America does not automatically lead to collective decisions about how they are to be used and how this effort relates to the rest of the discipline. Some researchers proceed by systematic search for specific materials. Others (and I confess to being among them) turn over each sheet of paper in search of the document not predicted from the catalog or ostensible focus of the collection. The latter kind of reading unveils the overall context of anthropological research in a given period and is more likely to make sense of its constituent pieces.

The aspiring anthropological historian should expect that almost any subject, whether personal or ethnographic, will lead from one archival collection and one physical location to others. Correspondents often preserve items that do not exist in the papers of the original subject. Correspondence involving a series of persons commenting on the same topic may clarify relationships among contemporaries. Sufficient materials may be available to follow a meandering trail through associative tendrils for a given individual, but there is never a cutoff point at which all documents have been located.

Historians of anthropology attempting to justify their work as a legitimate professional specialization have emphasized archival documents and methods. It should be remembered, however, that the history of professional anthropology in North America has a remarkably limited time depth. Many practitioners are still living who knew the prominent elders—Boas, Kroeber, Lowie, Sapir, Benedict, Mead and others. Their stories do not always agree with the archival record, and their memories are certainly colored by their own later experience and retrospective knowledge of ensuing events. But they link what we know about our elders in ways that do not surprise those of us who have studied oral traditions in our fieldwork. The historian of anthropology is obligated to use and preserve the records of oral history as well as published materials. Anthropologists are accustomed to sorting out the personal experiences and anecdotes that form part of the context of a culture, or an era, or a kind of anthropology. The personal transcends mere gossip to reflect a network of intertwined individuals and events. Historical accounts and interpretations based on oral as well as written records infuse them with an added dimension of reality and immediacy.

The history of professional anthropology in Canada has an even shallower time depth than in the United States. Edward Sapir established the Division of Anthropology under the Geological Survey of Canada in 1910. Academic anthropology began with Thomas F. McIlwraith at the University of Toronto and the Royal Ontario Museum in 1925. Many of these elders are still living, although most are now retired. One might expect the history of Canadian anthropology to be more accessible than that in the United States two to three decades earlier.

In practice, however, the more limited time depth has worked against acceptance of disciplinary history as significant for contemporary practice. I spent my sabbatical year of 1976–77 year seeking documents in the major regional centers in Canada. When I first discussed the history of Canadian anthropology in relation to questions of Canadian identity that were salient in the larger society at that time, I was frequently told, especially by graduate students, that anthropology in Canada had no separate identity as a national tradition (Darnell 1975). My efforts to problematize that history reflexively fell on deaf ears.

I located extensive archival documents at the Canadian Museum of Civilization that allowed me to document early professional anthropology in Ottawa, particularly during the Sapir years, 1910–25 (Darnell 1976). Other potential repositories had either no records, uncataloged records, or restrictive constraints on access and use. There were ethnographic archives but not personal ones; the institutional developments and social networks of the discipline had not yet entered the archives. Undeterred, I sought interviews with living elders; most were polite, appreciative of my interest in their experience, and superficially helpful but generally uninformative on controversial debates in disciplinary history. Catalogs of names and dates were offered, accompanied by bland anecdotes. Most felt obligated to protect colleagues' privacy lest potentially disruptive "gossip" cause harm to reputations, even of those deceased. A corresponding sense of historicism or obligation to record the disciplinary past was absent.

The intervening years have brought progress, but the intense reflexivity about the disciplinary past that characterized contemporary anthropology in the United States in the same period was still missing. Documentation of the histories of academic departments of anthropology over several years of sessions at the annual meetings of the Canadian Ethnology Society (now the Canadian Anthropology Society) proved more useful. Participants were comfortable describing their personal experience in their home locations, speaking "off the record" as it were to their peers. The concern for propriety and unwillingness to speak for other colleagues continued to take priority over history, however, including glossing over events that I as a participant remember as far more disputatious than in the retelling. Despite widespread collaborative support for the documentary project, the majority of the conference papers presented over several years of annual meetings were not submitted for publication (Harrison and Darnell 2006).

Contemporary Preservation Issues

This chapter has concentrated on currently available documents and their potential uses in contemporary anthropological practice. Without recognition that evidence of our disciplinary past serves future scholars, no project to preserve anthropological documents will be successful. Reflexivity, the key to much contemporary theorizing, strongly supports the significance of such preservation. Anthropologists who value the documents available from preceding generations must commit themselves to preserving materials in their own possession in order to ensure that a history of the anthropology of our time will be left behind for our successors.

The explosion of modern technologies, accelerating sharply since this chapter was written, raises questions about what documentation will be available in the future. Many anthropologists today conduct their careers primarily through the ephemeral media of telephone and electronic mail. Even the computer hard disks and backup files of those who still write letters may not survive or be readable beyond their immediate utility. Instant cross-country and cross-continental transportation permit many of us the luxury of waiting to see colleagues and talk things over rather than write a letter.

Despite these serious concerns, much can and should be done by all practicing anthropologists. Minimally, arrangements can be made for personal papers alongside fieldnotes and other research materials. The best choice of repository depends on individual circumstances.

Ideally, the anthropologist who nears retirement, moves to a smaller home or office, or finishes a given phase of their career will consult an archivist about how to arrange these materials and specify in advance where material in their possession would be most appropriately housed. For many, given the contemporary complexity of professional careers, this may involve more than one archive or institution. If an individual is or has been employed by several institutions, it is unclear that any one of them would undertake to curate the collection as a whole. Community institutions in or near local fieldwork site(s) may be most appropriate. An effort should be made to keep materials somewhere easily accessible to scholars and community collaborators, preferably alongside similar materials.

Many anthropologists convince themselves that their papers will be of limited interest to the discipline because they are not major figures. Most of us, however, have research materials of potential value, as well as correspondence with others whose careers, collectively or individually, concern the discipline as a whole. What seems unremarkable to the participant may become crucial and compelling a generation later. The work of perceived superstars is far more meaningful when framed in relation to that of their peers who do the bulk of disciplinary research. These peers are often more characteristic of the era in which they work than those whose ideas resonate more easily across generations.

Control can be exercised over what is preserved as well as where it is preserved. The anthropologist who organizes their own files before delivering them to an archive can ensure that intimate personal materials are removed or restrictions placed on their access. Such preliminary work is invaluable to the archivist who will eventually work with the collection.

Appointing a literary executor, whether a family member or colleague, is another way to ensure that one's wishes are carried out. Without specific instructions, families may do nothing with documents left at death or simply discard them, resulting in their loss to future researchers. There is nothing immodest about accepting a professional responsibility to preserve appropriate documents for the sake of future colleagues.

Most anthropologists are now aware of the importance of preserving documents about their careers and their participation in larger events within the discipline. This self-awareness has produced an enthusiasm for archival documentation of personal careers comparable to the longer-established commitment to preserving fieldnotes. The present effort (as of 1995) to preserve the anthropological record is timely and attuned to the increasingly widespread appreciation of the value of this record and of the need to save documents that will be lost if individuals do not take responsibility for materials in their possession or control while it is still possible.

Summary

1. The history of anthropology should be treated as an anthropological problem, an integral part of anthropology's study of human cultures across time and space.

2. The personal papers of anthropologists are crucial documents for the interpretation of field notes and other data records, for understanding the context of research and theory, and for tracing the intellectual and professional development of anthropology.

3. A computerized database and finding aids are needed to document the location of anthropological papers in archives.

4. All anthropologists should make arrangements for the appropriate archiving of their own papers and other materials in their possession. (Silverman and Parezo 1995:82–83)

Notes

1. Originally published as "Documenting Disciplinary History," in *Preserving the Anthropological Record*, ed. Sydel Silverman and Nancy J. Parezo, 73–84, 2nd ed. (New York: Wenner-Gren Foundation for Anthropological Research, 1995).

References

Clifford, James, and George Marcus, eds. 1986. *Writing Culture: The Politics and Poetics of Ethnography*. Berkeley: University of California Press.

Darnell, Regna. 1969. "The Development of American Anthropology, 1879–1920: From the Bureau of American Ethnology to Franz Boas." PhD diss., University of Pennsylvania.

———, ed. 1974. *Readings in the History of Anthropology*. New York: Harper and Row.

———. 1975. "Toward a History of the Professionalization of Canadian Anthropology." *Proceedings of the Canadian Ethnological Society*: 399–416.

———. 1976. "The Sapir Years at the National Museum." *Proceedings of the Plenary Session of the Canadian Ethnology Society*: 98–121.

———. 1990a. *Edward Sapir: Linguist, Anthropologist, Humanist*. Berkeley: University of California Press.

———. 1990b. "Franz Boas, Edward Sapir and the Americanist Text Tradition." *Historiographia Linguistica* 17:129–44.

———. 1998. *And Along Came Boas: Continuity and Revolution in Americanist Anthropology*. Amsterdam: John Benjamins.

Davis, Boyd, and Raymond O'Cain. 1980. *First Person Singular*. Amsterdam: John Benjamins.

Fabian, Johannes. 1983. *Time and the Other*. Chicago: University of Chicago Press.

Fowler, Don D., and Nancy Parezo. "Future Prospects." In Silverman and Parezo 1995:219–24.

Geertz, Clifford. 1988. *Works and Lives: The Anthropologist as Author*. Stanford CA: Stanford University Press.

Hallowell, A. Irving. 1965. "The History of Anthropology as an Anthropological Problem." *Journal of the History of the Behavioral Sciences* 1:24–38.

Harrison, Julia, and Regna Darnell, eds. 2006, *Historicizing the Canadian Tradition*. Vancouver: University of British Columbia Press.

Hymes, Dell. 1962. "On Studying the History of Anthropology." *Kroeber Anthropological Society Papers* 26:81–86.

Jackson, Jean. 1980. "'I Am a Field Note': Fieldnotes as a Symbol of Professional Identity." In *The Makings of Anthropology*, edited by Roger Sanjek, 3–33. Ithaca NY: Cornell University Press.

Koerner, Konrad, ed. 1991. *First Person Singular II*. Amsterdam: John Benjamins.

Kroeber, Alfred. L. 1950. "A Half Century of Anthropology." In *The Nature of Culture*, 139–43. Chicago: University of Chicago Press.

———. 1956. "The Place of Boas in Anthropology." *American Anthropologist* 58:151–59.

———. 1959. "A History of the Personality of Anthropology." *American Anthropologist* 61:398–404.

Lowie, Robert H. 1959. *Robert H. Lowie: An Autobiography*. Berkeley: University of California Press.

Mead, Margaret. 1972. *Blackberry Winter: My Early Years*. New York: William Morrow.

Ruwell, Mary Elizabeth. 1995. "The Physical Preservation of Anthropological Records." In Silverman and Parezo 1995:197–204.

Sebeok, Thomas, ed. 1963. *Portraits of Linguists*. Bloomington: Indiana University Press.

Silverman, Sydel. 1992. "Introduction." In Silverman and Parezo 1992:1–14.

Silverman, Sydel and Nancy J. Parezo, eds. 1992. *Preserving the Anthropological Record*. New York: Wenner-Gren Foundation for Anthropological Research.

———, eds. 1995. *Preserving the Anthropological Record*. 2nd ed. New York: Wenner-Gren Foundation for Anthropological Research.

6

Franz Boas's Legacy of "Useful Knowledge"

The APS Archives and the Future of Americanist Anthropology

It is a pleasure and privilege, though also somewhat intimidating, to address the assembled membership of the American Philosophical Society (APS) founded by Benjamin Franklin in 1743 "for the promotion of useful knowledge."[1] Like the august founders under whose portraits we assemble, members come to hear their peers share the results of their inquiries across the full range of the sciences and arenas of public affairs to which they have contributed "useful knowledge." Prior to the professionalization of science in the late nineteenth and early twentieth centuries, the boundaries between disciplines were far less significant than they are today. Those who were not experts in particular topics could rest assured that their peers were capable of assessing both the state of knowledge in each other's fields and the implications for society.

Benjamin Franklin, Thomas Jefferson, and George Washington were all polymaths, covering what we now separate into several kinds of science, humanities, and social sciences in ways that crosscut one another and illustrate the permeability of disciplinary boundaries. The study of the American Indian [*sic*] is a piece of the multidisciplinary heritage that constituted the APS and continues to characterize its public persona. The founding members of the society all had direct and seminal experience with the Indians [*sic*] and with the conflict between their traditional ways of life and the infringing world of settler colonialism. On the one hand, they felt justified in exploiting Indigenous resources, as surveyors, treaty negotiators, and land speculators. On the other hand, the Indians [*sic*] represented the uniqueness of the Americas, of the New World that defined itself apart from the decadence of old Europe. The gen-

Fig. 5. President Baruch Blumberg presides over an American Philosophical Society annual meeting under the portraits of Thomas Jefferson, Benjamin Franklin, and George Washington not long before his death in 2011. A Nobel laureate in biomedical sciences, he taught physical anthropology at the University of Pennsylvania for many years. American Philosophical Society.

tleman scholars [*sic*] of the New Republic identified with the Indians [*sic*] but also turned to the scientific study of their languages, cultures, and histories (the latter primarily through archaeology). Although most of Jefferson's linguistic vocabularies were lost, the works of Peter Stephen Du Ponceau, John Pickering, and Albert Gallatin established the American Indian [*sic*] linguistic collections that dominated the early scientific reputation of the APS. By the late nineteenth century, the specialist who interpreted the languages and myths of the American Indian [*sic*] for the membership of his day was Daniel Garrison Brinton, a Philadelphia physician who edited and published the multivolume *Library of Aboriginal American Literature*. The APS Library has continuously maintained a distinguished collection of Indian [*sic*] vocabularies accessible to successive generations of member-scientists who could classify the relationships of these languages and reveal the diversity of Native Americans, another instance of Franklin's vaunted "useful knowledge."

The continuity of this tradition is encapsulated today in the Boas collection that forms the core of the APS Library's Native American holdings. Franz Boas (1858–1942) was born and educated in Germany but is widely acknowledged as the founding figure of anthropology and linguistics in North America. Up until about 1905 when he resigned from the American Museum of Natural History to pursue a full-time academic career at Columbia University, Boas's career can be encompassed within anthropology as then understood. Originally trained in psychophysics in Germany, Boas turned to geography as the basis of his 1883–84 year of fieldwork among the Baffinland Eskimo, as they were then called. This experience convinced him that environment was a limiting rather than a determining factor in cultural development, and he soon acknowledged the rich expressive culture of the Eskimo despite their extreme environment. He reoriented his professional identity to anthropology and focused his fieldwork interests on the Northwest Coast, where the intersection of multiple linguistic groups borrowing from and enriching one another facilitated the reconstruction of particular histories in the absence of written records, based on mutual borrowings and reintegration of cultural traits by each group.

The Boasian paradigm later known as historical particularism explicitly countered the eugenics and social evolutionary theories of so-called primitive culture that were pervasive at the time. Increasingly, however, Boas's scientific work expanded from anthropology into fields we now separate out as linguistics, folklore, psychology, education, and such emergent standpoint–based disciplines as Indigenous studies, Afro-American studies, Jewish studies, and women's studies. He took public stands on war, science, and patriotism that were unpopular in his own time, wrote to newspapers, spoke to non-academic audiences, prepared museum exhibits for public pedagogy, encouraged minority group scholars, and supported Indigenous and Afro-American communities in combating racism and marginalization.

Boas's studies of immigrant head-form demonstrated the plasticity of human groups and the permeability of racial types. He was a pioneer in breaking down American isolationism with its incumbent intolerance and misinformation about cultural, linguistic, and biological diversity, offering cultural relativism as an alternative to evolutionary racism. He argued passionately for academic and intellectual freedom and for science as a civilizational value transcending the short-term goals of nation-states. He was among the strongest supporters of European scholars displaced by Nazi politics in their efforts to resettle in America and helped reunite families devastated by political turmoil across the Europe of two world wars. Boas models for us today the capacity of the public intellectual to call citizens to attend to social justice, environmental degradation, systemic discrimination, and other ills of contemporary society. The appearance of Boas's picture on the cover of *Time* magazine not long after his retirement from Columbia University in 1936 attests to his stature far beyond the boundaries of his nominal discipline of anthropology.

The American Philosophical Society holds Boas's personal and professional papers, as well as those of other Boas family members. The core collection consists of fifty-nine linear feet or forty-six reels of microfilm plus graphics dating from 1869 to 1940. The papers were cataloged and indexed by Carl Voegelin and Zellig Harris in the 1970s, and further finding aids have been issued in the interim. Nonetheless, omissions and misorderings in the microfilms as well as inadequacies in the finding aids themselves have impeded ongoing scholarship. The originals have been available only in the APS Library and only to scholars.

In 2008, even before he took up his official appointment as Native studies and western history editor at the University of Nebraska Press, Matthew Bokovoy invited me to spearhead a project to publish the Franz Boas Papers (FBP) held at the American Philosophical Society. As a member of the society, chair of its Phillips fund for Native American research, and sometime denizen of the archives since 1966, I concluded after some soul-searching that my work with Native North Americans, primarily Cree and Ojibwe [Anishinaabeg] in Canada, as well as in the history of Americanist anthropology, situated me ideally, perhaps even uniquely, to bring the pieces together. My commitments to community collaboration in ethnographic and linguistic research sustained over substantial periods of time were well entrenched.

Nonetheless, I worried lest the project decline into the communicative morass of the legendary six blind men poking at the elusive anatomy of an elephant. My biography of Boas's most distinguished linguistic student Edward Sapir (Darnell [1990] 2010) had convinced me that no single scholar could encompass the range of Boas's interests. But I was intrigued by the possibility that a team of scholars might pool the pieces of Boas's life and work that each of them knew in detail. The juxtaposition of partial perspectives offered the exciting potential for a fuller overall portrait. My prior historical scholarship on Boas had eschewed biography in favor of peeling the contextual onion, of unraveling his paradigm, the institutional context within which it evolved, and the social networks he initiated and sustained. A primary focus on Boas's own words as reflected in his correspondence would permit him to speak for himself, albeit to a future audience that he could not have envisioned.

Matt and I initiated negotiations with Martin Levitt, then librarian of the APS, and I invited Boas scholars who reflected the range and continuing significance of his oeuvre for anthropology, linguistics, Native American studies, and American and Canadian public life to join me in considering the feasibility of a documentary edition. This inaugural conference assembled in London, Ontario, in December 2010, amid a blizzard that extended the stay of many contributors by several days and exceeded the budget by several thousands. The revised proceedings (Darnell et al. 2015) serve as the framing volume for *The Franz Boas Papers: Documentary Edition.*

With the contributors as the core of the initial editorial advisory board, I assembled a Canadian-based research team designed to be attractive to the Partnership Grants program of the Social Sciences and Humanities Research Council (SSHRC) of Canada. SSHRC had supported the initial conference. After a leisurely process including an extensive preliminary application, we were invited to prepare an even more extensive final application. In March 2013 SSHRC awarded the Franz Boas Papers Documentary Edition Series at the University of Western Ontario $2.5 million dollars (Canadian) over seven years, in partnership with the American Philosophical Society, the University of Nebraska Press, the University of Victoria, and the Musgamagw Dzawada'enuxw Tribal Council of the Kwakwaka'wakw (the people that Boas called "Kwakiutl").

I serve as project director and general editor, assisted by a core research team of anthropologists, linguists, historians, and Native Americans (called "First Nations" in Canada) that includes the APS librarian, an international editorial advisory board, and an Indigenous advisory council (IAC). The APS has contracted with the University of Nebraska Press to produce a joint print and electronic documentary edition of fifteen to twenty-five thematic volumes that will present and recontextualize the remarkable breadth of Boas's life, scholarship, and public stature.

Boas did the vast majority of his ethnographic research in Canada, on the North Pacific (not Northwest) Coast of Canada and among the Inuit (as Eskimo call themselves and are called in Canada), facts that are virtually ignored by existing U.S. scholarship and in considerable need of historiographic redress. The national contexts of Indigenous experience are distinct in the United States and Canada. Our research team includes a number of Indigenous scholars who aspire to interpret documents collected by Boas and his students because they form part of their own history and can be juxtaposed with knowledge held in contemporary oral tradition to revitalize languages and cultures.

The project is governed by an Indigenous advisory council that has evolved, under the leadership of Susan Hill (Mohawk Nation, Wolf Clan), based on a loose coalition of advisers from descendant communities to a more formal membership of community-based scholars and scholars-in-training. The members represent relational collaborative perspectives rather than individual communities and are available to advise and mediate with relevant communities. The IAC mandate is to adjudicate the protection of culturally sensitive materials, return intellectual property to the communities of its origin through Digital Knowledge Sharing (DKS), and create scholarly and professional capacity within Indigenous communities.

The magnitude of available material mandated a selective edition since even twenty-five volumes could not possibly include the full contents of the Boas Papers, more than forty thousand documents. The decision was made to organize the selective edition thematically for several reasons: (1) A chronological edition, more usual for documentary editions, would have begun with Boas's early life and the rather narrowly anthropological engagements of his early career; this period, however, has been covered extensively by anthropologists writing the history of their discipline. The late Douglas Cole's meticulous biography, posthumously published in 1999, ends in 1906. My own *And Along Came Boas: Continuity and Revolution in Americanist Anthropology* (1998) and *Invisible Genealogies: A History of Americanist Anthropology* (2001) focus on the first generation of Boas's students and the emergence of his distinctive paradigm. Herbert S. Lewis (2014) emphasizes Boas's theoretical position within past and present anthropological debates. Much less research has been done on Boas's later, more interdisciplinary work, so we decided to focus our initial efforts there. (2) Moreover, much of the early correspondence is in German, and our collaborations with German colleagues were in their early stages. We hope that the edition will be able to integrate documents remaining in Germany with those already held by the APS. (3) Separating the material thematically renders the volumes more accessible to Indigenous communities because readers can focus on the volumes of local relevance or personal interest. (4) Each volume aspires to present its theme in a revisionist framework. Because few contemporary scholars have returned to the originals in their citation of Boas or assessment of his lasting importance, errors and anachronisms abound in the existing scholarship. Letters and explanatory annotations will, in some sense, speak for themselves. A nonpolemic framing essay will introduce each volume and assess its historiographic import within Boas's oeuvre.

There is an inevitable fine line between what George W. Stocking Jr. long ago problematized as historicism versus presentism (Stocking 1968). Historicism attempts to portray past events as participants saw them, within their original historical context. Presentism goes beyond unmediated documents to interpretative interpolation based on contemporary standards and values. Applying this familiar conundrum to documentary editing, I rephrase the dichotomy, emphasizing that historicist verisimilitude requires seeing things in their original context and clearly separating that from what we now make out of it. Contemporary scholars cannot help but have presentist motives for pursuing disciplinary history and selecting the topics they do. The methodological challenge is to recognize the difference and balance anachronism against changing standards, taking for granted that full objectivity is an unobtainable standard because of the inevitable position of the observer but that objectivity nonetheless remains a goal to be pursued with self-conscious reflexivity. Accordingly, following A. Irving Hallowell (1965; Darnell 1977), an APS member and one of my earliest teachers of anthropology, I define the history of the discipline as a quintessential anthropological problem. As in ethnographic fieldwork, with its characteristic methodology of participant observation, the anthropologist, like the historian, moves back and forth between external analysis and contextualization. The latter incorporates the effort to capture what Boas called "the native point of view."

Each volume of the documentary edition aspires to be revisionist in its capacity to reframe Boas's work for a twenty-first-century audience. For example, with my colleagues, American historian Gregory Smithers and Canadian biocultural anthropologist Alexis Dolphin, I am editing a volume tentatively titled *From Anthropometry to Plasticity* as well as an annotated edition of *The Mind of Primitive Man* (MPM) with detailed comparisons of the 1911 and 1938 editions. This was Boas's paradigm statement about the universality of human capacity, both biological and mental, underscoring the importance of considering the effects of culture, environment, and history alongside racial or biological determinants. The centennial of MPM in 2011 was marked by at least three conferences, one of which was the prelude to the Boas documentary edition (Darnell et al. 2015). Others were held at Yale University and the Wenner-Gren Foundation for Anthropological Research.

Boas devoted much of his early career to anthropometry, what we would now call a physical or biological anthropology, measuring the skull ratios of diverse human populations as an index of their unwritten prehistory. The method presumed permanent or at least very stable racial status. Between his measurement of Kwakwaka'wakw performers at the 1893 Chicago World's Fair and the publication of MPM, Boas turned this racialist scientific reasoning on its head. His prior work measuring school children in Worcester, Massachusetts, at Clark University in the late 1880s and early 1900s brought a contract to study immigrant head-form for the 1910–12 United States census. The Dillingham Commission hoped and expected to hear that southern European immigrants, hitherto considered a separate race, could not be assimilated into American society. Instead, Boas demonstrated that "head-form" based on anthropometric measurement could change in a single generation after immigration to New York City. Such "plasticity" of human type fatally undermined the concept of race as then understood and reenvisioned it rather as what we now call rac*ism* or socially constructed prejudice. Boas acknowledged statistical differences among human groups but deemed them amenable to change in ways that could not be constrained in an evolutionary hierarchy. His studies based on particular family lines highlighted variability within so-called racial groups as well as between them. This work is reported in MPM, and it remained fundamental to Boas's theoretical position throughout his career. Detailed comparison of the 1911 and 1938 editions reveals surprisingly minor differences. The primary one is that Boas switched the title of his framing essay from the topic of race in America in 1911 to a critique of race in Hitler's National Socialism in 1938. The particular exemplars in the substance of this chapter, however, remained virtually unchanged, as did the abstract structure of his argument.

If one rereads MPM today, it does not say what disciplinary history recalls it to have said. Biology and culture were not binaries requiring different methods, as both biological and cultural anthropologists since Boas's day have tended to assume (Darnell 2015, 2017). Beyond his argument for plasticity of immigrant head-form, Boas reasoned that the relatively rigorous methods of the biological sciences could be extended by analogy to the study of cultural phenomena. Rather than a positivist versus mentalist dichotomy, he took for granted the scientific validity of both, as sides of the same coin. Charges of latter-day critics that he was a mentalist, and that this made him unscientific, are risible in this context. Moreover, Boas was not overly concerned with culture as such, although he has often been accused of defending a reified culture concept. Instead, drawing on his training as a geographer, he focused on environment (or environment-and-culture, using them almost as a single term) as the binary of biology. He argued that the plastic, the situational, and the historical applied in both domains. The distinction was arbitrary in that it depended on the observer and on the problem at hand. Science was the mode of attack in both cases. Recent epigenetic studies in hormonal gene expression are now beginning to provide a mechanism for Boas's prescient intuition about the nature of human plasticity.

My colleague and associate editor Joshua Smith is editing a volume titled *Sovereign Anthropologies* that examines Boas's activities as activist and mentor of Indigenous scholars, including his influence on Indian [*sic*] law and Indian [*sic*] policy during the interwar years (Smith 2015). These documents effectively counter the stereotype of Boasian salvage anthropology as oblivious to then contemporary Indigenous lives. The "action anthropology" that arose a generation later under the leadership of second-generation Boasian Sol Tax still manifests itself in emerging contemporary ethical standards for research and collaborative protocols. The Boas documentary edition builds directly on this legacy both by documenting how far back it goes in Americanist anthropology and in the capacity of the project itself.

Other volumes planned or in preparation provisionally include Boas's engagements with anthropologists and anthropologies in Mexico, Canada, and Russia; his museum ethnography and pedagogy; what he called "primitive art"; folklore and ethnomusicology; grammatical theory and historical inference; culture and personality; environmental studies on the Northwest Coast; the Northwest Coast as a culture area (and its possible ties to Asia); "organizing anthropological research in America"; Afro-American race and racism; myth and narrative; law and politics; German philosophy and American pragmatism; New York City Jewish culture; efforts on behalf of European refugees and immigrants; ongoing ties to Germany; German education and early employment; and family letters/childhood. The IAC has proposed a volume of essays on uses of the Boas Papers in contemporary Native American and First Nations communities.

In light of this evolving partnership, the American Philosophical Society attracted independent donor support to digitize the Boas Papers. Digitization began in October 2012 and was completed in November 2014. A new digital finding aid incorporates APS metadata for correspondent and date. The FBP project editorial team has had access to these digitized materials in preparing the documentary edition. Although the Boas papers at the APS remain our source texts, we have located and expect to include or paraphrase Boas materials from other documentary collections in the United States, Canada, Mexico, Russia, Scotland, and Germany. Each thematic volume will include an editorial introduction as well as annotations necessary for contemporary readers to reconstruct the context of Boas's correspondence and the significance of his personal and professional network. Community partners and the IAC called for more detailed metadata allowing them to search for place-names, personal and clan names, ceremonial terms—all appearing in local variants. Project manager M. Sam Cronk has developed an Omeka-based tagging system now available to the research team that will eventually supplement publicly available materials at the APS. The complexity of Boas's legacy emerges from the juxtaposition and balancing of these multiple perspectives.

It is time, perhaps even past time, for reassessment of Boas's six-decade career and its ongoing impact in the academy and in public life. Anthropological commentary on Boas is polarized between postwar positivists who descry his purported mentalism and accuse him of being atheoretical, thereby impeding development of the science of anthropology, and the Boas students and students of students who maintain his legacy monolithically against all challengers. I have referred to Boas elsewhere as "the elephant in the middle of anthropology's room." Despite the diversity of the present-day discipline, every practicing anthropologist must come to terms with the legacy of the founding figure of professional anthropology in America.

Plans for the documentary edition already have stimulated other research agendas. A research team based at Humboldt University in Berlin under the direction of Michi Knecht plans to collect and digitize Boas documents located in Germany with extended commentary; we hope to include this in the *Franz Boas Papers: Documentary Edition* in fully bilingual format. Rainer Hatoum has deciphered Boas's idiosyncratic shorthand, thereby rendering intelligible his previously inscrutable Kwakwaka'wakw fieldnotes (Hatoum 2016). Han F. Vermeulen's *Before Boas: The Genesis of Ethnography and Ethnology in the German Enlightenment* (2015) provides a magisterial treatment of the European philosophical underpinnings of the anthropology that Boas imported to North America. The synergy of these projects, enhanced by overlapping research personnel, underscores the timeliness and interest of the documentary edition. Although Boas's field notes and published works are primary in documenting the Indigenous cultures he studied, his correspondence contextualizes this material so that contemporary scholars and members of descendant communities can access it effectively for contemporary purposes.

Unpublished manuscripts on American Indian [*sic*] languages in Boas's possession at the time of his death were added to the APS collections by way of the American Council for Learned Societies (Leeds-Hurwitz 1985). This distinguished legacy is maintained and extended in the contemporary society. Ancillary collections are regularly enhanced by materials donated by grantees of the APS Phillips Fund for Native American Research, which provides grants for research in Native American linguistics, ethnohistory, and the history of studies of Native Americans in the continental United States and Canada. The APS Library also holds the related papers of Frank Speck, A. Irving Hallowell, Elsie Clews Parsons, John Alden Mason, Frank Siebert, Ella Deloria, Dell Hymes, and Anthony F. C. Wallace, among many others.

Under the leadership of Martin Levitt and Timothy Powell, the APS Library obtained two large grants from the Mellon Foundation to rearticulate materials on endangered Native American languages with the communities of their origin. This initiative is setting new priorities and standards for the collaboration of scholars with the communities of their research subjects and the expertise of their traditional knowledge. Linguistic materials from four tribes (Leech Lake and White Earth Ojibwe [Anishinaabeg], Tuscarora, the Eastern Band of Cherokee Indians, and Penobscot) have been reexamined by knowledge keepers and native speakers, thereby correcting and elaborating the meaning of the collections. Long-separated materials—photographs, music, field notes, correspondence, and so forth—are being reunited in accordance with the protocols and needs of their originary communities rather than by arbitrary cataloging criteria. The work of Maureen Matthews with Hallowell's Ojibwe [Anishinaabeg] photographs is exemplary

(Matthews 2016). Memoranda of understanding have been signed with each of these groups specifying collaborative projects of utility to contemporary tribal members. More recent Mellon funding supports capacity building for Indigenous undergraduate, graduate, and postdoctoral researchers. A permanent program to welcome Native American cultural experts to the APS as researchers and consultants on their own traditions is in nascent stages.

The Mellon project facilitated the establishment of a Native American advisory board to adjudicate the treatment of culturally sensitive materials in the APS collections (largely of a religious or ceremonial nature and accessible by cultural protocol only to those who have undergone appropriate apprenticeship). The majority of the members are Native Americans, but I serve on behalf of the APS membership. This advisory board has devised protocols to protect esoteric knowledge and to treat both texts and artifacts in the APS collections with appropriate respect. The APS has agreed to restrict reproduction and publication of materials according to the advice of this advisory board, thereby making a commitment to the producers of the ethnographic and linguistic documents and to their communities that was unique in the archival world at the time of its formulation and placed the American Philosophical Society at the forefront of contemporary scholarship. The establishment of the Center for Native American and Indigenous Research (CNAIR) in 2014 continues this work. Under the aegis of curator of Native American materials Brian Carpenter, CNAIR is expanding the number of Indigenous communities collaborating with the APS.

The Boas documentary edition builds directly on this initiative. The IAC, with Susan Hill and Robert Hancock (Metis) as cochairs, facilitates work with descendant communities. All members are Indigenous, and all are closely tied to their home territories. The proximate mandate of the IAC is to facilitate the protection of culturally sensitive materials. The longer-term goal is DKS or the return of digital materials to the communities of their origin. The location of documents in Philadelphia far from the home territory of their creators has posed a serious obstacle to the usefulness of this knowledge to its producers. Intellectual property transmitted in an oral tradition is not covered by copyright legislation. Furthermore, in many cases there is ambiguity about the propriety of transfer of ritual items or ceremonial knowledge to museums, archives, and libraries run by outsiders and not under community control. From the point of view of many communities, ownership continues to reside with the creators of these materials rather than with their contemporary archival stewards. In this view, the archives are merely stewards on behalf of the true owners. The establishment of cooperative relationships between archives, museums, and other repositories of cultural information and descendants of the makers is thus a potentially fraught matter calling for mutually respectful consensus-based protocols. Such trust is established only by working together collaboratively over time.

The FBP project protocols arising from the APS collaborative model are already making a difference and are ideally suited to the Boas documentary research. Our core research team includes several Indigenous scholars who are working on materials collected by Boas and his associates in their home territories: Angie Bain (Union of British Columbia Indian Chiefs; Lower Nicola Indian Band), Ryan Nicolson and Deanna Nicolson (Kwakwaka'wakw), Johnny Mack (Nuu Chah Nulth), Rachel Flowers (Lwungen), and Marianne Nicolson (Kwakwaka'wakw). Dawn Nicolson (Kwakwaka'wakw) is the communities liaison. The IAC meets regularly to maximize the usefulness of the emerging materials for the cultural and linguistic revitalization programs that are rampant across Indian country today. Its protocols and deliberations constitute transferable knowledge applicable to multiple communities. Operating on a consensus basis, the IAC has final authority to exclude sensitive materials from further dissemination or publication in the documentary edition. Omissions and their general character would be noted in the published text where appropriate.

The collaborative model fits well with widely shared Native American concepts of co-stewardship and relationality and promises a documentary product that breaks ethical as well as intellectual ground. Whether the issue is linguistic texts, grave goods including human remains, or authorship attributed to the speaker rather than to the recorder or collector, the standards have been evolving rapidly since Boas's time, building on his legacy even when his practice diverges from what is now considered best practice.

The FBP project has established and continues to sustain important community relationships. Six members of the core research team were invited to visit the Kwakwaka'wakw communities of Kingcome Inlet and Alert Bay, British Columbia, in the summer of 2014. Project members, plus Tim Powell and Brian Carpenter on behalf of CNAIR, returned in March 2015 for a potlatch at Alert Bay to honor the Willie Family of Kingcome Inlet and to witness Mikael Willie taking the chiefly name of Ol' Siwidi. We returned in March 2016 for the potlatch in which name keeper Gwi'molas (Ryan Nicolson) returned the product of his research to the assembled Kwakwaka'wakw community as part of an effort to reconstitute the traditional clan system as a mode of governance for all of the Kwakwaka'wakw communities. Boas's fieldnotes, diaries, and correspondence supplement the knowledge of contemporary elders. At these potlatches, CNAIR has returned to the communities by DKS important unpublished materials collected by George Hunt and others in collaboration with Boas. The Boas Project, by supporting the research of community members, is helping to create a generation of community-based scholars who move adeptly between community and academy.

In Boas's day, he most often worked with elders and ceremonialists whose children and grandchildren no longer wanted to learn what their elders knew. Many chose to speak to anthropologists and linguists, with the result that much was recorded that would otherwise have been lost. Some latter-day critics dismiss such research as mere "salvage ethnography" based on reconstruction of memories about times already long gone at the time of recording. Despite the devastating impact of forced assimilation by government- and church-run residential schools, however, contemporary communities are drawing on these documents, many of them held at the APS, alongside the knowledge of living elders that has been preserved through oral tradition, to bring back traditional forms, especially through the language revitalization programs active in many communities. The knowledge held at the APS is therefore available for contemporary use in new and still evolving ways. It is the "useful knowledge" Benjamin Franklin envisioned when he founded the society.

A particular kind of anthropology, a Boasian kind, arose in this context (Darnell 2001). Boas developed a mode of fieldwork that emphasized culture as a body of knowledge in people's heads rather than a thing that could be observed directly. He argued that language, thought, and reality were inseparable and that the best route into "the mind of primitive man" or "the native point of view" was through written texts based on the spoken words of native speakers in their native languages. The categories of Indo-European grammar and mainstream North American cultural assumptions could not be imposed without distortion. Collaborative research methods and recognition of the expertise of the "informants" arose naturally from these assumptions. Such fieldwork took, and still takes, a long time. Many of the texts Boas and Hunt collected were never translated, but they remain accessible to contemporary use because they were recorded. The meaning encoded in them, both form and content, is itself the primary evidence—not the analysis of the outsider anthropologist or linguist.

This Boasian documentary perspective, which I have elsewhere referred to as the Americanist tradition, is, I believe, key to the continued viability of anthropology as a discipline. It also should be a source of pride to the membership of the American Philosophical Society that its traditional commitment to the study of Native Americans is pioneering in new forms of rendering knowledge useful and extending the range of the audiences drawing upon it.

Notes

1. Originally published as "Franz Boas's Legacy of 'Useful Knowledge': The A[merican] P[hilosophical] S[ociety] Archives and the Future of Americanist Anthropology," *Proceedings of the American Philosophical Society* 162, no. 1 (2018): 1–14.

References

Cole, Douglas. 1999. *Franz Boas: The Early Years, 1858–1906.* Vancouver: Douglas and McIntyre.

Darnell, Regna. 1977. "History of Anthropology in Historical Perspective." *Annual Review of Anthropology* 6:399–417.

———. (1990) 2010. *Edward Sapir: Linguist, Anthropologist, Humanist.* Berkeley: University of California Press. Reprint, Lincoln: University of Nebraska Press.

———. 1998. *And Along Came Boas: Continuity and Revolution in Americanist Anthropology*. Amsterdam: John Benjamins.

———. 2001. *Invisible Genealogies: A History of Americanist Anthropology*. Lincoln: University of Nebraska Press.

———. 2015. "Mind, Body, and the Native Point of View: Boasian Theory at the Centennial of *The Mind of Primitive Man*." In Darnell et al. 2015, 3–18.

———. 2017. "Franz Boas as Theorist: A Mentalist Paradigm for the Study of Mind, Body, Environment, and Culture." In *Historicizing Theories, Identities, and Nations*, edited by Regna Darnell and Frederic W. Gleach, 1–26. Vol. 11 of Histories of Anthropology Annual. Lincoln: University of Nebraska Press.

Darnell, Regna, Michelle Hamilton, Robert L. A. Hancock, and Joshua Smith, eds. 2015. *The Franz Boas Papers, Volume 1: Franz Boas as Public Intellectual—Theory, Ethnography, Activism*. Franz Boas Papers Documentary Edition Series. Lincoln: University of Nebraska Press.

Hallowell, A. Irving. 1965. "The History of Anthropology as an Anthropological Problem." *Journal of the History of the Behavioral Sciences* 1:24–38.

Hatoum, Rainer. 2016. "'I Wrote All My Notes in Shorthand': A First Glance into the Treasure Chest of Franz Boas's Shorthand Field Notes." In *Local Knowledge, Global Stage*, edited by Regna Darnell and Frederic W. Gleach, 221–72. Vol. 10 of Histories of Anthropology Annual. Lincoln: University of Nebraska Press.

Leeds-Hurwitz, Wendy. 1985. "The Committee on Research in Native American Languages." *Proceedings of the American Philosophical Society* 129:129–60.

Lewis, Herbert S. 2014. *In Defense of Anthropology: An Investigation of the Critique of Anthropology*. New Brunswick NJ: Transaction.

Matthews, Maureen. 2016. *Naamiwan's Drum: The Story of a Contested Repatriation of Anishinaabe Artefacts*. Toronto: University of Toronto Press.

Smith, Joshua. 2015. "Cultural Persistence in the Age of 'Hopelessness': Phinney, Boas, and U.S. Indian Policy." In Darnell et al. 2015, 262–66.

Stocking, George W., Jr. 1968. *Race, Culture and Evolution: Essays in the History of Anthropology*. New York: Free Press.

Vermeulen, Han F. 2015. *Before Boas: The Genesis of Ethnography and Ethnology in the German Enlightenment*. Lincoln: University of Nebraska Press.

7

·········

Franz Boas

Scientist and Public Intellectual

Franz Boas (1858–1942) was without question the preeminent American anthropologist of at least the first half of the twentieth century.[1] Beginning with his pedagogical mission in the ranks of his adopted science and adopted country, Boas moved anthropology from the aegis of government and museum to the academy, where his stringent standards of professional training and peer judgment could be implemented more effectively (Darnell 1998; Cole 1999; Hinsley 1981). To characterize Boas as a public educator in a broader frame requires a rather dramatic reassessment of the discipline's inherited understanding of Boas and his role in the history of anthropology.

Boas's first commitments to public education were focused in the great educational museums with which he was associated, the Field Columbian Museum in Chicago and especially the American Museum of Natural History in New York City. When the scientific standards of professionalization clashed with those of public edification, Boas resigned from the American Museum and retreated to his teaching position at Columbia, a choice made in full realization of its likely costs, at least in the short term, for his own organizational control of the increasingly professionalized discipline of anthropology. He practiced what George W. Stocking (1992:98) has called "pragmatic academic activism" and was prepared to wait for a wider public voice until it could be grounded in adequate science. Boas laid the groundwork on multiple fronts: his first generation of students filled newly available academic and museum positions at a time when the scientific community and the gen-

Fig. 6. Franz Boas in the American Southwest, 1921. National
Anthropological Archives, Smithsonian Institution [86-1324].

eral public beyond it were coming to acknowledge the significance
of a Boasian paradigm for the scientific study of race, language,
and culture. Boas perhaps concentrated his efforts as a public
intellectual within his own discipline because anthropology was a
small science speaking from the margins of the academy. Scholars such as Thorsten Veblen and John Dewey had easier access to
broader audiences, as did Margaret Mead for a later anthropological generation.

Nonetheless, Boas's position of scientific authority was consolidated during the years between the world wars, allowing him to emerge as a public intellectual of a stature unequalled in the social sciences in the years leading up to World War II. His outspoken commentaries on Nazi racism in Europe built on his earlier immigrant studies demonstrating human biological plasticity and the influence of culture on environment, as well as on his longstanding commitment to the emancipatory struggles of African Americans, Native Americans, and other minority groups ([1911b] 1924; 1912). In the final years of his life, Boas chose to put aside his scientific work in order to pursue social justice, but the social justice he envisioned remained indelibly anchored in the scientific methodology of his lifelong studies of human biology, culture, and language. He believed passionately in the role of the scientist as public intellectual and was uncompromising in pursuing the causes he championed. Boas came to America to escape anti-Semitism and equated it with seeking freedom of thought. The more he lamented the absence of such freedom, the more eagerly he harangued his fellow anthropologists and fellow citizens to refashion a world in turmoil around the principles of anthropology. An examination of Boas's biography, publication record, and personal correspondence (available from the American Philosophical Society in Philadelphia on microfilm) would seem to make unassailable the above characterization of Boas's pedagogical commitments across a wide range of venues and social or professional issues. The intellectual successors of a seminal scientist often distinguish themselves from their mentor by deploying a rhetoric of discontinuity. Boas himself did this in rewriting the history of anthropology in 1904 so that it began de novo with his own position.

Boas's reputation suffered considerable eclipse during the postwar years in a rapidly changing scientific and social climate. Scientific positivism dominated an academy expanding to absorb returning veterans who were drawn to anthropology in an effort to come to terms with the implications of their enforced cross-cultural encounters abroad. The Cold War era generated government support for research on a global scale in defense of American hegemony, with the study of the American Indian [*sic*] relegated to an increasingly marginal position, leading many among the new generation of anthropologists to dismiss "Boasian" anthropology as merely antiquarian, a descriptive rather than a theoretical enterprise. Important action now was thought to lie in dismantling colonial empires on a global scale. Theoretical and methodological parallels between the internal colonialism of North America and the emerging postcolonial nation-states of Africa and the Pacific were rarely explored. The majority of anthropologists seemingly ignored non-Americanist Boasian ethnographic field sites and public commitments. The Americanist tradition cast its net far more broadly than the inherited stereotype of nonjudgmental and apolitical relativism would suggest, both in terms of ethnographic forays outside native North America and in the use of ethnographic data to critique American society (Hymes 1972; Valentine and Darnell 1999; Darnell 2001).

Consensus among the postwar Boasian revisionists was that Boas set back American anthropology by half a century because he was not a theoretician. Among the most virulent critics were Murray Wax (1956), Leslie White (1963, 1966), and Marvin Harris (1968). Boas was alleged to have eschewed the possibility of scientific "laws" in anthropology, to have restricted his attention to descriptive facts about specific American Indian [*sic*] cultures culled from texts and "informant" memory rather than from observation of contemporary behavior. "Historical particularism" was not coined as a compliment. Although Boas's late nineteenth-century critique of social evolution was acknowledged to have performed a useful service for anthropology, he was castigated ex post facto for remaining mired in the negativity of deconstructing an inadequate paradigm.

The complexity of Boas's actual position has resurfaced only recently in professional visibility, in great part through a persistent strain of Americanist work acknowledging its continuity with the Boasian paradigm (for examples of this reflexive building upon it, see Valentine and Darnell 1999; Darnell 2001, 2015, 2017; Hymes 1972; Lewis 1999). More nuanced interpretations of Boas's role in the discipline have been around for a while, particularly from a historicist standpoint in the work of George W. Stocking Jr. (1968, 1992, 2001) and from an Americanist and linguistic viewpoint in the works of Hymes (1983) and Stephen O. Murray (1994). It is remarkable then that Cole's posthumous biography of Boas's early years (from his birth in 1858 to 1906) ignores a whole line of scholarship that suggests a more theoretical and activist Boas and accepts at face value an atheoretical and outmoded characterization of Boas's anthropology as a result of his "temperamental difficulty with making sustained and sweeping generalizations" (Cole 1999:160).

Boas was a theorist, educator, and public intellectual of major significance in his own historiographic context. His skills as an organizational leader built the premier department of anthropology in North America at Columbia, set a standard of professionalism and credentialism for the discipline, put a stamp on emerging national institutions for anthropology, entrenched the four-subdiscipline structure of the discipline, and maintained himself at the center of a close group of students and protégés who increasingly controlled the discipline. The Boasians were perceived by outsiders in terms of in-group identification, exclusionary practices, and cohesiveness in pursuit of common interests centered around Boas as a patriarchal father figure.

Boas was a positivist with a skeptical approach to explanation or generalization. He was not a systematic theorist, and his paradigm remained largely implicit and internal to the emerging discipline. But his theoretical ideas were monumentally influential both within and beyond anthropology. Transcending a narrow definition of education, Boas insisted more broadly that science must speak to social values and must function pedagogically, both within and outside of formal institutions. In museum exhibition, he interpreted this to mean that only tribal rather than typological (i.e., evolutionary) classification could meet the educational challenge: "the main object of ethnological collections should be the dissemination of the fact that civilization [*sic*] is not something absolute, but that it is relative, and that our ideas and conceptions are true only so far as our civilization goes" (Boas 1887a:589). The disputes that these beliefs evoked with the American Museum administration centered around his conviction that the museum-going public must be educated through the exhibits to understand unbowdlerized science. Ultimately these differences led to his retreat to Columbia in 1906.

Boas was outspoken even before he had the power to effectively make his case when confronted with the scientific establishment.

Documents from the time reflect "what would become Boasian thought" (Hyatt 1990:22). Both in his debates with Otis T. Mason and in his insistence on research as well as popular education at the American Museum, Boas displayed considerable courage, with the outcome by no means certain.

Hyatt (1990:61) contends that Boas "was reacting to his own experiences with prejudice," attacking social evolution because it merely justified white Western Christian superiority, a sensitive rebuke when addressed to an upstart Jewish immigrant. The anthropology Boas was developing, however, would establish common cause for Jews, women, Blacks, and immigrants. Hyatt contends that Boas's inclusive science arose from the personal career disappointments of these early years (cf. Cole 1999), and that his activism targeted bigotry toward African Americans "rather than call attention to his own plight and risk accusations of subjectivity. . . . This camouflage became part of Boas's raison d'être for attacking all forms of human prejudice" (Hyatt 1990:33–34).

Whatever his personal motivations, Boas persisted in taking political positions that made him unpopular in powerful circles. Prior to American entry into World War I, he energetically supported neutrality. Science for him was rational, whereas nationalism and patriotism were irrational. During the course of the war, he was utterly silent and thus did not suffer active persecution for his views. He did attempt to protest the dismissal of various academics opposed to the war effort, including J. McLean Cattell at Columbia. The faculty "revolted" in support of the dissident colleagues when Columbia threatened to investigate faculty "political sentiments" (Hyatt 1990:126); Boas responded defiantly by reading six principles of science in the interests of mankind to his classes.

In 1919 Boas wrote to the editor of *The Nation* scathingly attacking scientists who acted as spies in Mexico. His allegations were accurate but highly unpopular at the time. Boas saw such action as a perversion of science; the scientific establishment in American anthropology labeled it as sedition (Stocking 1968; Darnell 1969, 1990, 1998). Boas's political enemies within the discipline used the letter as an excuse to curb his increasing organizational power across American anthropology. In this case, the issues were also external. Hyatt concludes that Boas became "disturbed with

America" after this incident and that his "public respect for science" suffered as a result; he had not yet achieved the role of "scientist-statesman" (Hyatt 1990:131) and would do so only during the prelude to World War II.

After the peace, Boas's next "crusade" was against the unjust settlement at Versailles; he correctly singled out a legacy of mistrust and dissension. His protests against the restrictive immigration act of 1924 identified it as a "new destructive type of nationalism" (Hyatt 1990:134, 136). Boas appeared personally before the congressional immigration committee without effect. Social Darwinism was in the ascendancy in the United States, and many Americans felt threatened by the decreased homogeneity of their own society as a result of immigration and the wartime breakdown of isolationism. Boas countered that racism restricted individual self-actualization and had undesirable consequences for society. The underlying ideology of American anthropology thus became one of cultural pluralism even though superficially marked by the language of objectivist science (MacDonald 1998:22–23). Boas's larger pedagogical role in American society became increasingly important as his professional stature increased and his discipline brought its message of cultural pluralism and tolerance to a general public caught up in an ever more complex world, both domestically and internationally.

As an organizational leader par excellence, Boas created a national network of his students that effectively controlled the discipline by about 1920 (Darnell 1969, 1998; Stocking 1968). Many were ambivalent about the control Boas maintained over former students and protégés in what he perceived to be the larger interests of American anthropology, about his sink-or-swim pedagogical method of graduate training, and about his lack of openness to some of their forays away from the shared paradigm (Darnell 1998, 2001). He was tireless in insisting that students repeat courses, study each subdiscipline, and receive training "in all facets of research" (Hyatt 1990:75). Student discontent, however, was articulated mainly in private correspondence and must be interpreted in the context of an overarching loyalty both to Boas as mentor and to anthropology as he taught them to understand it.

Edward Sapir wrote to Lowie (May 20, 1925: RHL) characterizing their former teacher in terms of Carl Jung's psychological types as a feeling introvert for whom science continually struggled to exclude personal subjectivity and to value thinking over feeling. Stocking (1992:110) also privileged ambivalence in reading Boas's personality and personal style, the "ice-cold flame of truth" warring with the emotional and irrational facet of his character as scientist and activist. Margaret Mead reported that she persuaded Boas to let her go to Samoa for her first fieldwork in 1925 by accusing him of behaving like a Prussian autocrat rather than the liberal democrat that was his ideal and self-image (MacDonald 1998:24).

"The Study of Geography" (1887b) demonstrated that the sides of Boas's temperament were inseparable from the sides of his science. Methodologically and theoretically, he distinguished the purportedly objective sciences of the natural world from the historical or cosmological approach to science characteristic of geography, the discipline from which he came most directly to anthropology. Stocking (1968) discusses the continuity from Boas's disillusion with materialist physics to incorporating an observer effect in human geography among the Eskimos, as the Inuit were then called in Canada, and to his rejection of environmental determinism in favor of ethnology (with its inherent cultural specificity). Boas's first point was that science (producing "laws") and history (producing interpretations) were equally legitimate enterprises; a problem arose only when the differences were not distinguished. Logic or aesthetics provided a proper discipline for science, whereas affect, feeling, and emotion came to the fore in the social sciences. The cosmographer "lovingly tries to penetrate" the secrets of the phenomena studied "until every feature is plain and clear." This preoccupation with the object of his affection affords him a delight "not inferior to that which the physicist enjoys in his systematical arrangement of the world" (1887b, quoted in Stocking 1996:14).

Despite the warmth of the erotic metaphor, however, it would be a mistake to assume that Boas intended to restrict his anthropology to a science of the subjective. The necessary other side of the coin was the rationalism of science whereby even social activism must be judged. He saw himself as speaking for science, in method as well as content, to a general public. But to choose between the two forms of "science," the cover term on which he always insisted, was for Boas a matter of personal "standpoint" or "mental disposition" (Stocking 1996:15). Boas's own disposition encouraged him to shift his standpoint systematically, from the historical to the psychological, from the analyst's model to what he called "the native point of view" (Darnell 2001).

Boas grew up with the ideals of the failed 1848 revolution in Germany, accepting without question the ideal of *Bildung* or self-realization (Liss 1996). He acquired in childhood the idea of the importance of an intelligentsia, of public intellectuals who would serve as avatars of cultural change (see Stocking 1992:105). Boas was drawn to America by the "freedom of the American intellectual world" (Herskovits 1963:7), although he was soon and often to deem it illusory.

The charge that Boas's work was atheoretical can be easily countered by noting his dual paradigm statements of 1911—the introduction to the *Handbook of American Indian Languages* (1911a), in which he distinguished race, language, and culture as analytically independent variables, and *The Mind of Primitive Man* ([1911b] 1924), in which he attacked the scientific validity of racial types and as a consequence the hierarchical distinction among human races and cultures based upon them (see Stocking 1974).

Boas had been building toward this theoretical synthesis of race and culture for some time. Surprisingly to many of his intellectual heirs, his argument began with the biological and universal rather than with the cultural and historically particular. As early as 1894, Boas tackled the "human faculty as determined by race" in his vice-presidential address to the American Association for the Advancement of Science (Boas 1895). The critique of evolution would soon be thoroughly grounded in statistical evidence of changes in head-form or cephalic index from Boas's work for the Immigration Commission then underway and reported in *Changes in Bodily Form of Descendants of Immigrants* in 1912. His conclusions, doubtless expected by the commission to justify exclusion of immigrants, subverted the agendas of the eugenics and scientific racism dominant in the first decade of the twentieth century. Boas's data revealed that head-form could change in a single generation, leading to the inescapable conclusion that environment strongly modified heredity and that racial types were therefore arbitrary.

Consequently, the study of race gave way to the study of racism, the social construction of a purportedly biological category. At the time, however, Boas's work was ignored by government officials in favor of eugenicist agendas, and his work drew only limited attention in university circles; changing the dominant paradigm would take time. Lee D. Baker argues persuasively that the paradigm shift usually attributed to Boas within anthropology depended upon the conjunction of his empirical work and academic stature with the political economy of race as articulated by African American activist W. E. B. Du Bois and others (Baker 1998:106,107).

Boas was only one among a group of liberal reform intellectuals in America, not all of them native born, who challenged what they perceived as a smug isolationism and melting-pot image of potential homogeneity based on social Darwinism. Baker (1998:99) identifies Boas in anthropology, Du Bois in sociology, Charles A. Beard in history, Louis Brandeis in law, Veblen and John R. Commons in economics, and Dewey in education as "muckrakers in an ivory tower." Their pedagogy was aimed at educating the general public to join them in seeking social reform.

Although most anthropologists remember Boas primarily as an apolitical student of the American Indian [sic] (for exceptions see Williams 1996; Baker 1998), his collaboration with Du Bois and early activism on behalf of the American Negro [sic] apply a shared German "methodological orientation that emphasized inductive reasoning and the empirical gathering of descriptive and historical data"; Baker further suggests (1998:119) that Du Bois and Boas clicked so well in their balancing of scholarship and activism because both had "firsthand experience with persecution and discrimination." Boas's Jewishness has been central to most discussions of his activism, perhaps because he and many of his early students were Jewish and immigrants and because he became a powerful critic of Nazi anti-Semitism at the end of his life.

Framing Boas's public statements of political position alongside those of his intellectual contemporaries, however, renders the Jewish explanation less persuasive. Boas's immigrant studies focused on southern Europeans more than Jews, and his activism centered around African American political struggles; anti-Semitism did not become his primary target until the rise of the

Nazis. Whatever the sensitivization entrained by his personal experience, Boas was consistent in his commitment to unmasking racism and bigotry in all their forms.

Nor can the anthropological contribution to liberal reform be attributed to a Jewish bias among the Boasians and their allies across the social sciences. John Dewey, philosopher and educator, espoused anthropological relativism in its Boasian form, arguing that enculturation or socialization should be the focus of pedagogical attention. Education and science could lead to positive reconstitution of society. Dewey wrote the foreword to Paul Radin's influential *Primitive Man as Philosopher* in 1927. Although both Boas and Radin were Jewish anthropologists seeking to foreground culture rather than biology as the root of human differences, Dewey and Boas's sociologist colleague at Columbia, William Fielding Ogburn, were not. Along the same lines as Baker, Eric Wolf (1982:256) emphasized in the link between Boas and Dewey because Boas's intellectual defense of liberal reform required attention to the practical constraints of power in order to ensure real-world effects.

In his foreword to the 1963 reissue of the second edition of *The Mind of Primitive Man*, Boas's former student Melville Herskovits stressed the importance of the volume's initial appearance. Like Boas, Herskovits had shifted from the study of race to culture (of African, Caribbean, and [African] American worlds), finding Boasian precedents at each stage of his career. In Herskovits's view, Boas's magnum opus was the "first single work which, in the best scientific tradition, derived its conclusions from measured, objective analysis, and presented its data in terms of their wider implications, marshalling the known facts to bring them to bear on disputed questions" (1963:6). Boas attacked American racial bigotry and mustered science in support of equality. He challenged the racial determination of "human faculty" and its influence of physical on mental processes, dedicating his final chapter to the problem of race in Nazi Germany as he had to American society in 1911.

Although the term "racism" was coined only during World War II, Boas had long protested "the utilization of the concept of race for political ends" (Herskovits 1963:5). For the second edition in 1938, Boas rewrote the book substantially to incorporate new research and new social applications in a changed political context. He waged a campaign directed to the general public against the spread of Nazism to America, speaking widely "to attack anti-Semitism, pseudo-scientific race theory and the suppression of free thought" (Hyatt 1990:146). These issues were all interrelated, part of his long-standing contention that race, language, and culture had to be treated as distinct variables. Now Boas was explicit about anti-Semitism rather than prejudice in general. Hyatt argues: "No longer was he able to appear the detached, objective scientist, for he was no longer utilizing a surrogate cause to mask his true concern." The implicit accusation belies the fact that the critique of scientific racism of the end of Boas's career also targeted the persistent aftermath of slavery in the United States, alongside assertions of Aryan superiority in Europe (1990:146, 147). Hyatt claimed that Boas was never particularly interested in American Indian [*sic*] political issues, apparently content to leave this side of his work to ethnological "science" rather than its activist interface, although he did protest Canadian legislation outlawing the potlatch and intervened in local matters on behalf of George Hunt and other Northwest Coast collaborators. But he did not make political activism an explicit tenet of ethical Americanist fieldwork. Since most of his students were Americanists, his omission of Indigenous issues from his definition of American cultural politics doubtless contributed to the retrospective sense that Boas was fundamentally apolitical. Politics, like theory, was implicit and largely unsystematic for Boas almost to the end of his life and the Nazi critique.

The Mind of Primitive Man weathered well, and Boas did not change his core argument over the rest of his career. He concluded in his preface to the 1938 edition as he had in 1911: "There is no fundamental difference in the ways of thinking of primitive [*sic*] and civilized man [*sic*]. A close connection between race and personality has never been established. The concept of racial type as commonly used even in scientific literature is misleading and requires a logical as well as biological definition" ([1938b] 1966:17). Therefore, environment and culture still must be considered inseparable from race. Boas might well have taken pride in the burning by the Nazis of the German edition (published in

1914 under the title *Kultur und Rasse*) in 1933. The danger of ideas was clearly recognized by the totalitarian regime.

There are embarrassing difficulties in contemporary terms with the position Boas articulated in 1911 and consistently maintained for the rest of his career. The paramount critic of evolution was ironically trapped in some of its categories. Herskovits (1963:10–11) acknowledged that Boas's definitions of "the primitive" and of "race" retained evolutionary overtones that his own argument should have rendered obsolete. His commitment was to progress, to a distinction between culture(s) and "civilization," which seemed to contradict the cultural relativism that has been the hallmark of the Boasian position. Cultural relativism, in this reading, reflects the characteristically Boasian dualism of science and history. On the one hand, the surface diversity of culture forms resolves itself into a universal humanity based on scientific studies of race, language, and culture. On the other hand, "the role of emotional association in shaping judgments" led Boas to the threshold of the "comparative study of values" that would soon be constructed upon his pioneering work. Boas's intellectual heirs would finally transcend the lingering remnants of his evolutionary certainty about the nature and hegemon of civilization.

The Mind of Primitive Man is not an easily accessible book for a lay audience. Boas was disinclined to compromise "in his feeling that no concession to his readers should obscure the stark scientific quality of his data and his concepts" ([1911b] 1924:xi). Even as a public intellectual, Boas insisted on scientific credibility and detailed evidence. He refused to talk down to the public. The evidence had to be presented to back rational scientific conclusions based in science.

The 1938 preface shifted from the conclusions of his scientific research to academic freedom and the public's right, even obligation, to apply science to the persistence of racism in American society. He aspired to educate Americans about the critical importance of freedom of thought and the need for a politics of science. Science could not be divorced from its supporting social infrastructure. Boas simultaneously lamented the increasingly disturbing events in Europe and worried that similar dangers could threaten American society:

Still worse is the subjection of science to ignorant prejudice in countries controlled by dictators. Such control has extended particularly to books dealing with the subject matter of race and culture. Since nothing is permitted to be printed that runs counter to the ignorant whims and prejudices of the governing clique, there can be no trustworthy science. When a publisher whose pride used to be the number and value of his scientific books announces in his calendar a book trying to show that race mixture is not harmful, withdraws the same book after a dictator comes into power, when great [en]cyclopedias are rewritten according to prescribed tenets, when scientists either do not dare or are not allowed to publish results contradicting the prescribed doctrines, when others, in order to advance their own material interests or blinded by uncontrolled emotion follow blindly the prescribed road no confidence can be placed in their statements. The suppression of intellectual freedom rings the death knell of science. ([1938b] 1966:17–18)

Boas's position rested on the applicability of scientific method to the study of human culture. His argument was both theoretical and remarkably contemporary in its openness to continuous scientific revision of contingent and provisional results:

In scientific inquiries we should always be clear in our own minds that we embody a number of hypotheses and theories in our explanations, and that we do not carry the analysis of any given phenomenon to completion. If we were to do so, progress would hardly be possible, because every phenomenon would require an endless amount of time for thorough treatment. We are only too apt, however, to forget entirely the general, and for most of us purely traditional, theoretical basis which is the foundation of our reasoning, and to assume that the result of our reasoning is absolute truth. ([1938b] 1966:201)

After the tepid public response to *The Mind of Primitive Man* in 1911, Boas directed his next theoretical statement of his paradigmatic method, *Anthropology and Modern Life* in 1928, to a more popular audience. He defined the science of man[kind], taking for granted its relevance to "modern life," before plunging into the heart of the matter: "the problem" of race and the interrelations of races, dealt with scientifically. Boas then discussed nationalism before turning to eugenics, the nation-state's perversion of the scientific study of race, and moving on to abuses of racial typing in criminology (lamentably reminiscent of the "ethnic profiling" of our own day). Somewhat over half the book preceded its turn to culture. Although the rate of change in so-called primitive societies was quite gradual, culture could be understood as stable. Moreover, both "primitive" and "civilized men" [*sic*] were wont to rationalize the forms of their culture. Rational and irrational elements coexisted in both.

Boas turned next to education in the narrow sense of schooling and socialization, gradually broadening his definition to include the lifelong education of citizens. This pedagogical alignment of the definition of education immediately followed the all-important topic of race and racism. Boas emphasized variability within groups and the pedagogical needs of the individual, citing with approval "the pedagogical anthropology" of Maria Montessori on behalf of the *Bildung* or self-realization of the individual student. Evidence of physical growth was related to social class and sex, with a view to "laying out a standard of demands that may be made on boys and girls of various ages and belonging to a certain society" (1928:168, 177). Since it is impossible to sort out the relative roles of environment and heredity, the question ceases to be interesting for issues of social reform and educational policy. The causes are necessarily social.

"Anthropology throws light upon an entirely different problem of education" (Boas 1928:184). Individuals in "primitive tribes" were trapped by their "customary forms of thought" but considered themselves free. Our own society also followed habits learned in childhood. Educational methods were dependent upon "our ideals" (1928:187), despite rare consciousness of the conflict in democratic society between individual freedom and the teaching of shared symbols that restricted such freedom. In the same year that his former student Margaret Mead claimed in *Coming of Age in Samoa* in 1928 that traumatic adolescence might be a product of such cultural conflict for the individual rather than a cultural universal. Boas cited Mead's work among other contributions by his students or protégés. He seemed to believe that a stable society changing gradually could avoid such conflicts. His position was contrastive: the children of immigrants to America had no such sense of continuity and security. American pluralism raised challenges unimagined by so-called primitive societies.

Traditional teaching was insidious even within scientific specializations, because established ideas were acquired by "infusion" especially through socialization within a small-scale and presumably homogeneous society. The "critical faculty" was entrained within a narrow range, leaving the educated classes without an overall critical standpoint. Even intellectuals were inclined to be "conventional" because "their thoughts were based on tradition"; only a few escaped to true freedom of thought. This was more likely in a heterogeneous society. Education, then, should be a continual process of evaluating the past and breaking free of it to create new ideals. The major problem of modern society was its "conflict of ideals," which might be avoided in a simpler, more homogeneous society (1928:195–97, 202). He largely ignored rapid cultural changes and increasing complexity of Native American societies relative to change in the mainstream. His second generation of students such as Herskovits incorporated such change.

The method of the anthropologist demanded "emancipation from our own culture," which was difficult because everyone was inclined to see his or her own behavior as natural. "Scientific anthropology" began with the physical or organic side of things in order to determine universals. The "objective study" of historically distinct traditions produced "a standpoint that enables him to view our own civilization critically, and to enter into a comparative study of values" (Boas 1928:207). Boas equated "freedom of judgment" with the ability to distinguish cultural and biological causes, always a fraught task because of the observer's own standpoint. The social sciences could never become exact or predictive because of the complexity of variables and our inability to experiment on human societies. But the anthropologist could understand, if not explain, social phenomena—the very distinction of science and history that Boas had embraced in 1887. Absolute progress was impossible, although some recurrent tendencies in values and moral standards were identifiable across civilizations. "Simple tribes" and "closed societies" could offer alternative models for the critique of the anthropologist's own society. Anthropology could guide policy in modern life (1928:245) even in the absence of a single theory to which social phenomena could be reduced. Boas asked his targeted popular audience to accept a remarkably postmodernist view of knowledge and science. The moral commitment of the anthropologist as social critic acknowledging and amplifying voices from the margins of the dominant society guaranteed that the practice of anthropology would be a profoundly political and pedagogical endeavor.

Anthropology and Modern Life (1928) preceded the traumas of the Nazi rise to power in Germany and the virtual inevitability of war. Through the late 1930s, Boas continued to seek an anthropological voice in the public domain. Although the wartime and postwar work of Margaret Mead and Ruth Benedict on cultures at a distance now seems more salient, Boas took his legacy seriously. Public education was at the core of his final political commitments. After Boas was forced to retire from teaching in 1936 because of his age, he became increasingly critical of the academy, first at Columbia and later beyond. He believed it an urgent matter that power should be retained in the hands of teachers because administrative priorities limited freedom both to teach and to learn (Hyatt 1990:149). Education, centered in the academy where public intellectuals were most often produced, was the most effective way to counteract prejudice. His academic politics remained closely tied to his antiracism. University education was a means to this end.

> It was in the area of race that Boas had his greatest impact on American society and on future intellectual thought. By emphasizing the importance of each culture's values and by promoting "an understanding of the human misery, degradation and demoralization that can result when one people imposes its way on another," Boas changed many minds both within academic circles and in the general community. (Hyatt 1990:155)

In 1938 Boas consolidated his position in *General Anthropology*, a textbook directed to general readers with some chapters written by former students and protégés. Because it was impossible for a single person to cover the full scope of anthropology, he asserted that the collectivity could do so and speak with a single [Boasian] voice:

> Anthropology covers such a wide range of subjects that it is difficult for one person to be equally conversant with all its aspects. For this reason cooperation of a group of students, most of whom have worked in close contact for many years, seemed a justifiable solution of the task of preparing a general book on anthropology. Thus a greater number of viewpoints could be assembled, and the unavoidable divergence in the handling of diverse problems by a number of authors is, we hope, offset by the advantage of having the special points of view in which each author is interested brought out. (Boas 1938a:iii)

Taken together, the papers encapsulated the Boasian paradigm. The volume simultaneously co-opted the collaborators to maintain their shared position with Boas as the intellectual center and paterfamilias. Despite his disclaimers of sole authority, Boas reserved a number of key theoretical topics for himself: the brief introduction on the scope of anthropology, plus the chapters on race; language; invention; literature, music, and dance; mythology and folklore; methods of research; and the conclusion (considerably more elaborated than the introduction).

In 1940, two years before his death, Boas collected his major papers in *Race, Language and Culture*—the triangulation of independent classificatory variables already identified in 1911 that remained crucial to his theoretical thinking thereafter. He included twenty papers on race, five on linguistics, thirty-five on culture, and three miscellaneous. The definition of "race," succinctly stated in the brief preface, presumably on the assumption that the papers spoke for themselves, reflected changing language in biological anthropology but remained consistent with the substance of the immigrant head-form studies of the early century: "The terms 'race' and 'racial' are throughout used in the sense that they mean the assembly of genetic lines represented in a population" (Boas 1940:v).

Professional opinion of the quality of Boas's immigrant head-form studies remains hotly debated today, on ideological as well as methodological grounds. Corey S. Sparks and Richard L. Jantz

(2002; see also Wade 2002) attribute to Boas an environmental determinism that they believe is disproved by contemporary sociobiology. They seek to rehabilitate cranial typology as an accurate method for studying both fossil and living human populations. Their reanalysis of Boas's results invalidates his conclusions about plasticity of bodily form in descendants of immigrants. In contrast, Clarence C. Gravlee, H. Russell Bernard, and William R. Leonard (2003) praise Boas's studies of human plasticity for their effective challenge to scientific racism. Their reanalysis of Boas's data confirms his results and even strengthens some of them using inferential statistics and computational methods not available when he did his work. For these authors, Boas remains a heroic figure, both in his science and in his politics.

Whatever the intentional legacy of Boas's pedagogy, within the academy and beyond its gates, the historiographic question of continuing influence remains. I identity three such exemplary continuities here, although other exemplars could have been chosen.

First, Dell Hymes's edited collection *Reinventing Anthropology* suggests that Boasian activism is best remembered among Americanist anthropologists and linguists but defines anthropology in terms that continue to apply more widely: "interest in other peoples and their ways of life, and concern to explain them within a frame of reference that includes ourselves" with a view to "ultimate fulfillment of human potentiality" (Hymes 1972:11). The volume as a whole reflects 1960s optimism that anthropology has something to say to the larger world and that anthropologists can move effectively between scholarship and activism, between observation and participation. Such political and scholarly commitments were reclaimed by many.

Second, Eric Wolf's *Envisioning Power* (1999) builds on the insights of his contribution to the Hymes volume, calling politically committed anthropologists to consider relations of power as well as to respect the diversity and integrity of all cultures. His method is deeply ethnographic, choosing three societies at different scale of social complexity, each with an extreme driving preoccupation. This political economy approach was lacking in the early Boasian work but is not inconsistent with the refashioning of global society that Wolf envisions.

Third, Michael Ignatieff's summary of human rights issues (2001) reflects contemporary stresses in the anthropologically designed United Nations Declaration of Human Rights but nonetheless acknowledges a useful continuity to the Boasian positions on citizenship, public responsibility, and activism informed by science. This Boasian package has become so commonplace that it is hardly acknowledged as having Boasian roots, politically or methodologically. Paradigmatic success often engenders "invisible genealogies" (Darnell 2001).

These contemporary works reinforce the sense that the Boasian legacy is alive and well. Anthropologists today are reexamining their Americanist genealogies (Darnell 2001) and finding in Boas a theoretical sophistication, methodological rigor, pedagogical commitment, and political activism that is far from outdated. Rewriting the history of Boas as public intellectual and model for anthropological praxis is long overdue.

Notes

1. Originally published as "Franz Boas: Scientist and Public Intellectual," in *Visionary Observers: Anthropological Inquiry and Education*, ed. Jill Cherneff and Eve Hochwald, 1–24 (Lincoln: University of Nebraska Press, 2006).

References

Baker, Lee D. 1998. *From Savage to Negro: Anthropology and the Construction of Race, 1896–1954*. Berkeley: University of California Press.

Boas, Franz 1887a. "Museums of Ethology and Their Classifications." *Science* 9:587–89, 612–14.

———. 1887b. "Study of Geography." *Science* 9:137–41.

———. 1895. "Human Faculty as Determined by Race." *Proceedings of the American Association for the Advancement of Science* 43:301–47.

———. 1904. "The History of Anthropology." *Science* 20:513–24.

———. 1911a. Introduction to *Handbook of American Indian Languages. Bureau of American Ethnology Bulletin* 40:1–83. Washington DC: Government Printing Office.

———. (1911b) 1924. *The Mind of Primitive Man*. New York: Macmillan. Reprint, Norwood MA: Norwood Press, J. S. Cushing.

———. 1912. *Changes in Bodily Form of Descendants of Immigrants*. New York: Columbia University Press.

———. 1928. *Anthropology and Modern Life*. New York: W. W. Norton.

———. 1938a. *General Anthropology*. Boston: D. C. Heath.

———. (1938b) 1966. *The Mind of Primitive Man.* 2nd ed. New York: Macmillan. Reprint, New York: Macmillan.

———. 1940. *Race, Language and Culture.* New York: Free Press.

Cole, Douglas. 1999. *Franz Boas: The Early Years, 1858–1906.* Vancouver: Douglas and McIntyre.

Darnell, Regna. 1969. "The Development of American Anthropology, 1879–1920: From the Bureau of American Ethology to Franz Boas." PhD diss., University of Pennsylvania.

———. 1990. *Edward Sapir: Linguist, Anthropologist, Humanist.* Berkeley: University of Nebraska Press.

———. 1998. *And Along Came Boas: Continuity and Revolution in the History of American Anthropology.* Amsterdam: John Benjamins.

———. 2001. *Invisible Genealogies: A History of Americanist Anthropology.* Lincoln: University of Nebraska Press.

———. 2015. "Mind, Body, and the Native Point of View: Boasian Theory at the Centennial of *The Mind of Primitive Man.*" In *The Franz Boas Papers,* vol. 1, *Franz Boas as Public Intellectual—Theory, Ethnography, Activism,* edited by Regna Darnell, Michele Hamilton, Susan Hill, and Joshua Smith, 3–18. Franz Boas Papers Documentary Edition Series. Lincoln: University of Nebraska Press.

———. 2017. "Franz Boas as Theorist: A Mentalist Paradigm for the Study of Mind, Body, Environment, and Culture." In *Historicizing Theories, Identities, and Nations,* edited by Regna Darnell and Frederic W. Gleach, 1–26. Vol. 11 of Histories of Anthropology Annual. Lincoln: University of Nebraska Press.

Gravlee, Clarence C., H. Russell Bernard, and William R. Leonard. 2003. "Heredity, Environment, and Cranial Form: A Reanalysis of Boas's Immigrant Data." *American Anthropologist* 105:125–38.

Harris, Marvin. 1968. *The Rise of Anthropological Theory.* New York: Thomas Crowell.

Herskovits, Melville. 1963. Introduction to Boas 1938b.New York: Collier Books.

Hinsley, Curtis. 1981. *The Smithsonian and the American Indian: Making a Moral Anthropology in Victorian America.* Washington DC: Smithsonian Institution Press.

Hyatt, Marshall. 1990. *Franz Boas, Social Activist: The Dynamics of Ethnicity.* New York: Greenwood.

Hymes, Dell, ed. 1972. *Reinventing Anthropology.* New York: Pantheon.

———. 1983. *Essays in the History of Linguistic Anthropology.* Amsterdam: John Benjamins.

Ignatieff, Michael. 2001. *Human Rights as Politics and Idolatry.* Princeton: Princeton University Press.

Lewis, Herbert S. 1999. "The Misrepresentation of Anthropology and Its Consequences." *American Anthropologist* 100:716–31.

Liss, Julia. 1996. "German Culture and German Science in the *Bildung* of Franz Boas." In Stocking 1996:155–84.

MacDonald, Kevin. 1998. *The Culture of Critique: An Evolutionary Analysis of Jewish Involvement in Twentieth Century Intellectual and Political Movements.* Westport CT: Praeger.

Mead, Margaret. 1928. *Coming of Age in Samoa.* New York: Morrow.

Murray, Stephen O. 1994. *Theory Groups and the Study of Language in North America.* Amsterdam: John Benjamins.

Sparks, Corey S., and Richard L. Jance. 2002. "A Reassessment of Human Cranial Plasticity: Boas Revisited." *Proceedings of the National Academy of Sciences* 99 (223):14,636–39.

Stocking, George W., Jr. 1968. *Race, Culture and Evolution: Essays in the History of Anthropology,* New York: Free Press.

———, ed. 1974. *The Shaping of American Anthropology, 1883–1911.* New York: Basic Books.

———. 1992. *The Ethnographer's Magic and Other Essays on Culture and Personality.* Madison: University of Wisconsin Press.

———, ed. 1996. *Volksgeist as Method and Ethic: Essays on Boasian Ethnography and the German Ethnological Tradition.* History of Anthropology 8. Madison: University of Wisconsin Press.

———. 2001. *Delimiting Anthropology: Occasional Inquiries and Reflections.* Madison: University of Wisconsin Press.

Valentine, Lisa Philips, and Regna Darnell, eds. 1999. *Theorizing the Americanist Tradition.* Toronto: University of Toronto Press.

Wade, Nicholas. 2002. "A New Look at Old Data May Discredit a Theory on Race." *New York Times,* October 8, F2, F3.

Wax, Murray. 1956. "The Limitations of Boas's Anthropology." *American Anthropologist* 58:63–74.

White, Leslie. 1963. *The Ethnography and Ethnology of Franz Boas. Texas Memorial Museum Bulletin* 6. Austin: Texas Memorial Museum.

———. 1966. *The Social Organization of Ethnological Theory.* Houston: Rice University Press.

Williams, Vernon J., Jr. 1996. *Rethinking Race: Franz Boas and His Contemporaries.* Lexington: University of Kentucky Press.

Wolf, Eric. 1982. *Europe and the People without History.* Berkeley: University California Press.

———. 1999. *Envisioning Power: Ideologies of Dominance and Crisis.* Berkeley: University of California Press.

8

....

Franz Boas, Edward Sapir,
and the Americanist Text Tradition

The collection of native texts was foundational to the practice of Boasian anthropology and linguistics because it preserved for posterity the understanding of a culture by its members—not just the ethnographic facts but their integration into the lives of particular individuals.[1] Edward Sapir went far beyond his mentor Franz Boas, however, in exploring the connection between text collections from which grammatical and ethnological information could be extracted and the integration of cultural information by the individual narrator of a given text. Revisiting the text tradition, then, provides a link between Sapir's conventionally Boasian early career in linguistics and ethnology and his later theoretical work on the interrelationship between language, personality, and culture. Because linguistic and cultural theory are usually considered far apart today, this continuity in Sapir's thinking has been eclipsed in professional memory.

Collection of linguistic texts constituted the stereotypic cornerstone of what Charles F. Voegelin called "the Boas plan for the study of American Indian [sic] languages" (Voegelin 1952; cf. Stocking 1974). Having arrived at ethnology by way of psychophysics, geography, and the influence of culture on perception of environment, Boas was a self-taught linguist. Nonetheless, much of his resolute effort to professionalize North American anthropology revolved around the status of language and linguistics within it.

In his position as honorary philologist of the Bureau of American Ethnology, Franz Boas edited the *Handbook of American Indian Languages*, the first volume of which appeared in 1911. He intended its grammatical sketches to provide a data base for the typological comparison of American Indian [*sic*] languages.[2] The *Hand-book* further attempted to provide a model for brief grammatical description that could be adopted by nonprofessional linguists, often missionaries, traders, or amateur ethnologists with minimal training. Boas was committed on theoretical grounds to devising what would now be called "emic" categories, employing a minimum of externally imposed grammatical apparatus. In practice, however, the urgency of recording dying languages in the absence of adequately trained observers forced him to develop a standardized format for grammatical description.

After Boas began teaching at Columbia in 1899, he was able to emphasize the more systematic training of ethnologists in linguistics. In later years, many of them recalled Boas's sink-or-swim pedagogy without enthusiasm. Boas, however, was firmly convinced that all anthropologists should do linguistics because of its centrality to the study of culture itself. Alongside their diverse ethnological interests, therefore, his early students were expected to produce a standard grammar, a dictionary and texts of the languages they recorded in the field. A surprising number of them did so.

Only one of Boas's first generation of students showed any real flair for linguistics. Edward Sapir was being groomed by the Columbia Germanics Department for a career in Indo-European philology when he was sidetracked by Boas into the more compelling and urgent task of recording American Indian [*sic*] languages. Sapir began Boas's two-year seminar in linguistics while he was still technically enrolled in Germanics. The Eskimo, as they were then called, and Native American examples incidental to his MA thesis on Herder's theory of the origin of language (Murray and Dynes 1986; Darnell 1990) indicate that he was already firmly committed in principle to applying Indo-European methods to the analysis of data from unwritten languages. Sapir's fellow Boas student Robert Lowie recalls Sapir's "conversion" when Boas was able to provide a North American counterexample to every fact he thought he knew about language (Lowie [1956] 1984:124). He found firsthand fieldwork a heady challenge to what he now perceived as the dry scholasticism of Germanic philology.

After testing Sapir's analytic capacity on his own Kwakiutl [Kwakwala] texts,[3] Boas sent Sapir to the field to work with the Wishram

Chinook in the summer of 1905. Each of the four major field languages Sapir studied in his years of apprenticeship (through 1910, when he moved to Ottawa to become chief of the newly established Anthropological Division of the Geological Survey of Canada) resulted in a volume of published texts: Wishram in 1909, Takelma in 1909, Yana in 1910, and Ute/Southern Paiute in 1930.[4]

Texts provided the evidence upon which adequate, that is, language-specific, grammatical descriptions could alone be based. This was a part of the Boasian agenda, which Sapir embraced wholeheartedly.[5] In fact, his style of writing ethnography came to be perceived by his fellow Boasians as unique because of its emphasis on the labeling of cultural facts by linguistic forms. Sapir wrote to his friend Frank Speck that "songs, rituals and modes of myth-telling" (June 11, 1912: APS) can hardly be studied except linguistically. He concluded ruefully: "Oh well, I suppose I'm a crank on linguistics." Alfred Kroeber told Sapir (July 8, 1922: ALK) that his (Sapir's) fragmentary Takelma notes had an "intensive" quality that made them far more useful than the more usual "generic" or normative descriptions.

Sapir attempted to explain to Clark Wissler that ethnologists missed many important points if they were not trained in linguistics: "A good linguist can find out more, along certain lines, in five hours' honest work than the average ethnologist in six months of weary questioning" (October 3, 1920: NMM). Sapir's most explicit statement about the necessity of linguistics as the bedrock to adequate ethnography was written to Wilson Wallis (June 10, 1913: NMM), who had no formal training in linguistics:

It is highly useful, I think, for one making sociological studies among primitive [*sic*] peoples, to know enough about linguistic matters to take down Indian [*sic*] words and even texts with reasonable accuracy. . . . [i]t is always highly important, even from a strictly sociological point of view, to ascertain the native classification. . . . Aside from this special point of relationship terms, there are, of course, many other topics which are not easy to get at except through the medium of native terminology. Songs and much of social organization and religion generally can hardly be got at otherwise. I have always been struck by a certain externality about all such studies that were not based on linguistic knowledge. I always have an uneasy feeling that misunderstandings bristle in such writing. . . . [W]hat we are after in studying primitive [*sic*] peoples is, to a large extent, to get their system of classification. This scheme must be more or less reflected in their own language.

Linguistic methods became even more critical in the all-too-common situation among American Indians [*sic*] in which traditional cultural patterns were being lost rapidly. To his Ottawa colleague Diamond Jenness, Sapir noted (January 18, 1913: NMM) his conviction that

one cannot hope to do serious work with these badly disintegrated Athabascan tribes of the north unless one uses the linguistic approach. I doubt whether direct questioning on ethnological matters leads to much. One might still be able to obtain something if one followed up the hints given in personal narratives of various kinds.

During the period of Sapir's apprenticeship, Boas recommended him to Kroeber (May 24, 1906: ALK) for a research fellowship in California as "a born linguist" whose linguistic work was "about the best that any of my students have done." For Boas, a master of understatement, this was high praise indeed. Boas emphasized that, although Sapir knew little about ethnology, he learned quickly. That is, Sapir was so outstanding a linguist that he was encouraged to specialize, as Boas's ethnology students were not. Boas's hidden agenda, he told Kroeber, was to keep Sapir at Columbia "to relieve me of part of the work of linguistic instruction," a remarkable indication that Boas was prepared to surrender his hard-won primacy in teaching American Indian [*sic*] linguistics, at the only North American university to do so at the time, to a student who had not yet carried out his doctoral research.

Despite Boas's obvious respect for Sapir's linguistic ability and training in philology, it was not long before the two were at loggerheads. Boas assumed that his protégé would carry out the program of cultural and linguistic description of the American Indians [*sic*] within his mentor's framework. Sapir, because his priorities were linguistic rather than ethnological, emphasized different aspects of the Boasian agenda.

Sapir's grammar of Takelma, his dissertation research, was scheduled by Boas for inclusion in the first volume of the *Handbook of American Indian Languages*. Boas undoubtedly expected his prize pupil to set a new professional standard that could be emulated by less talented or trained observers. Sapir's four-hundred-page submission was singularly inappropriate to Boas's purposes of standardization, less an exemplar of the Boas plan than a demonstration of its inherent inadequacies. Sapir declined to modify his work, and Boas, justifiably in terms of his own project, postponed its appearance until the second volume in 1922. This compromise allowed both to win: the first volume remained the methodological exemplar Boas needed, but Sapir's work retained its integrity. A decade later, there were more anthropologists with sufficient training to appreciate Sapir's more elaborated model.

There were two linguistic issues: First, Sapir treated diachronic as well as synchronic questions in a way that most of Boas's contributors to the first volume could scarcely understand, much less emulate. Second, Sapir wanted to include multiple texts to illustrate his grammatical points. In spite of his commitment in principle to texts, Boas objected that they did not belong in the grammar. Boas considered texts essential in providing the evidence to back up grammatical arguments, but he expected them to be published separately. Sapir, in contrast, took for granted that the reader of a grammar would need the evidence of the accompanying texts for immediate cross-reference.

Sapir considered "a somewhat elaborate grammatical study of a language in which no adequate text material is available" to be "something of a joke" (to George B. Gordon, September 13, 1908: UPM).[6] To Boas (August 26, 1912: APS), Sapir insisted on the need for "rather full treatments" and argued that most of the *Handbook* sketches were "inadequate as final presentations." Boas was incensed when Sapir asserted that the "critical standpoint" he envisioned (September 3, 1912: APS) should not be compromised *merely* to obtain standardization. Boas was concerned primarily in this context with disciplinary organization; Sapir, with his greater linguistic expertise and lesser institutional responsibility, implicitly challenged his former teacher—with surprising success given that the issue was publication of his dissertation research.

Sapir's next challenge to Boas's self-appointed role as arbiter of American Indian [*sic*] linguistics was a more public one. In a 1912 review of Boas's *Kwakiutl Texts*, Sapir praised the Columbia series in which the texts appeared as a significant precedent for a university press and a major step forward for the text-oriented descriptive method espoused by Boas and his students. Still, Sapir could not resist a sideswipe at Boas's *Handbook* sketches—accepting his former teacher's general approach but calling for more rigorous implementation and implying that he, rather than Boas, would be the arbiter. Sapir shared Boas's goals[7] but criticized the inadequate means he pursued to implement them:

> phonetic variation, word-structure, and sentence-building will receive increased attention. The necessity of extensive linguistic materials in the form of native texts will then become apparent. A true psychology of language, as of every other form of human thought and endeavor, is possible only on the basis of a close study of its minutiae. (Sapir 1912:194)

Ethnological data were scattered throughout Boas's texts "in a specifically native setting." The "great psychological significance" of the textual material was that it preserved the native style of expression. In spite of inadequate annotation of the texts by Boas, they provided the "raw material" for generalization from language and culture to psychology (Sapir 1912:197–98). Sapir was in complete accord with Boas when he defined the ultimate problems of anthropology as psychological in *The Mind of Primitive Man* in 1911.

Sapir faced similar obstacles of cross-purpose with Kroeber over the painstaking standards for the text method that he wanted to apply to his study of Yana during his 1907–8 fellowship year in California. Kroeber, constrained by the urgency of his ethnological survey mandate to maintain California state funding, wanted Sapir to place Yana relative to other California Indian [*sic*] languages as quickly as possible. In this effort, Roland Dixon had recorded some linguistic data on Yana, a highly endangered language, in the course of his ethological work, which Kroeber included on a par with Sapir's own; Sapir accepted this practical necessity without protest. When it came to Boas's goals of standardization for linguistic descriptive method, however, Sapir held out for the ideal procedure for his own work—which meant texts.

Sapir's next job was at the University of Pennsylvania Museum in Philadelphia, where he and his student John Alden Mason initiated a survey of the Ute. Sapir collected myth texts from Charley Mack in Ute, while Mason elicited a larger body of myth materials in English. In spite of Sapir's extensive proposal, the Ute research program was never carried out by the University Museum. Instead, Sapir turned to work on the related Uto-Aztecan language Southern Paiute in Philadelphia with Tony Tillohash, a student from the Carlisle Indian School (Fowler and Fowler 1986). Tillohash was the ideal Sapir "informant." His English was adequate for basic translation, but he still knew about traditional language and culture. Moreover, Tillohash proved to have valuable intuitions about the structure of his native language, which helped Sapir (1925) formulate his phonemic theory foreshadowing "the psychological reality of the phoneme" in 1933:

> If the phonemic attitude is more basic, psychologically speaking, than the more strictly phonetic one, it should be possible to detect it in the unguarded speech judgments of naive speakers who have a complete control of their language in the practical sense but have no rationalized or consciously systematic knowledge of it. (Sapir [1933] 1949:47)

This productive collaboration with Tillohash posed a sharp contrast to Sapir's work in 1915 with Ishi, the last survivor of the Yahi tribe of southern California, who spoke the previously unrecorded southern dialect of Yana. Ishi never learned much English and was unable to provide English translations of his texts. Sapir, who had worked on the northern dialect of Yana during his year in California, proceeded by brute recall of stems and elaborate paraphrases. His summer with Ishi was intensely frustrating for Sapir because he could not rely on native speaker intuitions to confirm his grammatical hypotheses.

The text-oriented approach of the American Indian [*sic*] linguists trained by Boas depended to a remarkable degree on the accident of locating a particular "informant" or a small number of informants [*sic*]. Most grammars of the period are based on the speech of very few speakers, in some cases a single speaker. One aim of Boasian salvage linguistics was to train native speakers to write their own language and record texts after the ethnographer-linguist returned to his [*sic*] own institution. Among the examples of such effective collaboration are Boas with George Hunt (Kwakiutl [Kwakwala]), Marius Barbeau with William Beynon (Tsimshian), and Sapir with Alex Thomas (Nootka) and Albert "Chic" Sandoval (Navajo).

Jean Canizzo argued convincingly in 1983 that Kwakiutl culture as known to anthropology actually reflects the uniqueness of Hunt's atypical experience of it; her priority in this analysis is rarely credited due to its publication in a small Canadian journal. The potential difficulty of variability in representation of a culture by different members was never adequately addressed within the Boasian text tradition, which implicitly accepted a Kroeberian definition of culture as "superorganic." Boas assumed that oral tradition would provide the most specific statement accessible to the ethnographer of the culture from the point of view of its members, as though they were interchangeable. Although myths could not be assumed to reflect cultural facts directly, they were set in the background of the culture and indirectly provided important insight toward understanding it.

Boas's most explicit statement of the value of texts came in *Tsimshian Mythology* (1916:393): "Material of this kind does not represent a systematic description of the ethnology of a people but has the merit of bringing out those points which are of interest to the people themselves. They represent the autobiography of the tribe."

In his effort to produce a generalized, impersonal "autobiography" of the tribe, Boas recorded narratives that were widely known and therefore culturally representative. As a result, he paid less attention to esoteric knowledge that was not broadly distributed. Although Boas certainly recognized the value of a good informant [*sic*] (the term is problematic today but was used universally when Sapir and Boas did their fieldwork), his conviction that cultural knowledge was held largely unconsciously encouraged him to look for widespread and typical formulations of the "native point of view," that is, the native speaker's first language. He believed that such emphasis would avoid imposition of Eurocentric bias on the cultures described. Even in the case of grammatical analysis, texts avoided culturally inappropriate categorization by eliciting grammatical forms in the context of natural discourse.

From a purely linguistic standpoint, most Boasians assumed that it did not matter whether texts were mythological, ethnological, or autobiographical. In ethnological or psychological terms, however, the style and meaning of different kinds of texts might be quite different. Sapir's earliest work reflects an unusual sensitivity to nuances of style and sociolinguistic variation that would lay the groundwork for contemporary sociolinguistic studies of discourse and variability. Boas's texts emphasized detail; Sapir, who responded more quickly to linguistic patterning, attempted to describe underlying patterns of the expressive speech in his texts.

This is where Sapir began to rework the Boasian text tradition in terms of its implications for the role of the individual in culture. In each of his most extensive fieldwork studies (Nootka and Navajo), at least one key "informant" shared to some extent Sapir's enthusiasm for linguistic patterning. Not only could such informants dictate the texts on which analysis was based, but they could also analyze them at both linguistic and cultural levels.

Sapir's earliest statement about the native speaker's tendency to perceive linguistic phenomena focused on the perception of sound patterning. He wrote to Kroeber (September 8, 1916: ALK) that an "informant" who failed to learn a writing system for his own language might be hearing different distinctive sounds other than the ones the orthography provided notation for:

I have had enough experience with teaching Indians [*sic*] to write their own language to know that there is nothing simpler if one has only mastered the organically significant types of sounds. . . . I would go so far as to say that if one finds that he can make no progress with a native in the matter of teaching him to record a particular class of sounds, that the reason will nearly always, in the wash, be found to be a lack of adequate analysis on the part of the instructor. I am a firm believer in the consciousness, or if you like, the sub-consciousness, in native speakers of the organic phonetic elements of their language.

This statement foreshadows Sapir's formulation of the concept of the phoneme a few years later.

Working with one or a limited number of individuals gave Sapir (and others who adopted the text method) considerable insight into the relationship between the individual and culture. In practice, most Boasians emphasized texts with traditional ethnological content in their grammatical analyses. Such texts would serve a dual purpose. Many text collections also included descriptions of material culture, everyday social relations, and life history.

In the intersection of native speaker intuition for the structure of a language, the intense relationship of "informant" and linguist necessitated by the text method, and the dual theoretical relevance of texts to linguistics and ethnography, Sapir made his conceptual break from Boasian historical particularism into a cultural theory that focused on the creative role of the individual in culture.

Sapir's theoretical writing incorporating the individual into the anthropological concept of culture began with his 1917 critique of Kroeber's reification of culture as superorganic. Kroeber, primarily an ethnologist, sought a normative statement of group culture. Sapir, encouraged to listen to his "informants" by recording linguistic texts and by analyzing them in collaboration with a single native speaker, came to appreciate the variability in the integration of cultural facts among individuals in the "same" culture.[8]

When Sapir moved to the University of Chicago in 1925, he found himself surrounded by social science colleagues eager to explore interdisciplinary collaboration with the psychological and psychiatric sciences. Sapir became particularly enamored by the interactional psychiatry of Harry Stack Sullivan. The two, sometimes aided and abetted by political scientist Harold Lasswell, came to argue for a cross-cultural psychiatry dependent on the life history method for the study of individual personality. Sapir, as a Boasian anthropologist, already knew that life history could reveal variability in culture (for further discussion of the life history method see Leeds-Hurwitz and Nyce 1986; Murray 1986).

Curiously, Sapir himself never attempted to carry out personality studies of American Indians [*sic*] (cf. Murray 1986). In the interdisciplinary conferences of the late 1920s and 1930s, he was more likely to use examples from modern American society and to confound the role urged on him by colleagues from Chicago sociology and psychiatry as a purveyor of the exotic. Indeed, Sapir had long argued that the challenge facing the anthropologist was to provide the cultural context that would remove the exotic from the description of alien societies. Everyday behavior was always commonplace from the point of view of a member of the culture. Unlike many of his contemporaries who lacked Sapir's linguistically conditioned attention to the details of an individual's expression of their cultural world, Sapir challenged the adequacy of the theoretical apparatus of the social sciences to deal with the perspective of the individual. In reviewing a volume of life histories by anthropologists based on societies where they had worked (Sapir 1922), he argued that the "conscious knowledge of the ethnologist [should] be fused with the intuitions" of individuals within a culture, giving full due to the "traces of the individual consciousness." He concluded that "the exotic is easily mistaken for subject, when it should be worked as texture."

One of the last things Sapir wrote before his death in 1939 was a foreword (Sapir 1938) to his student Walter Dyk's Navajo autobiography, *Left-Handed: Son of Old Man Hat.* In spite of his fifteen-year involvement with emergent personality studies,[9] Sapir was adamant that he valued the sequence of individual memories as a means of conveying the reality of a culture, *not* as an analysis of personality per se. The impersonal genres of ethnographic reporting were best transcended in a linguistic text, especially a biographical one. Sapir made the same point in a 1927 review of Paul Radin's *Crashing Thunder.* The works of Dyk and Radin have been remembered as exemplars of Sapir's method of studying culture through the individual. Neither Dyk nor Radin, however, was primarily concerned to systematically work out the consequences of Sapir's foregrounding of the individual rather than culture.

While he did not fully espouse the growing enthusiasm in anthropology for psychologically oriented ethnology of various kinds, Sapir remained committed to the text method. His most passionate defense came through his collaboration on Navajo with Father Berard Haile (1874–1961) and Albert "Chic" Sandoval. Sapir was in the field in the summer of 1929 as director of the first summer field school of the Southwest Laboratory of Anthropology. Thereafter, he wrote frequently to Haile regarding points of grammar and interpretation and encouraged Haile to publish his exhaustive ceremonial texts. Haile, who lived in the field, was for Sapir the culmination of the relationship he had sought with key linguistic informants [sic] from Tony Tillohash on. Haile stood somewhere between colleague and informant [sic], never fully a peer.[10] When Sapir left the University of Chicago for Yale in 1931, Haile and the Chicago southwestern research program, lavishly funded by the Rockefeller Foundation, were left behind. Sapir was succeeded as the central theoretician of the Chicago program (the only academic program in pre–World War II North American anthropology to maintain appreciable independence of Boas) by British social anthropologist A. R. Radcliffe-Brown (1891–1955). It was hard enough to get texts published in this period.[11] But Radcliffe-Brown professed not to understand why anyone would value texts in the first place. In a memorandum in the University of Chicago anthropology department files in May 1932, he stated:

> What are such texts as these for? I wish Sapir had enlightened me on this. I read his letter over without finding out just what one does with such texts. . . . Authoritative it will certainly be. But just what will be done by scholars with these texts? . . . I am clear on this: that if they are to be treasured merely because they are disappearing, and because they are accurately transcribed . . . their publication would then be supported by mere antiquarian sentiment.

Sapir was horrified at the challenge to the very premises of the Boasian method. He considered texts, in some very serious way, as sacrosanct. Sapir wrote to departmental chair Fay-Cooper Cole that Haile's texts were "a priceless linguistic document," and he was unwilling to "see a beautiful piece of work made hash of because of the hostility of a supercilious gentleman" (May 22, 1932: UC). Radcliffe-Brown did not know what he was talking about when he attacked established North American methods. Cole (May 25, 1932: UC) was equally horrified at the intensity of Sapir's reaction and suggested that he exaggerated Radcliffe-Brown's position. Cole thought there was already enough text material available for linguistic analysis and wanted more on "what the ritual means to the Navajo," information that Haile could readily add. This further inflamed Sapir.

Sapir had no objection to additional ethnological notes and responded more calmly (June 2, 1932: UC), but he continued to insist that "Brown"[12] had seemed to suggest turning Haile's texts into a general treatment of Navajo ritual:

> You see, from my standpoint that meant not only was the priceless linguistic material as such to be disregarded . . . but that all my own Navaho[13] field work was, by implication, judged a waste of time, that I might, so far as he was concerned, never have trained Father Berard . . . that nobody cared for elaborate accounts of specific Navaho rituals anyway, and that we in America had better get busy and learn something from functionalism as to how a truly readable volume should be prepared. . . . It was all as if some Smart Aleck were to put the proffered texts of the Homeric poems aside with a supercilious remark.

Both Haile and Sapir believed that Cole was trying to evade the obligation and cost of publishing masses of text material for a limited audience. The dispute went on for years, eliciting Sapir's most lyrical defense of the text method (to Cole, April 25, 1938: UC):

> I'm not particularly interested in "smoothed-over" versions of native culture. I like the stuff in the raw, as felt and dictated by the natives. . . . The genuine, difficult, confusing, primary sources. These must be presented, whatever else is done. . . . There are too many glib monographs, most of which time will show to be highly subjective performances. We need to develop in cultural anthropology that anxious respect for documentary evidence that is so familiar to the historian, the classical scholar, the Orientalist. We'll *have* to do this, willy nilly, if we are to keep the respect of our colleagues. . . . If we're not careful, thoughtful and essentially not unfriendly, colleagues will be getting more and more restive and saying, "Yes, this is all most interesting and I admire the beautiful synthesis that you have made, but where is the raw evidence? I can't tell whether a given statement is common native knowledge or is merely your interpretation of one man's say-so."

This statement is thoroughly Boasian in its commitment to allowing members of so-called primitive cultures to speak in their own words through texts. Sapir's passion for the authenticity of texts, however, comes from the additional significance he accorded them. Texts expressed the unique lifeworld of individual members of particular cultures and allowed for the contextualization of individual lives within their cultures. Texts, for Sapir, always functioned at two levels. Linguistically, they preserved the pattern of expression that was unique to a language. Culturally, they showed how the world was integrated in the understanding of a particular narrator. The existence of a single narrator foregrounded integration and patterning, whether or not their version of the culture was shared by other members. The anthropologist's search for patterning, in both language and culture, relied first and foremost on the existence of adequate texts. The text tradition was not merely descriptive; it was the best possible basis for explanation.

Notes

1. Originally published as "Franz Boas, Edward Sapir and the Americanist Text Tradition," *Historiographia Linguistica* 17 (1990): 129–44.

2. Despite his early interest in the historical classification of these languages, Boas came to believe that the influences of borrowing were difficult if not impossible to distinguish from those of prior genetic relationship. He had long been interested in linguistic typology. Like the normative study of unconscious patterning in culture, linguistic typology focused on the uniqueness of each language. This emphasis fit well with Boas's increasingly areal interests in his Northwest Coast fieldwork and did not commit him to the same historical causes in each instance.

3. Kwakiutl [Kwakwala] was the language on which Boas himself worked most extensively during his long career.

4. The texts from his later fieldwork were published only after Sapir's death (Nootka by Morris Swadesh and Navajo by Harry Hoijer) or remain in manuscript (Kutchin, Sarcee, Hupa).

5. Few American Indian [*sic*] texts were published before Boas began to emphasize their collection. Thereafter, both in British and America anthropology and linguistics their importance was accepted at least until the advent of transformational grammar in the late 1950s.

6. The ideal situation was to publish grammar, dictionary, and texts together. Sapir was able to do this only with his Southern Paiute materials. But Southern Paiute was not published until 1930, when Sapir's reputation was unassailably established.

7. For example, his 1921 *Language* used a Boasian organization around grammatical categories and processes and included an extensive discussion of linguistic typology.

8. The text method was not the only cause of Sapir's reorientation toward the individual, although it may have been the decisive one. More directly biographical factors determining the timing (e.g., poetry, aesthetics, the illness of his first wife, and exposure to psychology) are discussed in Darnell (1986, chapter 9, this volume, 1990).

9. Sapir avoided the term "culture-and-personality," considering it overly simplistic and reductionistic.

10. Sapir chose Harry Hoijer rather than Haile as the executor for his Navajo materials.

11. Compare Boas's efforts through the American Council of Learned Societies Committee on American Indian [*sic*] languages (Leeds-Hurwitz 1985, Darnell 1990).

12. Most Boasians in this period referred to Radcliffe-Brown simply as "Brown," presumably an expression of their ambivalence toward him and toward British anthropology.

13. Sapir used the spelling "Navaho." "Navajo" is customary today.

References

Boas, Franz. 1911. *The Mind of Primitive Man*. New York: Macmillan.

———. 1916. *Tsimshian Mythology (Annual Report of the Bureau of American Ethnology for 1909–1910)*. Washington DC: Government Printing Office.

Canizzo, Jeanne. 1983. "George Hunt and the Invention of Kwakiutl Culture." *Canadian Review of Sociology and Anthropology* 20:44–58.

Cowan, William, Michael Foster, and Konrad Koerner, eds. 1986. *New Perspectives in Language, Culture and Personality*. Amsterdam: John Benjamins.

Darnell, Regna. 1986. "The Emergence of Edward Sapir's Mature Thought." In Cowan, Foster and Koerner 1986:553–58.

———. 1990. *Edward Sapir: Linguist, Anthropologist, Humanist*. Berkeley: University of California Press.

Fowler, Catherine, and Donald Fowler. 1986. "Edward Sapir, Tony Tillohash and Southern Paiute studies." In Cowan, Foster, and Koerner 1986:41–66.

Leeds-Hurwitz, Wendy. 1985. "The Committee on Research in Native American Languages." *Proceedings of the American Philosophical Society* 129:129–60.

Leeds-Hurwitz, Wendy, and James M. Nyce. 1986. "Linguistic Text Collection and the Development of Life History in the Work of Edward Sapir." In Cowan, Foster, and Koerner 1986:432–95.

Lowie, Robert H. (1956) 1984. "Comments on Edward Sapir, His Personality and Scholarship." In *Edward Sapir: Appraisals of His Life and Work*, edited by Konrad Koerner, 121–30. Amsterdam: John Benjamins. Originally published in *American Anthropologist* 58 (1956): 995–1015.

Murray, Stephen O. 1986. "Edward Sapir and the Chicago School of Sociology." In Cowan, Foster, and Koerner 1986:241–92.

Murray, Stephen O., and Wayne Dynes. 1986. "Edward Sapir's Coursework in Linguistics and Anthropology." *Historiographia Linguistica* 13:125–29.

Sapir, Edward. 1912. Review of *Kwakiutl Tales* by Franz Boas. Columbia University Contributions to Anthropology. *Current Anthropological Literature* 1:193–98.

———. 1917. "Do We Need a 'Superorganic'?" *American Anthropologist* 19:441–47.

———. 1922. Review of *American Indian Lives*, edited by Elsie Clews Parsons (New York: B. W. Huebsch, 1922). *The Dial* 73:568–71.

———. 1925. "Sound Patterns in Language." *Language* 1:37–51.

———. 1927. Review of *Crashing Thunder*, by Paul Radin (New York: D. Appleton, 1926). *American Journal of Sociology* 33:303–4.

———. (1933) 1949. "La realité psychologique des phonèmes." *Journal de Psychologie Normale et Pathologique* 30:247–65. Reprinted in English translation as "The Psychological Reality of Phonemes," in *Selected Writings of Edward Sapir in Language, Culture and Personality*, edited by David G. Mandelbaum, 46–60. Berkeley: University of California Press.

———. 1938. Foreword to *Left-Handed: Son of Old Man Hat*, by Walter Dyk, iv–x. New York: Columbia University Press.

Stocking, George W., Jr. 1974. "The Boas Plan for the Study of American Indian Languages." In *Studies in the History of Linguistics*, edited by Dell Hymes, 454–84. Bloomington: Indiana University Press.

Voegelin, C[harles] F[rederick]. 1952. "The Boas Plan for the Presentation of American Indian Languages." *Proceedings of the American Philosophical Society* 96:439–51.

9
....
The Emergence of Edward Sapir's
Mature Thought

Introduction

Edward Sapir was interested, in a more than passing way, in Germanic philology, American Indian [sic] linguistics, ethnology and folklore, poetry, literary criticism, music, mathematics, psychology and psychiatry, and theoretical linguistics.[1] The question remains of which, if any, is the "real" Edward Sapir. Scholars in a range of present-day disciplines and subdisciplines acknowledge him as a founding father [sic]; most are only minimally aware of his contributions in areas that, for them, are unrelated. I suggest that the whole of Edward Sapir best emerges when he is considered from a biographical perspective. That is, the concrete events and influences of Sapir's life reveal the integration of his thought over the span of his career. Sapir came to his range of interests over a temporal process of events (some planned, others accidental) and interactions with friends and colleagues, all in the institutional context of his day. Retracing this process elucidates why Sapir pursued certain problems at particular times, and why others were continuous throughout his career. The key biographical question is whether this range of interests was consecutive and compartmentalized, or interactive within and across particular periods with changing emphasis at different times. I believe that the latter is the case.

This chapter focuses on the single decade from approximately 1915 to 1925 in which Sapir's mature thought solidified in its scope and range. Up to 1915, Sapir was one of the most promising of the first generation of scholars trained by Franz Boas, and the only one with special expertise in linguistics. By the time he completed

Time Perspective in 1916, Sapir was actively dissatisfied with then current theoretical models of both linguistics and anthropology. He was growing unaccountably bored with the compilation of ethnological data. Boasian anthropology had initially appealed to Sapir because it so greatly broadened the scope of philology, which was up to that point almost exclusively Indo-European. Within this framework, he carried out fieldwork with four major American Indian [*sic*] languages before 1910. His appointment as director of the government anthropology program in Ottawa was an honor for such a young man (he was only twenty-six at the time), and he relished the challenge to establish and organize a major program of anthropological research in Canada along Boasian lines, as Alfred Kroeber was already doing in California. Ottawa provided Sapir with a few years of contented and productive euphoria. Soon, however, things began to settle into a rut. Boasian anthropology had become what Thomas S. Kuhn calls a "normal science," in which everyone knows what to do to "make a contribution," but the innovative "paradigm" is already firmly in place. Sapir, who was easily bored, began to find much of his work onerous.

By the time he left Ottawa in 1925 to begin his university teaching career, Sapir had vastly expanded the scope of his scientific investigations. His major literary output, including his poetry, was essentially complete. He had begun to publish on psychological topics, elaborating the emphasis on culture and the individual that first appeared in print in 1917 as his rebuttal to Kroeber's concept of the "superorganic." The later Ottawa years were a time of experimentation with intellectual scope and scientific relevance, despite personal pressures that are well known. Sapir's discontent aside, the productivity of this period is greater than that of any other in terms of theoretical writing, fieldwork, poetry, and personal correspondence.

In this significant decade, Sapir the linguist cannot be separated from Sapir the whatever-else. His mind was churning with possibilities as he alternated and intermixed methods and models. I focus on these years of ferment because they shed light on the nature of Sapir's oft-cited "genius" or "intuition." An undercurrent of distrust underlies the admiration when such terms are used, a faint suspicion that scientific respectability is somehow threatened.

Sapir's genius is more concretely intelligible as a tendency to combine novel sources of information and insight, to adopt new models from juxtaposed solitudes. He was a better linguist because he worked with unwritten as well as with written languages, and with languages situated in unfamiliar cultures. He was a better anthropologist because he extended Boasian models for historical reconstruction on the basis of phonetic evidence for genetic relationships at the same time that he left the door open for evidence of both areal and genetic connections. His psychological work addressed the overabstraction of culture as the organizing concept of Boasian anthropology. His poetry refused to be bound by the canons of scientific formalism, as did his experiments with genres of ethnographic presentation. Sapir's genius was that while other people stayed in their boxes, he did not seem to notice the existence of the boxes. This protean scholarly and artistic activity became the hallmark of his intellectual style.

To discover where Sapir's most innovative ideas came from requires retracing the connections and overlaps of the work done in that formative decade in which his formidable output included *Time Perspective* in 1916 (summarizing, making explicit, and extending the potentials of the Boasian program for the reconstruction of culture history); his critique of the superorganic and formulation of the concept of "genuine" culture (foreshadowing later work in culture and personality); experiments in writing ethnography in literary form between 1918 and 1922; his single volume of published poetry in 1917; his only book, *Language,* in 1921; the first formulation of the six-unit classification of American Indian [*sic*] languages in the same year; and, finally, the first explicit formulation in print of the concept of the phoneme in 1921. All this was in addition to numerous reports on particular American Indian [*sic*] languages and problems in theoretical linguistics. The magnitude of this output reflects the culmination of different kinds of thought by Sapir as an individual scholar, as well as his contributions to the consolidation of the Boasian paradigm by the first generation of Boas's students. The changes that occurred in Sapir's thought after 1925 are already foreshadowed in this decade. His university years brought contact with academic colleagues, particularly Indo-Europeanists, but also interaction with psychologists and psychiatrists, most notably Harry Stack Sullivan, and development of a cadre of students, primarily in linguistics. Continuities with Sapir's earlier thought persisted.

The Boasian Spirit

The maturing of Sapir's thought was coterminous with the coming of age of Boasian anthropology. I have argued elsewhere (Darnell 1969; 1971, chapter 2, this volume) that Boas and his students came to dominate the discipline only around 1920. One major factor in that emerging dominance was the production of what Kuhn (1962) calls "paradigm statements" that came to serve as textbooks for anthropology. Boas initiated the synthesis with *The Mind of Primitive Man* and the introduction to the *Handbook of American Indian Languages*, both in 1911, but, as Sapir noted to Wilson D. Wallis (March 5, 1913: NMM), he made no attempt to present the subject in an accessible and palatable style:

> It has always seemed a pity to me that Boas has not given more time to making known his general views on anthropological method. He is certainly one of the very best thinkers on the subject that we have altogether, though most people might hardly suspect this to be the case from the chiefly concrete material that Boas has published. I am always rather reticent about cracking up in that I have stood in rather close personal relation to him, but to be frank it has always seemed to me that the very best of the English and German writers on anthropological method cut a rather sorry figure in comparison with Boas. If Boas could only realize the necessity of putting his work into some kind of acceptable form and of dealing with things in a more complete and rounded manner, his influence would be increased many times.

Boas's first generation of students took it upon themselves to remedy what they perceived to be a gap. Collectively, they produced the general syntheses that would dominate the North American discipline until at least the Second World War. The first of these was Sapir's *Time Perspective* in 1916, closely followed by Lowie's *Culture and Ethnology* and Clark Wissler's *The American Indian* in 1917, Lowie's *Primitive Society* and Kroeber and Thomas T. Waterman's *Sourcebook in Anthropology* in 1920, Sapir's own *Language* in

1921, Alexander Goldenweiser's *Early Civilization* in 1922, and Kroeber's *Anthropology* and Wissler's *Man and Culture* in 1923. Sapir's work was central to the consolidation and popularization of the Boasian program.

Time Perspective

Sapir's monographic essay on time perspective was a Boasian product that cast Sapir as a spokesman for other Boasians. The essay was undertaken not on Sapir's own initiative but at the request of Kroeber, who wanted Sapir to write on the question of time perspective to support his own linguistically conditioned attention to genetic relationship and change through time. Kroeber wrote to Sapir (December 7, 1914: NMM):

> What we had in mind was an attempt to grapple with the accumulating but unorganized evidence on the time element in the history of the American race and civilization. . . . On the American side we have now reached a pretty thorough understanding of the several local types of culture and their interrelations. This may make possible an attempt to estimate the length of time involved in these local developments, as well as in such general cultural traits as may be specifically American. . . . What I had in mind was any treatment of the ethnological material which would emphasize its historical bearings more than has been customary. We in this country have been particularly remiss and unimaginative in this respect. The average American anthropologist, even if he [*sic*] is an archaeologist, treats his data with an almost punctilious avoidance of the factor of time.

This was ten years before the Pecos classification in the American Southwest would provide the first temporal sequence based on archaeological data. Sapir was uncertain that he was the best person to carry out this synthesis, but he stepped up to the challenge of infusing history into American archaeology (Golla 1984:164–65; Sapir to Kroeber, December 14, 1914: ALK):

> I think you are right in your remark about our timidity in grappling with the time element in the history of culture. I think that it is historically due to the fact that so many of our men are

trained in descriptive or psychological comparison rather than in strictly historical comparative work. We do not, for instance, most of us, fully realize the importance of eliminating many ethnological and linguistic features even if extraordinarily complex, when it can be shown that they are quite probably of secondary origin. . . . Pointing out anomalies is not in itself reconstructing history. . . . . I think that one of the most important things to realize at present is that all culture areas, despite the fact that we, in supposed contrast to many English ethnologists, pride ourselves on a historical sense, are, to a large extent, after all, of a purely descriptive rather than historical value. . . . This type of reasoning is, of course, perfectly familiar to us in linguistic work. In comparing various Indo-Germanic languages among themselves we are not moved entirely by considerations of descriptive resemblances and differences, but we evaluate these historically at every step. . . . It is always, of course, easier to do this in linguistics than in culture anyway.

That is, Sapir used his linguistic model in consciously analogic ways to reason his way to time depth in American ethnology. He did not reject the postulates of Boasian diffusional studies but supplemented and extended them based on his own training in linguistics. In the same letter, Sapir warned explicitly that his argument would have to be abstract because concrete evidence was not yet available. The work was intended to be programmatic so that it could serve to organize more systematic future research along these lines.

Time Perspective was reviewed by Lowie, who wrote to Sapir praising the linguistic portion of the argument as a needed antidote to Boasian particularism. Sapir, the linguist among them, had models that could provide the needed revitalization (Lowie to Sapir, January 4, 1916: ALK):

I think your views on culture areas are thoroughly sound and the insistence on their non-equivalence and on their *historical* evaluation, while carrying immediate conviction, has not yet been made before in definite form, so far as I remember. Further, all you say on the ethnological inferences from linguistic data, while perhaps *only* [emphasis mine] an adaptation of Indo-

Germanic methods to the American field, is most suggestive and ought to have a direct influence on working anthropologists.

Other anthropologists shared the concern of Kroeber, Lowie, and Sapir for this topic. Wissler, best known for his culture area classification of American Indians [sic], praised Sapir's illustration that linguistics had something to contribute to Boasian anthropology (Wissler to Sapir, February 9, 1916: NMM). Radin, the trickster among them, expressed the ambivalence most Boasian anthropologists felt for linguistics as a method of cultural inference requiring detailed reconstruction of particular instances (to Sapir, December 23, 1919: NMM):

> My interests are primarily historical; I am a linguist in so far as my colleagues care to consider me one, only as a means, to further my ethnological-historical studies. The bare fact of the interrelationship of the N[orth] A[merican] Indian [sic] languages is of overwhelming importance to me, for it means so much ethnologically, even granting that many Indian [sic] cultures are of secondary origin. . . . Ethnology, to any person valuing precision and accuracy is the fuzziest and most unsatisfactory subject in the world—scientists please keep out. What is wanted is a person with an historical imagination and one who isn't afraid to have all his conclusions overthrown every ten years. But just think of the fun building these insecure structures! Of course it would be better if we could build secure structures, but that cannot be done in history or still less in ethnology, which is simply history without an authenticated chronology.

Concern over the limitations of ethnological method in the absence of corollary data from history had been around for a long time; for example, Radin wrote to Sapir considerably before the essay on time perspective was completed (January 27, 1914: NMM):

> But unfortunately that is the one thing in which ethnology differs from history . . . that chronology is and will always be impossible in primitive [sic] culture and any attempt to reconstruct one will be artificial, or what is more, vague. It is essential to recognize this fact and the corollary it entails, that corollary being—turn to the other aspect of ethnology—that of complete, comprehen-

sive and sympathetic interpretation. From this point of view ethnology can be made a real human science. . . . It is only from this angle that she can stimulate history.

Sapir, in contrast to his colleagues who were primarily ethnologists, was more sanguine about the unique possibilities opened up by linguistic methods of reconstruction relative to the rest of culture. In *Time Perspective* he had dealt with the areal and geographical logic of Boasian anthropology and its stress on diffusion as a cultural process in an attempt to move ethnologists toward linguistics. The Boasian ethnological method was equally unfamiliar, even alien, to his colleagues in linguistics who were accustomed to languages with written history. Sapir applied areal logic to numerous problems of American Indian [*sic*] linguistics throughout his career, most saliently to the northern origin of the Navajo. Linguists, however, are more likely to remember his work in the 1930s on Tocharian, an Indo-European language of Central Asia that Sapir demonstrated to have been heavily influenced by Tibetan. It seemed natural to him to apply insights about cultural process derived from anthropology to classical Indo-European arenas.

Despite its linguistic focus, the work on time perspective was compatible with and an extension of the Boasian model—at least in Sapir's opinion. The other Boasian problem of Sapir's early career was the classification of American Indian [*sic*] languages. In this arena, the assumptions of the linguistic model put him at greater divergence from his colleagues, and particularly from Boas himself.

Classification of American Indian [*sic*] Languages

The six-unit classification of American Indian [*sic*] languages that Sapir put forth in a one-page note in *Science* in 1921 was not solely a product of his own research. Rather, it was a systematic compilation of the work of others, augmented by his own efforts to fill in the gaps. As director of the Canadian government program in anthropology, Sapir was able to fund substantial fieldwork, including his own, and to set priorities for research, a position of power that he wielded effectively. Colleagues often failed to realize he had an agenda, much less to see how their work might facilitate it. For example, J. Alden Mason wrote to Sapir (March 23, 1913:

NMM): "Someone told me once you had said you would never go into the field without a definite object in view. Now open up—just what is the object of my summer trip?" Sapir wanted to know more about northern Athabaskan languages for his comparative work on Na-Dene, although he did not convey this to Mason, presumably because of his awareness that preconceptions tend to be self-fulfilling.

In addition to careful choice of the languages on which he personally did extensive fieldwork, Sapir made a point of learning something about language families more distantly related to his major descriptive work. As early as 1911, he wrote to Truman Michelson, the Bureau of American Ethnology's distinguished Algonquianist (July 20, 1911: NMM):

> I hope that I will be able to get first-hand acquaintance with several Algonkin dialects. . . . Of course, you understand that I have not the remotest intention in the world to work at these thoroughly. All that I mean to do is to get some sort of bird's eye view [the same phrase used in the title of his first formulation of the six-unit classification] in order to help me in better appreciating your own and others' work on Algonkin dialects.

In 1921 he was still attempting to reassure Michelson that he did not intend to call himself a student of this language family, except insofar as it could be related to other languages and language families (October 27, 1921: NMM):

> You must, of course, always bear in mind that my standpoint is not that of an Algonkinist; that is to say, I would not dream of expecting all the familiar Algonkin features to turn up in Yurok and Wiyot. The question is simply one of determining if there are enough lexical and morphological links to justify us in grouping Yurok and Wiyot [into Ritwan] as a parallel development to Algonkin from some remote prototype of both.

In the same year, Sapir also attempted to expand his knowledge of various Athabaskan languages. He wrote to Frank Speck (April 9, 1921: NMM): "I want to get into personal touch with the Athabaskan field so as to have a more live first-hand feeling for Na-Dene.

Eventually I shall probably, if my plans are realized, do field work on Haida and Tlingit linguistics as well."

Sapir realized he could not expect to do all the concrete work of describing American Indian [*sic*] languages himself. He corresponded with colleagues working on other languages and language families and applied their data to his own formulations of genetic relationships. He established particularly fruitful collaborations with Leo Frachtenberg, Radin, Mason, Kroeber, Roland Dixon, John Swanton, William H. Mechling, and Speck. Sapir made a clear distinction between firsthand fieldwork and competence in comparative generalization. He wrote at length to Pliny Earle Goddard, a conservative Athabaskanist at the bureau, detailing his Uto-Aztecan work (June 25, 1914: NMM) and added a characteristically self-denigrating disclaimer: "I give you these facts merely to humor you. I did not imagine before receiving your letter that you estimated the value of one's contribution to American linguistics by the number of pages of text that he had collected."

The reason for this concern over method and the source of data revealed a fundamental conflict with Boasian ethnological method. Boas himself was extremely negative, both in correspondence and in print, about many linguistic relationships that Sapir considered demonstrated. Boas was much more interested in diffusion as a cultural process. Areal and distributional studies had proved productive in his work with folklore elements on the Northwest Coast, and he could not accept that sound correspondences in language provided irrefutable evidence of genetic relationship. Boas's attitude was a subject that rankled in Sapir's correspondence. For example, Radin wrote to Sapir (March 3, 1913: NMM):

> It seems that there are many of us in now for proving relationship between independent stocks. . . . It has always seemed very evident and curious to me that while Boas'[s] interest in ethnological matters was primarily historical rather than purely descriptive, when it came to linguistics, his interest is exactly the reverse, merely descriptive or "psychological," hardly at all historical or reconstructive. To my mind this is a fundamental error in method of approach, though I fully recognize that both historical and psychological interests have their place.

Sapir's response leaves no question about his fundamental, methodological disagreement with Boas (June 10, 1913: NMM):

> I thoroughly agree with you in regard to Boas'[s] attitude towards establishing larger linguistic groups of a genetic character. It is one of the cases in which, in my opinion, he allows his judgment to be influenced by a preconceived like or dislike. For some mysterious reason he simply does not like to think of an originally small number of linguistic stocks, which have each of them differentiated tremendously, but prefers, with [John Wesley] Powell, to conceive of an almost unlimited number of distinct stocks, many of which, in the course of time, become extinct. To me the former alternative seems a historical necessity. There must, in the nature of things, come a time when the members of a linguistic group have diverged so much that their genetic relationship is difficult to detect. I believe that there are many languages that at last analysis are genetically related where we shall never be able to establish such a relationship. Language is conservative, of course, but conservative is only a matter of degree, not an absolute fact.

Although this comment is compatible with his outline of time perspective in that its intentions and procedures are basically Boasian, Sapir faced a barrage of attacks with each major reduction of the number of linguistic stocks that he proposed. For example, Boasian conservativism was lyrically defended by Frachtenberg (October 20, 1914: NAA):

> You must not forget that "correspondences," no matter how interesting, are far from proving genetic affiliation. . . . We must, therefore, be very careful in applying the methods that have given us such splendid results in the Indo-European, Semitic and Ural-Altaic fields to the domain of American Indian [*sic*] linguistics. . . . The best we can do at the present time, to my mind, is the simplification of stocks, not in accordance with their seeming points of resemblance, but with their relationship of type. I mean by that, that we ought to tabulate at first such stocks that express identical psychological concepts by similar grammatical devices and see what this will prove. Of course, in such a tabulation, the question of geographical contiguity will play a very important part.

This is the position of someone not trained in Indo-European, as Boas himself was not, who is unprepared to apply the methods of philology to unwritten languages. Kroeber and Dixon initially applied a similar conservatism in California.

Boas's principled conservatism continued to frustrate Sapir throughout his classificatory work. He wrote to Speck (October 2, 1924: APS):

> At last analysis these controversies boil down to a recognition of two states of mind. One, conservative intellectuals, like Boas . . . who refuse absolutely to consider far-reaching suggestions unless they can be demonstrated by a mass of evidence. . . . Hence, from an over-anxious desire to be right, they generally succeed in being more hopelessly and fundamentally wrong, in the long run, than many more superficial minds who are not committed to "principles." . . . The second type is more intuitive and, even when the evidence is not as full or theoretically unambiguous as it might be, is prepared to throw out tentative suggestions and to take it as it goes along. . . . I have no hope whatever of ever getting Boas and Goddard to see through my eyes or to feel with my hunches. I take their opposition like the weather, which might generally be better but which will have to do.

From their enthusiasm and the rapidity with which Sapir and his associates were revamping the linguistic map of North America, Boas and other conservatives concluded that Sapir must not have been sufficiently cautious about methods. They failed to recognize that he was following a fundamentally different method and that it had its own standards of rigor. Sapir frequently counseled caution in his correspondence with other linguists and was far from enthusiastic about relationships that were not clearly demonstrated by Indo-European criteria of lexical and morphological similarities. The linguistic comparative method was simply not a familiar one in North America. For example, Sapir wrote to Frachtenberg (January 8, 1915: NMM):

> I believe, of course, in reasonable caution in assuming larger linguistic stocks than indicated on Powell's map, but I am convinced that the attitude Boas is taking in this matter is much

overdone, and is at last analysis due simply to the fact that he has had no personal experience in historic grammar or comparative linguistics. His main linguistic interest is purely psychological and the bias that this interest gives all his linguistic work may as well be recognized once for all. You probably realize as I do to what an alarming extent personal training and interest influence one's scientific point of view. I feel most decidedly that the study of American Indian [*sic*] linguistics is these days turning over a new leaf, as it were, and that the purely historic study of languages as based on comparative evidence must more and more be brought to the fore.

When Frachtenberg protested that he was not all that conservative, in spite of being trained by Boas, Sapir responded (January 9, 1917: NAA):

Well, we are evidently progressing in the same general direction. After all, the logical facts cannot be long withstood. It is only a question of whether one prefers to be a conservative as long as he respectably can, or has a bit more courage than the crowd and is willing to take a look ahead.

Sapir did look ahead. His vision invariably deployed linguistic method to elucidate problems of ethnology. In 1918 he wrote to Speck (August 1, 1918: APS):

Great simplifications are in store for us, but we must be critical and not force our evidence. Besides we must try to work out genealogically degrees of relationship. Only so will fascinating perspectives appear. It seems to me that only now is American linguistics becoming really interesting *at least in its ethnological bearings*. [emphasis mine]

The most explicit statement of Sapir's idea of competent method comes in his strictures to Radin, who was inclined to gloss over the detailed work of providing specific evidence for his sweeping contentions. In 1913 he wrote to Radin (April 2, 1913: NMM):

As to writing up grammars, I may say that I consider it dangerous to rely on one's general knowledge, no matter how fresh it may be in one's mind. The only plan that seems to me to be worth a moment's consideration is to make careful collectanea under various heads, phonological and morphological. In this way the material boils itself down to systematic shape, and the actual writing is hardly more than putting facts and ideas into connected form that are already worked out for you inductively.

He continued to caution Radin about the pitfalls of classificatory work at a superficial level (July 17, 1918: NMM):

> In general, I think that you do not allow enough for the possibility of borrowing between neighboring languages. I also believe that you would gain a great deal from closer adherence to tentative phonetic laws, instead of seizing hold of everything that looks in the least comparable. . . . Of course, I do not for a moment dream that we have by any means reached the last state in our process of disentangling the relationships of North American languages. Much remains to be done; but I do not think we ought to prejudice our general case by making far-fetched comparisons or going at it too precipitously. What we need more than anything else is careful reconstruction of such groups as do belong together. . . . You can't dodge the labor of synthesizing at every step. Reconstruction forms are invaluable aids. You can't get along without them.

Radin was not alone among American Indian [*sic*] ethnologists and part-time linguists in looking to Sapir for guidance in analyzing field materials and pronouncements about the larger picture. In fact, Radin urged Sapir to organize the group of potential workers and settle the relationships once and for all (December 16, 1919: NMM). Sapir did not respond directly, but he had actually served in an informal coordinating role for some years. Radin however, went out on his own and argued that all North American languages were genetically related (Radin 1919). Sapir was forced to repudiate this contention, although he personally thought about how one might obtain evidence for certain suggestive "Proto-American" features. Sapir announced his conclusions only when he felt the evidence was sufficient to convince his colleagues. Nevertheless, his habit was to leak his latest theories in correspondence, usually to nonspecialists who would not be threatened or perhaps would not challenge him as he thought out loud in hope of affirmation. For example, he wrote to Radin the same year that his Algonquian-Ritwan article appeared in the *American Anthropologist* (July 18, 1913: NMM):

> The process of slaughter of linguistic families, upon which several of us seem to have embarked of late, is going on apace. . . . I now seriously believe that Wiyot and Yurok are related to Algonkin. I have been more frank with you in regard to this than with others to whom I have given only dark hints. Please treat this information as strictly confidential, as, should it turn out that I have been hasty, I will present a rather sorry picture. There really are some astonishing points of contact both morphologically and lexically. . . . The consequences of this latest theory are so great that I am hesitating very considerably, even in my own mind, about committing myself, and want to get more and more evidence before I confess to myself that I am convinced. Had Wiyok and Yurok been, let us say, Eskimo or Siouan, I would not have hesitated for a moment, but when you have that vast expanse of country separating the Californian stocks from even the westernmost Algonkin tribes, one may well hesitate.

As time went on, of course, Sapir proposed connections that were even more startling to the ethnographic understandings of the time. Sapir became convinced that the Na-Dene would prove to be connected to Indo-Chinese and announced this in correspondence at the same time his six-unit classification was made public. He wrote to Wissler (October 3, 1920: NMM) commending National Research Council (NRC) proposals for anthropological research in Polynesia:

> Polynesian may have a significance we hardly dream of at present. The whole thing is perhaps to be beautifully correlated with race. Indo-Chinese may originally have belonged to specifically Mongolian peoples; the real problem requires an acquaintance with surrounding linguistic groups (particularly Dravidian and Indo-Chinese). Finally, let me say (this is confidential!!) that I would not be surprised if reconstructed Indo-Chinese, originally a northern language within a stone's throw of certain individ-

uals who were to take a trip to N[orth] America, showed significant analogies to Na-dene. . . . Perhaps it is not for nothing that Tsimshian Indians say Haida sounds like Chinese! And so we come back to our Indians [*sic*].

In the same period, Sapir corresponded extensively with Sinologist Berthold Laufer on the same postulated relationship, although he never published his evidence. An unsigned note in *Science* in 1925 was the closest he came (Sapir 1925b). In reporting on the success of his paper announcing the six-unit classification at the American Association for the Advancement of Science in December 1920, Sapir remarked to Wallis (January 8, 1921: NMM):

> I do not know if I shall publish my map and findings just at present, as I may prefer to make my ground more secure before I commit myself in print. The Na-Dene is the one that most particularly interests me at present, as I consider it highly probable that it represents a tremendous wedge into the American field, possibly from the Asiatic continent. I am hoping to devote myself to this particular problem for the next few years.

Sapir had already considered the extended Na-Dene hypothesis in his 1920 paper! He wrote to Radin (December 5, 1919: NMM) that he planned a paper on the status of linguistic classification in North America and noted: "There are a certain number of what may be called proto-American elements that have so wide a currency as to bring up the question of much more far-reaching syntheses than most of us have dared to suggest. I may bring out some of these fundamental elements in my Cambridge talk." Sapir, however, elected to wait until further evidence was available. For the rest of his life, he focused most intensively on the Na-Dene languages that had the potential to provide such evidence.

In any case the six-unit classification, despite Sapir's protestations that it reflected work in progress, with no expectation of closure, was received by most of his colleagues, especially the ethnologists, as a rigid pronouncement. Sapir himself was explicit that he expected further simplifications and that the classification was "presumably" rather than necessarily genetic. He presented his six units in a form that made it clear subgroupings were intended;

TABLE 2. North American linguistic classifications

Sapir 1929	Sapir (Implicit)	Powell 1891
I. Eskimo-Aleut	Eskimo	Eskimo
II. Algonquian-Ritwan	*Algonquian-Riwan	Algonquian, Beothukan, Wiyot, Yurok
	*Mosan	Wakashan, Chemakuan, Salish
	Kootenay	Kootenay
III. Na-dene	*Tlingit-Athabascan	Haida, Tlingit, Athabascan
	Haida	
IV. Penutian	*California Penutian	Miwok, Costanoan, Yokuts, Maidu, Wintun
	*Oregon Penutian	Takelma, Coos (-Siuslaw), Yakoanan, Kalapuya
	*Plateau Penutian	Waiilatpuan, Lutuamian, Sahaptin
	Chinook	Chinook
	Tsimshian	Tshimshian
	(Mexican Penutian)	—
V. Hokan-Siouan	*Hokan	Karok, Chimariko, Salinan, Yana, Pomo, Washo, Yuman, Esselen, Chumash
	*Coahuiltecan	Tonkawa, Karankawa, Coahuiltecan
	*Tunican	Tunica, Atakapa, Chitimacha
	*Iroquois-Caddoan	Iroquois, Caddoan
	Yuki	Yuki
	Keres	Keres
	Timucua	Timucua
	Muskhogean	Muskhogean
	Siouan	Siouan, Yuchi
VI. Aztec-Tanoan	*Uto-Aztecan	Nahuatl, Pima, Shoshonean
	*Tanoan-Kiowan	Tanoan, Kiowa
	?Zuni	Zuni

* Twelve units Sapir considered accepted by most of his colleagues. The reduction of Powell's fifty-five stocks to twenty-three reflected the work of Sapir's generation. The further reduction to six units he considered to be his own work.

he expected that more conservative linguists would probably recognize the legitimacy of the subgroupings, many of them resulting from Sapir's own fieldwork.

With the exception of his 1929 version (differing only in the inclusion of Beothuk, Waiilatpuan-Lutuami-Sahaptin, and Zuni), Sapir did not, after 1921, return to the subject of classification of American Indian [*sic*] languages. In his book *Language* in the same year, Sapir's interest in typology is clear, suggesting that he perhaps came to see this alternative to genetic relationship as another method of classifying language similarities (although typology also interested him for its own sake). In any case Sapir and his students concentrated on the description of particular languages and the development of new modes of description, particularly what we now call morphophonemic. After 1925 Sapir apparently concluded that the linguistic map of North America had been filled in, at least in its essential character. Ethnological implications could be inferred as a result of the application of Indo-European methods, and Sapir felt he had done his part in the herculean task of Boasian anthropology to delineate the culture and history of American native peoples.

One further sideline of filling in the Boasian paradigm from the standpoint of language remains: Sapir showed considerable interest in kinship as the semantic domain of language most likely to shed light on genetic relationship because it was most language-like. As early as 1916, he wrote to Speck (November 10, 1916: NMM) that Lowie failed to understand the possible linguistic ramifications of kinship terms, especially in relation to the levirate. By 1918 he thought that kinship studies might reinforce linguistic classifications, such as in a letter to Edward Gifford (November 12, 1918: NMM):

> I myself am more skeptical than ever now of the validity of any
> attempt to seek close and far reaching correlation between socio-
> logical phenomena and types of kinship systems. There is no
> doubt that sociological features have their more or less definite
> reflexes in these systems and that there is no shadow of doubt
> that Rivers and for that matter Lowie have tremendously over-
> done the correlation. I am much more inclined to make my
> stand with Kroeber than with anyone else and he again is per-

haps a little extreme in minimizing the influence of sociological factors. The really interesting point in the whole business . . . is the tracking of the subtler psychological attitudes revealed in kinship systems. The evident feeling displayed for different types of symmetry or asymmetry or diverse handlings of categories and intercrossings of categories. There is a mathematical-like formal sense, perhaps very obscure but none the less real, involved in these attitudes which place kinship systems pretty much in the category of linguistic phenomena generally.

The psychology Sapir is talking about here is the patterning that makes a people distinctive, and it reflects changes already under way in his thinking. Nonetheless, conventional Boasian concerns persist, as he pointed out to Mechling (July 15, 1919: NMM): "I am at present working on a detailed discussion of the kinship systems of Wiyot, Yurok and Algonkin. Some really astonishing things are coming out and I believe that the present investigation is in every way confirmatory of my linguistic hypothesis."

Rethinking the Premises

Sapir's period of personal and professional crisis began about 1916 and was correlated directly with the depression and increasing mental illness of his wife, neé Florence Delson, after the birth of their third child in that year. Sapir found it more difficult to concentrate on his work and increasingly found satisfaction in other areas, reexamining the nature of his commitment to anthropology. For example, he wrote to Frachtenberg, who was considering leaving anthropology to earn a decent living in business (November 28, 1916: NAA): "As a matter of fact, I do not know that purely scientific work is necessarily the sine qua non of personal happiness in any way. I imagine that almost the best thing that you could do would be to make your living out of something entirely different and take up anthropology as a free lance's hobby." This is a remarkable comment from a man whose professional success was as obvious and complete as Sapir's at that time.

Disaffection, on the other hand, seemed to be in the air. Angst was in fashion. Radin expressed similar sentiments to Sapir at about the same time (February 19, 1916: NMM):

We anthropologists, i.e. the four Semites who graduated under Boas, are either an unusual aggregation of men or a self-centered set who insist on giving in to their intellectual whims whenever the spirit prompts them. Here I am inveighing against the tyranny of modern science which insists that you do original research and hack work, when it is so much better for your soul and your mind to lie on your back and gaze into a New Mexican sky, walk into the mountains or, still better, read history or Greek and Latin, while Lowie until recently wanted to write and read philosophy and Goldie wanted to read books like [Lucien] Lévy-Bruhl and [Emile] Durkheim. Now come you with your composing and delight in modern literature! Thank the lord it is so. . . . To cultivate anthropology in the old way has not, as you know, appealed to me for the last two years.

Correspondence reflects the ongoing dialogue, although Sapir's replies were not preserved in the files of the National Museum.[2] In relation to the illness of Sapir's wife, Radin saw the two subjects as related and remarked (March 28, 1917: NMM):

I can sympathize with you in your attitude toward anthropology as it is currently understood and "practiced." I must confess however that I have not lost my interest in it, from an interpretive point of view, if you know what I mean. What irritates me is the hopeless inadequacy and inaccuracy of our data.

Radin found Sapir entirely too dedicated to the self-discipline of scientific work and suggested to him that he should have done something else (August 17, 1918: NMM):

It's also true, in my opinion, that you are not in the proper profession. The idea of a man of your brains being a philologist or ethnologist! You should have studied mathematics. Why the hell didn't you? How could a man with any red blood in him, conscious of possessing brains, turn to philology? That is something one can stumble into, as one falls into a deep ditch, in which one stays because it is hard to get out and because man adjusts himself even to living in ditches. The trouble with linguistics is that it consumes too much time to do it properly and to do it in a general vague way is always aesthetically repulsive to a real man with linguistic ability.

Sapir's own musings on his proper role in life were best expressed in a long philosophical letter to Lowie (September 29, 1916: RHL; Lowie 1965:20–21) in which he considered reasons for his disillusionment with his work:

> Why do I engage in music? I suppose I could call it recreation and be done with it, but I do not think it would be quite sincere for me to put off your query like that. I feel I can do not only eminently satisfactory linguistic work but also satisfactory ethnological work, as I proved to myself in my two Nootka trips. I have now an enormous amount of linguistic and ethnological data on my hands from various tribes, certainly enough to keep me busy for at least five years of concentrated work. But (and here's the rub and the disappointment) I don't somehow seem to feel as much positive impulse toward disgorging as I should. A certain necessary enthusiasm, particularly towards ethnological data and problems, seems lacking—lacking beyond a mild degree, anyway. I somehow feel in much of my work that I am not true to my inner self, that I have let myself be put off with useful but relatively unimportant trifles at the expense of a development of finer needs and impulses, whatever they are. A chafing of the spirit, the more annoying because there is externally so little excuse for it! I know, as no one else can, that it is this profound feeling of dissatisfaction and disillusionment which hardly ever leaves me, that is mainly (not altogether, for I must waste much time on office routine, but mainly) responsible for my relatively unproductive scientific career up to date. To amass data, to write them up, to discuss "problems"—how easy, but cui bono? Do not misunderstand me. My "cui bono" is not grounded in any philosophy of relative values. I have no theoretical quarrel with anthropology. The fault lies with me. Being as I am, for better or for worse, the life of an Americanist does not satisfy my inmost cravings. To be frank, I do not believe this discontent is due chiefly to the unhuman aspect of our discipline, to its narrow range of appeal. I am afraid I may have too

much of the "shut-in" personality about me to feel that sort of limitation as keenly as a [Harlan] Smith or perhaps yourself.

I find that what I most care for is beauty of form, whether in substance or, perhaps even more keenly, in spirit. A perfect style, a well-balanced system of philosophy, a perfect bit of music, the beauty of mathematical relations—these are some of the things that, in the spheres of the immaterial, have most deeply stirred me. How can the job-lot of necessarily un-coordinated or badly co-ordinated facts that we amass in our fieldwork satisfy such longings? Is not the incessant pouring over such facts a punishment to the liberty loving spirit? Does not one most "waste time" when he is most industrious? And yet one always feels relieved and a bit pleased to have done with some bit of "scientific" work. I do not really believe that my temperament is so very unscientific either, for I am surely critical and almost unreasonably analytical. A scientific spirit but an aesthetic will or craving! A sort of at-cross-purposes-with-oneself type of temperament that entails frequent inhibitions, frustrations, anything but a smooth flow of self-satisfied and harmonious effort. Shucks! my self analysis may be all wrong, but the inner dissatisfaction is there.

Sapir was becoming increasingly disenchanted with Ottawa, a feeling intensified by his wife's loneliness and isolation there. He was convinced that a change of scene would improve her health but was unable to obtain a university position in the United States. Sapir had outlets in Ottawa that his wife did not. He was active in government and literary circles and a popular public speaker; these contacts were enhanced by his own increasing interest in the world of *belles lettres*. On the other hand, his attempts to secure a part-time teaching position in Canadian universities near enough to Ottawa for commuting were unsuccessful. The grass looked greener on the other side of the international boundary and in a university context. Moreover, World War I was not kind to scientific funding, and the Victoria Memorial Museum was no exception. Sapir had realistic reason to feel disillusioned (Sapir to Radin, December 5, 1919: NMM):

The atmosphere here is just as unfavorable to anthropology as it was during the war and we are likely to continue to mark time for an indefinite period. I was never so discouraged about the progress of the Division as I am today; even the puny Summary Reports for our Division that I prepare every year have not been published the last two years. The only real hope for the Division is in a radical change of administration and, though interesting rumours are afloat, there is no great reliance to be put in them. The sad fact is that we have not only not progressed, but have to a considerable extent retrograded. It is delightful to hear from Kroeber, what a contrast is afforded in this respect by the Department of Anthropology at the University of California, that evidently has a lot going on in the way of research and publication. I envy you your contact with a bunch of enthusiastic students.

In the writing of poetry, Sapir found his most satisfying answer to the dissatisfactions of ethnological work. He exchanged poetry with a number of colleagues and actively sought their criticism of his own poems. Not all were enthusiastic. Radin reacted predictably to the new enthusiasm with amazement (June 23, 1917: NMM): "Your literary ambitions frighten me. Are you doing it in order to make money or because you like it? . . . What you say about a volume of free verse astonishes me. However what is happening to your ethnology and philology? Hope you are not throwing it overboard?" Radin professes not to be able to express himself as well as Sapir does and urges him to return to interpretive ethnology (August 17, 1918: NMM). When Sapir sent a copy of his poetry volume (1917b, published at his own expense and reviewed in *The Dial* without enthusiasm), Radin (December 6, 1917: NMM) affirmed his own appreciation of modern poetry: "However, you do me a great injustice in insisting that I don't understand and to a certain extent appreciate the new movement in poetry. . . . I enjoy minor expressions of art. They require so little mental strain to enjoy them." Radin, however, insisted that his own poetry, unlike Sapir's, was not "experimental" (April 3, 1922: NMM). Subsequent correspondence finds Radin jumping on the bandwagon (September 30, 1920: NMM):

Like you I feel myself turning toward literature and art. What form this new interest will take I don't know. I feel something brewing in me but I don't exactly know what it is. Poetry! I doubt it. More likely it will be a cross between a semi-philosophic essay and a play of phantasy. All I know is that I want to be rid of the crushing pressure of facts, "scientific! established" data when I write. I want to write without worrying about whether I am contradicting myself or not.

Sapir's most intense poetic interaction was with Ruth Benedict, who assisted him in an arrangement for a potentially publishable volume in 1928. Their relationship cooled, however, after Sapir's second marriage in 1926. In Ottawa, a frequent confrere was Duncan Campbell Scott of the Office of Indian Affairs. After the publication of *Dreams and Gibes* in 1917, there is considerable correspondence indicating Scott's interest in discussing Sapir's poetry with him. After Sapir left Ottawa, Scott wrote him (July 16, 1925: NMM): "I enjoyed your sonnet in the last number of *The Nation*, but I wish I had you here to explain to me."

In addition to the poetry per se, Sapir made a few experiments with genres of ethnographic writing, attempting to make ethnology intelligible to a general audience in a way that scientific reports did not. These efforts were not overly successful, which Sapir himself realized. To an Ottawa acquaintance who had read his poems Sapir noted (to Madge Macbeth, January 20, 1922: City of Ottawa Archives, courtesy of William Cowan): "'The Blind Old Indian [*sic*] and his Names' was an experiment, and not a truly successful one. The treatment of Indian [*sic*] material is a problem—at least for me. I may be able to do something later. I have not the key to the solution of the difficulty inherent in remotely exotic matter—probably because my own natural handling of subjects has already something of the remote about it." Poetry was Sapir's escape from ethnology, his assertion of personal creativity and incompatible with ethnological work despite his intentions. Both his poetry and literary criticism attempted to mediate between science and personal perception.

Sapir's concern with form was not restricted to poetry. In 1918 he experimented with perception of design elements and asked a diverse group of colleagues and their relatives to comment on an American Indian [*sic*] design. He explicated some of the aesthetic issues involved to Leslie Spier (May 13, 1918: NMM):

The fact that your brother and sister reacted towards the design in about the same way you did yourself would suggest one rather important inquiry, namely, whether the design strikes the subject as essentially complete in itself, or as fruitfully capable of development. . . . I would like, if possible, to get at the aesthetic process proper, both appreciative and creative. . . . [This] may well ultimately persuade us that much of our conventional art teaching is but little in harmony with psychological fact. . . . One of the things that most strikes me is the apparent lack of relation between experience and aesthetic conception. . . . A surprisingly large number of designs suggested by people familiar with art are astonishingly dull.

In the following year, Sapir offered a paper on the same subject (to Miriam Finn Scott, March 17, 1919: NMM):

It occurred to me some time ago that it would be an interesting study both psychologically and aesthetically to take a relatively simple design and ask a number of people, selected more or less at random, to make up a series of developments from the given design, in each case following their natural spontaneous bent as much as possible. My main idea was to test the varying types of aesthetic conception revealed in these different series.

As in his poetry, Sapir focused on the creativity and individuality of individuals within the same cultural context. This experiment was carried out not long after his critique of the superorganic, where he argued that culture had its locus in the individual, with the obvious implication that diversity among individuals was to be expected (and celebrated).

Fascination with form rather than content preoccupied Sapir in this period. It is manifested in his book *Language*, as is his tendency to seek an audience wider than his scientific colleagues. A number of these colleagues failed to share his fascination with linguistic form. Radin (April 20, 1922: NMM) charged that Sapir was prone to "vastly exaggerate the cognitive appeal of language." Wallis, in response to Sapir's comments on his own manuscript (March 13, 1922: NMM), was unable to accept the aesthetic tone of Sapir's critique:

I must confess that I have no great interest in form as such, no aesthetic response, as you would term it. I am interested in social data from the point of view of their meaning or content, rather than form or function pure and simple. I do not see what you mean by the aesthetic undertone, unless you refer to this search for a meaning. No doubt this last is most elusive, but it is worth searching for. . . . Yet, though I have no sympathy for your view-point—if I understand it—your many comments have really aided me greatly.

Sapir's comments centered on the role of the individual as the creative force in culture. He had just completed his formulation of the concept of a "genuine culture," which owes more to his poetic and literary works than to the anthropological theories of his training.

Despite the oral tradition within the discipline that *Language* was written in only a few weeks, off the top of Sapir's head so to speak, the project actually developed more gradually. In August 1920, Sapir wrote to his Ottawa colleague Marius Barbeau (August 10, 1920: NMM), "My book on language is progressing rather slowly." Only two of the twelve chapters were completed. Sapir complained about the "very considerable concentration in thinking that it demands." Only a few months earlier, he had optimistically assumed that it would take him two or three months in Ottawa, simply delaying the start of his summer fieldwork (Sapir to Harlan I. Smith, June 22, 1920). In November he noted to Spier (November 8, 1920: NMM): "In fact, I make a point these days not to read other people's general works on language. I am interested only in source material, that is, first-hand accounts of specific languages. Unfortunately, my own textbook is moving along very slowly. In fact I have not done anything on it of late. I slowed up a bit when I learned that the publishers were in no hurry on account of present publishing conditions, but I must get back to work quickly, or I shall find myself way behind."

Sapir intended *Language* to function at several levels. He told Truman Michelson (August 7, 1920: NAA) that "It is a book that I hope will be of some use to linguistic students generally by way of widening their perspectives." That is, Sapir still longed for students and chafed at the isolation of his museum post. He did not want to write entirely for a specialized audience. And he wanted to present data from unwritten languages alongside that from the more traditional, Indo-European languages, to be able to take for granted that the same methods applied to both and that the exotic nature of anthropological examples was only superficial. The emphasis on the beauty of form in every language was deliberate and served to resolve Sapir's conflict between his science and his aesthetic perception. He was fully aware of the difficulty of the treatment (Sapir to Wallis, November 23, 1923: NMM): "Thank you for your flattering remarks about my book on language. I feel it is rather compactly written, and is likely to withhold some of its contents on a first reading." Sapir was delighted at the book's warm reception and carefully preserved letters and reviews. He seems to have felt that the volume successfully presented his mature viewpoint about language from his standpoint at the intersection of two disciplines. By the time of its publication, his specifically literary production had tapered off, being no longer necessary to his own psychological re-evaluation.

From Aesthetics to Psychological Reality

The illness of Sapir's wife was a major drive in his introduction to psychology. He was unable to explain to himself why she rather than anyone else became ill or to suggest a lasting cure. Reading in psychology posed at least the possibility of a cure. On the other hand, Sapir quickly became intrigued by this reading for its own sake. His correspondence with one doctor who treated Mrs. Sapir moved back and forth between discussion of her condition and exchange of professional commentary. F. Lyman Wells, also a friend of Boas's, asked Sapir about symbolism in folklore, hoping to find the reversions to the "primitive" that Freud predicted in *dementia praecox*. In turn, Wells recommended readings in psychology for Sapir. Sapir's personal disillusionment was transposed into an increasingly professional interest in psychology for its own sake. Its insights fit well with the progression of his own thought at the time.

Sapir preferred Carl Jung to Sigmund Freud, being particularly fascinated by Jung's classification of psychological types. He attempted to convince Lowie (May 20, 1925: RHL) that the classification was feasible by applying it to various colleagues. He classified himself as an intuitive introvert, a classification he did not apply to anyone else. Lowie was a thinking extrovert, Kroeber a sensation-intuitive introvert with an inconsistent extrovert compensation, Radin a sensation extrovert, Benedict a thinking-feeling introvert, and Boas a feeling introvert with a strong and only partially successful thinking compensation. All are perceptive judgments of these colleagues.[3]

The Jungian categories provided a comparative framework for individual differences without imposing value judgment. Sapir acknowledged that it is "difficult, of course, to feel through to the essential personality because of the screening effects of cultural adaptation." He recognized that if culture could not be separated from personality, no system would be able to go beyond mere verbalism. Sapir never attempted to provide individual portraits of the range of variation within an Indian [*sic*] culture, except perhaps in his quasi-literary portraits of Tom, the Nootka.

William F. Ogburn provided another early stimulus for Sapir's thinking on psychological questions. The two met in the summer of 1915 when Sapir was in Berkeley working with Ishi. Like Wells, Ogburn hoped that Sapir, as an anthropologist, could help him broaden the base of psychology. Sapir was not yet able to do so (to Ogburn, January 14, 1918: NMM):

> I am sorry that I cannot give you any fruitful criticism about what the psychoanalysts have done in folklore and ethnological respects. I have hardly gone into these aspects of their work at all. . . . I would not go so far as to say that there is not much that is suggestive in the psychoanalytical handing of myths and religious ceremonial. I am frankly on the fence at the present, with a very lively doubt in my mind as to whether these people are just at present properly qualified to undertake the work. It seems to me that they know too little about the nature of the cultural phenomena to be able to add very materially to our insight just at present. None of them seems to recall the fundamental fact of all historical phenomena, that however their psychological origin may be explained they tend to persist as such and to take on entirely new meanings. In other words, the psychoanalysts arrive too rapidly at their goal.

The critique of psychoanalytic method is thoroughly Boasian, although Sapir is clearly intrigued by the possibilities for ethnological procedure. He quickly turns to Ogburn's "superorganic" notion of culture, arguing, characteristically, for the importance of the individual:

> I am not in the least surprised that you inclined rather to agree with Kroeber than with myself in our recent controversy. I have certain ideas about the meaning and value of individuality in history that I am afraid are rather heterodox. Much of the talk of social psychology that I run across from time to time strikes me, to be very frank, as simply bosh. The attempt to understand history in terms of book formulas that take no account of the individual is, to my mind, but a passing phase of our hunger for conventional scientific capsules into which to store our concepts. When all the experiments in massed action will have brought with them their due share of inevitable disappointments, there will be a very real reaction against this whole way of thinking, but in any event this reaction is not due for some time yet so you may as well have the laugh on me for the present.

Ogburn continued to find some of Sapir's work incompatible with his own and failed to understand that Sapir's intention was quite distinct from the thrust of his own work. In response to "Culture, genuine and spurious" he wrote (August 31, 1922: NMM):

> You and I seemed in previous talks to understand our meanings of art and science. You say that you like to keep them separate. It seems to me in this paper . . . [you] have them mixed. I feel that in this article your subjective colors your analysis and you almost drift into mysticism. You seem to be struggling to articulate something you feel emotionally rather than see coldly and scientifically.

The difference was irreconcilable. "Culture, genuine and spurious" was an aesthetic concept, expressing the search for balance that Sapir had been seeking in his own life and work. It is "inherently harmonious, balanced, self-satisfactory. It is the expression of a richly varied and yet somehow unified and consistent attitude toward life, an attitude which sees the significance of any one element of civilization in its relation to all others. It is, ideally speaking, a culture in which nothing is spiritually meaningless" (Sapir [1924] 1949:314–15). It was a synthesis of anthropology and art, not a separation of them.

Sapir's use of psychological studies to buttress his ethnological theory was characteristic of his career-long preoccupation with synthesis of methods and models from diverse sources that could be welded into a coherent whole. He could not keep his interests in separate boxes. In contrast, Kroeber turned to psychoanalysis in a period of personal crisis similar to that which plagued Sapir but responded by compartmentalizing anthropology and psychoanalysis. Most anthropological colleagues were appalled by Kroeber's perceived defection. Radin wrote to Sapir (July 14, 1920: NMM): "With regard to this psychoanalysis adventure I think it is a crime. My explanation is that he is trying to stave off the full recognition of his own inward condition by attempting to analyze others. It is a typical indirect Kroeberian trick." Kroeber had hoped that Sapir would realize why he had set up a lay practice as an analyst and abandoned anthropology, at least for a period (July 19, 1920: UCB): "Why are you so silent on the notice of my new undertaking? You are the one man in the profession that I counted on not to take the event either as a slap or as a morsel of gossip." Kroeber saw himself and Sapir as working through similar problems (July 29, 1920: NMM):

> I don't plead any preponderating [*sic*] objective scientific motive, of course. I'm not so rotten an analyst as that. But I do want a larger "pediment," more varied interests and contacts, a leverage to prevent one from rutting even deeper into my little job, and, if I can pick it up, any legitimately earned money. Is it any different, except from the last factor perhaps, from your writing poetry? It's a healthy instinct that leads us to try to break the bars that tend to close in on us with the momentum of years; healthy, if the effort is not spasmodically hysterical.

Self-control was important to Kroeber. He made no effort to combine the insights of the two disciplines that drew him in different directions in this period, whereas for Sapir, the cross-fertilization was what brought satisfaction.

The emerging integration of Sapir's thought still did not reconcile traditional linguistic methods with his developing aesthetic and psychological concerns. The shift in his thinking is complete with the publication in 1925 of "Sound Patterns of Language" in the inaugural issue of *Language*. This essay marked the first explicit definition of the phoneme in American linguistics. Oral history has it that this monumental insight into the nature of linguistic patterning emerged gradually from fieldwork with a number of American Indian [*sic*] languages, building on the insights of Boas's seminal article "On Alternating Sounds" (1889). Sapir framed his argument in terms that emphasized this continuity and held some hope of convincing Boasian colleagues. He did not emphasize the sense in which he went beyond Boas, who merely stated that native speakers learn another language in terms of sound categories already familiar from a native language, resulting in what are perceived as "mistakes" or accents. Sapir showed that perception of sounds is structured within a single language, such that the phonemic inventory of a given language will manifest internal consistency. This insight opens the door to a whole new way of organizing grammars and comparing languages. It is a new level of structure that leaves Boas's argument (and his linguistics) far behind. The founding of the Linguistic Society of America (LSA) intensified the widening dichotomy, giving Sapir an outlet for his identity as a professional linguist independently of anthropology. In addition to Boasian anthropologists, the LSA membership included classical philologists unaccustomed to working with unwritten languages. Bloomfield was prominent among the Germanists for his Indo-European work; his Americanist forays, including firsthand fieldwork, were of minimal relevance to them. Boas's role in the LSA was honorary rather than constitutive.

The concept of the phoneme is an outgrowth of the period in which Sapir broadened the base of his thinking. He had long been concerned with the use of appropriate linguistic categories for the language studied and argued that culture could best be understood in terms of the language (e.g., to Wallis, June 10, 1913: NMM): "I have always been struck by a certain externality about all such studies that were not based on linguistic knowledge. I always have an uneasy feeling that misunderstandings bristle in such writings." In good Boasian fashion, Sapir insisted that languages should be described in terms of their own categories, rather than those of Latin or Greek. He wrote to Father Morice about his practical Carrier grammar (January 21, 1918: NMM): "As far as I myself am concerned, I find any arrangement of linguistic material that proceeds from the standpoint of the reader's language irksome. As a scientific student of language I am always primarily interested in the native viewpoint." The Boasian argument, however, was formulated in terms of grammatical structures, *not* sound patterns. "Sound Patterns" begins with precisely this question:

> There used to be and to some extent still is a feeling among linguists that the psychology of a language is more particularly concerned with its grammatical features, but that its sounds and its phonetic processes belong to a grosser physiological substratum. . . . The sounds and sound processes of speech cannot be properly understood in such simple mechanistic terms. (Sapir 1925a in 1949:33)

Sapir goes on to discuss the "intuitive placing" of sounds relative to one another, suggesting that phonetic processes make sense only in pattern terms. The idea of psychological integration of language, as of genuine culture, brings into linguistic theory arguments that Sapir raised initially out of his explorations of psychology and aesthetics. Nonetheless, he remained primarily a linguist and frequently brought linguistic models and analogies to anthropology, particularly early in his career; in this case Sapir, however, borrowed from culture and psychology into linguistics. In 1925 he made the argument for the phoneme in abstract terms, using examples familiar to linguists. In 1933 he referred to the "psychological reality of the phoneme" and focused on the linguistic intuitions of his Southern Paiute and Nootka consultants to show the nonmechanistic perception of sound pattern. This formulation is most characteristic of what Sapir meant by phonemics.

Sapir's work with Tony Tillohash and Alex Thomas preceded his analysis of their patterns of hearing their native languages by a substantial period. Only in the context of his increasing focus on the individual in culture and on the aesthetic integration of culture did his recognition of the important consequences for linguistic theory cause him to reevaluate the intuitions of the individual "informants" with whom he had worked. Sapir preferred to work with "informants" who had a substantial degree of insight into their native languages. Ishi, with whom Sapir found it excruciatingly painful to work, did not have this ability. Whatever his intuitive practice, however, Sapir had to look at these experiences with language speakers in a new way before he could conclude that they belonged in a grammar. In 1933 Sapir specifically acknowledged that his claim for the phonemic level of structure arose from his field experience: "In the course of many years of experience in the recording and analysis of unwritten languages, American Indian [*sic*] and African, I have come to the practical realization that what the native speaker hears is not phonetic elements but phonemes" (Sapir 1933 in 1949:47). This idea was not new to Sapir in 1925; in *Language* (1921a:174) he had referred to "that unconscious sound patterning which is ever on the point of becoming conscious." The innovation in 1925 was his formal statement of the internal consistency of sound patterning of which speakers were unaware.

Retrospect

This chapter argues that the decade from 1915 to 1925 produced an amalgam of models and methods from a range of sources and turned Edward Sapir from a competent Boasian anthropologist into an interdisciplinary theoretician. The experiences of his personal life led him to a serious questioning of his profession, culminating in a focus on aesthetics and psychology that fed back into his linguistics and set the stage for his later work on culture and personality. The seeds were all present by the time he left Ottawa in 1925. This combination of interests and their interconnection in the study of particular problems make Edward Sapir unique in the histories of both anthropology and linguistics.

Discussion

Michael Silverstein: A chronological comment. I was delighted to find in reading the Sapir-Kroeber letters that in early 1916 Sapir formulated the paper "Psychological Reality of Phonemes" with the Tony Tillohash example about the fact that Ute speakers and Paiute speakers are going to hear not the sounds, but the inner sounds, and write them as well. And he goes through the entire analysis that then appears in formal terms in the paper so many years later (see Golla 1984:220–22 [Sapir to Kroeber, September 8, 1916: ALK]). And Kroeber writes back, totally misunderstanding everything and says, in effect, "Yes, it is difficult to train people in subtle phonetic differences."

Regna Darnell: I guess the time wasn't right for the phoneme yet. I did not cite either the Kroeber or the Lowie correspondence particularly here because they are fairly easily available. Bruce Nevin (personal communication) reported from his work on Sapir's Yana texts that Sapir's initial phonetic recordings in the field quickly became implicitly phonemic as he began to see patterns in the language and no longer needed to record the phonetic detail. But this was not yet formulated in theoretical terms.

Notes

1. Originally published as "The Emergence of Edward Sapir's Mature Thought," in *New Perspectives in Language, Culture and Personality,* ed. William Cowan, Michael K. Foster, and Konrad Koerner, 553–88 (Amsterdam: John Benjamins, 1986).

2. Letters addressed to Sapir at the museum were automatically cataloged in the files there. His replies to personal as opposed to purely professional letters were not retained. Many of these, however, are preserved in the papers of his correspondents, sometimes in duplicate copies by both sender and recipient.

3. Interestingly, Lowie omitted this characterization of colleagues in his 1965 private publication of Sapir's letters to him. The full text remains in the Lowie papers at Berkeley. A documentary editing of the various versions is forthcoming from Piero Matthey.

References

Boas, Franz. 1889. "On Alternating Sounds." *American Anthropologist* 2:47–53.
———. 1911a. Introduction to *Handbook of American Indian Languages. Bureau of American Ethnology Bulletin* 40. Washington DC: Government Printing Office.
———. 1911b. *The Mind of Primitive Man.* New York: Macmillan.
Darnell, Regna. 1969. "The Development of American Anthropology, 1880–1929: From the Bureau of American Ethnology to Franz Boas." PhD diss., University of Pennsylvania.
———. 1971. "The Professionalization of American Anthropology." *Social Science Information* 10:83–103.

Goldenweiser, Alexander. 1922. *Early Civilization: An Introduction to Anthropology*. New York: Knopf.

Golla, Victor. 1984. "The Sapir-Kroeber Correspondence." *Survey of California and Other Indian Languages* 6:183–88.

Kroeber, Alfred L. 1923. *Anthropology*. New York: Harcourt, Brace.

Kroeber, Alfred L., and Thomas T. Waterman, eds.1920. *Sourcebook in Anthropology. University of California Syllabus Series* 118. Berkeley: University of California Press.

Kuhn, Thomas S. 1962. *The Structure of Scientific Revolutions*. Chicago: University of Chicago Press.

Lowie, Robert H. 1917. *Culture and Ethnology*. New York: Liveright.

———. 1920. *Primitive Society*. New York: Boni and Liveright.

———. 1965. *Letters from Edward Sapir to Robert H. Lowie; with an Introduction and Notes by Robert H. Lowie*. Berkeley: privately printed.

Radin, Paul. 1919. "The Genetic Relationship of the North American Indian Languages." *University of California Publications in American Archaeology and Ethnology* 14:489–502.

Sapir, Edward. (1916) 1949. "Time Perspective in Aboriginal American Culture: A Study in Method." *Anthropological Series 13, Memoirs of the Canadian Geological Survey* 90. Ottawa. Reprinted in Sapir 1949:389–462.

———. 1917a. "Do We Need a 'Superorganic'?" *American Anthropologist* 19:441–47.

———. 1917b. *Dreams and Gibes*. Boston: Poet Lore.

———. 1921a. *Language: An Introduction to the Study of Speech*. New York: Harcourt, Brace.

———. 1921b. "A Bird's-Eye View of American Languages North of Mexico." *Science* 54:408.

———. (1924) 1949. "Culture, Genuine and Spurious." *American Journal of Sociology* 29:401–29. Reprinted in Sapir 1949:308–31.

———. (1925a). 1949. "Sound Patterns in Language." *Language* 1:37–51. Reprinted in Sapir 1949:33–45.

———. 1925b. "The Similarity of Chinese and Indian Languages." *Science* 62:112.

———. (1929) 1949. "Central and North American Languages." *Encyclopedia Britannica* 5:138–41. Reprinted in Sapir 1949:169–78.

———. (1933) 1949. "La realité psychologique des phonèmes." *Journal de Psychologie Normale et Pathologique* 30:247–65. Reprinted English translation as "The Psychological Reality of Phonemes" in Sapir 1949:46–60.

———. 1949. *Selected Writings of Edward Sapir in Language, Culture and Personality*. Edited by David G. Mandelbaum, 46–60. Berkeley: University of California Press.

Wissler, Clark. 1917. *The American Indian*. New York: Douglas McMurtrie.

———. 1923. *Man and Culture*. New York: Thomas Crowell.

10

Indo-European Methodology, Bloomfield's Central Algonquian, and Sapir's Distant Genetic Relationships

Introduction

This paper attempts to pin down the precise nature of Konrad Koerner's considerable influence on my longstanding engagement with the intersecting histories of linguistics and anthropology, particularly in North America.[1] Konrad and I have spoken of these matters intermittently since the early 1970s. We collaborated in various contexts around the Edward Sapir centennial celebrations of 1984. More recently, through the North American Association for the History of the Language Sciences (NAAHOLS) and the various publications he edits so elegantly for John Benjamins, Konrad has challenged me to formulate historiographic problems in Americanist anthropology to address the concerns of linguists who are not Americanists as well as of my anthropological and linguistic colleagues who are.

As a graduate student at the University of Pennsylvania in the late 1960s, I audited historical linguistics with Henry Hoenigswald. Henry welcomed me to his seminar but apologized in advance that he knew very little about Native American comparative linguistics and would not often be able to cite examples relevant to my work. He mused for a moment and added that the genetic relationships involved in American Indian [*sic*] historical work were either so distant that the mere fact of relationship was all that could be ascertained or so shallow in time depth that the details were almost trivially obvious. What interested him was the middle ground, so characteristic of Indo-European, in which the fact of relationship could be taken for granted and the detailed history reconstructed and confirmed by independent documentary evidence.

He did not imply that absence of written records would invalidate the comparative method. Nor, however, did he have any personal reason to explore alternative sources of evidence from firsthand fieldwork on contemporary Indigenous languages.

The seminar was about the emergence of Indo-European methodology and the results it produced. It emphasized the phonemics of Indo-European classification, with implications for the social causes of accumulated phonetic variations within segments of a population until a threshold was reached in which the mainstream pattern flipped to a qualitatively different form. I found this methodological insight more useful than the promised occasional Native American example that turned out to be a single case, Leonard Bloomfield's Central Algonquian. I later learned that this was the sole exemplar for most non-Americanist linguists that Indo-European comparative method could be applied successfully to the study of unwritten languages. Such languages are now more appropriately referred to as "exotic" than as "primitive"; both terms, however, entail inferiority and induce a dramatic alterity for those to whom they are applied.

I am left with unanswered historiographic questions: What happened to eclipse linguists' memory of the equally rigorous phonetic laws proposed by Sapir for Athabaskan, Uto-Aztekan, and Ritwan? Why did Sapir and Bloomfield need to argue explicitly that methods derived from the study of Indo-European were applicable to Indigenous languages in North America, a claim which in retrospect seems to involve flogging a long-dead horse? How was this claim related to the increasing professional autonomy of North American linguistics after the founding of the LSA and its journal *Language* in 1925? What did all this have to do with the place of linguistics in Boasian anthropology in the early twentieth century?

Alternative Interpretations of the Role of Indo-European in American Indian [*sic*] Linguistics

While musing over these matters, I consulted Lyle Campbell's then recent definitive review of the history of American Indian [*sic*] linguistics (1997). Campbell explicitly aspires to set to rest what he considers misconceptions in both the historiography and the contemporary practice of American Indian [*sic*] linguistics. He fore-grounds the continuous and longstanding mutual influences of Indo-European and Americanist linguistics and asserts that "the historical linguistic study of Native American languages was usually up to date with the linguistic methods and theories of the day and not infrequently contributed to them" (1997:4). Campbell's extensive documentation is persuasive; indeed, much of it relies on my own work over the past three decades. My assertion in 1971 (quoted by Campbell 1997:378fn) that Indo-European techniques were not applied to American Indian [*sic*] languages because they were unwritten, that there were no European-trained linguists to make such applications, and that Americanist linguistics depended on observation of lexical similarities is certainly an overstatement. I plead only that my remarks were in the context of discussing the 1891 linguistic classification of John Wesley Powell for the BAE (Darnell 1971a), not Native American linguistics as a whole. Even so, my reading arises from a quite literal reading of the words of various late nineteenth- and early twentieth-century participants about the uniqueness of American developments. Powell, for example, was either unaware of or unwilling to acknowledge the roots of his linguistic practices in European comparative method.

At this point the differences between my standpoint and Campbell's cause us to emphasize different sides of the same coin. I am not suggesting that I am correct and Campbell is wrong. Rather, I am intrigued by the multiple interpretive possibilities opened up when scholars approach the same historical events and personalities from different angles. The resulting picture is more complex than either of us would see by working in isolation. Indeed, given that disciplinary history is usually a fairly solitary enterprise, we are fortunate that there is now sufficient literature in the history of Amerindian [*sic*] linguistics to support such interpretive debates.

(1) Campbell is a linguist; I am an anthropologist. He depicts a discipline of linguistics located in North America but autonomous from the study of American Indian [*sic*] languages, "not merely a Johnny-come-lately stepchild of American anthropology, but rather [with] an independent history of its own" (1997:28). This dual disciplinary affiliation plays through the professionalization of American anthropology and linguistics. The dichotomy is

recapitulated in the relatively strong retrospective identification of Leonard Bloomfield with linguistics and of Edward Sapir with anthropology, resulting, at least for some linguists, in the virtual eclipse of much of Sapir's comparativist work.

(2) Campbell is interested in relating the search for linguistic family relationships and sound changes to the international history of comparative linguistics. This leads him to focus on pre-professional work by such American scholars as John Pickering, Peter Stephen Du Ponceau, Albert Gallatin, and Thomas Jefferson, who were undeniably in touch with their European counterparts. Even earlier, Roger Williams and Jonathan Edwards identified the Algonquian linguistic family and proposed what we would now recognize as sound correspondences. I have focused on the professionalization of anthropology (which in North America includes linguistics) and with continuities across the paradigm shift from the BAE to Boasian anthropology between 1879 and about 1920 (Darnell 1998) whereas Campbell emphasizes the earlier continuity between Powell and his predecessors, particularly Albert Gallatin.

(3) Campbell strongly supports a conservative linguistic classification, correctly noting that Campbell and Mithun (1979) still represented at that time the conservative consensus in American Indian [sic] linguistics, confirmed by its use two decades later in the languages volume of the *Handbook of North American Indians* (Goddard 1997). Campbell is at pains to counter the challenge to this conservative classification by Joseph Greenberg's *Language in the Americas* (1987). In the process he seems to equate pitfalls inherent in the alternatives of Powell's fifty-eight units in 1891 and Sapir's six in 1921 with those separating Campbell and Mithun's sixty-two linguistic families in 1979 and Greenberg's three super-stocks in 1987. This seems to me to paint with rather too broad strokes of the historiographic brush. Interestingly enough, the seeds of alternative interpretation are present in Campbell's analysis. It is a question of emphasis.

Limitations of the Powell Classification

Campbell's interest in the Indo-European linkages of early Americanist work leads him, in my view, to overestimate the linguistic sophistication of the Powell classification. He attributes the drive to achieve a comprehensive linguistic classification of the continent to the Indo-European strain of the tradition Powell inherited, asserting, for example, that it is shared with Thomas Jefferson.

> The methods employed in research on the classification of native languages in the Americas, not surprisingly, were the same as those employed in Europe and elsewhere to establish family relationships and to work out their linguistic history. . . . American Indian [*sic*] linguistic studies were consistently in tune with developments in European linguistics and Indo-European studies, and frequently contributed significantly to methodological and theoretical linguistic discussions in Europe as well as in America. . . . The enormous linguistic diversity in the Americas aroused a desire for classification, to bring the vast number of distinct languages into manageable genetic categories. (1997:28)

Campbell (1997:43–44) quotes Gallatin's 1836 definition of a linguistic family as having "at some remote epoch . . . a common origin . . . in the same way" as various Indo-European languages. Gallatin, like the linguists on the bureau staff, J. Owen Dorsey and Albert Gatschet, was indeed attuned to Indo-European developments. In spite of their Indo-European training, both Dorsey and Gatschet were conservative with regard to genetic relationship, perhaps precisely because the evidence for unwritten languages seemed to them less conclusive in the absence of the written records that could usually be taken for granted in Indo-European. Their work did not, therefore, lead directly to the desired comprehensive classification.

Powell, who needed a classification for ethnological purposes and the applied work on the bureau mandated by Congress, enthusiastically compared Gallatin's work to that of Carl Linnaeus in biology. Citing Kroeber (1953), Campbell reports (1997:60) that Powell actually favored biological rather than philological training for anthropology. Because his linguists refused to commit themselves on classificatory matters, Powell assigned a taxonomic biologist, Henry Henshaw, to transform his extensive vocabulary lists, culled from Smithsonian Institution manuscripts and collected through fieldwork by bureau staff, into a systematic classification.

There has been considerable retrospective debate over the authorship of the Powell classification. It appeared under Powell's name; the fieldwork was done by various bureau staff, particularly Dorsey and Gatschet; Henshaw was the primary synthesizer. Campbell (1997:58) acknowledges that Powell's method was "not very refined," being "a rather impressionistic inspection of rough word lists and vocabularies." He cites William Sturtevant's observation in 1959 that the hard part was getting the vocabularies. In Powell's view, anyone could look at them and arrive at the correct genetic classification. In this light it is difficult to interpret Powell's methodology for the 1891 classification as derived from Indo-European.

Campbell's fascinating discussion of Powell's increasing doubts about his ability to distinguish between areal and genetic causes of linguistic similarity (1997:55, 59) further discredits the philological or comparative character of his reasoning about language classification. Sound correspondences were not part of his linguistic model. Powell's linguistic stocks were intended to establish the fact of relationship within his postulated units. He did not attempt subclassification and apparently thought that the fifty-eight units of the 1891 classification were "equally dissimilar" (Campbell 1997:62, quoting Darnell 1988). That they range from far-flung linguistic families such as Algonquian or Athabaskan to linguistic isolates such as Zuni, Beothuk, or Kootenay was insignificant in Powell's understanding of linguistic classification.

Campbell further notes that Powell sided with Otis T. Mason of the U.S. National Museum against Franz Boas in 1907 about arranging museum exhibits according to evolutionary typology rather than by cultural units. Boas sought particular tribal histories, while Mason preferred to formulate universals reflecting the broad evolutionary development of "civilization." Again, Powell's concerns are ethnological rather than linguistic per se. He wants to make sense out of the cultural and linguistic diversity of the continent and seizes upon linguistic classification as the most expedient means to this end.

Linguistics as Handmaiden to Boasian Ethnology

Franz Boas, whose early linguistic work was supported by the Bureau of American Ethnology, came to share Powell's disquiet about his ability to distinguish borrowing from prior genetic relationship among distantly related languages. Unlike Powell, however, Boas acted upon his disquiets, repudiating earlier genetic proposals resulting from his Northwest Coast fieldwork and protesting the more confident reconstructive work of his students, particularly Indo-European–trained Edward Sapir (Boas 1920).

Boasian anthropology implicitly laid claim to an Americanist linguistic tradition indigenous to the continent. Although many first generation Boasians were of recent European origin, they challenged an anthropological establishment longer settled on American soil and proud of New World achievements they claimed as their own. Campbell (1997:28) cites "Kroeber's view that Indo-Europeanist methods were too philosophical-typological, too concerned with 'inner form' . . . whereas the Americanists' methods reflected the practical ethnological expediency of classifying native [*sic*] groups." Kroeber (1913) was not inclined to accept that Indo-European methods could solve the problems of North American linguistic classification. Fieldwork and visual inspection were sufficient for practical classification, in Kroeber's case of the linguistic and cultural diversity of the state of California.

Indeed, Kroeber's own classificatory ventures, in collaboration with Roland B. Dixon of Harvard, began with the assumption that they were observing lexical similarities resulting from borrowing; they moved only gradually to a genetic interpretation *of the same data*. Although Campbell (1997:67) attributes to me (Darnell 1971a, 1971b) the argument that they proceeded "only with reluctance," I think we must also recognize the possibility of dissimulation. This is certainly what Kroeber said. But his motivation, in addition to his lack of philological training to properly assess Sapir's proposals, included disinclination to confront directly Boas's classificatory conservatism. Kroeber emphasized the increasing impossibility of any explanation other than prior genetic relationship for the postulated Hokan and Penutian stocks. Sapir's work between 1903 and 1913, the period of Kroeber's interpretive shift, buttressed the claims of the comparative method to elucidate American Indian [*sic*] linguistic data and perhaps enhanced Kroeber's willingness to challenge Boas's conservatism on historical matters.

Despite his acknowledgment of the influence of Hermann Steinthal during his German university years, Boas was a self-taught linguist, who learned to describe Eskimo (now called Inuktitut) during his Baffin Island fieldwork in the early 1880s. His immersion-based pedagogy confirmed for his students that the linguistics necessary for an anthropologist could be learned by trial and error. Students took Boas's seminar analyzing his own fieldwork texts from various languages until they understood what was going on (e.g., Lowie 1959). Many of them, who did not aspire to become linguists, actually produced dissertations consisting of a grammar, dictionary, and texts of various languages that Boas felt in need of immediate salvage. The urgent commitment to record disappearing languages mitigated against extensive training in comparative Indo-European. Sapir, the exception among those trained directly by Boas, came to Boasian anthropology *after* his Indo-European training. Pliny Earle Goddard of the bureau received his Indo-European training from Benjamin Ide Wheeler at the University of California, and John Peabody Harrington studied philology in Europe. The rest were amateurs in linguistics as it was understood outside of anthropology.

Boas became disenchanted with Indo-European because of its evolutionary undertones. Around the turn of the century, his major theoretical project was the critique of evolution. Whereas Campbell (1997:48) deemphasizes the evolutionary ethnocentrism of Du Ponceau, William Dwight Whitney, Daniel Brinton, and, indeed, Powell himself (and is undoubtedly correct to do so from a contemporary point of view), I would note that, for Boas at the time, anything smacking of evolution was apt to be dismissed summarily.

Campbell argues persuasively that the comparativist work during this period of "reductionist frenzy" (1997:72) centered not on the kind of evidence cited but on the amount of evidence that would warrant conclusive proof of genetic relationship. He suggests that the debate over areal and genetic causes of similarity has resulted in the incorporation of areal perspectives "now so prominent in most reliable work on proposals of remoter relationship" (1997:72).

This incorporation seems to me a peculiarly Americanist methodological tendency, resulting precisely from the application of Indo-European method in the absence of independent confirmation from written records. The methodology was formulated elegantly by Sapir in *Time Perspective in Aboriginal American Culture: A Study in Method* (1916). This is perhaps the most extreme example in Boasian anthropology of linguistics serving as handmaiden to ethnology, and it came from the lone Boasian trained as an Indo-Europeanist. Sapir argued to his colleagues in ethnology that linguistic method could reliably distinguish genetic from areal relationship because sound changes were by definition characteristic only of the former. The rest of culture was patterned in a way that failed to preserve historical development in contemporary forms that were distinguishable as resulting from common origin or borrowing.

Campbell does not emphasize Sapir's reliance on Indo-European methods in this context, presumably because it led Sapir to what he considers unjustified genetic hypotheses based on overzealous application. Campbell cites Kroeber's assertion (1940) that Sapir's six-unit classification of 1921 was not scientific (i.e., systematic) in its method (quoted by Campbell 1997:75):

> From one point of view such a procedure is nothing less than forecasting. . . . . It is in no sense whatever a definable or controllable method of science or scholarship. The danger . . . is that its prophecies may be mistaken especially by non-linguists for proved or probable findings. Tremendous havoc can be worked when archaeologists or ethnologists begin to built [*sic* in Campbell] structures of inference on Sapir's brilliant but flimsy gossamer web of prophecies as if it were a solid foundation.

There is no discussion of Kroeber's turn away from linguistic classification in the intervening years of his career. Campbell continues to rely on Kroeber's retrospective repudiation decades later of his own complicity in Sapir's drastic reduction of the number of linguistic stocks in North America. He concludes (1997:76): "Later, it came to be assumed that this classification [Sapir's six units] had been established by legitimate linguistic methods, and thus it became entrenched in the literature."

After further detractions from the conclusions of the six-unit classification, Campbell (1997:76) implies that Sapir, later in his life, implicitly recanted by citing [in an article not devoted to his applications of the comparative method] large numbers of unrelated linguistic stocks in North America. Sapir indeed turned away from dramatic reduction of the number of linguistic families in the continent after presenting his own classification. He had, after all, had his say. Americanist linguistics, partly as a result of his classificatory work, was less obsessed with classification after the 1920s. I am uncomfortable, however, with the conclusion that Sapir changed his mind about the ability of genetic relationship to persist identifiably at great time depth and about the utility of postulating distant relationships even without complete or fully convincing evidence. Still in the six-unit classification, Sapir allowed for an intermediate level acceptable to the more conservative among his contemporaries. There was room for further research to clarify the proposed more distant relationships.

When Campbell turns to Bloomfield (1925, 1928, 1946) to demonstrate that sound change is regular in unwritten or exotic languages (1997:77), it is difficult to escape the conclusion that he considers Sapir's application of Indo-European method to both demonstrable and merely suggestive cases of putative linguistic relationship to have tainted all of his comparativist work. This conclusion seems to me perverse. I am not prepared to dismiss the legitimacy of Sapir's linguistic methods in a cavalier fashion.

How Bloomfield Came to Provide the Exemplar

In 1931 Sapir was invited to write about methods of linguistics for a case book in the social sciences, representing the successes of the interdisciplinary synthesis that crystallized around the Chicago School of Sociology in the 1920s. With a rare display of modesty undoubtedly motivated by his intent to persuade his readers that he presented consensus rather than a personal synthesis, Sapir made his point about the special properties of the comparative method for studying American Indian [*sic*] languages with reference to the work of Bloomfield rather than his own. Sapir stressed ([1931] 1949:73) that Bloomfield's contribution was to have "tested" the Indo-European–derived "concept of phonetic law" in relation to what were then called "primitive" languages. Such phonetic laws were, in Sapir's view, foundational to "the scientific study of language."

Sapir's initial illustrations of regular sound change were conventional Indo-European ones. But he went on to assert that evidence was rapidly accumulating, presumably through Boasian fieldwork, that the same methods could be applied to any languages: "If these laws are more difficult to discover in [so-called] primitive languages, this is not due to any special characteristic which these languages possess but merely to the inadequate technique of some who have tried to study them" (Sapir [1931] 1949:74). He was explicit in claiming that the methodology of Bloomfield's Proto-Central Algonquian reconstruction "is precisely the same as the methodology which is used in Indo-European linguistics" (75). Sapir also implied that many of his colleagues, with or without training in Indo-European, lacked the historical imagination to trust sound changes as reliable evidence for distant relationships among American linguistic families (cf. Darnell 1990). Yet his reliance on Bloomfield to make the case about the regularity of sound change, in general and in American language families in particular, suggests that he may have found it politic in the immediate context to associate this work with narrowly comparative reconstruction rather than with his own more speculative proposals over the previous two decades.

Sapir illustrates five phonetic laws from Bloomfield (1925), particularly praising a sixth law based on a single set of correspondences, noting that later information from his own fieldwork on Swampy Cree confirmed the analysis, as well as the predictive capacity of the comparative method (Bloomfield 1928). Only after considerable discussion of Bloomfield's work on Central Algonquian did Sapir turn to his own work ([1931] 1949:78): "Bloomfield's experience with the Central Algonquian dialects is entirely parallel to my own with the Athabaskan languages."

Sapir chose his historical problems differently than did Bloomfield. Central Algonquian was a tidy geographically contiguous unit, wherein genetic relationship had long been recognized. Sapir, in contrast, was fascinated with Athabaskan partly because of its irregular distribution across North America. Ritwan (Wiyot and Yurok) intrigued him because its distant relationship to Algonquian was geographically anomalous; these languages were spoken in California, far from the Algonquian center of gravity, and had been treated as linguistic isolates. Uto-Aztekan was puzzling because of the range of cultural development separating Nahuatl, the language of the Aztec civilization, from the "root-digging savages" of the southwestern desert.

Sapir's comparative Athabaskan sound patterns were presented in terms of three "representative" languages: Navajo, Chippewyan, and Hupa. He emphasized "pattern" (that is, phonemic contrast) rather than particular sounds. His form of presentation is fully parallel to that used for Bloomfield's Central Algonquian. We may infer that Sapir intended to stake a claim for his own comparative work to the same rigorous application of the Indo-European method practiced by Bloomfield. He realized that his six-unit classification would be misunderstood (in his view) by many of his more narrowly focused linguistic colleagues in both disciplines and chose in this paper to go on the offensive.

Sapir was not the only Americanist linguist to acknowledge the exemplary status of the Central Algonquian reconstruction. Charles Hockett (1948:599) saw "the descriptive and comparative structure of Algonquian" as "one of Leonard Bloomfield's life works." Nonetheless, those linguists who praised it usually did so on "indirect evidence" derived from Bloomfield's stature as a Germanicist: "since Bloomfield's other work proves him a sound scholar, his Algonquian studies must be sound too. Algonquian, after all, is an out-of-the-way language family, and few have concerned themselves with it." Hockett presents sixteen principles of the comparative method illustrated in Bloomfield's Algonquian work, optimistically concluding (1948:609):

> Yet if, for any one of the sixteen, Bloomfield's Algonquian evidence stood alone—if there were no comparative Germanic, comparative Romance, comparative Indo-European, comparative Semitic, and so on—that isolated support for the principle would still be persuasively solid.

Hockett does not directly address the implicit ethnocentrism of European linguistics, particularly its assumption that the important languages of the world are those with written traditions. Regardless of the quality of Bloomfield's reconstructions, for many non-Americanist linguists they could not, in principle, hold the paradigmatic potential of the classic Indo-European cases from which the comparative method was derived. During the interwar years, even in North America, Americanist linguists still had to defend the importance of work on unwritten languages and the validity of their applications of Indo-European methods to them. Otherwise, Sapir, Bloomfield, and Hockett could have spent less time making their case.

This was particularly crucial with the professionalization of linguistics in North America, since Americanist linguists found themselves engaged with colleagues whose priorities were quite different and whose attention to Native American languages was perfunctory at best. It is unclear how many of Sapir's colleagues agreed with him in this period that "when it comes to linguistic form, Plato walks with the Macedonian swineherd, Confucius with the head-hunting savage of Assam" (1921:234).

Hockett himself stressed in retrospect that the methods of the anthropological linguists [i.e., fieldwork] were unfamiliar to the philologists and comparativists. The Americanists could not draw on "inherited bodies of texts" as Bloomfield had been trained to do in Germanics. Rather, "he transferred the [Indo-European] method bodily—as also, indeed, did Boas, Sapir and every other investigator of such languages . . . since there were no texts, they had to be gathered by writing down accounts from the lips of native speakers" (1989:5). Then and only then could the anthropological linguist proceed philologically, using the comparative method.

Hockett (1989:4) continues to assert that Bloomfield's Central Algonquian, with "reconstructions . . . as full, realistic and convincing as any in Indo-European," demonstrates the absolute universality of neogrammarian regular sound change. Hockett argues that a single counterexample would render the entire comparative method a "mistake." This sense of testing the comparative method against data from widespread and historically independent linguistic families does not seem to me to have characterized linguistics overall, in Europe or North America at any time. Although the equivalence in principle of all human languages can no longer be denied, the last four decades demonstrate that not all linguists turn in practice to the study of the widest possible sample of such languages.

A fundamental discontinuity separates American linguistics and European. Hymes and Fought (1975:917) cite "the inhospitability to European theory" of various American structuralist linguists, in part because European refugees were getting jobs during the Depression while American linguists remained unemployed. Postwar linguistics was even more isolationist and self-consciously American. Hymes and Fought conclude that European models are unnecessary to account for the grammatical and comparative work of Sapir and Boas. What they find particularly fascinating is that

> in the United States . . . the scholars who participated in the founding of structural description participated also in the founding of the comparative historical linguistics of a great many language families. Comparative philology was effectively introduced to these families by structuralists—Bloomfield in Algonquian, Sapir in Uto-Aztecan, Athabaskan, etc. (1975:952)

The Americanist emphasis on grammatical categories is not present in the European tradition of the same period. The synthesis of synchronic and diachronic analysis arose in good part from the local exigencies of Amerindian [*sic*] fieldwork. In this Americanist tradition, Indo-European was only one of the methods employed.

Conclusion

In spite of a long history of comparative linguistics of American Indian [*sic*] language families, both Leonard Bloomfield and Edward Sapir considered it necessary to argue in the 1920s and 1930s that Indo-European methods could be applied reliably to the study of unwritten languages; furthermore, this application was taken to demonstrate the universality of the method itself. In the view of its most prestigious practitioners, American Indian [*sic*] linguistics had much to contribute to general linguistics. Both Sapir and Bloomfield were adamant that the autonomous American discipline of linguistics must apply itself to the study of all languages.

Hymes and Fought define a "first Yale school" of linguistics that emerged around Sapir in the 1930s, a decade before the widely acknowledged Yale school associated with Bloomfield thereafter. The principles of Sapir's linguistics (1975:997) begin with the application of structuralist methods "to both exotic and well-known languages." The professionalization of linguistics and the rescue of what we now call endangered languages are the next foundation points. These three principles do not distinguish Sapir from Bloomfield. Sapir and Bloomfield shared a concern with genetic relationship of linguistic families, although they had somewhat different notions of how this should be approached. Both also wanted to tie linguistics to other disciplines and to practical applications, in education for example; again, however, their approaches were quite different in practice.

The substantial overlap in goals demonstrates that Sapir and Bloomfield deployed the methods of Indo-European to similar ends and with similar rigor. Sapir's Athabaskan, Uto-Aztekan, and perhaps Ritwan have stood the test of time, alongside Bloomfield's Algonquian, despite the failure of Sapir's work to attain the same paradigmatic status for general linguistics. The major difference between the two efforts appears to be that Sapir also attempted more speculative reconstructions, which have been embraced by ethnologists and archaeologists but usually rejected or reformulated by linguists, especially those outside anthropology.

On Ritwan, for example, Ives Goddard (1986) argues that Sapir was correct in linking California Wiyot and Yurok to Algonquian, although sometimes for the wrong reasons. Goddard would have been happier with fewer correspondences, each unassailable. Sapir, however, chose to list all possible evidence, realizing that some uncertain cognates might yield to further study by other researchers who would correct and expand upon his work. He did not share the neogrammarian assumption that a single apparent counterexample would disprove a postulated genetic relationship. Specific historical circumstances might apply to change observed in process at a particular point in time; "all grammars leak."

The continuity of Indo-European influences on the study of American Indian [*sic*] languages as accessible to contemporary historiography, however, must be distinguished from the perceptions of actors at any given moment of that history. Neither Sapir nor Bloomfield evidenced extensive knowledge of prior work (extensively discussed by Campbell 1997), which in retrospect seems foundational. The Boasian/Americanist emphasis on fieldwork may have foreshortened this history of the application of Indo-European methodology to the study of American Indian [*sic*] languages.

Notes

1. Originally published as "Indo-European Methodology, Bloomfield's Central Algonquian and Sapir's Distant Genetic Relationships," in *The Emergence of the Modern Language Sciences: Studies on the Transition from Historical-Comparative to Structural Linguistics in Honour of E. F. K. Koerner*, ed. Sheila Embleton, John Joseph, and Hans-Josef Niederehe, 3–16. Vol. 2, *Methodological Perspectives and Applications* (Amsterdam: John Benjamins, 1999).

References

Bloomfield, Leonard. 1925. "On the Sound-System of Central Algonquian." *Language* 1:130–56.

———. 1928. "A Note on Sound Change." *Language* 5:99–100.

———. 1946. "Algonquian." In *Linguistic Structures of Native America*, edited by Harry Hoijer, 85–129. New York: Viking Fund.

Boas, Franz. 1920. "The Classification of American Languages." *American Anthropologist* 22:367–76.

Campbell, Lyle. 1997. *American Indian Languages: The Historical Linguistics of Native America.* Oxford: Oxford University Press.

Campbell, Lyle, and Marianne Mithun, eds. 1979. *The Languages of Native America: Historical and Comparative Assessment.* Austin: University of Texas Press.

Darnell, Regna. 1971a. "The Powell Classification of American Indian Languages." *Papers in Linguistics* 4:71–110.

———. 1971b. "The Revision of the Powell Classification." *Papers in Linguistics* 4:233–57.

———. 1988. *Daniel Garrison Brinton: The "Fearless Critic" of Philadelphia.* Publications in Anthropology no. 3. Philadelphia: University of Pennsylvania.

———. 1990. *Edward Sapir: Linguist, Anthropologist, Humanist.* Berkeley: University of California Press.

———. 1998. *And Along Came Boas: Continuity and Revolution in Americanist Anthropology.* Amsterdam: John Benjamins.

Goddard, Ives. 1986. "Sapir's Comparative Method." In *New Perspectives in Language, Culture and Personality*, edited by William Cowan, Michael Foster, and Konrad Koerner, 191–214. Amsterdam: John Benjamins.

———, ed. 1997. *Handbook of North American Indians.* Vol. 17, *Languages.* Washington DC: Smithsonian Institution.

Greenberg, Joseph. 1987. *Language in the Americas.* Stanford: Stanford University Press.

Hockett, Charles F. 1948. "Implications of Bloomfield's Algonquian Studies." *Language* 24:117–31.

———. 1989. "Leonard Bloomfield: After Fifty Years." *Yale Graduate Journal of Anthropology* 2:1–11.

Hymes, Dell, and John Fought. 1975. "American Structuralism." In *Current Trends in Linguistics 10: Historiography of Linguistics*, edited by Thomas A. Sebeok, 903–1174. The Hague: Mouton.

Kroeber, Alfred. 1913. "The Determination of Linguistic Relationship." *Anthropos* 8:389–401.

———. 1940. "Conclusions: The Present Status of Americanist Problems." In *The Maya and Their Neighbors*, edited by Clarence L. Hay et al., 460–87. New York: D. Appleton-Century.

———. 1953. "Concluding Review." In *An Appraisal of Anthropology Today*, edited by Sol Tax, 357–76. Chicago: University of Chicago Press.

Lowie, Robert H. 1959. *Robert H. Lowie, Ethnologist.* Berkeley: University of California Press.

Powell, John Wesley. 1891. *Indian Linguistic Families of America, North of Mexico: Seventh Annual Report of the Bureau of Ethnology.* Washington DC: Government Printing Office.

Sapir, Edward. 1916. *Time Perspective in Aboriginal American Culture: A Study in Method.* Ottawa: Department of Mines, Geological Survey, Memoir 90, Anthropological Series 13.

———. 1921. *Language: An Introduction to the Study of Speech.* New York: Harcourt, Brace and World.

———. 1931. "The Concept of Phonetic Law as Tested in Primitive Languages by Leonard Bloomfield." In *Methods in Social Science: A Case Book*, edited by Stuart A. Rice, 297–306. Chicago: University of Chicago Press. Reprinted in Sapir 1949, *Selected Writings of Edward Sapir*, edited by David G. Mandelbaum, 73–88. Berkeley: University of California Press.

Sturtevant, William C. 1959. "The Authorship of the Powell Linguistic Classification." *International Journal of American Linguistics* 25:196–99.

11

········

Camelot at Yale

The Construction and Dismantling of the Sapirian Synthesis, 1931–1939

For a brief shining moment in the 1930s, Edward Sapir stood at the forefront of a new synthesis of Boasian ethnology and linguistics, centered on the study of the American Indian [*sic*] and incorporating the insights of what was then cutting-edge interdisciplinary study of the relationship between the culture and the individual, what Sapir called "the impact of culture on personality."[1] Nowhere else in North America at the time was there such a distinctive emphasis on the symbolic nature of culture and the need for qualitative ethnological fieldwork geared to revealing the point of view of the individual. Linguistics was crucial both to the fieldwork and to explication of the native standpoint. Anthropologists and linguists alike needed to study language in its technical aspects.

Despite his initial euphoria at the opportunity to develop his own program in anthropology and linguistics, Sapir's call to Yale in 1931 was a mandate taken up against formidable odds. On the surface he was the superstar, the darling of the Rockefeller Foundation philanthropists who controlled the research purse strings for a small number of elite graduate universities competing for their limited resources. James R. Angell, newly appointed outsider president of Yale, chose Sapir to catapult his institution into the major leagues, alongside Chicago, Harvard, Berkeley, and Columbia. Minor Rockefeller Foundation support for Yale's IHR began in 1929, but it could not yet challenge the well-established Chicago school of sociology, wherein Sapir's superstar appointment in 1925 had been crucial to establishing a separate department of anthropology four years later.

It was not long, however, before the grand synthesis began to unravel. The IHR was dominated by psychologist Mark May, who touted Clark Hull's behaviorist psychology as the key to interdisciplinary synthesis, and by Sapir's Boasian nemesis Clark Wissler, who had previously represented anthropology at Yale without contest. For both May and Wissler, the political stakes were firmly established before Sapir arrived. Sapir brought with him John Dollard, an ambitious young academic trained more in sociology and psychology than in anthropology who was to implement the Rockefeller-sponsored seminar on the impact of culture on personality, presumably while Sapir collected kudos for its visionary scope and prestigious sponsorship. The late Fred Eggan emphasized that Sapir had long dreamed of a department of his own; he "took Dollard with him," and "Yale was not impressed by this invasion" (personal communication, October 1984). The Rockefeller Foundation international fellows were expected to provide insider perspective on the development of personality in their own diverse home culture settings. Dollard, not surprisingly, found more congenial allies for his own career in the IHR establishment.

Angell's mandate to Sapir included an independent department of anthropology with Sapir at its helm. He apparently made no effort to consult, much less inform, Albert Keller, distinguished chair of the Yale sociology department and heir apparent to the William Graham Sumner folkways tradition. Sumner's comparative evolutionary sociology was well ensconced at Yale and ran counter to everything Sapir believed about an Americanist anthropology grounded in the study of symbolic culture approached through text-based linguistic fieldwork and followed by comparative analysis.

Keller's protégé, George Peter Murdock, had been hired to teach physical anthropology in the sociology department; Sapir thought physical anthropology belonged in anatomy and had nothing to do with anthropology. Indeed, Yale did not hire a physical anthropologist until the 1970s. Murdock (1965) retrospectively acknowledged his hostility to Boasian anthropology, having retreated to Yale for his doctoral work after Boas reputedly snubbed him as a dilettante in anthropology. Documents suggest somewhat more complexity than his own apologetic.

Matters proceeded more smoothly in linguistics. Sapir was the fourth distinguished linguist (alongside Franklin Edgerton, Eduard Prokosch, and Edgar Sturtevant). His appointment allowed the program to become independent of its constituent language departments. Sapir encouraged his linguistic students to take their degrees in linguistics rather than anthropology, in line with the increasing autonomy of linguistics from anthropology signaled by the establishment of the Linguistic Society of America and its journal *Language* after 1925. At Chicago, Sapir's failure to establish flexible working relations with Carl Buck in classical philology had effectively restricted anthropological linguists to working in anthropology.

The linguistics that Sapir wanted his students to learn was not anthropological in the sense proselytized by Boas. The "first Yale school" in linguistics developed around Sapir and the advanced graduate students he brought with him from Chicago, with Morris Swadesh, Stanley Newman, and Mary Haas as the core, later joined by Charles Hockett, George Trager, Benjamin Lee Whorf, Charles Voegelin, Zellig Harris, George Herzog, and others (Darnell 2001, 1990; Hymes and Fought 1975). Sapir's classic papers on the concept of the phoneme in 1925 and 1933 called for more abstract representations of sound patterning, to the acute distress of Boas, who believed that phonetic detail was lost irretrievably by such a methodology. The movement toward morphophonemics and process grammar was equally alien to the descriptive linguistics Boas had taught himself in the course of his Native American linguistic fieldwork.

Although Sapir's linguistic interests had moved away from historical problems after his 1929 six-unit classification of American Indian [*sic*] languages (Sapir 1929), his students continued to carry out comparative philological studies on a variety of American language families. In the decade between 1911 and his first version of the synthetic classification in 1929, the small band of Sapir's linguistic protégés recapitulated the intellectual ferment of Boas's own intense collaboration with Alfred Kroeber and others. Boas, however, continued to oppose the application of the Indo-European comparative method to unwritten languages. For Sapir, the independent linguistics program offered a refuge in which to pursue his own version of the linguistics of the future in collaboration with colleagues also trained in linguistic methodology.

Despite the personality conflicts and political squabbles endemic to the history of any academic institution, the Sapirian synthesis held its own as long as Sapir stood staunchly at the helm. His first heart attack, while teaching at the LSA Summer Institute of Linguistics in Ann Arbor in 1937, however, marked the beginning of its disintegration. Leslie Spier took over as chair of anthropology while Sapir was on sabbatical in 1937–38. Sapir was forced to spend the year in New York under medical care and returned to a much-circumscribed future in the fall of 1938. He died February 4, 1939.

In the resulting departmental realignment, Spier resigned as chair and was quickly replaced by Murdock. Murdock's four years as chair dramatically reconstituted the anthropology program, with archaeology rather than linguistics as its secondary focus. Although Sapir and Murdock were in agreement that the core of any anthropology program was necessarily ethnology, they envisioned ethnology quite differently. While Sapir encouraged intensive studies of particular societies geared to getting at the "native point of view," Murdock envisioned a worldwide comparative database to support quantitative, scientific generalizations. His aspirations were epitomized in the Cross-Cultural Survey established in 1935, which was the forerunner of the Human Relations Area Files.

Murdock's expansion of Yale ethnology beyond the boundaries of Indigenous North America was facilitated during World War II. Yale anthropologists were active in government service and demonstrated the usefulness of their knowledge in the practical political arena. For Murdock, and possibly others, the Sapirian version of the Americanist/Boasian tradition was relegated to a quaint backwater of the discipline. Jobs, according to Murdock, were in archaeology rather than linguistics. Even today, more than half a century later, the surviving principals are reticent to explore details of this transition. Stories of anti-Semitism and Sapir's exclusion from the Yale faculty club (actually the graduate club) abound in the oral tradition of American anthropology, reinforcing the sense that there was a basis for this understandable reticence. Several insist that they perceived no discontinuity.

Without attributing unprofessional actions or motives to any of the participants, I would like to explore the crucial transition as recorded in documents from the 1930s and early 1940s preserved in the archives of Yale University and the Department of Anthropology and from my own interviews conducted while preparing my biography (Darnell 1990). Both the theoretical and the institutional consequences of the rapid dismantling of Sapir's linguistic-psychological-ethnological synthesis seem to me to resonate into the present day. I identify a contemporary resurgence of the continuous Americanist, Sapirian alternative that was eclipsed at Yale by the anthropology of Murdock and by the structuralism of Leonard Bloomfield (Darnell 1997, 2001). Sapir's students maintained his legacy, underground as it were, awaiting future generations with renewed commitment to the psychologically real and to the study of language, culture, and society from an epistemological standpoint.

The Sapirian Synthesis

President Angell made it clear to Provost Charles Seymour that Sapir was to have a free hand: "I am very anxious, of course, to try and hold up the hands of the anthropology folk in their effort to get some progress in their field" (February 15, 1932, Presidential Papers: YU). Sapir's appointment included $5,000 annually for cultural anthropological fieldwork through the IHR. Before long, Sapir complained (to Angell, October 17, 1933, Presidential Papers: YU) that the division in interests between psychology and sociology in the IHR and the "strictly ethnographic field" made it difficult for him to support his own students' research. He further warned that the Department of Anthropology should not "dissipate our energy" by trying to cover all subdisciplines. Archaeology could be left to Cornelius Osgood in the Peabody Museum. Physical anthropology should be relegated to the "biological disciplines." Sapir wanted "primitive [sic] linguistics" to be developed "in connection with a general linguistic program." He requested $60,000 over five years to support work in North and South America, Oceania, Africa, and Asia "as opportunity arises." Angell dutifully conveyed Sapir's request to David H. Stephens of the Rockefeller Foundation (November 29, 1933, Presidential Papers: YU), but the response was discouraging. Sapir wrote directly, but ultimately unsuccessfully, to Stephens (June 18, 1934, Presidential Papers: YU) about "our own melancholy plight at Yale" with "no special fund for anthropological research" and lamented the need to cannibalize from the IHR.

Sapir did succeed in obtaining funding for the series Yale University Publications in Anthropology (YUPA), to which all members of the department contributed until the funds ended in 1938. Dean Furniss wrote to Spier (November 24, 1937: YUDA) that the foundations did not normally support publication and that additional money would not be forthcoming: "When the project was started, I attempted to make it clear to Professor Sapir that there was no support in sight beyond the few years remaining of the Foundation's grant for research in language and literature." Yale had no publication fund, making the outlook "gloomy" at best. Both Spier and Sapir resigned from YUPA editorship in mid-1938, although Spier (to Ruth Bernier of Yale Press, June 11, 1938: YUDA) agreed to complete the three volumes then in press.

Since its inception in 1902–3, Yale's sociology program had included a substantial anthropological component centered on William Graham Sumner's "science of society." In 1903–4, Sumner was joined by Albert Keller, establishing the perspective that would characterize Yale sociology until Keller's retirement in 1940. The program included such anthropological topics as "the earliest forms of the industrial organization, marriage and the family, property, religion and government" (YU: n.d.). The catalog for 1906–7 listed a course on "the anthropological evidence of legend and folktale" based on Homer. This was a far cry from the ethnological evidence emanating from the participant-observation fieldwork that was valorized by Sapir and other Boasians.

By 1907–8 the sociology curriculum had moved toward geology, emphasizing "the general character of the evolutionary theory and its special application to man and society" and culminating in "the science of society" as defined by Sumner and Keller (YU: n.d.). The catalog for 1929–30, just before Sapir's arrival, identified

both theoretical and applied courses in Anthropology, Ethnology, and the Science of Society. The controlling viewpoint of the department is evolutionary adjustment. The theoretical courses deal with the forms and evolution of institutions as adaptations of societies to their life conditions; the applied courses review and assess methods of adjustment to contemporary conditions. (YU: n.d.)

In 1930–31 Murdock was entrusted with the undergraduate introduction to anthropology, ethnology, and physical anthropology, as well as graduate courses in sociological systems, ethnology, and physical anthropology.

In spite of the established gravitas of this baseline, Sapir had strong views of his own about how the graduate program should develop. He incorporated Murdock's ethnology, but simultaneously served notice of a substantial change in tenor. According to the 1931–32 catalog, anthropology graduate students

> are expected to have a general acquaintance with the social science field and with psychological and sociological points of view. The aim is not to train technicians in some one narrowly selected aspect of anthropological work. The emphasis throughout will be on culture and its historical and psychological interpretation.
>
> The work offered includes courses and opportunities for research in ethnology, cultural theory, primitive [*sic*] linguistics, and, to some extent, archaeology and physical anthropology. No student will be accepted for the doctor's degree who does not show a reasonable acquaintance with all of these fields, although in his research work he is expected to specialize in only one or two of them.
>
> Concentration may be on descriptive and historical ethnology; or primitive [*sic*] linguistics; or cultural theory; or, in particular cases, on archaeology or physical anthropology. Those who take ethnology or cultural theory as their major field are strongly advised to supplement their work with courses in the departments of Sociology and Psychology. Those who specialize in primitive [*sic*] linguistics should also take up work within the department of Linguistics and in one or more other departments offering courses in languages.
>
> Students are expected to use the anthropological resources of the Peabody Museum. They will be given some opportunity to undertake ethnological, archaeological, or linguistic field work, or to share in the researches of the Institute of Human Relations. In general, a student will not be expected to come up for his doctor's degree until he has had firsthand contact with a field project. (YU: n.d.)

The new emphasis on empirical fieldwork and historical ethnology was thoroughly Boasian, as was the four-field scope of anthropology. Primitive [*sic*] linguistics and collaboration with interdisciplinary research in the IHR were part of Sapir's vision of a new kind of program to emerge at Yale under his leadership.

Although faculty turnover was considerable during the 1930s, each continuing faculty member developed their own courses. Sapir, consistent with the breadth of his research interests and his dual responsibilities for graduate instruction in anthropology and linguistics, offered the broadest range of subjects, including primitive [*sic*] languages, the impact of culture on personality, the psychology of culture, phonetics, problems in anthropology, research in cultural anthropology, research in linguistics, primitive [*sic*] society, primitive [*sic*] religion and art, advanced phonetics and phonemics, comparative problems in primitive [*sic*] languages, Tocharian (parts of the team-taught course), languages of the world, introduction to general linguistics, and problems in ethnology (with Spier).

Murdock's range was narrower, including ethnology, physical anthropology, sociological systems, and systematic ethnography. Only the last moved beyond his contribution to the scope of sociology under the Sumner-Keller umbrella. "Systematic ethnography" appeared only in 1935–36, the year the Cross-Cultural Survey was founded.

Osgood remained based primarily in the Peabody Museum and adopted a descriptive Americanist agenda for his teaching, including prehistoric archaeology, the American Indian [*sic*], American archaeology, research in archaeology, and museum methods. Sapir was thus freed to concentrate on theory, in both linguistics and ethnology.

Wissler was more researcher than instructor. His research courses in ethnic psychology and anthropology had to be arranged individually. Presumably due to his work with the IHR, Wissler was cross-listed in sociology although Sapir was not. He developed a course in culture and environment.

Spier, who was appointed in 1932–33, taught types of culture growth, methods of ethnology, ethnography of the Southwest, and ethnography of North American culture areas. Again, theory was left primarily for Sapir.

Although the departmental center of gravity remained Americanist, George Herzog taught primitive [*sic*] music, American Indian [*sic*] music, and African ethnology, while Peter Buck covered the Pacific. Sociology maintained additional cross-listed graduate courses in Africa, the Pacific, the science of society, the individual and society, marriage and the family, and societal evolution, while the geography department concentrated on climatology and geography. Sapir's linguistics courses were also cross-listed; only in 1933, however, were the linguists actually listed in the anthropology catalog.

The anthropology program was successful, particularly insofar as it was student focused. Sapir identified more as a teacher than as an administrator. He wrote to his wife Jean about his pleasure in receiving an office in Trumbell College, tying him to the coveted Yale undergraduate program (from which Sapir was otherwise excluded by virtue of being Jewish):

> I have a feeling this office will be a godsend, if only it gives me a good way to escape from the graduate office. What crazy divinity ever picked me out for an administrator? There are so many excellent Herskovitses and Dollards in the world it seems poor planning to pick on me. (September 20, 1933: YUDA)

Weston La Barre recalled Sapir's enthusiasm for "student contact":

> One stupid colleague stated that "Sapir wastes himself on his students." Sapir used to go off in some corner of the university to talk with a bright or interesting student, and for hours he would be incommunicado while his secretary frantically sought his whereabouts for some august bureaucratic reason. This kind of thing happened to me once or twice, and I found it immensely ego-enhancing. Sapir just cared more for a student and for anthropology than he did for the busywork that has now swamped universities.[2]

Sapir held a weekly open house for graduate students at his home. They remembered that he was not doctrinaire in imposing his own interests on them. William Fenton took Sapir's courses in social organization, primitive [*sic*] religion, the impact of culture on personality, and phonetics, reporting that each proved useful to his fieldwork.[3] It was Sapir who "shepherded" him through preliminary exams (with honors) and his dissertation defense in 1937. All of the anthropology graduate students took linguistics, and the more advanced linguistics students explained it to the ethnologists. La Barre, Eggan, and David Mandelbaum also reported their inability to comprehend the linguistics.[4]

Sapir encouraged students to work in the interstices of ethnology and linguistics. For example, he hoped Voegelin would work on several Algonquian languages in addition to his Shawnee fieldwork, so that "he can begin to work out something rather full about the nature of the Algonquian vocabulary from the point of view of its relation to American Indian [*sic*] culture" (August 17, 1934: YUDA). Sapir worried about whether Voegelin had "a realistic enough sense of environment in the physical sense as well as in a cultural sense" to move beyond "the ordinary linguistic preliminaries" (August 17, 1934: YUDA). Sapir's approach demonstrates how thoroughly his linguistics was grounded in anthropology.

Sapir collided directly with the IHR establishment over his support for Hortense Powdermaker's "Mississippi Delta Negro" community study over that of Dollard, which was far more sociological in its method. Powdermaker (to Mark May, September 27, 1933: YUDA) was interested in directed conversations about life history and the attitudes of both Blacks and whites. She hoped to obtain a comparative New Haven sample, arguing for the desirability of a social anthropology of "our own culture" and maintaining "the same detached attitude" as in her prior Melanesian fieldwork directed by Bronislaw Malinowski.

Sapir was enthusiastic about Powdermaker's reflexive symbolic analysis of southern culture and wanted her book published by the IHR. Mark May (February 12, 1936: YU), acting on advice from Murdock (January 27, 1936: YU) and Leonard Doob (January 16, 1936: YU), informed Powdermaker that the book did not meet the institute's scholarly or editorial standards. Although Sapir reiterated his enthusiasm (to May, February 6 and 13, 1936, and April 27, 1936: YU), the IHR terminated Powdermaker's appointment in the summer of 1937. There is no indication that the manuscript was read by anyone outside the IHR ingroup, which by this point, no longer included Sapir. *After Freedom* was published elsewhere in 1939 after a substantial delay.

Dollard wrote to Margaret Mead that Powdermaker had been "doing some unpleasant yammering" about his book and that her departure from the institute "is one of the reasons why Sapir is so sore" (June 7, 1937: YU). Dollard's rigid sociological emphasis on class corresponded to the IHR party line. The qualitative research favored by Sapir and his associates was easier to attack through Powdermaker than through Sapir directly.

Sapir also confronted May (June 15, 1935: YU) in defense of Pearl and Ernest Beaglehole's Polynesian work carried out under Yale's affiliation with Maori scholar Peter Buck and the Bishop Museum in Honolulu. Decisions were made in Honolulu without consulting the Yale committee. Murdock was pushing Clellan Ford, who "comes from Sociology, though his project is strictly ethnological" (June 15, 1935: YU). Sapir preferred to support work already underway by experienced personnel. He blamed Dean Furniss, who "had no right to ask me to come to Yale to be made a fool of" (June 15, 1935: YU), for his exclusion from the process. The Beagleholes worked in a more Sapirian frame than Ford; Sapir felt a personal obligation to them as well.

Sapir and Murdock shared responsibility for some students, especially after Sapir's illness prevented his hands-on attention to details of their programs. Murdock supported Hockett's wish to switch from Potawatomi to Kickapoo (July 30, 1938: YUDA), on Sapir's advice that "a man does best what he most wants to do." Sapir (to Murdock, May 7, 1938: YUDA) reported his "decidedly good impression" of Hockett's Potawatomi work. Sapir also supported his switch to ethnology rather than linguistics:

> My feeling in matters linguistic is never to force the pace. The work is minute and, to most people, soon becomes boring and the returns are relatively slight. So as soon as a man like Hockett shows the least sign of preferring ethnological work, he should by all means be encouraged to go ahead with that because such an interest is far more likely to be rewarding in terms of his career. (Sapir to Murdock, August 8, 1938: YUDA)

Murdock rather than Sapir ran out of patience when Hockett proposed yet another switch, this time to a psychiatric project with Adolf Meyer at Johns Hopkins: "Personally. I am rather committed to your Mexican Kickapoo plan and hope you will be able to follow it through without premature diversion to something else" (October 14, 1938: YUDA). Sapir (to Murdock, October 8, 1938: YUDA) simply assumed that Hockett was not making a specific proposal and might pursue the new idea at a later time.

Murdock (to Bloomfield, April 19, 1939: YUDA) arranged for Leonard Bloomfield to serve as external examiner for Hockett's dissertation, after Sapir's death left the department "short of qualified authorities on primitive [sic] linguistics." It was, to say the least, an understatement.

Although his thesis had been a linguistic one, Hockett remained a protégé of Murdock insofar as he was an ethnologist. Murdock praised Hockett's Kickapoo ethnological work:

> His interests have always struck me as more sociological and scientific than purely historical [i.e., Boasian], and he habitually views present day social and economic problems from an ethnographical perspective. I know that Sapir regarded him as highly as I do, both as an ethnologist and as a linguist. (Murdock to Willard Park, May 17, 1940: YUDA)

Park responded, "Unfortunately there is little demand for instruction in the field of linguistics, and we do not have the resources to specialize in linguistic research. Perhaps some day" (November 21, 1940: YUDA). By this time it was clear that Hockett was going to be primarily a linguist. Indeed, when Fay-Cooper Cole asked about linguists (May 7, 1941: YUDA), Murdock replied that Hockett "has not kept in touch with me," and Bloomfield could best comment (though he noted that both Sapir and Bloomfield valued his linguistic work highly).

Already during Sapir's lifetime, there was considerable debate over how to prepare students to find employment in the doldrums of the Great Depression. Dollard considered the job market "a sore point." His own position on the desirability of interdisciplinary training was implicitly critical of the Sapirian vision of Yale anthropology:

Some think it is just a function of the field itself, others feel that the type of training is too narrow and should be amplified to meet a wider possible market. In the latter case some psychology and sociology might be mixed in for places where a double type of training would go over but a single strand, historical, Boasian type is not needed. (Dollard to Margaret Mead, June 7, 1937: YU)

In response to inquiries from Dean Furniss, Spier noted as acting chair (January 24, 1938: YUDA) that of the nine Yale PhDs since the inception of the program, two were still at Yale (A. E. Hudson as a research assistant in anthropology and La Barre as a Sterling Fellow), E. G. Burrows (who would have to "get over" his determination to remain in Honolulu) had no present position, and the rest were all employed.[5] He emphasized that "not one of these men [and they were all men] was without anything whatever when he got his degree." When necessary, the department had provided "a fellowship or some stopgap job," moreover in anthropology. Three of the eighteen to twenty students at that time would return to permanent positions: Vern Ray at the University of Washington, W. S. Stallings at the Laboratory of Anthropology, and Jane Garrettson at Connecticut College. Three of the women students would be financially independent and "will probably not be calling on us for help to secure jobs!" Erminie Voegelin was about to begin teaching at DePauw University, although she "is married and does not need a position." Spier was confident of placing the one or two students completing their degrees each year. Yale's record on this front was better than California, Chicago, Harvard, and, particularly, Columbia, where "quantity production" produced "rather shocking" results.

Spier explicitly defended the Sapirian synthesis of ethnology and linguistics, to which Boasian culture theory was fundamental, in light of "some disquieting rumors that have reached me." He insisted that in his twenty-five years in anthropology,

I do not recall in all that time an anthropologist being asked to teach anthropology and sociology. . . . This must not be taken to mean that I am against interdisciplinary training. Quite the contrary. But I want our students to be taking courses in classics or whatever because they have a real interest in the subject.

I do not want to see them taking a couple of courses in another field just so they can pretend they are equipped to teach or do research in another subject besides anthropology. The time in residence is all too short for giving adequate training in one field to have it cut into in this fashion. (Spier to Furniss, January 24, 1938: YUDA)

Despite the existence of archaeology positions in local museums, "which are not to be sneered at," Yale was "not equipped to train our people in this field." A "first-rate archaeologist" would be needed, which would also benefit the program as a whole. Furniss's response the following day praised the department's employment record but conveyed his sense of "a demand for students trained in Anthropology and some kindred subject. . . . As I see it, the demand is for Sociology and perhaps for Psychology, and . . . our students would be well advised to prepare themselves in these lines" (Furniss to Spier, January 25, 1938: YUDA).

Furniss, influenced by Dollard and Murdock, dismissed Spier's protest that he knew of no such interdisciplinary positions on grounds that inquiries came to him directly and to the Yale appointments office. He proposed that Yale "strengthen" its work in archaeology "without much delay." This was Murdock's agenda, not Sapir's or Spier's. The new direction from the administration proceeded despite ample evidence that the existing program had successfully placed its students. Aware of the difficulties in maintaining his program in his absence, Sapir wrote to Robert Lowie thanking him for sharing a report of his conversation with Dean Furniss:

> It confirms certain hunches I had had about how that gentleman's mind was working. He seems to have been trying to trap you into saying something which he might construe as indicating a belief that anthropology and sociology ought to combine! Murdock has tried similar insinuations with me in the past. (Sapir to Lowie, January 17, 1938: YUDA)

There is no evidence that Furniss ever seriously considered this. He did, however, allow Murdock to redefine his sense of the needs of Yale anthropology, whether in response to the realization that

Sapir would not be able to return to his active role in the department or in a genuine commitment to alter the institutional intellectual priorities.

Ironically, at about the same time, Erminie Voegelin wrote to Spier about rumors that DePauw University was considering appointing "a real anthropologist." She confirmed by negation the Sapirian sense of what this meant: "I am so in hopes they will get a professionally trained anthropologist, not a semi-one who is steeped in sociological theories" (November 19, 1937: YUDA).

The Murdock Revisions of Sapir's Program

Revisions to the program began during Sapir's sabbatical and illness in 1937–38. Spier, as acting chair, appointed George Vaillant to teach Mexican archaeology and Robert Lowie to offer South American ethnology and history of ethnology (presumably based on Lowie's *History of Ethnological Theory*, which appeared in 1937 [Lowie 1937]). Charles Seligman taught courses on New Guinea and the Nile Valley. Alfred Hudson was assigned to Murdock as an assistant. George Trager and Benjamin Whorf taught Sapir's linguistics courses (phonetics and American Indian [*sic*] languages, respectively) after Morris Swadesh left to take up a position at the University of Wisconsin (Spier to Furniss, August 12, 1937: YUDA).

Murdock attempted retrospectively to rationalize his relationship to Sapir's program as represented by Spier. In an interview with Denise O'Brien in 1976, he emphasized Spier's administrative incompetence, such that "the dean had to ask me to take over the chairmanship. This was a blow to Leslie, and he resigned from Yale in a huff. And I did my level best to induce him to stay, but he'd thought I knifed him in the back" (June 4: YUDA). Murdock gave two examples. First, Spier allegedly took his dislike for Osgood out on Murdock's protégé Vaillant, who was hired to teach archaeology in 1937–38. Further, Beatrice Whiting was not permitted to take a course outside the department until she appealed to the dean. "Personal views" affected Spier's administrative decisions, and the administration was not impressed.

Nonetheless, Murdock protested his innocence, insisting that he was "closer to [Spier] than anybody else in Anthropology" and admired his ethnographic work. Spier was thoroughly steep[ed] in his Boas approach and considerably more articulate than Boas himself, and it was Spier to whom I owe recognition of the virtues of the Boasian approach. I'd never agree with him that history was the only thing and science was not or anything of that kind, but our relations were good. (Murdock to O'Brien, June 4, 1976: YUDA)

Spier was an effective editor, and Murdock learned from him. Murdock professed that Spier's leaving "was a blow to me because of course I had to make new appointments and fill the gap and remake the department, that was the time when we got Malinowski" (Murdock to O'Brien, June 4, 1976: YUDA). Murdock glossed over his own promotion to full professor when he succeeded Spier as chair of anthropology.

After Sapir's death, Murdock shamelessly employed the rhetoric of "irreparable loss" to the department in his negotiations with Dean Furniss (February 6, 1939: YUDA). Sapir's salary as a Sterling Professor was not guaranteed to the department, and various research funds would revert to the university or the IHR. After considerable departmental discussion, Murdock reported:

> The senior members of our staff have agreed that the focal center of any department of anthropology is ethnology and that physical anthropology, archaeology, and primitive [sic] linguistics are marginal by comparison. All should be represented by at least one basic course, but no university should expect to be able to specialize in more than one of the peripheral subjects in addition to its basic ethnological offerings. Hitherto our Department has specialized in ethnology with primitive [sic] linguistics as its secondary specialty, archaeology being represented in the person of Osgood and physical anthropology not at all. Our plan calls for the development of archaeology as our secondary specialty, the introduction of basic courses in physical anthropology which we have always lacked, and the reduction of primitive [sic] linguistics to the giving of basic courses only. (Murdock to Furniss, February 6, 1939: YUDA)

The underlying reasoning was that archaeology could be developed around Osgood for far less cost than replacing Sapir with someone of equal caliber. Sapir's linguistic colleagues, Edgerton and Sturtevant, felt "a dearth of really outstanding men obtainable below the status of a Sterling Professorship and [there was] a marked lack of enthusiasm on their part with the candidates our department would prefer" (Murdock to Furniss, February 6, 1939: YUDA). Most telling was Murdock's assessment of the job market:

> Experience shows that there is almost no demand for PhDs in primitive [*sic*] linguistics compared to a demand for trained archaeologists which greatly exceeds the supply. Very few indeed of Professor Sapir's PhDs in primitive [*sic*] linguistics have permanent jobs today [confirmed by Haas in Murray 1997] whereas I have had several urgent inquiries already this year for young archaeologists. (Murdock to Furniss, February 6, 1939: YUDA)

Murdock considered his budget a conservative one, deploying two basic strategies: "using part of the time of outstanding men [again, they were all men] now at Yale in other capacities" and "bringing in capable men from outside for individual courses." It would cost more (as much as $3500) to bring in "a single young man competent perhaps in two fields."

Murdock proposed that Wissler teach for one year, postponing his retirement. Irving Rouse (from the Peabody Museum), "who by consensus of opinion [unspecified] is the ablest man to be turned out by the Department since its inception," would teach archaeology. Yale anatomist William Greulich could teach physical anthropology, and Vaillant would continue to teach archaeology. Clellan Ford, who held a split appointment with the IHR, would teach primitive [*sic*] technology and Melanesian society in alternate years. Murdock intended to do more graduate teaching himself, at least for the present. An appointment was needed for "two basic courses" in linguistics, phonetics, and "primitive languages" to be taught in alternate years. Herzog and Whorf had previously taught at Yale and could be trusted to do so again.

Murdock was eager to entice Edward E. Evans-Pritchard to Yale on grounds of "a considerable group of anthropologists, not to mention an even larger group of sociologists and social psychologists with whom we maintain cordial and cooperative relationships" (November 2, 1938: YUDA). Evans-Pritchard responded that he already knew the work of the department and had "for a long time wished to become more familiar with anthropological work and thought in America" (December 26, 1938: YUDA). He knew nothing about Africa and so preferred to teach Arab social organization instead. Unfortunately, the outbreak of World War II caused Evans-Pritchard to cancel at the last minute in order to go to the Sudan for the British government (to Murdock, September 23, 1939: YUDA). He regretted "missing the chance to meet American *sociologists*" [emphasis mine].

Murdock's initial prospectus for the department ended with a plea for fieldwork research funds, especially for sabbatical research time "in rotation" for all members of the department. "A professional anthropologist stagnates unless he [*sic*] occasionally quits teaching for a period to engage in the field work" (Evans-Pritchard to Murdock, September 23, 1939: YUDA). Further, "little that is significant can be done in less than a year." Murdock was more worried about faculty than about student research, at least in this context.

Murdock wrote to Furniss (December 4, 1939: YUDA) requesting a permanent appointment for Bronislaw Malinowski, "one of the greatest living anthropologists," as Bishop Professor at Yale. The proposed appointment was tied to the impending retirement of Albert Keller (Murdock to Furniss, January 16, 1941: YUDA). Murdock emphasized that Yale sociology "has always characteristically been based on an Anthropological orientation." He even proposed himself as a collaborator to ease Malinowski into substituting for Keller!

> Since I have myself been trained in sociology under Professor Keller and am personally most sympathetic to his approach, I could, in collaborating with Professor Malinowski, assure students . . . of an adequate grounding in Sumner-Keller theory. [Moreover, this would] conform to Yale College usage and to the tradition set by Professor Keller in the past. (Murdock to Furniss, January 16, 1941: YUDA)

Murdock wanted to continue the existing warm collaboration of anthropology with sociology. It "seems to us to be the most promising road to the realization of Yale's extraordinary opportunities for the achievement of a sound and integrated social science."

In his eagerness to bring Malinowski to Yale, Murdock also argued (to Furniss, July 16, 1940: YUDA) that Malinowski's interest in race relations might allow him to replace recently deceased Sterling Professor Charles Loram. The administration, however, closed down work in this area, given that it had been so closely associated with Loram as an individual.

Malinowski, not surprisingly, came highly recommended. Peter Buck wrote to Murdock (September 27, 1940: YUDA) of his "dynamic personality" and "magnificent work in the past." Were his health better, he would be ideal as "an essential replacement of Sapir." Malinowski died not long after his arrival in 1942, leaving his potential role in Murdock's realignment of Yale anthropology away from Boasian anthropology largely unfulfilled.

Fay-Cooper Cole wrote to Murdock with some reservations that Malinowski would bring great prestige to Yale. During his time at Chicago, he used to be "very much of a lone worker" and "rather intolerant of other points of view," so that "his students were not as well grounded in the fundamentals of anthropology as a whole as we generally expect American students to be" (September 21, 1940: YUDA). Malinowski had mellowed recently but would probably be happiest as the "sole figure" with students coming "to get his viewpoint" in a place where he would be free to do research. Ironically, Cole, a fellow Boasian who might have been expected to sympathize, was the administrator who had hired British social anthropology's other guru, Alfred R. Radcliffe-Brown, to replace Sapir when he moved from Chicago to Yale in 1931. Based on that experience he indirectly predicted pitfalls ahead for integrating academic versions of the American and British traditions, at Yale as at Chicago.

By 1939–40, Murdock had rewritten the program description. As in the case of Sapir's prospectus of 1931–32, it is a notice of intent, to be tenaciously worked out in the program. Murdock agreed with Sapir that the aim was not to train technicians

> in some narrowly selected aspect of anthropological work but rather to produce broadly oriented social scientists with a specialty in anthropology. Students are therefore expected to acquire a general acquaintance with the entire social science field. (YU)

There is no mention of culture or of the "historical and psychological interpretation" foregrounded in Sapir's proposal. Although Sapir also privileged interdisciplinary collaborations with sociology and psychology, he never intended that graduate students would cease to be primarily anthropologists.

The emphasis on the "worldwide" ethnological perspective of the department was also a change in focus. The department had always offered work in various ethnological areas, but the Sapirian synthesis included a core of Americanist work to which Murdock assigned no special priority. Under Sapir's regime, graduate students studied unwritten languages to use them in their fieldwork. As the 1939–40 catalog shows, Murdock, in contrast, envisioned "more than a minimal facility in foreign languages" because "the important [scholarly] materials on many areas are in languages other than English" (YU). Ability to assimilate materials from a range of world cultures for the Cross-Cultural Survey was an asset in the new program emphasis.

Work in ethnology was treated separately from that in culture theory, with archaeology, primitive [sic] linguistics, and physical anthropology trailing behind. Courses in other departments were recommended for all students. Students could expect "some opportunity to carry on original fieldwork" (1939–40 catalog: YU) through the IHR or the Peabody Museum, but fieldwork was not mandatory to the training of an anthropologist as it was for Sapir.

The new emphases encouraged Murdock to bring John Dollard into the Department of Anthropology. He wrote to Furniss that Dollard was "probably the leading single figure in culture and personality" (December 4, 1939: YUDA) and with no mention of ensuing tensions credited Sapir for bringing him to Yale. Although psychology and sociology had contributed to culture and personality,

> its greatest development . . . has probably been in anthropology. When Sapir came to Yale and brought Dollard with him, . . . Yale assumed the unquestioned lead in this field, and everyone here and elsewhere expected forward strides of considerable magnitude. Owing to personal estrangements of various sorts, however, development was curtailed, being confined almost entirely to

the IHR. Although it has gained headway and influence on the research side under the sponsorship of the Institute, the field of culture and personality has long been hampered on the instructional side. (Murdock to Furniss, December 4, 1939: YUDA)

No one objected to Dollard's moving to anthropology, as long as it was not perceived as "at the expense of the more strictly anthropological aspects of the Department's program." With Murdock and John Bennett, a "balanced and unified department" would easily result, allowing the potentials of Dollard's work to be realized.

Dollard was duly appointed. Beginning in 1940–41, he taught the transmission of culture. Life history, the catalog notes, is "the means by which the culture of the group becomes the habit system of the individual" (YU). His culture and personality course description in 1941–42 combined Freudian life history and field interview techniques, presumably with a view to sending students into the field to test psychoanalytic insights into the relation of culture and personality. As described in the 1940–41 catalog, social structure and the individual emphasized "methods and techniques derived in the main from the study of modern communities" (YU). Neither Murdock nor Dollard saw anthropology as restricted to the study of the "primitive" or exotic. Sapir had also wanted to apply the insights of anthropology to contemporary society, but he assiduously employed the methods devised for the qualitative study of small, isolated, face-to-face communities to do so.

In Murdock's view, the new synthesis was now in place, supported by the IHR. He wrote enthusiastically to John Gillin about coming to Yale with a Carnegie fellowship:

You will find at Yale, I think, a very live and stimulating group of fellow spirits. Several of us in anthropology are very much interested in the borderline between individual and group behavior, and we have profited enormously by our contacts with Hull and his stimulus-response colleagues and with Dollard and others in the psychoanalytic field. (April 4, 1940: YUDA)

In the preface to *Social Structure*, Murdock reiterated that "most of what other anthropologists have subsequently learned from Malinowski had already become familiar to the present author through the influence of Keller" (1949:xii). He acknowledged with qualification the influence of the "American historical anthropologists of whom Franz Boas was the pioneer and intellectual leader" by virtue of clearing away the "intellectual debris" of evolutionism:

> The school accomplished distressingly little, however, toward the advancement of cultural theory. . . . Boas himself, who has been extravagantly overrated by his disciples, was the most unsystematic of theorists, his numerous kernels of genuine insights being scattered amid much pedantic chaff. He was not even a good field worker. He nevertheless did convey to his students a genuine respect for ethnographic facts and for methodological rigor. In the hands of some of his followers, however, his approach degenerated into a sterile historicism consisting of rash inferences concerning prehistory from areal distributions. (1949:xiv)

Sapir was credited for "such linguistic knowledge" as Murdock possessed and for his "initiation into fieldwork." Sapir's "extraordinary intuitive flair and verbal facility" had provided the "initial stimulus" to culture and personality. But "the permanent contributions of Sapir to cultural theory are relatively slight in comparison to those he achieved in linguistic science" (Murdock 1949:xiv). With this faint praise, the Sapirian synthesis was relegated to the past, a position fully consistent with Murdock's genuine differences of anthropological vision from Sapir.

In spite of the fairly dramatic changes in general approach, students whose primary loyalty ended up being to Murdock continued to acknowledge considerable debt to Sapir. Those who pursued projects in life history and culture and personality under Murdock's supervision included Leo Simmons and Clellan Ford. Beatrice and John Whiting recalled Sapir's "humanistic point of view" and his emphasis on

> the importance of knowing the native language for understanding culture. His stress on the importance of metaphor anticipates the position of the present symbolic school. His explication of the phonemic analysis of language was a model for the emic approach developed in ethnoscience. . . . Sapir inspired us to isolate the expressive-projective domain of magic, religion and

art as a potential index of the modal personality of a culture. (Whiting and Whiting 1978:44)

Weston La Barre recalled that Sapir had a great linguist's "almost preternatural sense of dynamic pattern" (1952:159). He was among the first to become "restive with traditional Boasian anthropology" and its hostility to generalizations other than diffusionist historical ones; it was "on the whole a science of atomistic behaviorism centered on establishing descriptive culture patterns" (159–60). There was value in this, but Sapir had ventured further. In "cultural studies," Sapir emphasized psychoanalysis as preparation for fieldwork on personality and culture. Anthropologists, far more frequently than "comparable social scientists like sociologists and psychologists," were trained as analysands (160).

Irving Rouse was matter-of-fact (personal communication, January 18, 1986) in reporting that he did not know Sapir well because he was a protégé of Sapir's former student, Cornelius Osgood, and Rouse was busy working his way through graduate school. But everyone took culture and personality with Sapir. La Barre and Rouse took Navajo linguistics with "all professional linguists"; Rouse did not even know linguistic notation. "At the last session, Sapir remembered that he had two graduate students . . . and asked each of us a question, which we could not answer. In retrospect, however, it became clear that I had absorbed more linguistics than I realized and that it has benefited my archaeology." Sapir was not very interested in artifacts, but he advised Rouse to apply linguistic technique to their study. Sapir also suggested a career covering "all the cultural (as opposed to linguistic) groups whose prehistory I was attempting to reconstruct." He advised concentrating on a specialty "until he had acquired the reputation to speak with authority on broader issues." Rouse believed that Sapir had followed this advice in his own career, moving from linguistics to culture theory.

The departmental definition of ethnology as the "glue" of anthropology was the study of contemporary cultural and social behavior. Rouse believed that Sapir compartmentalized linguistics and ethnology, expanding into the latter without being "oriented towards origins. Instead, he sought to understand the cultures of the people under study." Asian origin is an example of a linguistic problem that requires linguistic methods.

"Murdock's appointment as chairman [*sic*] did not in my observation change the intellectual outlook of the department." Chairs have very little power. Students had to develop their own point of view because "each of my professors had a different point of view and . . . their views often conflicted." Murdock was "not dogmatic" about the positions taken by the culture-and-personality and life-history students. Murdock and Dollard were the only ones in the department interested in the IHR approach. Business proceeded as usual in other areas:

> The conflict within the department was in my observation partly a clash of personalities and partly a reflection of the shift in policy within the IHR from Sapir's linguistically oriented program to Mark May's emphasis on behavioral psychology.

Murdock got Dollard into the department, but he later moved to psychology and was "more at home" there.

For Rouse, the appointment of Floyd Lounsbury after World War II, "when linguists were still not widely included in anthropology departments, is an indication that the [Sapir] tradition was still alive." Rouse believed that a linguistic position was offered to Harry Hoijer after Sapir's death but that he refused it, and the department decided to wait. (There is no documentation of such an offer, although inquiries about linguists were made.) The ethnoscience tradition that characterized Yale later (Harold Conklin, Ward Goodenough, and Charles Frake) also had its "roots in Sapir."

During World War II, a president's memo to department chairs (April 8, 1941: YUDA) enjoined Yale departments to cut back dramatically on course offerings to save money, "covering only the essentials of their respective subjects." Murdock accepted this necessity and emphasized the relevant ongoing work of the department, particularly in Latin America: "Every faculty member . . . has devoted some time and interest to Latin American studies, although obviously all are not Latin Americanists" (to Furniss, May 12, 1941: YUDA). Murdock had done this during his five years of directing the Cross-Cultural Survey.

Both Murdock and Ford found themselves in the U.S. Navy in

1943. Ralph Linton and A. Irving Hallowell were proposed (to Furniss, April 7, 1943: YUDA) to cover the ethnology and cultural theory that were "the core of any department of anthropology," especially given the ties to sociology and the IHR at Yale. Ford and Murdock had been doing all of this since Malinowski's death in May 1942. The appointments would cost very little, and nothing long range, sparing Yale "an unbalanced unit consisting of three archaeologists and one social psychologist." Ironically, Murdock's insistence on developing archaeology instead of linguistics as the secondary specialization briefly threatened the primacy of ethnology, his own area of greatest commitment.

Murdock pleaded for the future:

> It is highly desirable that Yale maintain its position in anthropology during the war, so that it may be in a position to play a leading part in the expansion of anthropological teaching and research which seems certain to come with the return of peace. Postwar reconstruction and colonial administration will create an unprecedented demand for anthropologically trained personnel, which Yale should be in a unique position to fill. (Murdock to Furniss, April 7, 1943: YUDA)

Murdock's cross-cultural assumptions moved anthropology toward science and "verified theory" about which anthropology had previously been "extraordinarily naive" (Gillin 1954:26). Murdock believed that anthropology provided "the ideal ultimate testing ground for theories of human behavior." Indeed, "anthropology has at its disposal, in the riches of ethnography, evidence concerning an immensely wider range of variation in human behavior than has any other discipline."

It is perhaps in this sense that John Whiting, in a session honoring Murdock at the 1987 Annual Meeting of the American Anthropological Association, told Kenneth Pike that Sapir was (merely) a poet and that Murdock "was a scientist." The science in Sapirian culture theory was not visible to the protégés of the Cross-Cultural Survey. Indeed, Murdock once described Whiting as "the best-trained young social scientist in the United States" (to Gillin at Ohio State, April 4, 1940: YUDA). That he was an anthropologist was apparently, for Murdock, secondary.

The syntheses proposed by Murdock and Sapir disagreed on fundamentals. Sapir's program was not revived in the immediate postwar period, although its legacies persist in the Yale ethnoscience and linguistic anthropology of the 1960s. The tensions between qualitative and quantitative, ethnographic and comparative, cultural and social continue to wind in and out of institutional politics and career commitments of individual anthropologists. The genealogy of the Sapirian synthesis remains an available option in Americanist anthropology into the new millennium.

Notes

1. Originally published as "Camelot at Yale: The Construction and Dismantling of the Sapir Hypothesis, 1931–1939," *American Anthropologist* 100 (1998): 361–72.

2. La Barre to Robert Allen, February 24, 1971; via Allen personal communication, October 1984.

3. Fenton to Robert Allen, February 24, 1971, via Robert Allen, personal communication, October 1984. Also: Eggan, personal communication, October 1984 and Mandelbaum, personal communication, October 1984.

4. La Barre to Robert Allen, June 25, 1971, via Robert Allen, personal communication, October 1984.

5. H. Scudder McKeel as the director of the Laboratory of Anthropology in Santa Fe, Froelich Rainey at the University of Alaska, W. W. Hill at the University of New Mexico, Willard Park at Northwestern University, and David Mandelbaum was a National Research Council Fellow with a permanent job expected in the spring.

References

Darnell, Regna. 1990. *Edward Sapir: Linguist, Anthropologist, Humanist.* Berkeley: University of California Press.

———. 1997. "The Anthropological Concept of Culture at the End of the Boasian Century." *Social Analysis* 41:42–54.

———. 2001. *Invisible Genealogies: A History of Americanist Anthropology.* Lincoln: University of Nebraska Press.

Gillin, John, ed. 1954. *For a Science of Social Man: Convergences of Anthropology, Psychology and Sociology.* New York: Macmillan.

Hymes, Dell, and John Fought. 1975. "American Structuralism." In *Current Trends in Linguistics 10: Historiography of Linguistics,* edited by Thomas A. Sebeok, 903–1176. The Hague: Mouton.

La Barre, Weston. 1952. "Family and Symbol." In *Psychoanalysis and Culture,* edited by George B. Wilbur and Warner Munsterberger, 156–67. New York: International Universities Press.

Lowie, Robert H. 1937. *The History of Ethnological Theory.* New York: Holt, Rinehart and Winston.

Murdock, George Peter. 1949. *Social Structure.* New Haven CT: Yale University Press.

———. 1965. "Autobiographical Sketch." In *Culture and Society: Twenty-Four Essays.* Pittsburgh: University of Pittsburgh Press.

Murray, Stephen O. 1997 "A 1978 Interview with Mary R. Haas." *Anthropological Linguistics* 39:566–75.

Sapir, Edward. 1929. "Central and North American Languages." *Encyclopaedia Britannica* 5:138–41.

Whiting, John, and Beatrice Whiting. 1978. "A Strategy for Psychocultural Research." In *The Making of Psychological Anthropology,* edited by George Spindler, 41–61. Berkeley: University of California Press.

12

....

Benedictine Visionings of
Southwestern Cultural Diversity

Beyond Relativism

Although Ruth Benedict has been remembered within American-ist anthropology primarily for the cultural relativism expressed in terms of pattern integration in her best-selling *Patterns of Culture* (1934b), her later work moved beyond the culture-specific study of small-scale societies like those of the American Southwest to encompass cross-cultural examination of modern nation-states.[1] Her anthropology became an explicit tool for multicultural aware-ness, anti-racism, and humanistic cultural critique in ways that remain relevant today. Reexamination of these ideas is overdue.

My career, both as practitioner and as historian of anthropol-ogy, has arisen from a conscious effort to rehabilitate and reengage some fundamental tenets of Boasian anthropology in the context of contemporary disciplinary practice, particularly in the study of Indigenous North Americans (Darnell [1990] 2010, 1998, 2001, 2002; Harrison and Darnell 2006; Valentine and Darnell 1999). I distinguish "Americanist" anthropology from the larger set of all anthropological practice in North America in order to empha-size the coherence of this paradigm. It is not narrowly Boasian, although there are manifold continuities. A rather perverse cri-tique of Boas as atheoretical, mounted by proponents of proposed successor paradigms built around neo-evolution, positivism, and materialism (Harris 1968; Steward 1955; White 1963, 1966), con-tinues to be cited unreflexively despite revisionist historiographic work by myself, George W. Stocking Jr. (1974, 2001), and others. I suggest that the shared theoretical commitments of the Boasian paradigm inspired several generations of talented students and enumerate seven of its distinctive features (Darnell 2001:12–20):

1. Culture is a set of symbols in people's heads rather than the behaviors that arise from them.

2. Language, thought, and reality are mutually entailed and accessible to scientific investigation.

3. The ideal database for ethnology and linguistics is texts from native speakers of native languages.

4. Recording the knowledge encoded in oral traditions is urgent because they are a valuable and irreplaceable part of the permanent record of human achievement.

5. Indigenous "tradition," like the anthropologist's "culture," is constantly changing and adapting. It is a moving target.

6. Indigenous people are subjects and collaborators rather than merely objects of study.

7. Fieldwork, the core method of the discipline, takes a long time.

I have concentrated on the superstars of the "classic" generation (in the sense used by John Bennett [1998]), including, for example, Alfred Kroeber, Robert Lowie, Paul Radin, and Edward Sapir. They were the first generation to be professionally trained in American universities, and they divided the broad scope of the discipline according to Boas into more manageable specializations.

The member of that initial cohort who has received the most distorted rendering in professional memory is Ruth Fulton Benedict. After her death and during the post–World War II scramble for recognition of anthropology as a "science," and with the expansion of its focus beyond Native North America, more recent colleagues have glossed over Benedict's work during the interwar years. Insofar as she is remembered today, it is as a mere popularizer, a poet and aspiring critic of interwar American culture (Geertz 1990), or as a feminist icon whose closet lesbianism continues to titillate (Caffrey 1989; Lapsley 1999), or as a minor satellite of Margaret Mead (1974, 1959) in the theoretical fuzziness of a now-outdated culture and personality "school" (Harris 1968).

Mead, convinced that Native Americans lacked functioning cultures, thought Benedict was not a "real" fieldworker because she considered herself the standard for what fieldwork ought to

Fig. 7. Ruth Benedict (1887–1948), 1937. Library of Congress Prints
and Photographs Division.

be. Benedict's partial deafness and seemingly aloof personality
precluded fieldwork of the sort that Mead herself practiced and
valued. Therefore, she implicitly dismissed Benedict's ability to
synthesize the work of the colleagues and students she knew well
as a second-best substitute for the real thing (although this sort
of integration was a skill Mead herself did not cultivate). In introducing her selections of Benedict's writings for *An Anthropologist*

at Work, Mead retrospectively relegated her teacher, friend, and former lover to the past, asserting that she "became a figure of the broken sureties of a past age, to which she was full heir, to the uncertainties which precede a new integration in human thinking" (1959:xxii).

I will not deal with Benedict's sexuality or with why it was (and perhaps still remains) nearly a sin among anthropologists to write well, especially for the general public. I argue in contrast that Benedict best exemplifies the purported shift from Boas's notion of history to that of psychology or "the native point of view." I emphasize the continuity in her analysis of trait and pattern and the degree to which this perspective was shared among Boasians of the founding generation. I then turn to the analytic apparatus of *Patterns of Culture* (1934b) and its grounding in her southwestern experience. Benedict's later work emphasized how anthropology could be applied to modern ethical problems of international conflict, especially anti-Semitism, Nazi imperialism, and the Holocaust. Her leadership in policy-directed interdisciplinary research on cross-cultural diversity during and after World War II was highly influential in the public domain despite the marginalization of national character studies within anthropology itself. Contemporary globalization studies raise parallel questions of resistance to homogenization of difference and the nature of the social conditions that produce freedom and self-fulfillment (or their antitheses). Benedict's mature work repositioned her earlier "primitive" ethnography in ways that counter recent interdisciplinary challenges, particularly from cultural studies, to the anthropological concept of relativism as a defamiliarization strategy and precursor to politically relevant critique in favor of a so-called postmodern nihilism with its arguably fundamentalist need to define rigid moral universals. Benedict faced a similar critique (1934b, quoted in Daniel Rosenblatt 2004:467):

> The sophisticated modern temper has made of social relativity . . . a doctrine of despair. It has pointed out its incongruity with the orthodox dreams of permanence and identity and with the individual's illusions of autonomy. It has argued that if human experience must give up these the nutshell of existence is empty.

That this was not Benedict's position is only one persistent mis-conception that calls for reexamination.

Trait, Pattern, Integration

For Benedict, the story began with Boas—her mentor and friend, whose professional assistant and caretaker she became in his later years. Boas distinguished between "history," based on inference from trait distributions within geographical regions or culture areas, and "psychology" or "the native point of view," which moti-vated the borrowing and integration of such traits into complexes. On methodological grounds, history had to be dealt with prior to psychology because of the depth of ethnographic information needed to answer psychological questions. Boas himself began to provide such ethnographic "thickness" (in the language of Clif-ford Geertz's later interpretivism). Benedict took up her compara-tive work at a time when the first-generation Boasians had amassed a considerable database of "objective" descriptions with substan-tial time depth. By "objective" they meant "empirical" rather than independent of observer standpoint. Integration or "pattern" was to be found at the level of the particular culture. Robert Lowie's much-misread reference to "that planless hodgepodge, that thing of shreds and patches called civilization" (1920:440–41) referred to the historical accident of traits available for selection by a given culture at a given point in time, not to their place within a partic-ular culture or civilization. He saw his own society as intensively shaped by the same historical processes that influenced Native American societies.

I have argued elsewhere that the classic Boasian trait studies—for example, A. Irving Hallowell on bear ceremonialism (Darnell 1977, chapter 16, this volume), Leslie Spier on the Sun Dance, Alexander Goldenweiser on totemism, Ruth Benedict on the vision quest and the guardian spirit complex—already combined historical and psy-chological explanations for observed patterns. Variation in traits, for them, simultaneously reflected the history of culture contact and the process of adaptation of borrowed materials. Sapir implic-itly acknowledged the consensus underlying this method when he congratulated Benedict for her guardian spirit paper as "a notable addition to that body of historical critiques that anthropology owes to Boas" (Sapir to Benedict, June 25, 1922: APS).[2] Benedict dealt separately with the vision quest in Plains cultures (1922) and the more specialized guardian spirit complex (1923), clarifying that the associated traits of the complex found across North America were neither stable nor consistent. Rather, they were adapted to the cultures in which they were found.

In retrospect, Boas himself (1940:311) dated the transition from the completed historical project to the psychological one of "cultural dynamics" as taking place around 1910. The shift from comparison on the basis of limited data to intensive descriptive study of particular cultures with less emphasis on comparative generalization was actually more gradual than reflected by the arbitrary date. Despite her primarily psychological interests, Benedict preserved the salience of the cross-cultural comparative perspective and drew it into her later work on complex societies (i.e., postwar nation-states).

Benedict emphasized "the fluid recombination of cultural elements" (1923:8) and the psychological questions of "what happens in the inner life . . . of beliefs and practices assimilated into diverse tribal complexes" (7). She began with religion and turned to the guardian spirit complex as its primary North American form. Her two volumes of Zuni mythology in 1935 followed the Boasian program of increasing the ethnographic database for comparative work while simultaneously generalizing an adequate methodology for studying traits and their integration in the domain of religion. Incidents from diverse sources were combined in plot sequences that allowed considerable creativity to the narrator operating within a particular cultural framework. Benedict moved from seeking maximal integration in the study of religious phenomena in her earlier career to realizing that "almost every aspect of culture equally reflected psychological factors" (Young 2005:10).

Benedict's fieldwork, like that of most of her contemporaries, took place during summer vacations from university teaching. She visited Zuni Pueblo in 1924, Zuni and Cochiti Pueblos in 1925, the Pima in 1927, the Mescalero Apache as director of the Southwest Laboratory of Anthropology field school in 1931, and the Blackfoot of Montana and Alberta in 1939, where she again directed a field school (Mead 1974:30). Interestingly, Mead does not mention her Serrano fieldwork in conjunction with her supervision of the field school students in 1922. Boas, Elsie Clews Parsons, Margaret Mead, and Ruth Bunzel visited or accompanied Benedict in parts of her southwestern work. Her publications, particularly in folklore, drew heavily on this personal fieldwork, as did her sense of the emotional quality of everyday life in these places, confirming her conviction that the latter must remain the basis for meaningful cultural comparison.

Patterns of Culture

When she turned to comparative questions in *Patterns of Culture* (1934b), the data came from "reworking of raw material" (Mead 1974) from her own fieldwork and that of trusted colleagues: Boas himself and Mead's then husband Reo Fortune. *Patterns of Culture* was written "out of a sense of social responsibility"; she suggests that it "confirmed anthropology as a source of moral authority in American life, superseding history" (Caffrey 1989:206, 213). Benedict envisioned a flexible definition of science that would facilitate the study of patterns and themes. Although the version of the argument published in the *American Anthropologist* two years earlier had covered virtually the same ground with a somewhat more analytic style of presentation, the very success and accessibility of *Patterns of Culture* ensured that it would remain the epitome of Benedictine anthropology. She aspired to transcend the "anecdotal" character of most existing ethnography. Her strongest version of the relativity hypothesis reads:

> Fundamental and distinctive configurations in culture . . . so pattern and condition the emotional and cognitive reactions of its carriers that they have become incommensurables, each specializing in certain selected behavior and each ruling out the behavior proper to its opposites. (1932:4)

Benedict's later work would qualify the incommensurability of such patterns and seek mechanisms of respectful communication across fundamentally different cultures.

Patterns observed by the analyst provide the "emotional background" for individual action within the culture. Borrowed traits are by definition reworked in relation to patterns. Although cultures are in one sense "individual psychologies" writ large, they are also "incomparably" more integrated than personalities (1932:24). As in her trait studies a decade earlier, Benedict attributed to cultures a collective capacity to theorize, to develop dominant concepts, to philosophize (cf. Radin 1927).

Among the Pimas, Benedict was first struck by the deep gulf between the Pueblo cultures and those of the Plains. She first spoke of "pattern"—"a cultural, open system" (Caffrey 1989:155)—in relation to her shock at the differences in "psychological type" within the Southwest culture area (Benedict 1930). Mead cites the "metaphor" in which Benedict applied Nietzsche's Apollonian and Dionysian categories to cultural patterns, adapting the philosopher's terms to her own purposes (Mead 1974:35, 42). Elvin Hatch (1973:81) argues that this metaphor was quintessentially Boasian, combining her mentor's location of the "primary creative forces of culture" in "the tendency toward consistency within the subjective sphere" and "his view that custom is at bottom emotional."

In 1932, however, Benedict considered the dichotomies, as well as the terms she borrowed from abnormal psychology for the Kwakiutl [Kwakwala] and Dobuans, as heuristic devices rather than as absolutes. She crosscut the Nietzschean distinction with an intersecting one of realism and nonrealism. The Plains and the Southwest culture areas, although differing on the Apollonian-Dionysian dimension, were both strong realists, as opposed to the Northwest Coast. Indeed, the choice of terms from abnormal psychology, given her view that cultural standpoint provided the appropriate standard for defining normality and abnormality, should not be read as adapting a universal pathological typology to a culturally relative nomenclature. Rather, she matter-of-factly framed difference relative to psychological and historical context, thereby simultaneously relativizing the psychiatric typology. Benedict (1934a) appeared in a psychological journal and brought her argument to an audience beyond anthropology.

In *Patterns of Culture*, Benedict argued that each culture "selected" the dominant ideas that rendered it intelligible, both to itself and to the analyst, from an "arc of cultural possibilities" (1934b:34). She seems to have adopted this idea of selection on analogy to her friend Edward Sapir's emergent concept of the phoneme (Darnell

2001:193), although it was for her a question of "attitude" rather than of linguistic structure, or even structure in a more general sense. Whereas Sapir situated the locus of creativity in the individual operating within a linguistic or cultural pattern, Benedict was attracted by the possibilities of freedom, at both societal and individual levels.

Benedict was acutely concerned with the question of the cultural relativity of the normal and the abnormal (1934a, 1934b). She worried about the plight of the individual stigmatized by the ideal forms of their own culture—for example, the Zuni consultant whose creativity would be welcome in Benedict's society but would have brought witchcraft accusations in his own without the protective intervention of her collaboration. Benedict's sense of being abnormal within her own culture has been cited by most commentators as underlying this preoccupation.

Benedict was a relativist when it came to precipitous judgment of the cultural patterns revealed through fieldwork and urged her fellow Americans to incorporate tolerance for difference into their own cultural pattern. She was far less a relativist about the plight of the individual isolated as abnormal by culture-specific, and therefore parochial, attitudes and practices. One of the crucial standards of freedom was how a society treated those outside its ideal or typical pattern. Her later work would move "beyond relativity" to a presumably universal judgment of harm done to individuals or societies, measured largely in terms of "freedom." Her relativism, then, was both methodological and epistemological.

Not every culture could be expected to have a clear or dominant pattern; some cultures were inherently "genuinely disoriented" (1934b:196). Benedict's fieldwork among the Serrano had taught her, quoted as the frontispiece of *Patterns of Culture*, that the uniquely different "cup" of a people's culture might be broken. Not every culture, at every point in time, would be amenable to integrational analysis; the historical stability of cultural patterns could never be taken for granted. Caffrey (1989:244) suggests that engagement with the culture and personality seminars of psychiatrist Abram Kardiner reflected a search for what happened in cultures without a dominant focus (Cora DuBois's Alorese study was the preeminent exemplar).

In his introduction to *Patterns of Culture*, Boas wrote that "the more intimate our knowledge of the cultural drives that actuate the behavior of the individual," the more likely that apparently bizarre practices "when viewed from the standpoint of our civilization" could be accounted for (Boas 1934b:xv). Boas supported Benedict's isolation of these "extreme" cases as having a special character. The Zuni, Kwakiutl [Kwakwala], and Dobuans were extreme because each held such a dominant idea along the arc of human possibilities that was unfamiliar to American society. Understanding a few cultures well was preferable to superficial sampling (Benedict 1934b:61). Interestingly, Benedict's former student Eric Wolf adopted a similar methodological principle in choosing three "extreme" cases at different scales of sociocultural complexity—Kwakiutl [Kwakwala], Aztec, and German National Socialist—while "envisioning power" (Wolf 1999).

Benedict was not the only one of her generation to pose dichotomies that might put American culture into new perspective. Sapir's distinction between "spurious" and "genuine" culture was unintelligible to many of his colleagues in the Chicago School of Sociology (as well as to many anthropologists) (Darnell [1990] 2010), but it resonated for Benedict. She wrote to Mead (October 16, 1932 in Mead 1959) that "centrifugal cultures" were spurious, and "centripetal, well-coordinated ones" were genuine. For both Benedict and Sapir, however, integration may have been less at stake than the satisfaction possible for the individual under these conditions.

From "Primitive" Ethnography to Cross-Cultural Commentary

After *Patterns of Culture*, Benedict analyzed several specific cultural cases chosen to accentuate the ability of cultures to choose within the options available to them. "Two patterns of Indian [*sic*] acculturation" (1943) contrasted the former high civilizations of the Americas that still form the majority of the population and its primary labor force and what she called the "free tribes" who favored resistance or escape and were largely exterminated. Mode of production conditioned different approaches to imposed political sovereignty. Subordination arose from historical circumstances reinforced by culture. She insisted that empirical dimensions of production had to be read relative to dominant cultural attitudes.

In the Southwest, therefore, the same environment was exploited differently by Pueblo farmers and Athabascan herdsmen.

In my own work in southwestern Ontario, the relatively settled Iroquoian farmers and the more recently nomadic Algonquian-speaking settlers (Ojibwe [Anishinaabeg], Pottawatomi, Odawa, Delaware) sustain quite different modes of being in relation to contemporary resources of education, employment, and social and medical services. I have been exploring the "nomadic legacy" of making decisions—for example, about alternating urban versus reserve (reservation in the United States) residence—by moving people to resources without ceding commitment to a home territory. In both southwests, the contrast between fundamentally different cultures highlights the agency within ongoing tradition that is still operative for each of these groups.

Race: Science and Politics (1940) was Benedict's first foray into the politics of World War II racism and anti-Semitism, her first effort to break down American political isolationism. Always something of an outsider among the German or Jewish men around Boas in the early years of her career, Benedict ironically found herself the ideal, "objective" spokesperson for this new politics of culture grounded in anthropology. As "a white Anglo-Saxon descendant of the Mayflower Pilgrims and 'daughter' of the American Revolution," she could speak to America at its core (Caffrey 1989:202).

Reviewers, however, emphasized her description of racism and ignored the underlying social vision that had been implicit already in *Patterns of Culture*. Benedict went on to coauthor a pamphlet on race with Gene Weltfish and a children's book on the "green devils" of prejudice. *In Henry's Backyard* (1948) wrote large her personal anxieties in terms of America's urgent need for cultural hygiene.

For the commentaries of her later career, Benedict was comfortable with the term "applied anthropology" as it developed during the 1930s. She was a founding member of the Society for Applied Anthropology in 1941 and applauded the interdisciplinary community and industry studies typified by Robert S. and Helen M. Lynd's study of Middletown (1929). Anthropologists working for the government during the war saw themselves as applied anthropologists in that sense.

Benedict and Boas planned a comparative study of contemporary North American Indian [*sic*] "acculturation" based on the fieldwork of her students and expanding the evidential basis of the methodology of the interwar years. By 1937 twenty tribes were studied in Project No. 35 of the Columbia University Council on Research in Social Sciences. The groups were chosen for their continued functioning and lack of disruption to traditional practices in order to highlight the adaptation and integration of new culture traits. Pueblo incorporation of Spanish traits illustrated the possibility of cohesion and even freedom. Extension of "security" to as many individuals as possible became another important comparative dimension. The students were trained to go beyond traits to their functioning in contemporary cultures. The program both foreshadowed *Patterns of Culture* (Young 2005:77) and built upon its successful paradigm.

By 1938 the project title had changed to "problems of culture and personality," although Benedict retained her emphasis on the costs to the individual of institutional arrangements. This is what she meant by culture and personality. Her proposed summary book on the range of human behavior was set aside with the immanence of war, fascist victories, and the critical need for scholars to advise policymakers. American Indian [*sic*] acculturation studies continued to be salient in her classes.

International Forays beyond Nationalism

In accepting an Achievement Award from the American Association of University Women in 1946, Benedict clarified that her wartime work had attempted to bring an anthropologist's definition of problem to the international context:

> These ways of stating problems of human behavior and the solving them had been worked out, for several decades, in anthropological studies of small tribes, usually without written language, whose traditional ways of conducting life owed very little indeed to the influences of Western civilization. I had believed for a long time before the war that the same kind of research would help us to understand civilized nations. (Quoted in Mead 1974:66)

Like most Boasians prior to World War II, Benedict initially took for granted the Durkheimian logic of the so-called primitive as a laboratory for sociology because modern society was too complex in scale for ethnographic studies (1934b:204). The "local arrangements" of subcultures, however, could be analyzed using standard ethnographic methods. Methodological obstacles posed the only gulf between "primitive" and modern. Her address continued, elaborating her faith in knowing the other and finding a scale at which the anthropologist could work effectively:

> I believe we can try out in little [*sic*] some of the problems which face the United Nations. I have the faith of a scientist that behavior, no matter how unfamiliar to us, is understandable if the problem is stated so that it can be answered by investigation and if it is then studied technically by suitable methods. And I have the faith of a humanist in the advantages of mutual understanding among men [*sic*]. (Quoted in Mead 1974:66)

What Benjamin Lee Whorf called "multilingual awareness" applied also to culture. The anthropologist learned to accept more than one way of seeing the world through contact with other cultures. Faced with "cultural diversities in the postwar world," anthropology foreshadowed the aspiration of the United Nations to build "enduring world understanding" (Benedict 1943, quoted in Mead 1959:440). Americans would have to learn that other cultural patterns were coherent in their own terms.

In the Anna Shaw Lectures on nature and social institutions at Bryn Mawr College in 1941,[3] Benedict relied heavily on the concept of "synergy," defined as combined action that exceeded its parts. High-energy cultures reinforced the individual, thus producing social cohesion, whereas their low-synergy, atomistic counterparts pitted individuals against one another and discouraged social solidarity. The former were preferable—more "genuine" in Sapir's terms. Benedict did not use the term "synergy" again after the Shaw lectures, perhaps because she worried that its cybernetic resonances threatened to efface human agency.

Benedict's cross-cultural studies of war challenged her long-held commitment to cultural relativity. On the one hand, she believed cultures should be left to their own ways as long as they caused no harm to others; on the other, relativity was essential "in the face of a conservative movement to return to a system of absolutes" (Caffrey 1989:309). Her concerns remained methodological as well as ethical. In an unpublished paper on "ideologies in the light of comparative data" written around 1941–42 (quoted in Mead 1959:385), Benedict wrote:

> The fundamental problem before all the sciences—physical and social—is still to learn the conditions which do bring about a designated outcome. The prime lesson the social sciences can learn from the natural sciences is just this: that it is necessary to press on to find the positive conditions under which desired events take place, and that these can be just as scientifically investigated as can instances of negative correlation. This problem is *beyond relativity* [her emphasis].

The goal, derived from outside the standpoint of any particular culture, including her own, was social cohesion that minimized individual aggression and frustration. In Benedict's 1946 seminar on social organization, she put it: "Traits beyond cultural relativity are a common denominator of ethical moral sanctions" (Young 2005:23).

Benedict defended democracy as the system most likely to produce but not ensure freedom. "Primitive Freedom" in the *Atlantic Monthly* in 1942 contrasted the atomistic, perpetually dissatisfied Chuckchee of Siberia, who lacked social mechanisms for solidarity, with the Canadian Blackfoot, who felt themselves to be free. She concluded that the accountability of a privileged group of leaders might lead to the perception of freedom or its absence under superficially similar institutional arrangements. Political freedoms had to be utilized to enhance individual agency and satisfaction if a concept of public good were to thrive.

Benedict's work for the Office of War Information built on her previous ethnographic and comparative methods. "The study of national character was a bold undertaking, an attempt to bring methodological order to the ad hoc ventures of anthropologists in wartime and it was much criticized within her profession" (Young 2005:162). Wartime work by anthropologists had moved the discipline irreversibly away from the study of isolated, small-scale societies. Benedict's direction in generalizing the anthropological method was "configurational, thematic and value-oriented," while her colleagues, particularly at Columbia after Boas's retirement and her failure to succeed him, turned to more "ecological and stratificational" modes of analysis (Mintz 1981:152). Sidney Mintz, for the most part in the latter camp, emphasized in retrospect Benedict's "insistence on the study of culture as a way to explain" (1981:154).

Benedict's studies of four complex societies—Japan, Thailand, Romania, and the Netherlands—all began with the sociopolitical system and history. These societies differed from the ones she had studied previously because of the "written texts and legends" by which contemporary cultures kept their history accessible to its members. "These histories, and ideas of history" (Young 2005:105) then entered into the formation of cultural patterns. Nonetheless, the divide was not absolute: Thai moderation and Romanian individualism were "parallel" to her Pueblo-Plains contrast from *Patterns of Culture* (albeit without historical and geographic context she could provide for the southwestern cases).

Benedict no longer expected to discover a single dominant theme. Her Thai work, for example, was multithematic: enjoyment of life, minimization of anxiety, and male domination were all critical. The continuity of Thai child development produced "psychic security," whereas the Japanese pattern exemplified discontinuity from childhood to adulthood. Socialization and the continuity of life cycle transitions offered a direct mechanism for dynamic intersection of the individual with the culture. Because she was not interested in the individual per se, she found psychologically oriented life histories an inefficient way of obtaining cultural data.

Benedict deliberately employed an open-ended analytic of "psychological type" bringing cohesion to a culture rather than seeking any kind of rigid typology. Virginia Heyer Young's class notes in 1946 (2005:192) talked about a "core culture" to which individuals reacted rather than a "basic personality type" as Abram Kardiner suggested, in what she considered a closed typology that might limit the possibilities of individual agency.

The Chrysanthemum and the Sword (1946) has been widely criticized for its "culture at a distance" approach, albeit this was necessitated by the exigencies of war. Benedict talked about Japanese "character" more than about culture pattern per se. Mead (1974:74) rather cavalierly labeled her methodology as "imaginative realism"—a method in which "Japan comes to look, somehow, erratic and arbitrary while the United States comes to look somehow, more and more so"; Geertz's "somehow" is his key to the analytic quality of the method applied to the "dismantling of American exceptionalism" through contrast to the "spectacularized other" (Geertz 1990:121–22). Both Margaret Mead and Clifford Geertz remained apparently oblivious to the empirical data that produced convergence of evidence from Benedict's interviews in North America with "Americans of Japanese ancestry" ("whether born in Japan or America") drawn into the wartime research projects, childhood studies (considered reliable at the time), and expressive products of the culture deployed to reveal its dominant pattern.

The book, with the subtitle *Patterns of Japanese Culture*, was seminal in determining American disarmament and economic reconstruction policies (and incidentally spurred a second wave of public influence for *Patterns of Culture*, its analysis of the range of human possibilities now writ on an international scale). Benedict's title came from two principles of Japanese life: the honored self-responsibility of the Samurai sword and the passively entrained chrysanthemum plant (Young 2005:21). The tension between these superficially contradictory cultural themes at different times in history produced the distinctive Japanese character.

Benedict extended her analysis to the United States: "Knowledge of tribal society was clearly necessary for understanding modern America" (Young 2005:113). Virginia Young's notes from Benedict's seminar in 1946 apply the concept of the "primitive [*sic*] segmented society" to understanding the social problems arising in America from the tension between the symmetrical behavior necessary to democracy and the actual widespread hierarchical organization of much of American society.

The Columbia University Research in Contemporary Cultures (RCC) project, casually known as the National Character study, began in 1947 as Benedict's final grand project. Five contemporary nation-states (Russia, Czechoslovakia, France, Eastern European Jews, and China) were chosen for particular problems and points of comparison. They were not expected to be directly comparable but were selected for their contrastive potentials. Eastern European Jews, although not a nation until the formation of Israel in 1948, were included because their transnational mobility provided a unique standpoint toward the effects of multiple hosting cultures.

After Benedict's death in 1948, Margaret Mead and Rhoda Métraux completed the project. Meanwhile, at Columbia and across American anthropology, cultural ecology was increasingly the dominant integrating concept. Caffrey (1989:332) attributes this to its grounding within the discipline of anthropology, a retreat from "the decentralization and diffusion of interdisciplinary work." RCC was deemed unscientific and was dissociated from the discipline in general, just as culture and personality had long been dismissed by many anthropologists as "historical," "subjective," or "soft" (Caffrey 1989:342, 334).

The prescient interdisciplinary social science that developed around Edward Sapir under Rockefeller Foundation auspices in the 1930s, with Benedict as an occasional participant, was similarly abortive within the discipline and of limited application outside it (Darnell [1990] 2010). Despite Sapir's charismatic leadership, there was by then less urgency for anthropological advice.

In the renewal application for what she now called the "national cultures" project in December 1947, Benedict argued that the groundwork had been established for national character studies "refined and corrected by region, occupation, class, sex, and age groups, and by period." The cultures are complex, but their "basic themes" are clear (quoted in Young 2005:129). The term "character structure" seems to mean "simply the cultural configuration expressed in the individual" largely through socialization (Young 2005:140).

Conclusion

In sum, then, Benedict is an honorable precursor of an anthropology of globalization and resistance thereto. She studied American Indian [*sic*] societies and generalized the methods of her studies to a deeply moral and humanistic yet simultaneously analytic and scientific anthropology encompassing all human societies regardless of their degree of complexity. Her model foregrounded their culture change, process, and agency. The coherence of cultures was provisional and contingent, to be understood historically as well as through contemporary attitudes and practices. Yet cultures could remain integrated while responding to changing conditions, whether by resistance or assimilation.

Benedict was far from unaware of the structures of power constraining the contacts of cultures. Indeed, she successfully entered the corridors of power in her own society to argue that respect for cultural difference was the only possible framework for sustained political coexistence. She persuaded the U.S. government to administer postwar Japan through its own social institutions and "the usefulness of anthropology in thinking about practical and political questions" (Rosenblatt 2004:461). She moved beyond the naive relativism attributed to her today in order to begin formulating cross-cultural and universal standards of well-being, both for cultures and individuals. Her early relativism remained intact; to move beyond relativism required moving through relativism itself. We can still learn much from this Benedictine legacy.

Notes

1. Originally published as "Benedictine Visionings of Southwestern Cultural Diversity: Beyond Relativism," *Journal of Anthropological Research* 64 (2008): 469–82.

2. Ruth Benedict's papers are at Vassar College. Extensive Benedict materials also are found in the Margaret Mead Papers (Library of Congress) and the Franz Boas Papers (American Philosophical Society). The same letters are often present in the multiple collections.

3. Copies of most of the Anna Shaw Lectures are included in the Benedict Papers at Vassar College. Virginia Heyer Young (2005) discusses these manuscripts in detail.

References

Benedict, Ruth. 1922. "The Vision in Plains Culture." *American Anthropologist* 24:1–23.

———. 1923. *The Concept of the Guardian Spirit in North America*. Memoirs of the American Anthropological Association No. 29. Menasha WI: George Banta.

———. 1930. "Psychological Types in the Cultures of the Southwest." *Proceedings of the 23rd International Congress of Americanists, 1928*, 572–81.

———. 1932. "Configurations of Culture in North America." *American Anthropologist* 34:1–27.

————. 1934a. "Anthropology and the Abnormal." *Journal of General Psychology* 10:59 82.

————. 1934b. *Patterns of Culture*. Boston: Houghton Mifflin.

————. 1935. *Zuni Mythology*. 2 vols. Columbia University Contributions to Anthropology 21. New York: Columbia University Press.

————. 1940. *Race, Science, and Politics*. New York: Viking.

————. 1942. "Primitive Freedom." *Atlantic Monthly* 169:756–63.

————. 1943. "Two Types of Indian Acculturation." *American Anthropologist* 45:207–12.

————. 1946. *The Chrysanthemum and the Sword: Patterns of Japanese Culture*. Boston: Houghton Mifflin.

Benedict, Ruth, and Gene Weltfish. 1948. *In Henry's Backyard: The Races of Mankind*. New York: Henry Schuman.

Bennett, John. 1998. *Classic Anthropology: Critical Essays, 1944–1996*. New Brunswick NJ: Transaction.

Boas, Franz. 1934. Introduction to *Patterns of Culture*, by Ruth Benedict, xiii–xv. Boston: Houghton Mifflin.

————. 1940. *Race, Language and Culture*. New York: Free Press.

Caffrey, Margaret M. 1989. *Ruth Benedict: Stranger in This Land*. Austin: University of Texas Press.

Darnell, Regna. 1977. "Hallowell's Bear Ceremonialism and the Emergence of Boasian Anthropology." *Ethnos* 5:13–30.

————. 1990. *Edward Sapir: Linguist, Anthropologist, Humanist*. Berkeley: University of California Press.

————. 1998. *And Along Came Boas: Continuity and Revolution in Americanist Anthropology*. Amsterdam: John Benjamins.

————. 2001. *Invisible Genealogies: A History of Americanist Anthropology*. Lincoln: University of Nebraska Press.

————, ed. 2002. *American Anthropology: Selected Papers from the American Anthropologist, 1976–1990*. Lincoln: University of Nebraska Press.

Geertz, Clifford. 1990. "Us/Not-Us: Benedict's Travels." In *Works and Lives: The Anthropologist as Author*, 102–28. Stanford: Stanford University Press.

Harris, Marvin. 1968. *The Rise of Anthropological Theory*. New York: Thomas Crowell.

Harrison, Julia, and Regna Darnell, eds. 2006. *Historicizing Canadian Anthropology*. Vancouver: University of British Columbia Press.

Hatch, Elvin. 1973. *Theories of Man and Culture*. New York: Columbia University Press.

Lapsley, Hilary. 1999. *Margaret Mead and Ruth Benedict: The Kinship of Women*. Andover: University of Massachusetts Press.

Lowie, Robert H. 1920. *Primitive Society*. New York: Harper.

Lynd, Robert S., and Helen M. Lynd. 1929. *Middletown: A Study in Contemporary American Culture*. New York: Harcourt Brace.

Mead, Margaret, ed. 1959. *Writings of Ruth Benedict: An Anthropologist at Work.* Boston: Houghton Mifflin.

———. 1974. *Ruth Benedict.* New York: Columbia University Press.

Mintz, Sidney. 1981. "Ruth Benedict." In *Totems and Teachers,* edited by Sydel Silverman, 141–70. New York: Columbia University Press.

Radin, Paul. 1927. *Primitive Man as Philosopher.* New York: Dover.

Rosenblatt, Daniel. 2004. "An Anthropology Made Safe for Culture: Patterns of Practice and the Politics of Difference in Ruth Benedict." *American Anthropologist* 106:459–72.

Steward, Julian. 1955. *Theory of Culture Change: The Methodology of Multilinear Evolution.* Urbana: University of Illinois Press.

Stocking, George W., Jr., ed. 1974. *The Shaping of American Anthropology, 1883–1911: A Franz Boas Reader.* New York: Basic Books.

———. 2001. *Delimiting Anthropology: Occasional Essays and Reflections.* Madison: University of Wisconsin Press.

Valentine, Lisa Philips, and Regna Darnell, eds. 1999. *Theorizing the Americanist Tradition.* Toronto: University of Toronto Press.

White, Leslie. 1963. *The Ethnography and Ethnology of Franz Boas. Bulletin of the Texas Memorial Museum* 6. Austin: Texas Memorial Museum.

———. 1966. *The Social Organization of Ethnological Theory.* Rice University Studies 52. Houston: Rice University.

Wolf, Eric. 1999. *Envisioning Power: Ideologies of Dominance and Crisis.* Berkeley: University of California Press.

Young, Virginia Heyer. 2005. *Ruth Benedict: Beyond Relativity, Beyond Pattern.* Lincoln: University of Nebraska Press.

13

Benjamin Lee Whorf and the Boasian
Foundations of Contemporary Ethnolinguistics

The role of Benjamin Lee Whorf (1897–1941) in contemporary
ethnolinguistics is an unusually complex one from the standpoint
of the histories of anthropology, linguistics, and psychology, not
to speak of philosophy.[1] Whorf has been thoroughly misread as
unscientific because his institutional credentials were not in anthropology or linguistics. And yet his musings on the relationships
among language, thought, and reality continue to be cited—largely
under the interdisciplinary rubric of cognitive science—with the
respect due to a pioneer whose work is foundational to what is
being done today.

Anthropologists and linguists remain curious about Whorf; they
want to know whether he was right about linguistic relativity and
the critical importance of grammatical categories to differences
in the potential for the organization of the thought of individuals speaking a given language, relative to speakers of another language. The question, even stated in this simplistic form, continues
to fascinate. That there would be no such relationship is counter-
intuitive; to demonstrate the precise nature of the relationship,
however, remained an elusive prospect for Whorf's immediate successors. In my view, however, the kinds of experiments devised more
recently by cognitive scientists have very little to do with Whorf's
actual formulation of the problem of linguistic relativity. Rather,
he has been taken as a straw target for contemporary arguments,
thereby producing a discontinuity—or at least an unacknowledged
selectivity in contemporary readings—that has received little historiographic notice and calls for explanation.

Cognitive scientists have consistently acknowledged their debt

Fig. 8. Benjamin Lee Whorf (1897–1941). Benjamin Lee Whorf Papers,
Yale University Library [MS 822-4344755].

to Whorf and his intellectual genealogy stretching back through
his mentor Edward Sapir to his teacher Franz Boas to the German
Romanticism of Johann Herder, Wilhelm von Humboldt, and Hermann Steinthal. It is an honorable genealogy, deeply enmeshed
in the moral imperative of North American anthropology, which
moved back and forth between the tolerance for diversity associated with the notions of cultural relativism or linguistic relativity

and the obligation of the anthropologist as public intellectual to direct the fruits of cross-cultural investigation back to the critique of their own society. The consensus of such acknowledgments has been that Whorf raised questions of contemporary concern but lacked sufficiently rigorous methodology to resolve them. Such pro forma acknowledgment of Whorf as a predecessor too often fails to reexamine his actual work or the specific claims he made about linguistic relativity. A reexamination of his contribution and its subsequent appropriation by quite different research agendas is, therefore, long overdue.

This chapter returns Whorf to center stage and examines how his ideas are grounded in the general approach of Boasian anthropology to the study of North American Indigenous languages and cultures (Darnell 1998, 2001), a task that requires addressing a number of stereotypes about Whorf's position in the group around Edward Sapir at Yale in the 1930s and framing his formulation of what he called "the linguistic relativity principle" in relation to the larger body of his own linguistic work and that of his contemporaries.

Dell Hymes and John Fought, in their monumental discussion on American structuralism (1975:997) identify a "first Yale school" around Sapir, discontinuous from the better-known Yale school that emerged there around Leonard Bloomfield in the 1940s and 1950s. The distinctive features of the first Yale school were:

1. to develop methods of structural description and "to test their application in the analysis of both exotic and well-known languages";

2. to develop the discipline of linguistics;

3. to continue the urgent task of recording disappearing languages;

4. to continue the work of demonstrating precise genetic relationship among American Indian [*sic*] languages;

5. to link linguistics to other disciplines and to practical affairs.

Bloomfield agreed on the importance of all of these tasks, although few of his students took up questions of genetic relationship, and the balance among them was different from that of the Boasians.

Bloomfield's view of the relation of linguistics to other fields, particularly psychology and anthropology, was considerably narrower than Sapir's. Whorf's position was closely tied to the Boasian-Sapirian package recapped above. Despite the overlap in questions and methods, his broad humanistic orientation to linguistics would have been alien to the ethos of the second Yale school under Bloomfield and even more so to its most ardent disciple, Bernard Bloch. The post-Bloomfieldians moved even further from Boasian roots of Americanist linguistics than did Bloomfield himself. Postwar positivism further eclipsed the humanistic linguistics that neither Sapir nor Whorf were around to defend.

Our disciplinary oral traditions focus on several reasons not to take Whorf seriously.

First, he is often dismissed as an amateur linguist because he never held an academic degree in anthropology or linguistics; his only teaching position was in 1937–38 when he replaced Edward Sapir, who was on sabbatical, for a single course in American Indian [*sic*] linguistics. These indices of professional credentialization were indeed important by the 1930s. Whorf stood out among his contemporaries in never attempting to obtain formal credentialization from his apprenticeship with Sapir or to earn his living as a linguist.

Second, much of his writing appeared in unconventional journals, directed to engineers or theosophists, and aimed to make technical linguistic material accessible to educated but nonprofessional audiences. North American linguistics was still becoming professional, its disciplinary autonomy dating back only to the founding of the Linguistic Society of America. Whorf's publication outlets challenged these newfound respectabilities and disciplinary specializations. Moreover, linguists based in anthropology no longer seemed central to mainstream North American linguistics. The increasing isolation of the two disciplines accelerated during and after the Second World War, an increasing hiatus that culminated in the contemporary marginalization of linguistic anthropology within the four-field structure of the North American discipline.

Third, Whorf's Theosophical Society leanings and fascination with Asian philosophies have inspired charges that an already highly suspect mentalism degenerated into mysticism. Whorf's religious preoccupations were readily dismissed in an intellectual climate emphasizing the superficial appearance of science. Science was understood to be self-consciously and unequivocally secular.

Fourth, there has been some question of how much Whorf actually knew about Hopi. He worked intensively with the language in New York City with Ernest Naquayouma, a bilingual native speaker of Hopi. Whorf's exposure to the Hopi language in its proper cultural context and among monolingual speakers was extremely limited. If grammatical categories highly influenced or even determined thought, as Whorf suggested, then a bilingual "informant" could hardly be taken to represent unproblematically the thought-world of their natal community. Whorf was rarely able to carry out conventional fieldwork except on an occasional vacation from his non-academic employment, even though he attracted prestigious and highly competitive funding from the Social Science Research Council for fieldwork. His contemporaries were able to spend much more time "in the field," and this was considered part of the mystique of being a "real" anthropologist.

Although all of these things are true, they do not add up to an accurate picture of Whorf's professional stature as it was perceived by his contemporaries. Whorf's career was indeed anomalous, but such issues arise in the context of assessing his ideas about linguistic relativity virtually without attention to the structure of his ideas as a whole (what Penny Lee [1996] calls "the Whorf theory complex"), his reputation among his contemporaries, or the degree of complicity of Sapir in his supposedly mystical or mentalist formulations about the relationship of language and culture.

Whorf was well educated, albeit not within the disciplines in which we remember his work today. A generation earlier, virtually everyone had been trained in something else. But for Whorf's professional generation, doctoral credentials in anthropology were becoming de rigueur. Although contemporaries and successors judged him by the emerging standards, Whorf's university degree in chemical engineering from the Massachusetts Institute of Technology (MIT) served him well in his lifelong employment as a fire insurance claims adjustor. Practical experience taught him, as it had Sapir, to distrust disciplinary boxes. He did not separate his scientific training in engineering from his work in linguistics and was wont to employ examples from his work to illustrate the relationship between linguistic categories and real-world experience. There was nothing mystical about Whorf's belief in the real world.

His best-known example is the cautionary tale of the empty gasoline drum, treated as no longer dangerous because of a linguistic label but still containing sufficient fumes to cause an explosion. Although the story arises from his personal experience and has consequences of particular urgency to a fire insurance company employee, his experience taught him, as it did Sapir, the irrelevance of disciplinary boxes. Whorf never claimed that the explosion of an empty gasoline drum caused him to arrive at what his successors have called "the Whorf hypothesis." The story serves not as evidence but as a representative anecdote, illustrating how what he called "habitual thought" relies on unexamined linguistic categories. Whorf took for granted that any speaker of a given language could bring such categories to conscious awareness and articulate them in words. This insight arose from his long-term work on Hopi but also from what Sapir called the "psychological reality" of the "multilingual consciousness" that it inculcated in him (as well, presumably, as in his key consultant).

Employment was a problem for Whorf's entire generation. They came of age professionally in the midst of the Great Depression when there were few academic jobs in any field and even fewer in so new and apparently insignificant a discipline as linguistics. Whorf was almost alone in holding steady employment, and he was careful to avoid decreasing resources available to his fellow students.[2] Linguistics in North America did not come into its own until the Second World War demonstrated its practical utility in dealing with unfamiliar but suddenly politically significant cultures and languages, particularly in Asia and the Pacific.

The turn of the 1940s was a time of loss for the kind of linguistics in which Whorf's ideas developed. The world was girding itself for war. Sapir had his first heart attack in the summer of 1935 and died in 1939 at the relatively young age of fifty-five. Whorf learned that he had cancer late in 1938; he underwent surgery but continued to write until his death in 1941 at the age of forty-four (Lee 1996:13). Had he lived to a normal life span, Whorf would have had the opportunity to elaborate the ideas for which he is castigated today as having provided little empirical evidence. These are the stereotypes that have drowned out more measured assessment. Here is what he said:

> We dissect nature along lines laid down by our native languages. The categories and types that we isolate from the world of phenomena we do not find there because they stare every observer in the face; on the contrary, the world is presented in a kaleidoscopic flux of impressions which has to be organized by our minds—and this means largely by the linguistic systems of our minds. (Whorf 1956:213)

> The phenomena of language are background phenomena, of which the talkers are unaware or, at most, dimly aware. . . . These automatic, involuntary patterns of language are not the same for all men [*sic*] but are specific for each language and constitute the formalized side of the language, or its "grammar." . . . From this fact proceeds what I have called the "linguistic relativity principle," which means, in informal terms, that users of markedly different grammars are pointed by their grammars toward different types of observations and different evaluations of externally similar acts of observation, and hence are not equivalent as observers, but must arrive at somewhat different views of the world. (Whorf 1956:221)

Whorf was forced to concentrate on getting into print his ideas on how to approach linguistic questions, with the hope that others would choose to follow up (as indeed they did). We are left with programmatic and suggestive formulations.

Sapir's version of process grammar and his concern with the relations of language, thought, and reality were not followed up at Yale after his death; the students, mostly what we would now call postdocs, were not senior enough to succeed him, and the department of anthropology turned away from linguistics almost totally (Darnell 1998, chapter 11, this volume). Boas and Bloomfield tried, in anthropology and linguistics, respectively, to mentor Sapir's former students, but the collective unity and sense of shared mission dissipated after his death. In the period after Whorf's death, North American linguistics under the leadership of Bloomfield veered sharply toward behaviorism and experimentalism, explicitly striving for the status of science and equating science with the exclusion of meaning from the purview of linguistics. This definition of science would have made sense to Whorf.

Ironically, given persistent accusations that he was unscientific, Whorf knew more about science than any of his fellow Boasian linguists because of his training in engineering. He read voraciously in the physical sciences and frequently applied scientific metaphors and analogies in his linguistic work. Albert Einstein's theory of relativity was the most significant scientific discovery of Whorf's lifetime, and he followed its technical elaboration as well as extending it metaphorically to the at least superficially incommensurable thought-worlds associated with different languages. His comment in the MIT *Technology Review* in 1940 (1956:214) suggests that Whorf expected this audience to follow the process by which his own train of thought had moved from Einstein's physics to questions of linguistic form: "We are thus introduced to a new [application of the] principle of relativity, which holds that all observers are not led by the same physical evidence to the same picture of the universe, unless their linguistic backgrounds are similar, or can in some way be calibrated." The reference to calibration entails a method of scientific experiment that Whorf found highly congenial. He wanted linguistics to be more scientific.

Whorf was not alone in his fascination with the physics of relativity. As early as 1924, Sapir had explicitly cited "the relativity of the form of thought" grounded in the "incommensurable analyses of experience in different languages" (in 1949:158). It was "not so difficult to grasp as the physical relativity of Einstein" in spite of the blinders imposed by "our naive acceptance of fixed habits of thought" (159). Yet Sapir's flirtations with linguistic relativity were not received with the same skepticism as Whorf's. The sheer magnitude and quality of his other work allowed him to be taken seriously in ways that Whorf never was.

In the eyes of linguists in the 1940s and 1950s, however, what was unscientific about Whorf's work was the methodology underlying his comparisons of Hopi and what he called "Standard Average European" (SAE). Whorf did not intend his pronouncements to be interpreted literally as having resulted from controlled scientific comparison of the two languages; detailed evidence was still forthcoming. Robin Ridington (1991) has glossed some of Whorf's most lyrical theoretical statements in poetic lines to indicate the assemblage of his argument in terms to which scientific experiment in the narrow sense is irrelevant. Rather, Whorf's work explored directions for further investigation of how meaning is expressed in language and in particular languages.

Despite their skepticism toward anything that talked about "mind," the Bloomfieldians and neo-Bloomfieldians who dominated Yale linguistics after the deaths of Sapir and Whorf expended considerable energy in attempting to formulate the Whorf (or Sapir-Whorf) hypothesis in terms amenable to unambiguous testing. Harry Hoijer, a Sapir student from his pre-Yale days at the University of Chicago, edited an influential collection of conference papers in 1954 that deemed the experimental results inconclusive. Thereafter, linguistic relativity retreated as a topic for serious investigation, although lip service to its underlying insight was retained.

Whorf as a Linguist among His Peers

In his own time, "Ben" Whorf was acknowledged as one among a group of peers, most of whom had followed Edward Sapir from Chicago to Yale in 1931. In addition to Whorf, the cohort included Morris Swadesh, Stanley Newman, Mary Haas, George Trager, George Herzog, Zellig Harris, and later Carl Voegelin, Charles Hockett, and indirectly Joseph Greenberg. Whorf joined the group only after Sapir arrived in New Haven. He could not have been singled out in 1931 for the crucial idea now identified as the "Whorf hypothesis" because it did not yet exist. His dramatic formulation of the relationship of language, thought, and reality came only at the end of his lifetime. Whorf's best-known paper on linguistic relativity, "The Relation of Habitual Thought and Behavior to Language," appeared in a memorial volume for Sapir (Hoijer 1946). Of necessity, its influence on linguistics, anthropology, and psychology was subsequent to that publication and proceeded without further input from the author. The elegiac tone of the volume suggests that he chose a subject whose importance to him was shared with Sapir and reflected the latter's much-touted "genius."

During his lifetime Whorf was acknowledged as an American

Indian [*sic*] linguist in the Sapirian vein. He was the only Sapir student to contribute two grammatical sketches (on Milpa Aztec and Hopi) to the linguistic memorial volume edited by Hoijer in 1946 reporting his extensive work on comparative and classificatory problems in historical linguistics. With George Trager, he succeeded in linking Sapir's Uto-Aztecan stock to Tanoan. Mary Haas wrote to Whorf (February 16, 1937: YU) that the Tanoan connection followed up well on "Sapir's intuitions." Both Whorf's synchronic and diachronic work were respected among his peers.[3]

Ironically, Sapir's students were more interested in linguistic classification in the 1930s than was Sapir himself; he turned to other problems after presenting his six-unit classification in 1921 (revised to its more familiar form in 1929). The students saw themselves as taking over where Sapir left off, linking linguistic stocks to produce a culture history of the continent that could be read in broad strokes (Darnell [1990] 2010; Murray 1997). Sapir was apparently not much involved in the collective's revised synthesis. His own professional identity evolved toward linguistics as an autonomous discipline, whereas his students continued to embrace the Boasian view of his early career.

There can be no question that Sapir thought highly of Whorf. He wrote to Alfred Kroeber (April 30, 1936: ALK):

> Whorf is an awfully good man, largely self-made, and with a dash of genius. He is sometimes inclined to get off the central problem and indulge in marginal speculations but that merely shows the originality and adventuresome quality of his mind. . . . [He] is one of the most valuable American Indian [*sic*] linguists that we have at the present time.

For Sapir, if not for many of his contemporaries, imagination was a desirable quality. After the onset of Sapir's illness in 1937, Whorf increasingly served as the focal point of the Yale cohort as they dispersed for fieldwork and employment. Whorf's personal papers contain round-robin letters that he appears to have been responsible for keeping in circulation. All of the students were protective of Sapir, given his precarious health. Whorf, who had to stay in the area, was delegated and entrusted to decide what Sapir should be bothered with and what not.

During Sapir's sabbatical in 1937–38, when he was forced to cancel a sojourn in China as the guest of Fang-Kuei Li (where he doubtless hoped to pursue possible linkages of tone languages in Asia and America) to spend the year mostly in New York City attempting to recover his health, Whorf was hired to teach the required course on "problems of American Indian [*sic*] linguistics" to anthropology graduate students, many of whom were dubious about the relevance of such technical material to their ethnological interests. Whorf was elated by the opportunity to share his enthusiasm for linguistics in general and American Indian [*sic*] languages in particular. He wrote to Yale anthropology chair Leslie Spier, a Boas-trained Americanist ethnologist (August 4, 1937: YUDA): "I realize that . . . the students will have, for the most part, only the haziest notions of linguistics, and my idea would be to excite them in the linguistic approach as a way of developing understanding of the ideology of other peoples."

Whorf realized he would have to appeal to ethnological reasoning to hold the attention of his students. He knew that he had neither the stature nor the charisma of Sapir. Tolerance for cultural diversity, that is, cultural relativism, with or without the label, had been at the core of the Boasian program since *The Mind of Primitive Man* in 1911, and Whorf aspired to demonstrate this in terms of Native American linguistic data. Spier apparently agreed to this strategy, writing to Dean Edgar Furniss (August 6, 1937: YU) that Whorf

> has a very stimulating way . . . and I would like to take advantage of his interest in hooking up language and ethnology, for I think it would take with many of our students. They might thus be encouraged to give serious attention to linguistics, when a "straight" linguistics course might leave them cold.

To John Carroll, Whorf explained that he envisioned (August 1937: YU) "a psychological direction" to the examination of "the organization of raw experience into a consistent and readily communicable universe of ideas through a medium of linguistic patterns." This is the moment of origin of the Whorf hypothesis (Darnell [1990] 2010:381). It was less a new theory or methodology than a pedagogical hook to translate the linguistic work of Sapir and his students so that it would be both intelligible and relevant to non-linguists. The other members of Whorf's cohort shared the logic in this construction of their common agenda and responded to it as unremarkable.

Whorf's background was somewhat different from that of others in his cohort, in ways that perhaps explain why he was the only one to take up this pedagogical challenge. John B. Carroll, in his introduction to Whorf's selected writings in 1956 under the title *Language, Thought and Reality*, emphasizes Whorf's "contact with a small but earnest band of Sapir's students" (Carroll 1956:16) as the watershed in his recognition as a professional linguist. Whorf was accepted into the linguistics doctoral program in at Yale, but he chose to follow Sapir's courses rather than pursue the degree as such.

Whorf was introduced to Sapir as a protégé of several prominent Harvard archaeologists who worked in Mexico (Alfred Tozzer, Herbert Spinden, and Sylvanus Morley). He already had considerable experience with several languages, including Hebrew, Nahuatl, and Mayan, as well as a broad professional network in anthropology and had worked on Mayan and Aztec cryptography and iconography. His archaeologist mentors had a considerable stake in Whorf's acquisition of credentials in the cutting-edge linguistics of the day. Whorf, or someone like him, could help them interpret their archaeological data. Most of Boas's students, in contrast, were immersed in the study of the more acutely endangered languages of the Americas north of Mexico. Moreover, tension between Columbia and Harvard had resulted in an implicit division between cultural anthropology and linguistics under Boas in New York and archaeology and physical anthropology in Cambridge that maintained the naturalist, scientific tradition initiated by Frederic Ward Putnam in the late nineteenth century.

The Harvard archaeologists failed to recognize that American linguistics itself was changing, with an increasing division between Boas and Sapir over phonetic versus phonemic transcription (Darnell [1990] 2010). Boas held that the ethnologist qua linguist was responsible for recording the greatest possible detail of rapidly disappearing languages while it was still possible to do so. Sapir believed that the interesting facts about languages were contained in their underlying relational patterns rather than in their surface details. His formulation of the concept of the phoneme, which first appeared in print in 1925 in the first volume of *Language*, constituted a turning point in the affiliation of Sapir and his students with the discipline of linguistics rather than with its anthropological roots. Although Boas served as an early president of the LSA and was honored there as an elder statesman, he never became a linguist in this sense of primary professional identity. Linguistics, for him as for most of the cultural anthropologists he trained, was a handmaiden to ethnology rather than an end in itself.

Sapir's emphasis on phonemic patterning fed into his growing fascination with the relationship of culture and the individual. In language, this became "the psychological reality" of the phoneme. In ethnology, it drew on the long-established Boasian search, through the collection of native language texts, for "the native point of view." Whorf found this tradition of attention to linguistic creativity at the level of the individual, realized differently across languages and cultures, remarkably congenial. What first appeared as trivial technical details in the grammars (including sound systems) of particular American Indian [*sic*] languages provided entreé into the manifold thought-worlds of the speakers of those languages.

Whorf argued that the linguist could transcend the patterns of habitual thought characteristic of their first language by virtue of its contrastive pattern relative to languages learned in the field and described in their own unique terms. "Multilingual awareness"—what his Yale colleague George Trager would later call "metalinguistic" awareness—was the proper goal of linguistic science because it allowed the linguist to return to their own society and see it more clearly.

I have argued (Darnell 2001 and 2008, chapter 12, this volume) that Whorf's formulation of the linguistic relativity principle owes much to Ruth Benedict's *Patterns of Culture* (1934), whose goal was for the anthropologist to become "culture-conscious." The moral imperative toward critique of then-contemporary North America is pervasive in Benedict, albeit geared to the humanities rather than to linguistics as a science, and it is echoed repeatedly in Whorf's expectation of an audience among fellow scientists.

Ironically, these Benedictine passages are the very ones in which Whorf is accused of mysticism by linguists, most of whom do not read Benedict (Darnell 2008, chapter 12, this volume). Again, Whorf's most contentious positions are deeply grounded in Boasian anthropology, in the intersection of linguistics and ethnology around the study of the American Indian [*sic*]. This context has been obscured in recent readings of Whorf.

Whorf and Cognitive Science

Whorf's characteristic phrase "linguistic relativity" is retained by Gumperz and Levinson, albeit their edited collection on the state of the art in cognitive science simultaneously proposed that the concept needed "rethinking" (1996:2): "Readers will find that the original idea of linguistic relativity still live[s], but functioning in a way that differs from how it was originally conceived." The tone of papers and introductory discussions is resolutely revisionist.

Stephen C. Levinson is the most articulate advocate of a new synthesis provided by cognitive science. He emphasizes that the differences from Whorf's position are substantial. Whorf was interested in cultural and linguistic differences rather than in universals; cognitive science assumes a species-wide, wired-in explanation for cross-culturally attested similarities in the processing of linguistic and other communicative forms. Levinson characterizes the contemporary search for psychologically and biologically grounded universals as rationalist, with Whorf s position relegated to the status of mere empiricism. Whorf was unwilling or unable to arrive at the kind of generalizations in which Levinson is interested. Levinson further opposes the realism of cognitive science to the idealism of Whorf, that is, the mentalist concern with what was going on in people's heads, presumably to the exclusion of attention to the real world outside linguistically conditioned human minds.[4] "In this light, the Sapir-Whorf hypothesis [in its original form] seems uninteresting" (1996:177). Levinson suggests (134) that anthropology

> remains largely outside this current of thought: viewed from cognitive science it is a reactionary output of empiricist ideas with an outmoded stress on human ideational difference and

the importance of environmental learning [i.e., socialization into a particular culture and language].

Levinson is prepared to dismiss Boasian historical particularist emphasis on the unique grammatical categories of each human language, with the implication that organization of the discipline of anthropology around the concept of culture is an unproductive strategy given what we know today about universal cognitive structures. The emphasis on particular ethnographies as a result of participant observation fieldwork and extensive work with particular "informants" to produce native language texts seems rather a waste of time from this formulation of the cognitive science perspective. It is extreme in its explicitness about what is at stake but expresses widespread consensus.

Whorf, in contrast, took Boasian ethnographic particularity for granted. For him, the universals of linguistic form were of considerable interest but would be arrived at by a different strategy, one of adding up and comparing the commonalities among as many languages as possible. Levinson's strategy would have struck him as a case of the premature generalization that Boas habitually deplored in all fields of anthropology, not exclusively in his critique of evolution.

When Levinson calls for "a sophisticated theory of the co-evolution of mind and culture" (1996:41) in approaching the pragmatic inseparability of language and culture, his language is directly counter to the thrust of Boasian speculations on similar issues. For Sapir, for example, the binary opposition of interest was culture and the individual (or culture and personality), which he understood as "sides of the same coin." Agency and creativity were at the core of Sapir's theory of culture.

Boas's critique of the theory of evolution as applied to culture was essentially complete by 1894; he would have seen no reason to talk about evolution in the same breath as diversity of linguistic or cultural form. The biological overtones of Levinson's desiderata also were unacceptable in an Americanist anthropology that separated culture from biology and centered the discipline around the former. Boas's work on race was foundational to the move from arbitrary typological classification to plasticity and population adaptation (Boas 1911; Darnell 2001). But he moved on after about 1912 to concern himself more with racism than with race per se. Racism, for him, was a question of culture rather than of biology. When Levinson turns to his own data on spatial expression in the Mayan language Tzeltal based on his own fieldwork, his negative judgment of the Boasian agenda is mitigated. He deplores the unintentional ethnocentrism of semantic analysis based on unproblematized Indo-European categories. This formulation of how to characterize the uniqueness of a particular set of categories would have made perfectly good sense to both Boas and Whorf. When Levinson is not carving out an intellectual space for cognitive science among the disciplines and in relation to its arguable home base within Americanist anthropology as understood by Whorf, he remains very much interested in cross-linguistic variation of the sort that so fascinated Whorf. This is the "intermediate position" identified in the introduction to the collected volume, in which the cognitive synthesis results in "such diversity being viewed within the context of what we have learned about universals" (in Gumperz and Levinson 1996:3). Fair enough.

A more nuanced version of the rejection of Whorf's methods and conclusions alongside praise for his intuitive genius is found in John Lucy's insistence that Whorf did his best to test his ideas empirically (and indeed they have yet to be tested formally in the ways Whorf himself understood the empirical problem). Whorf, in Lucy's view, successfully produced "the nucleus of a procedure for establishing a neutral basis for the comparison of language-reality relationships" by playing off Hopi and "Standard Average European" (SAE) against one another without privileging either (in Gumperz and Levinson 1996:43; Lucy 1992). Moreover, Whorf adopted a moral framework for linguistics "which placed the science of language at the centre of all efforts to advance human understanding" (1996:64). This is what John Joseph (1996:372), in comparing Whorf's position to that of general semantics, identifies as the "magic key" view of language that linguistics inherited from Wilhelm von Humboldt.

It is possible to arrive at cognitive science by non-Americanist routes not associated with Whorf, some of which may rely less on a rhetoric of discontinuity (Murray 1994) to justify their own innovativeness. For example, Maurice Bloch, a British social anthropologist with strong ties to French structuralism, argues that contemporary anthropology is being torn apart by a dichotomy between, on the one hand, "the hermeneutic and literary dimensions of ethnography" and, on the other, by an "aggressively naturalist" insistence on the realism of the world as the grounding for mental constructs; he views these too frequently opposed strains of anthropological theory as "two fundamentalisms" (Bloch 1998:40) that have

> developed in the work of anthropologists who identify with only one side of this dual heritage and who consequently wish to "purify" anthropology of the other orientation. We are therefore faced with two movements which have in common their rejection of the hybrid character of the discipline.

Bloch suggests that anthropologists, especially in North America, have permitted their quest for "scientific credibility" to erode the discipline's reliance on an ever-continuing cross-checking of theory against data emerging from participant observation fieldwork; they have, he argues, simply accepted what their informants [*sic*] tell them about their worlds as authoritative and abdicated their own obligation to analyze and compare (1998:41).

Bloch argues persuasively that cognitive science provides a way out of the respective fundamentalist impasses because it informs ethnographic practice with some hope of objectivity in dealing with the traditional core subject matters of [social] anthropology; in his view, these are social structure, political organization, and ritual (1998:43). Unlike Levinson in his rhetorical mode, Bloch insists that the particularism of ethnography is crucial to testing cognitive schemas in cross-cultural contexts. He considers it inevitable that anthropologists will employ psychological theories in their efforts to interpret the behavioral patterns of other societies. Cognitive psychology offers more valid and replicable ways of interpreting alterity than an unreflexive folk psychology (usually applied naively) (1998:43–44). Although Bloch's position provides a plausible rationale for the ethnographic application of cognitive science, its internal concerns are less with discovery procedures for fieldwork and more with universal constraints on human thought across cultural and linguistic communities. His argument may persuade anthropologists to attend to cognitive science, but it is less clear that the reverse is true.

The Gumperz and Levinson collection provides a useful overview of the contemporary status of linguistic relativity debates in the mid-1990s because it includes contributors from a wide variety of disciplinary and theoretical backgrounds, with a substantial range of opinion among the contributors, although not all attempt to trace the continuities or discontinuities from cognitive science back to Whorf. The contributors most sympathetic to the Whorfian position are the fieldworking anthropologists whose work is mostly subsumed under the rubric of ethnography of speaking, that is, apart from the mainstream of linguistics.

The most powerful reformulation of Whorf's position has been Dell Hymes's "Two Types of Linguistic Relativity" (1966) wherein he suggested that Whorf's emphasis on variations in linguistic structure among languages entailed glossing over variability in favor of an assumed uniformity of such structures within each speech community. Reversing Whorf's argument but retaining his consideration of nontrivial relativity, Hymes called for attention to a second kind of linguistic relativity in the uses of language. Language functions, he argued, would prove to be universal, although they would take dramatically different surface forms in particular societies. Hymes has referred almost interchangeably to "the ethnography of speaking" and "the ethnography of communication," reflecting his commitment to ethnographic exploration of modalities other than language and their relative positions in a given communicative economy. The Whorfian tradition in Americanist anthropology, he concludes, is not necessarily incompatible with the rationalist and universalist agendas of cognitive science. Whorf, like Sapir, explored the foundations of what today is called ethnolinguistics in critical relation to his linguistic relativity principle and his understanding of linguistics as a science.

In sum, the Whorf caricatured as an ancestor or precursor to cognitive science is not a Whorf who would have been recognized in his own time. As Levinson astutely observes, the intellectual climate changed in the 1960s, allowing for reworking of the Boas-Sapir-Whorf position in ways that our erstwhile ancestors could not have imagined.

Notes

1. Originally published as "Benjamin Lee Whorf and the Boasian Foundations of Contemporary Ethnolingusitics." in *Language, Culture and Society*, ed. Christine Jourdan and Kevin Tuite, 82–95 (Cambridge: Cambridge University Press, 2006).

2. Mary Haas, in an interview with Stephen O. Murray in 1978 (Murray 1997), recalled that Sapir did his best to find short-term positions on research projects or in the field for his students. There were few academic positions. Stanley Newman (Darnell 1989, chapter 15, this volume) wanted to pursue Sapir's interests in "linguistic psychology" but moved into American Indian [*sic*] linguistics because he could find no other way to support himself and his family.

3. The situation is parallel to the reception of Sapir's *Time Perspective in Aboriginal America: A Study in Method* in 1916. Sapir's most powerful examples of how to reconstruct the past history of peoples without history were linguistic. Language differed from the rest of culture because sound changes made it possible to distinguish the results of genetic diversification from a common ancestor from those due to borrowing or diffusion. Sapir's colleagues in Boasian ethnology adopted this perspective, which culminated in his reduction of the linguistic families of North America to only six, as a framework for their studies of culture. Most were indifferent to the linguistic evidence as such, trusting Sapir, the linguist among them, to have gotten it right. The reception of glottochronology as a dating technique for unwritten languages by Whorf's Yale colleague, Morris Swadesh, met with a similarly unnuanced response.

4. This is emphatically not Whorf's position. The tripartite title of his collected papers, "Language, Thought and Reality," reinforces the significance of the third term "reality."

References

Benedict, Ruth. 1934. *Patterns of Culture*. Boston: Houghton Mifflin.

Boas, Franz. 1911. *The Mind of Primitive Man*. New York: Macmillan.

Bloch, Maurice. 1998. *How We Think They Think: Anthropological Approaches to Cognition, Memory, and Literacy*. Boulder CO: Westview.

Carroll, John B. 1956. Introduction to Whorf, *Language, Thought, and Reality: Selected Writings by Benjamin Lee Whorf*, 1–34. Edited by John B. Carroll. Cambridge: MIT Press.

Darnell, Regna. 1989. "Stanley Newman and the Sapir School of Linguistics." In *General and Amerindian Linguistics: In Remembrance of Stanley Newman*, edited by Mary Ritchie Key and Henry Hoenigswald, 71–88. Berlin: Mouton de Gruyter.

———. (1990) 2010. *Edward Sapir: Linguist, Anthropologist, Humanist*. Berkeley: University of California Press. Reprint, Lincoln: University of Nebraska Press.

———. 1998. "Camelot at Yale: The Establishment and Dismantling of the Sapirian Synthesis, 1931–1939." *American Anthropologist* 100:361–72.

———. 2001. *Invisible Genealogies: A History of Americanist Anthropology.* Lincoln: University of Nebraska Press.

———. 2008. "Benedictine Visionings of Southwestern Cultural Diversity: Beyond Relativism." *Journal of Anthropological Research* 64:469–82.

Gumperz, John, and Stephen C. Levinson, eds. 1996. *Rethinking Linguistic Relativity.* Cambridge: Cambridge University Press.

Hoijer, Harry, ed. 1946. *Linguistic Structures of Native America.* Viking Fund Publications in Anthropology 6. New York: Viking Fund.

———, ed. 1954. *Language in Culture: Proceedings of a Conference on the Interrelations of Language and Other Aspects of Culture. American Anthropological Association Memoir* 79.

Hymes, Dell. 1966. "Two Types of Linguistic Relativity." In *Sociolinguistics,* edited by William Bright, 903–1176. The Hague: Mouton.

Hymes, Dell, and John Fought. 1975. "American Structuralism." In *Current Trends in Linguistics: Historiography of Linguistics* 10, edited by Thomas Sebeok, 903–1176. The Hague: Mouton.

Joseph, John. 1996. "The Immediate Sources of the Sapir-Whorf Hypothesis." *Historiographia Linguistica* 23:365–404.

Lee, Penny. 1996. *The Whorf Theory Complex: A Critical Reconstruction.* Amsterdam: John Benjamins.

Levinson, Stephen C. 1996. Introduction to Gumperz and Levinson 1996:21–36.

Lucy, John. 1992. *Language Diversity and Thought: A Reformulation of the Linguistic Relativity Hypothesis.* Cambridge: Cambridge University Press.

Murray, Stephen O. 1994. *Theory Groups and the Study of Language in North America.* Amsterdam: John Benjamins.

———. 1997. "A 1978 Interview with Mary R. Haas." *Anthropological Linguistics* 39:695–722.

Ridington, Robin. 1991. "On the Language of Benjamin Lee Whorf." In *Anthropological Poetics,* edited by Ivan Brady, 241–61. Savage MD: Rowan and Littlefield.

Sapir, Edward. 1916. *Time Perspective in Aboriginal American Culture: A Study in Method.* Canadian Geological Survey Memoir 90. Ottawa: Government Printing Bureau.

———. 1949. *Selected Writings of Edward Sapir.* Edited by David Mandelbaum. Berkeley: University of California Press.

Whorf, Benjamin Lee. 1941. "The Relation of Habitual Thought and Behavior to Language." In *Language, Culture and Personality: Essays in Memory of Edward Sapir,* edited by Leslie Spier, A. Irving Hallowell, and Stanley S. Newman, 75–93. Menasha WI: George Banta.

———. 1956. *Language. Thought, and Reality: Selected Writings by Benjamin Lee Whorf.* Edited by John B. Carroll. Cambridge: MIT Press.

14
....

Mary R. Haas and the First Yale
School of Linguistics

When I first met Mary Haas, I didn't know who she was.[1] It was at a Berkeley party at the meetings of the American Anthropological Association in the late 1960s. She looked wildly out of place amid clouds of pungent smoke and too many bodies for the size of the room. Since no one else was talking to her, I thought I would have a go at it. So I found myself telling her about my dissertation work and was horrified when I realized who she was and how naively I had been babbling about my interpretation of the Boasian-Sapirian tradition in which she had been a core participant.

I had the privilege of taking my first field methods course with Mary at the LSA Summer Institute in 1970 after my first year of teaching in Alberta and of beginning fieldwork to learn Plains Cree. They couldn't find her a Thai speaker, so we worked on Aymara, a new language for Mary. It was the heyday of transformational grammar. People like me, who already had PhDs, were paid to come and get converted. There were fifteen or so of us. The already-converted syntax and phonology students were without a clue about fieldwork. I remember Juan, our native speaker of Aymara, listening patiently to one student's rather painful paraphrase of the inclusive-exclusive distinction; Juan finally sighed deeply and said, "It's the inclusive." Mary, on the other hand, was a joy to watch. She asked questions until it became clear that something else, or something more complex, was going on. Then she switched tacks, often abruptly. I loved it when I could see the plan, the structure emerging. Mary and I were the only ones who thought it was part of the course to go for coffee with Juan after

Fig. 9. Mary Haas in conversation at Berkeley, 1980. Mary R. Haas Papers, American Philosophical Society [Mss.Ms.Coll.94].

the class. So I got to know him a little too, as well as Mary. Toward the end of the course, she said thoughtfully over coffee: "You know, Morris [Swadesh] may've been right [about Aymara]—it feels Penutian."

Mary gave a couple of lectures at the institute that summer. Participants heady with "The Theory" were inclined to dismiss her as a mere descriptivist. Somebody tried to trip her up by asking about the phonetic quality of an obscure consonant cluster in one of the languages John P. Harrington had recorded in his characteristic idiosyncratic orthography. Mary began "Well, I can't answer that for certain." The questioner beamed with pleasure—there was something about a Native American language that she didn't know. But she continued: "However, given that Harrington mistranscribed a similar sound in a language I have heard, and given what several other linguists later recorded for closely related languages, I think it was probably [whatever the cluster was]." It had not occurred to her would-be tormenter that the question itself might be complicated, or that Mary would think through potential evidence to give a more serious and respectful answer than the flippancy deserved.

Knowing languages was not highly valued that summer, and in some circles perhaps still is not. But I found much to draw me to Mary's version of linguistics: its ties to my own discipline of anthropology, the urgency of fieldwork on endangered languages, and her appreciation for the beauty and integrity of both the languages studied and their grammars. I savored her auditory memory for forms in particular languages and her ability to cite them from memory to illustrate comparative points. I treasured her accessibility to students and her insistence that even anthropologists like me had a responsibility to the language, "to get it right." She was a fitting successor to her own mentor, Edward Sapir.

What I miss most of all is Mary's calling me "Linda" (as did many of her contemporaries who grew up on silent films)—the name seemed to go well with Darnell. I never corrected her and found it personal and quite charming; I was sad when someone told her and she stumbled through an embarrassed apology.

What Mary thought about her career and her participation in Americanist linguistics after 1930 is laid out in an interview with Stephen O. Murray (1997). This personal retrospective on the history of anthropological linguistics, however, is quite different from the glimpses of her participation in what Hymes and Fought (1975) have called "the first Yale school of linguistics" that are recorded in the Archives of Yale University (YU) and its anthropology departmental archives (YUDA). These archives document the coursework, fieldwork, and collegial interaction of Sapir's students, including both those who followed him from the University of Chicago in 1931 and those who were attracted to the group later. Due to the exigencies of the Great Depression, most of them were still around Yale when Sapir died early in 1939.

Their mentor's declining health after his first heart attack in the summer of 1937 encouraged his students to depend on each other for feedback and mutual support. They wrote round-robin letters from the field, facilitated back in New Haven by Benjamin Lee Whorf, whose continuing employment as an insurance investigator in nearby Hartford, Connecticut, made him the ideal homebody. In the department of anthropology, Leslie Spier took up the slack for Sapir, both with the students and with general administrative work.

The linguistic students formed a group distinct from the anthropologists. They were further along in their careers, and their work was too specialized for most of the ethnology students to follow. Weston La Barre, for example, came to Yale with some idea that he might be a linguist. But Sapir's course in Navajo sent him into "culture shock": "I never aspired to compete with these formidable older colleagues in linguistics" (La Barre 1978:280). La Barre found Sapir's insistence on psychoanalysis as necessary for students of psychology and culture more congenial.

The group of students around Sapir at Chicago had coalesced during Sapir's last year there (in which Mary not only switched from philology with Carl Darling Buck and Germanics with Leonard Bloomfield but also met and married Sapir's prize student, Morris Swadesh), but at Yale the linguists around Sapir were perceived as something of a closed circle. The Swadeshes, Mary and Morris, and Stanley S. Newman formed the core of the first Yale school, with Charles F. (Carl) Voegelin, Benjamin Lee Whorf, George L. Trager, George Herzog, Zellig S. Harris, Charles F. Hockett, and others joining them later. In retrospect, Mary expressed annoyance that many of the latter, who were not at Chicago, attempted to speak with authority about Sapir's Chicago years (Murray 1997).

Sapir soon came to consider Mary one of his most promising students. Not long after she received her PhD in linguistics, with a dissertation on Tunica (Haas 1935), he wrote to Alfred L. Kroeber: "She has grown steadily in my opinion and is actually, at the present time, an excellent linguist, entirely devoted to American Indian [*sic*] linguistic research" (Sapir to Kroeber, June 17, 1935: ALK). In addition to Tunica, she had "done a pretty complete job" on Natchez and had begun to work on comparative Muskogean. This assessment came in the context of recommending Morris Swadesh to Kroeber for a position at Berkeley. Sapir emphasized that Kroeber could get two linguists for the price of one. In a separate letter to Kroeber, Sapir pushed the Swadeshes rather than Newman, whose interests had turned increasingly toward linguistic psychology and who was "not particularly in love with fieldwork as such":

> Swadesh and his wife are more likely for an indefinite period— perhaps the rest of their lives—to be committed to specialist work in American Indian [*sic*] linguistics. . . . The Swadeshes love languages as you love decorative art and chess. Their combined energy is enormous. (Sapir to Kroeber, June 17, 1935: ALK)

Sapir's appreciation of Mary was not entirely contingent on her association with Swadesh. He wrote to Leslie Spier (June 25, 1937: YUDA), as Swadesh was preparing to leave for his new job at the University of Wisconsin, that "a casual remark of Morris'[s] seemed to imply that she might be available"; she was "by no means to be sniffed at, being a better phonetician than either Herzog or Whorf, and a better American Indian [*sic*] linguist than Herzog or Trager." Accordingly, Sapir wrote again to Kroeber (August 5, 1937: YUDA) since it appeared that Mary would now need a job to support herself:

> I learned today from Mary Haas Swadesh that she and her husband are expecting to get divorced as soon as she establishes residence in Oklahoma, which will be very soon. They are both excellent linguistic students but did not succeed in making much of it as husband and wife.

Mary would be ideal for "a geographical survey of American Indian [*sic*] linguistics in general or California linguistics in particular" (Sapir to Kroeber, August 5, 1937: YUDA). He continued: "My respect for her work has grown steadily from year to year. She is not as brilliant as Morris but more interested in historic problems and fully as accurate in her field methodology." Kroeber could get in touch with her in Eufaula, Oklahoma, that is, in the field.

For Mary, what made the Yale department unique in Americanist linguistics was the emerging professional standard for what was then called "primitive linguistics." The crucial combination was training in the methods of comparative philology, largely Indo-European, and fieldwork with unwritten languages. Previous generations, including Boas and most of his students in Sapir's cohort, were self-taught descriptive linguists without a grounding in the general study of language. The crucial thing, however, was the fieldwork, which kept structuralism from overwhelming "the culture." She criticized both Hockett and Harris for their failure to get the languages right and for their distaste for fieldwork. Theory was only useful in relation to the experience of working with the languages and their speakers. Thus, she respected Kroeber for his understanding of the relationship between language and culture, even though, in her opinion, he wasn't much of a linguist.

Mary's reports back from the field make it clear that she saw her task as ethnological, not narrowly linguistic. She wrote to Leslie Spier that her focus on obtaining Creek ethnological texts was the only way to proceed because her "informant's" English was "weak," although "his command of Creek is strong" so that "it will be difficult to get comparable material from him by other methods" (November 18, 1936: YUDA). Grammatical elicitation out of context was not practical.

The following summer Mary was determined to spend further time in the field working on Creek, although she also planned work with, "as far as I have been able to discover," the sole remaining speaker of Hitchiti (Haas to Spier, July 5, 1937: YUDA). By this point she considered herself entirely capable of evaluating possible field sites and their potential productivity. Sapir trusted her to do so without advice from the "home office," a distinct contrast to Boas's insistence on close control of field projects and detailed reports of his students (Stocking 1974).

Sapir did not teach field techniques or use "informants" to teach field methods in class, although he did teach techniques of organizing and analyzing the file slips resulting from fieldwork (Murray 1997). Nonetheless, it is clear that Sapir encouraged his students to take the intuitions of their consultants seriously. He wrote to Whorf (October 4, 1938: YUDA) that his choice of grammatical presentation could be justified by quoting his Hopi speaker: "I think that the feelings of natives about such matters are extremely important, even if they express themselves amateurishly." The fieldwork itself had to be figured out by each student in the course of doing it.

Mary was ambitious to pursue fieldwork in as many languages as possible, seeing the potentials as nearly endless. She wrote to Whorf (February 16, 1937: YUDA):

> The number of languages that one can make a serious study of is limited, but there is nothing I like better than to get "glimpses" of the ones I haven't the time to take up seriously. One of my secret ambitions [is to gain a] little firsthand knowledge of at least one language from every stock in North America—what an ambition!

Her letter goes on to discuss the work of other students. Although Sapir himself had largely turned away from comparative problems by this time, Whorf, Trager, and Haas were all engaged in a search for "superstocks" that would "prove to everybody the soundness of Sapir's intuitions along such lines" (that is, his six-unit classification of 1929; Darnell [1990] 2010). Mary envisioned her own contribution to this continued historical reconstruction as the "tentative" linking of Muskogean and Siouan. Whorf and Trager's connection of Tanoan to Uto-Aztecan "gives me new courage." It was a mutual reinforcement of genetic hypotheses that recapitulated Sapir's own intense collaboration with Kroeber on classificatory problems a generation earlier, especially from 1913 through 1915 (Darnell [1990] 2010). She also reported finding what might be tone rather than pitch accent in Creek (Haas to Whorf, June 19, 1937: YUDA). When she told Sapir, he said, presumably teasingly, that it sounded like she made it up because she liked tone languages!

A few months later, she wrote to Whorf from Eufaula, Oklahoma, enclosing some forms in San Blas from two boys, ages six and fourteen. The data were limited by the age of the boys and by her inability to work with them in Spanish (which she still did not speak when I took her field methods course in 1970). She had no comparative material with her in the field and hoped that the bits would provide Whorf with a "hunch" about genetic relationships:

It is just barely possible that you may be able to connect it up with your Uto-Tanoan or something. It has some of the "general American" characteristics with which we are familiar. (Haas to Whorf, November 13, 1937: YUDA)

The decision about her divorce from Swadesh finally made, Mary immersed herself in her fieldwork. Neither she nor Morris seemed greatly disturbed by the ending of their marriage. Mary insisted that they remained "still the best of friends" and were both much happier. The letter then turned to her work. She was delighted to have another year on Creek to complete her preliminary dictionary, which she planned to use "as a basis for obtaining quickly a lot of material on Hitchiti, Koasati, Alabama, and Choctaw, as I get around to them." She was "trying to get at this comparative problem scientifically" (Haas to Whorf, November 13, 1937: YUDA)—that is, by applying Indo-European methods.

Her field report to the Department of Anthropology (November 2, 1937: YUDA) justified the expenditure since July 1, 1937, of the princely sum of $250.00 ($75.75 for living and personal expenses plus sales tax, $52.00 for informants' fees, $37.09 for supplies, and $30.45 for car expenses). She had $54.71 left and was to receive an additional $250.00 at the end of November, for a total on hand of $304.71, which would enable her to continue the work. She explains that her Creek work had begun in 1936–37 with amassing considerable lexical, grammatical, and textual material. With the supplementary material from 1937, she expected to produce "a scientific grammar and dictionary of the language." She was attempting "in so far as was possible . . . in spare time, to organize this material systematically." Lexical slips were alphabetized and grammatical material sorted into categories of phonology, morphology, and syntax. These categories, however, were not rigidly discrete: "I have rechecked about one-third of the total lexical material from the point of view of phonetics and semantic range of usage." She had obtained another hundred pages of texts and begun grammatical analysis of previously collected texts. The final grammatical analysis would only be possible after leaving the field. Time remaining in the field would be devoted to checking lexical material and securing additional texts. Time, rather than potential available material, was the deciding factor. She planned to spend three or four weeks with the last speaker of Hitchiti:

> It is closely related to Creek and although its lexical elements are different, its basic grammatical structure is the same, and, inasmuch as I now have a pretty thorough understanding of this structure, it will be possible to obtain adequate material on this language in a comparatively short period of time.

Her paper on Muskogee (Creek) geminate consonant clusters had been submitted to *Language*.

Mary's contribution to the *Handbook of American Indian Languages*, edited by Boas for the Bureau of American Ethnology (Haas 1941), brings into focus the ways that the first Yale school around Sapir differed from the linguistics of the group around Boas at Columbia. She sought Whorf's response to her editing of her dissertation on Tunica, being eager to check the proofs "on some of my earlier hunches" about "the probable classification of the languages of the Southeast and Texas" (Haas to Whorf, November 20, 1939: YUDA). Several weeks later she wrote to Whorf that she was particularly annoyed by Boas's practice of recording "phrase-final melodies" in such a manner as to obscure the distinction between morphology and phonology. She was uncertain whether phrasal melodies actually existed in Tunica—an irresolvable question given that Tunica was a "mere remnant" of the time when "many speakers had the language as their only means of communication." Tunica and Natchez, to which she intended to turn next, were "dying languages" for which "there are no criteria by which it [melodic character] could be proven" (Haas to Whorf, December 14, 1939: YUDA).

Her definition of a dying language was a general one, although applied here to a particular case and speaker: "Tunica at present serves no sociological purpose [in everyday life] and when a language has reached that point it is to all intents and purposes a dead language"; her "informant" never learned the language from his mother (Haas to Whorf, December 14, 1939: YUDA):

> He is keenly aware of the fact that he does not have full command of the language. My information thus comes of a faulty

memory which works something like a phonograph record. It can repeat what it has heard but it cannot make up new expressions corresponding to what it has heard.

As the only woman in the first Yale school, Mary held her place by virtue of the work she did and the seriousness of her commitment to it. Following the assumptions of the day, Sapir felt no obligation to find her a job while she was married to Swadesh. Thereafter, he seems to have ignored her gender in seeking funding and positions for her. It was a time of transition, in which the professionalization and academic prestige of linguistics lagged far behind that of anthropology. This situation would persist until after World War II, when linguists in government service, among whom Mary was prominent, clearly demonstrated the utility of their work.

In the 1930s, however, the first Yale school was locally based, underemployed, and fighting an uphill battle against the established prestige of a Boasian linguistics located wholly within anthropology and conservative regarding distant genetic relationships of American Indian [*sic*] languages. Sapir confided to Whorf (October 8, 1938: YUDA) that Jules Henry and Gene Weltfish had the ear to be excellent phoneticians, "but Boas has simply never taught them the patterning of sounds. They can learn, of course, but their loyalty to Boas may interfere practically with the proper functioning of their cerebral cortices." Boas, in contrast, claimed that Sapir's phonemic representations failed to preserve the irreplaceable phonetic detail of the languages as spoken (Darnell [1990] 2010:69–74); he was not interested in deeper or more abstract structures.

The New Haven and New York linguists met regularly in the late 1930s. Some, with feet in both camps, hoped for rapprochement. Herzog wrote to Whorf (November 24, 1939: YUDA) downplaying the dichotomy and the inevitability of conflicting loyalties:

> If there is a Columbia "group" with a special point of view and approach with which you people disagree, the thing to do is to have discussion, rather than to sit back. Actually there is no integrated group with a group point of view. There is a certain amount of loose thinking here against which I cannot be too effective. Some of the people involved have modes of thought

too well established over the decades to change them. Others have very occasional contacts with Columbia. . . . Now I think that the fact that I have been for some years associated with Sapir should be an indication that some things or viewpoints might be taken for granted, at least as far as I am concerned.

Even from New York, Herzog continued to consider himself closely tied to the first Yale school.

Some of Sapir's linguistic students at Yale cast their lot with the new linguistics rather than with its anthropological roots. The winds of change were moving toward a more overtly structural linguistics. After his move to Wisconsin, Swadesh reported to Whorf that he was trying to re-create the energy of the New York–New Haven axis in the Midwest. He had arranged with Voegelin, Bloomfield, and Hoijer to meet in Chicago once a month and urged Whorf to do something similar in New Haven "so that there will be both an eastern and a western section of the Indian [*sic*] language group" (Swadesh to Whorf, September 3, 1937: YUDA).

Voegelin wrote to Whorf contrasting the LSA meetings in Chicago to those of the American Anthropological Association. He was dismayed by the conservativism of the former: "There was none of the rapport so common at the anthropologist meetings" (Voegelin to Whorf, January 2, 1938: YUDA). Bloomfield and Bernard Bloch were singled out among those "in the 30–40 age-class [who] met and joked" but seemed to believe themselves "the inheritors of a perfect technique [which] it is our duty to follow." Voegelin found Bloomfield himself uninterested in anything except Algonquian and "not all that informal." Sapir's students were spoiled by the kind of attention they received from him. (Mary was among those who mentored their own students in a similar way.)

After Sapir's death, Bloomfield was the only game in town; it was increasingly clear that his linguistics would be the way of the future. Bloomfield accepted a certain mentoring responsibility for Sapir's students and the progression of their careers. Voegelin wrote to Robert Lowie in 1939 that Boas had delivered Sapir's presidential address to the American Anthropological Association (Voegelin to Lowie, n.d. [but before Sapir's death February 4, 1939]: RHL):

He did not mince words, but said that an anthropologist who was not also a linguist was superficial. He cited as examples of men who had successfully combined ethnography and linguistics Edward Sapir and Leonard Bloomfield. This was all the more ironical for at that time he was speaking it was impossible for a graduate student to obtain modern training in linguistics, with a basic understanding in phonemics, say, either at Yale or at Columbia—probably no place except Chicago. Boas is magnificent just the same.

Although Voegelin could not predict the future, the absence of cutting-edge linguistics at Yale was confirmed as the Department of Anthropology moved rapidly away from linguistics after the death of Sapir. Archeology, rather than linguistics, would become the Yale specialization beyond the traditional ethnological core of Americanist anthropology. Linguistics necessarily moved, in this context, toward an autonomous professional identity. It was as a linguist, albeit one committed to anthropological concepts of culture and history rather than to an abstract structuralism, that Mary Haas took up a position at Berkeley a few years later. But that is another story.

Notes

1. Originally published as "Mary R. Haas and the First Yale School of Linguistics," *Anthropological Linguistics* 39 (1998): 566–75.

References

Darnell, Regna. (1990) 2010. *Edward Sapir: Linguist, Anthropologist, Humanist*. Berkeley: University of California Press. Reprint, Lincoln: University of Nebraska Press.

Haas, Mary R. 1935. "A Grammar of the Tunica Language." PhD diss., Yale University.

———. 1941. "Tunica." In *Handbook of American Indian Languages*. Vol. 4, edited by Franz Boas, 1–143. New York: J. J. Augustin.

Hymes, Dell H., and John G. Fought. 1975. "American Structuralism." In *Current Trends in Linguistics. Vol. 10, Historiography of Linguistics*, edited by Thomas A. Sebeok, 903–1176. The Hague: Mouton.

La Barre, Weston. 1978. "The Clinic and the Field." In *The Making of Psychological Anthropology*, edited by George D. Spindler, 258–99. Berkeley: University of California Press.

Murray, Stephen O. 1997. "A 1978 Interview with Mary R. Haas." *Anthropological Linguistics* 39:695–722.

Stocking, George W., Jr. 1974. "The Boas Plan for the Study of America Indian Languages." In *Traditions and Paradigms in the History of Linguistics*, edited by Dell H. Hymes, 454–84. Bloomington: Indiana University Press.

15

Stanley Newman and the Sapir
School of Linguistics

Stanley Newman was one of the graduate students who followed
Edward Sapir from Chicago to Yale in 1931 and became a key member of the research group that formed around him in New Haven
(along with Morris Swadesh, Mary Haas, Benjamin Lee Whorf,
Carl Voegelin, George Herzog, Walter Dyk, Murray Emeneau,
Zellig Harris, and George Trager).[1] Among these students and
associates, Newman most nearly bridged the gap between Sapir's
own interests in linguistics and in culture and personality. Newman specialized in psychology of language, which led him to work
in close collaboration with Sapir. Newman remains a key source
of Sapir's views because Sapir never wrote up his class notes for a
long-promised textbook on the psychology of culture (see Irvine
1994). Newman's work in the 1930s sheds light not only on his own
biography but also on the Sapir school of linguistics and the interdisciplinary studies of language that flourished in this period and
languished for many years thereafter.

Stanley Newman holds a virtually unique position among the
students of Edward Sapir because he was the only one to work seriously in both of Sapir's major areas of interest—American Indian
[*sic*] linguistics and the nascent field of personality in its relation
to culture. The two collaborated closely in what was then called
"linguistic psychology," with Newman quite independently following up Sapir's exploratory studies from the Chicago years (Sapir
1927, 1929). Both envisioned an interdisciplinary social science
linked to psychiatry as represented by Harry Stack Sullivan's social
interactionist perspective. The research tradition that the three
men developed was abortive, for reasons that included cutbacks

in research funding for the social sciences during the Depression, Sapir's death in 1939, and the Second World War turn to culture and personality studies characterizing whole cultures of nation-states in response to the breakdown of North American isolation-ism. Both Newman and Sapir took this work very seriously at the time. This chapter retrieves the context of their interdisciplinary effort, thereby illuminating a little-known side of Stanley Newman's lifework and simultaneously clarifying the integration of Sapir's later thought (cf. chapter 9, this volume).

The collaboration between Newman and Sapir took place in the context of what Dell Hymes's obituary of Morris Swadesh (in Hymes 1983) identified as the "first Yale school," centered on Sapir and preceding the better-known dominance of Yale linguistics from 1940 on by Bloomfieldian structuralism. When Sapir moved from Chicago to Yale in 1931, five students moved with him—Walter Dyk, Mary Haas, George Herzog, Stanley Newman, and Morris Swadesh. Research funding for work in American Indian [sic] linguistics and the impact of culture on personality was part of the package deal that lured Sapir to Yale's IHR to organize seminars sponsored by the Rockefeller Foundation on the latter topic. Fang-Kuei Li, although his doctorate was from Chicago, was at Yale from 1937 to 1939. Emeneau, Voegelin, Trager, Hockett, and Whorf joined the Sapir group at Yale during Sapir's tenure there. Zellig Harris was unofficially part of the inner circle around Sapir after they met at the Linguistic Institute in the summer of 1937 (cf. chapter 11, this volume).

Following Sapir's death in 1939, most of his students adapted in one way or another to the changing emphasis of linguistic science, particularly the structural and anti-"mentalist" tenets favored by Leonard Bloomfield. Research in American Indian [sic] linguistics continued, but Sapir's former students did not challenge the dominant paradigm of the period. A strange hiatus in the history of linguistics resulted, eclipsing Sapir's processual approach to language structure (most elegantly exemplified in Newman's *The Yokuts Language* in 1944) and his insistence on the necessity of link-ing linguistics and other social sciences, particularly psychology and psychiatry. His students have been remembered as "linguists" in a much narrower sense than that of Sapir himself. The broader context for the study of language to which Sapir devoted most of his later career has been effaced in the process. In the context of current directions in linguistic theory, however, there is much to be gained from reconstructing what Sapir and Newman wanted to study and how they proposed to go about it.

Sapir and Newman operated in a mutual admiration society based on both personal affection and intellectual style. The laudatory tenor is endemic to the genre, but the personal nature of his enthusiasm for the work of his young colleague shines through in Sapir's comments to a subcommittee of the NRC on training fellowships for the interdisciplinary study of culture and personality that was designed to fund Newman's work (December 21, 1935: NRC, via Robert Allen):

> Dr. Newman's career started off with the humanities. When I first came across him at the University of Chicago a number of years ago, he was concerned with literature. He wrote very acceptable poetry and was working in the Department of English. . . . For reasons which he could probably explain better than I, he ultimately found himself dissatisfied with the traditional academic training interests that he was in contact with in the Department of English and turned to anthropology.
>
> He took a great deal of work from various men [*sic*] at the University of Chicago and did very well. At the same time he took up work in linguistics, chiefly Russian, and developed a great interest and rather remarkable technique in that regard. His first field trip was a study of the Yokuts language of South Central California, and although that language had been studied in a preliminary way by Dr. Kroeber he was able to make a new study of it which completely supercedes the older work. The grammar which was eventually his thesis at Yale University is practically finished now, in revised form, and is, I think, perhaps the most beautiful—perhaps that is not the word some of you might use—story of an American Indian [*sic*] language that has ever been written, beautiful not only because the language is beautiful, but also because the treatment is highly balanced. I mention this to show that Dr. Newman is always aesthetic even when he seems most technical and formal. I can see direct con-

nections between his writing of poetry and this development of the American Indian [*sic*] language. After his first field trip, he took up further work among the Yokuts, covering, I think, six dialects in all and then worked in B.C. He hasn't had time to work up this material as yet.

Sapir went on to explain that Newman had found himself "gradually getting more and more interested in the psychological problems affecting language" and "the unconscious symbolism of vowels and consonants, a theme I had developed somewhat." Newman learned statistics (producing an "interesting" paper), although Sapir was generally highly skeptical of statistical analysis because of its inability to account for the role of the individual in culture. At Yale Newman had pursued "social psychology, whether linguistic or not, speech being his chief theme." Sapir obtained a two-year Social Science Research Council fellowship for him to do that work.

Newman was at the time working with Swadesh "on a new English grammar" for the American Council of Learned Societies (ACLS) (1934–36), "the idea being to profess complete ignorance of English grammar and take it from the ground up as though it were an unknown language." Newman had unearthed "many original things" in the stress patterns of English. Swadesh (personal communication, Mary Haas) considered the English grammar project primarily a means to fund Newman's American Indian [*sic*] linguistic work. Newman, in contrast, was most intrigued by Sapir's efforts to apply the discovery procedures of American Indian [*sic*] fieldwork to a written, well-studied language. He valued the psychological as well as the linguistic implications of the project.

Sapir stressed that Newman was "a great man for patterns." He felt "the relations of things, not merely the facts in a sensory sense." Sapir's own recent work on the phoneme (1925, 1933) had crystallized his longstanding concern with form and pattern in language. This was high praise indeed.

The way Dr. Newman came into the particular field we are discussing is as follows: I will begin with myself. For years I have been interested in the possibility of extending linguistic studies to include the psychological factors involved, and it seemed to me that a very careful study of all the unconscious personalities in the speech situation would be very revealing not only to the linguists but perhaps even more to the psychologists. . . . It occurred to me that [Newman] might be a man to have in mind for personality studies with a speech theme, and I asked him whether he would be interested in tying up with a psychiatrist who was interested in the larger aspects of personality formation and had in mind the cultural point of view.

When Newman agreed, Sapir sent him to Harry Stack Sullivan (who was also present at the meeting in 1935). Newman was "enthusiastic" about the possibility of funding for the training analysis that was just becoming sine qua non in psychiatric training. Sapir was concerned only that the analysis would provide insufficient material, since Newman was "a thoroughly normal person" without "the slightest trace of neurosis." Newman was willing to postpone his longer-range ambitions in order to acquire the training needed for serious work in the interdisciplinary field straddling linguistics and psychiatry.

Sapir went on to speculate about Newman's personality: "I have never met anyone like him. He is a kind of mystic." The closest he came to criticism was to mention a certain lack of practicality. Newman was married and had a family to support. Although he had completed his Yale degree, "he doesn't seem to realize that it is up to him to try to get connected with something immediate." Newman followed instructions to apply for things and continued his work on the resulting grants. His interests were intellectual, not political:

He is quietly taking things in and has no animosities that one can see. He is strangely objective, and yet you feel he has a lot of genuine feeling, you feel he would like nothing better than to be let alone and be given something intensely interesting, preferably of an aesthetic type, to do. He wants to understand people.

Sapir went to a great deal of effort in this period to get Newman an inside track on what he envisioned as the research program of the future. The NRC declined to finance training analysis for anthropologists to learn psychoanalysis prior to studying personality variation cross-culturally in the field. The scheme, largely a product of the joint theorizing of Sapir and Sullivan, was supported on the NRC committee by Johns Hopkins psychiatrist Adolf Meyer. Meyer was impressed by the discussion about Newman, writing to Sapir (December 23, 1935: NRC):

> I am particularly fascinated by the necessity of drawing history and linguistics as obligatory considerations into the field of the training of our own men [*sic*], although perhaps a little more from the point of view of principles and opportunities for organizing material than in any hope that the amateur can do any good to the fields himself.

Psychiatry was just emerging as a discipline with standardized professional credentials, among them training analysis, and anthropologists could not, in Meyer's view, be permitted to challenge the elite status of psychiatry as a science.

Sapir also sent Newman to see Sullivan and Henry Murray of Harvard, a more scientifically oriented student of personality. He assumed Newman would prefer the intuitions of Sullivan to Murray's more formal methods (to Newman, August 12, 1935: APS):

> Harry Stack is not a systematic thinker and he is a hornet's nest of prejudices but I know few people who have as keen perceptions of a personalistic character as he. He's really a sort of involved, lumbering, sensitive, inarticulate artist on the subject of personal relations. I feel you ought to get a lot out of him—more, probably, than out of [Henry A.] Murray, who has systematic ideas and a comprehensive viewpoint but suffers, I guess, from the system-maker's disease. The two together should be worth your while.

Despite Sapir's prestige in interdisciplinary social science circles and among granting agencies, funds were drying up, and established academics were defending their existing empires rather than expanding into new terrain.

Newman's retrospective account of Sapir's "psychology of human behavior" (Newman 1986:405) began with his interests in music and poetry, reflecting Sapir's early "dissatisfaction with conventional treatments and his restless search for more meaningful treatments." When Mary Haas planned a biography of Sapir, the project was abortive. At the time, Newman wrote to her (November 16, 1971: APS) about the power of the aesthetic in his view of Sapir:

> If you're planning to deal with the multiple interests that Sapir had, would you consider including some of his poetry? I may be prejudiced on this matter because my first meeting with Sapir was at the Poetry Club at the University of Chicago, where his remarks on the poetry being read seemed to me more incisive and apt than the things I'd been hearing from my English profs. (At the Poetry Club the meetings were conducted by the president's reading the unsigned poems written and submitted by the members, and after each poem those present would go at it hammers and tongs. We had some good arguments. Sapir, as you can imagine, entered into the spirit of things with his usual zest.) But he did write a lot of poetry and was serious about it. Certainly his experience with word polishing in poetry influenced his prose style. One of his poems is called "Zuni." Maybe there are others with anthropological relevance.

Newman did not propose Sapir's poetry for its anthropological content but rather for the concern they shared for the aesthetic.

Newman's respect for Sapir's intellectual breadth is reflected in the range of his writings. In a review of *Selected Writings of Edward Sapir* in 1951, he emphasized that the "absorbing interest" of Sapir's life went beyond his descriptive American Indian [*sic*] studies to seek "new perspectives for the phenomena of language that would relate it to other forms of human behavior." The concept of the phoneme had intrigued Sapir "not so much as a methodological tool for the linguist, but rather as a powerful and clear demonstration of the unconscious patterning of human behavior" (Newman [1951] 1984:61). This review devotes considerable attention to Sapir's prose style, honed by poetry but increasingly controlled by the "evocative overtones" of his topic. Unlike most academic writers, Sapir wanted to capture the imagination and attitudes of his audience, therefore alternating humor and sober argument. Sapir's use of language was "holistic"—"an attempt to write for the reader as a person rather than as a disembodied intellect" (63). Newman believed that language had become, for Sapir, less subject matter than a method to approach something else: "In short, language provided the clearest and most easily described evidence of the fundamental human tendency to mold behavior into unconscious patterns of form" (63). Newman lamented that the selection of Sapir's work was divided into separate segments dealing with language, culture, and personality, because Sapir himself did not acknowledge such boundaries, and they detracted from the ability of readers to see his thinking as a whole.

By 1951 Sapir's work had to be assessed in relation to the new dispensation. Newman stressed that Sapir wanted linguistics to become more "cosmopolitan" among the sciences, but he also shared Bloomfield's commitment to the development of an autonomous level of linguistic analysis. Sapir acknowledged that interdisciplinary work legitimately rested on the specialized competencies of its various contributors. Thus, language, with its "complete detachment from other types of cultural patterning" had enormous potential for both Gestalt and experimental psychology, as evidenced by the phonetic symbolism studies, although Newman does not mention his own contributions to these ([1951] 1984:64).

Newman was not alone among Sapir's students in arguing implicitly that Sapir did what Bloomfield did, but he also went beyond Sapir in his understanding of the proper scope of linguistics. Although this argument needed to be made, Newman's tone is often apologetic. Sapir's students struggled to reconcile the validity of both approaches (see Harris [1951] 1984). Newman's final reassessment of Sapir's contributions to linguistics and psychology in 1986 avoided reference to his personal contacts with Sapir. He argues on textual evidence that Sapir had been interested in the individual, culture, personality, and language at least since 1917 when he contested the common anthropological concept of culture as superorganic. The "scientific psychology" of his day "left Sapir cold" (1986:409) because it could not account for the submerged formal systems (largely linguistic) or elaborated symbolic constructs that characterized both individuals and cultures.

Newman elegantly clarifies Sapir's terminology in this period. He preferred the term "psychiatry," which he used in a nonclinical sense of total personality in relation to behavior and culture; he reserved the term "psychology" for studies that segmented behavior and treated it statistically (Newman 1986:422). Sapir did not trust statistics. Newman reports that he wrote to Sapir's son Philip (March 29, 1984) about his puzzlement over this apparent indifference to the bandwagon of the Chicago sociology department in 1930:

> I didn't know Edward Sapir very well. I'd shifted from English . . . to Anthropology only the year before. In talking to me in his office one day, he gave me a copy of his "A Study in Phonetic Symbolism." He asked me to read it and see if I'd like to carry on with the study. At the time, I was taking a course in statistics from L. L. Thurstone, a young Prof. in the Psychology Department, who later became one of the major figures in American statistics. I had read one of Thurstone's recent papers, in which he used an experimental technique very much like the one in Edward Sapir's article. . . . I was very enthusiastic about this clever statistical device.
>
> When I told Edward Sapir about Thurstone's statistical procedure and said that I'd like to apply it to further work with phonetic symbolism, I was disappointed that he didn't share my enthusiasm. In fact, he seemed rather cool toward the idea. But he didn't raise any objections, so I continued the phonetic symbolism experiments using the Thurstone statistics.

Not until Newman was preparing his paper for the Sapir Centenary Conference in Ottawa in 1984 (Newman 1986) and read the transcripts of the Second American Psychiatric Association Colloquium on Personality Investigation in 1930 did he fully understand Sapir's principled objection to Thurstone's emphasis on scientific laws as the priority for the social sciences. He was seeking rapprochement. Until then Newman had been puzzled why Sapir used such an elaborate statistical design in "his first and also his last venture into statistics." Interestingly, Fred Eggan (1974) also attempted to interest Sapir in Thurstone's statistics when he was a graduate student at Chicago and was met with the same lack of enthusiasm Newman describes.

The explanation lies in Sapir's changing audience for his theoretical writing after his move to Chicago in 1925. He was talking to psychologists, psychiatrists, and sociologists on the interdisciplinary conference circuit (Darnell 1986, chapter 9, this volume; Darnell 1990) who equated the objective, the formal, and the statistical with the significant. At the first American Psychiatric Association colloquium in 1928, Sapir was quiet during the discussions, although he tried to summarize the range of disciplinary views in a way that would make them potentially compatible. The following year he was prepared to present his own forays into the experimental realm (1927, 1929), intending to establish his credentials as a spokesperson for the synthesis that all participants hoped would emerge. He stressed the "scientific" character of his work in linguistics and refused to be relegated to the role of the anthropologist expert-on-the-exotic with a bizarre example illustrating the theoretical points of others. The battle for the status of research in the social sciences was fought on alien ground; Sapir was definitely in a minority.

In "Speech as a Personality Trait" in 1927, Sapir noted that people initially produce intuitive judgments of the personalities of others on the basis of their speech. He defined five levels of such potential evaluation, ranging from voice characteristics to stylistic arrangement and proposed that the individual and the culture had to be differentiated at each level. The result would be "a valuable lever in psychiatric work" (Newman 1986:418). Sapir did not suggest how this differentiation might be made and would have been hard put to demonstrate even potential application of this cumbersome scheme to clinical diagnosis.

In "A Study of Phonetic Symbolism" in 1929, Sapir argued that linguistics was useful for the analysis of speech because of its established methodology. His experiment presented five hundred Chicago high school students with a hundred "non-sense words" and measured their meaning changes when one sound was modified. He was dissatisfied with this methodology (acknowledging the help of a colleague in psychology other than Thurstone) because it obscured the significant individual variation in responses that he found more intriguing. When Sapir reported this research to the second American Psychiatric Association conference, he stressed a further experiment in which a single subject responded spontaneously to changes in sound with changes in meaning. Sapir was trying to get at unconscious symbolism rather than surface meaning, and he saw this patterning as integrated uniquely for each individual subject.

Having made his point, Sapir dropped this experimental stance and left Newman to pursue it in more detail. Newman (1986:421) attributes Sapir's compulsion, in collaboration with Sullivan, for "planning interdisciplinary projects that would permit making precise observations of interpersonal behavior" to the American Psychiatric Association colloquia of the late 1920s. The Depression was well underway by then, and money was not available to Sapir and Sullivan "even for their [own] research projects" (422). Newman himself would suffer repeatedly from the vagaries of funding and felt that the research he did in the 1930s was determined far more by the vicissitudes of available opportunities than by the evolution of his own interests; he did not pursue the linguistic psychology work because he could not support himself that way (personal communication). The next to follow up on these interests was Norman A. McQuown (1957), who cited Sapir but not Newman in arguing that psychiatry might eventually expect diagnostic help from the linguist. There is no evidence of a continuous research tradition from Newman to contemporary emphasis on the psychiatric interview as a method in social science.

During this transitional period, Newman alternated American Indian [*sic*] linguistic fieldwork and analysis with speech psychology research. His Yokuts work was sponsored by the ACLS Committee on American Indian [*sic*] Linguistics dominated by Boas, although Sapir and Bloomfield were his nominal equals in decision-making. Boas had felt strongly his responsibility as self-appointed doyen of salvage linguistics at least since he sent Sapir to study Takelma in 1906. Boas's patience for Sapir's forays into interdisciplinary social science was distinctly limited, and his irritation extended to Newman on occasion. In 1933, when Newman was working on Bella Coola, Boas wrote to Sapir (December 11: APS) protesting that Newman's obligations to the English grammar project and his grant applications in language psychology prevented him from writing up his Amerindian [*sic*] material for Boas. He wanted Sapir to "arrange" for the Bella Coola to be completed. Sapir's handwritten note to Newman on this letter declines to accept his former teacher's priorities, though pacification was in order out of both respect and expediency: "Could you fix up a brief statement that I could pass on to the old man? Perhaps an engagement to put in half an hour, before going to bed, on Bella Coola?" Both Sapir and Newman wanted the work done, but Newman could not afford to complete it without income from some other source. The ACLS could only support fieldwork, so the analysis and writing had to be sandwiched between other commitments (Leeds-Hurwitz 1985).

In his text contribution to Anna Gayton's collection of *Yokuts and Mono Myths* (Gayton and Newman 1940:4), Newman expressed the aesthetic dimension of his Yokuts grammatical work but presented only a sample of the material he had collected:

> In translating we come to the unhappy realization that each language, instead of shaping itself to our will, governs and directs the trend of our expression. We are sharply reminded that languages have an inner resistance. Their materials are already shaped into a system of formal and conceptual patterns. Within the patterns of a language other than our own, we are forced to make uncongenial distinctions that seem imperative to us.

Newman went on to discuss the grammatical "potentialities of style" in Yokuts and emphasized that the traditional, that is, Boasian, notion of an American Indian [*sic*] grammar failed to come to grips with the vast expressive power of a language or its psychological reality for speakers. A grammar

> tells what a language can do but not what it considers worth doing. To the native, a grammar is always unconvincing, for it ignores the most vital and ultimate part of his language—the intricate network of values, of attitudes and expectancies that guides his [*sic*] selection of expressive tools. (Gayton and Newman 1940:4)

The Yokuts' "feeling for simplicity," "scrupulous and unremitting attention . . . to form for its own sake," "formal balance and symmetry . . . rare among languages" were as important as the grammar in the more traditional sense. Like Sapir and Whorf, Newman valued the "collective quest" for stylistic integrity in a language that was virtually untranslatable (Gayton and Newman 1940:8). Admittedly, such statements were excluded by convention from grammars (cf. Newman and Whorf in Hoijer 1946, a collection of grammars edited by Sapir's students that appeared after his death).

Whatever the topic at hand, it was framed in Sapir's view of language as indivisible from its context and use. Like Sapir, Newman was not above purple prose. In the memorial volume for Sapir (Spier, Newman, and Hallowell 1941:94), for example, he addressed the "incredulity" of the average man's conception of linguistics (in a paper reporting on experiments in linguistic psychology):

> Those who have not been initiated into the somewhat esoteric concepts and methods of linguistics frequently express their incredulity at the picture of language presented by linguists. They find it very strange, for example, that a grammatical description can get along without any reference to the persons using the language. . . . As naive observers, they see language as it takes place in the context of human behavior, where it is merely one of the expressive and communicative activities of human beings in their everyday business of living. But the linguist seems to regard language as a huge autonomic mechanism and the language-using person as a passive thing coerced by the relentless operations of phonemic patterns, morphological processes, syntactic configurations, conceptual categories, and all the other paraphernalia of linguistic systems.

Linguists too often begrudged the intrusion of a fuller picture of language beyond the exclusive domain of their science. The tendency of linguistics to define itself in terms of "isolated methodology" rather than the subject matter of language was regrettable. The English grammar work made it clear to Newman that the linguist could not ignore usage (1941:95). Tone and other language phenomena

> undeniably intrude themselves upon the structure of English, and they are therefore within the province and responsibility of the linguist, even in his most restricted capacity as a student of formal linguistic structures.

Newman proposed to begin by studying the deviations in linguistic aspects of adolescent speech behavior. This work was sponsored by the General Education Board in New York City, but Newman approached it with the holistic view he had imbibed from Sapir. He considered this study of the personality problems of individual adolescents to be "the closest I've done to the kind of interest that Sapir had in the Yale years" (Newman to Stephen O. Murray, May 31, 1984, personal communication).

Newman's language psychology work was loosely channeled through the Yale IHR from 1932 to 1937, although Sapir obtained some outside funding for much of that period. Mark May, director of the institute, was less than enchanted with the research program, failing to understand how Sapir and Newman wanted to approach "the more realistic and practical problems of speech" (Newman to May, September 6, 1933: YU). Newman's fellowship renewal from the Social Science Research Council rendered May's objection essentially irrelevant.

Newman's proposal for the study of speech behavior suggested that the psychologists had avoided speech almost entirely, except in the most superficial and impressionistic way, and had failed to utilize the techniques of linguistics to their full potential. Linguists, in turn, had failed to study "the realistic factors involved in language as a type of human behavior." The clinical observations might later be useful for psychiatric diagnosis. Clinical results tended to confirm diagnosis, and clinicians were usually minimally concerned with experimental controls. Newman proposed that the applications for the study of individual speech should be pursued into several empirical areas:

1. Neurotic individuals tended to have "more extreme and conspicuous" speech characteristics than normal individuals, providing a rich research site with independent evidence from clinical treatment.

2. Newman proposed to teach English to foreigners by "adapting the teaching method to the individual situation," including attitudes toward the two languages. Culture, as Sapir insisted, had its locus in the individual.

3. English composition had been taught on an intuitive and haphazard basis. Newman wanted to describe the characteristics of acceptable prose style in "an objective, non-literary way." Writing classes were compared to a clinic where experiments could be conducted into corrective methods. The use of the psychiatric model for modification of normal behavior through learning is extremely interesting in this proposal (YU).

May professed himself unable to understand how the speech analyses were to be related to personality. He also had difficulty with the idea that "unconscious mechanisms reveal themselves in speech phenomena" (May to Newman, April 27, 1937: YU). The unconscious, for May, had nothing to do with linguistics. Part of the difficulty was that Sapir and Newman took these matters for granted, whereas May, heavily influenced by the behaviorism of Clark Hull and attempting to organize institute research around its integration with Freudian psychology, saw no way to provide "objective" proof of such fuzzy concepts. The positions were irreconcilable.

In an undated version of his proposal, Newman argued that a clinical study must not be bound by "an over-scrupulous insistence on a stereotyped approach" because the features of speech that were significant in one case might be completely irrelevant in the next one. His method consisted of describing whatever proved to be relevant in a particular instance. The study would lead not to larger samples for verification and replicability but to larger questions:

> The isolation of . . . fragments of speech behavior is frankly an artificiality, imposed for the purpose of developing an analytic technique. Even beyond this, the investigators fully appreciate that speech behavior is, in its turn, merely an arbitrarily delimited sphere within the larger context of interpersonal behavior. (YU)

In response to May (March 31, 1937: YU), Newman stressed that manifestation of "unconscious mechanisms" in speech was "my methodological assumption." Confirmation would come not from particular isolated details but from "a study of general tendencies actualized in a group of details." Newman applied a notion of patterning derived from the phonemic model in Sapirian linguistics. His justification for the use of linguistic rather than other behavioral data was the "greater refinement" of methodological tools already available than for "any other type of overt behavior." Behavior was inherently symbolic, and language provided the key to its symbolism. Even the distinction between normal and abnormal must be subordinated to "how unconscious mechanisms can, on the one hand, be expressed or disguised within the limits of culturally acceptable forms and, on the other, be actualized through cultural deviations."

Beginning in 1937, Newman collaborated with Vera Mather, a psychiatrist trained by Adolf Meyer, in studying patients at the New Haven Hospital associated with Yale. They hoped to improve clinical diagnosis by offering more precise terminology for speech aberrations that could be associated with particular affective states. The sample of forty cases was treated in a case history rather than statistical method (Newman and Mather 1938). Despite the collaboration of the researchers from both disciplines, the study did not lead psychiatrists to linguistic studies.

In 1937 Newman accepted a position with the General Education Board in New York City, finally removing himself from affiliation with the Institute of Human Relations. He wrote to May (May 8, 1937: YU) that he was eager to attack language problems in secondary schools and "get some realistic notion of the range and types of language problems encountered in such an applied field as education."

Newman's "Personal Symbolism in Language Patterns" (1939:177) used his case material from the adolescent study to show "how an individual's use of language, like his expression in other forms of interpersonal behavior, is symptomatic of his functioning and his adjustments as a person in a cultural setting." The paper appeared in the second volume of Sullivan's journal *Psychiatry* and dealt with written compositions of individual students to show how they addressed a practical need of the school system. The rhetoric Newman uses to describe the "depersonalized approach to human behavior" in the academic disciplines is straight out of Sapir and Sullivan.

When the adolescent study ended in 1939, Newman described his situation as "desperate" (to Murray, May 31, 1984: APS). Because he had gotten to know Boas during his two years in New York, he was supported briefly to write up his Bella Coola material. Although this was Newman's perception of the matter, Boas felt an obligation both to the Native American linguistic work and to a student of Sapir's; it is typical of him that personal acquaintance with Newman would have been somewhat secondary to these larger professional considerations. In any case, Newman eventually accepted an ACLS position designed to contribute to the war effort and worked on Iranian in New York City. In retrospect, he described (to Murray, May

31, 1984, in Murray 1986) his choices at the end of the Depression as "ruthlessly limited" and reflected on the lasting importance of the language psychology work and on distinguishing his own position from that of his mentor. Newman wrote that he had

> as much faith as Sapir did that the individual personality develops in contact with other people and has continuity through time. My main difference with Sapir (based, of course, on our different temperaments and histories) [is that] I sometimes felt uncomfortable in the adolescent study, feeling that I had reached conclusions in a kind of imaginative, free-wheeling flight, more appropriate and valid for writing poetry or for doing applied work, like treating psychiatric patients where the practitioner is forced to make decisions as best he can. I would have preferred to be part of a more elaborate interdisciplinary research team. An analysis of an individual's language would give only part of the picture; it would be more useful if combined with a life history. . . . It is significant, I think, that when I took over Sapir's phonetic symbolism study, I concentrated on the statistical approach in his paper and improved the methodology. But as I got to know him better and read his paper again later in the light of his other writings, I realized that he had a profound dislike of statistics . . . and would have preferred for me to continue with the more open-ended approach.

Much of Newman's reassessment of the language psychology work revolved around the importance of Sapir as his teacher and mentor, both professionally and personally. In retrospect (Newman to Haas, November 16, 1971), Newman stressed that Sapir had consistently used his professional contacts on behalf of his students. "On looking back, I realize that I didn't appreciate the loyalty and generosity that Sapir showed to his students." In his own case, Sapir had handed over his experimental data on phonetic symbolism; Newman had thanked him for the problem and experimental approach only in "a perfunctory footnote." When Swadesh and Newman failed to produce a book on English grammar, Sapir "should perhaps have taken a whip to us" but instead he "ran interference for us" and got them another grant to continue their own work. Sapir apparently did not expect more elaborate thanks.

Over the course of his career, Newman became increasingly aware of the broad and less easily characterized influence of the first Yale school of linguistics, particularly the impact of the personality and intellect of Edward Sapir on his thinking. He never returned to language psychology in its Sapirian sense, and this early work has been largely forgotten by scholars who know him only as an Americanist. The grand dreams of an interdisciplinary social science proved to be built on flimsy ground and disintegrated with Sapir's death, having depended on his charisma and capacity for synthesis as well as his reputation in order to obtain funding to work in language psychology. Given his lack of systematic interest in language, Newman was never particularly intrigued by the culture and personality work that coalesced around Ruth Benedict, Margaret Mead, Ralph Linton, and Abram Kardiner during the war years. In terms of his own career, language psychology was a dead-end for Newman. Nonetheless, his broad approach to the nature of linguistics and social science retains traces of its genesis in this work. The developing histories of both anthropology and linguistics have more recently revived the intellectual congeniality of the Sapirian tradition, and it invites revisiting.

Notes

1. Originally published as "Stanley Newman and the Sapir School of Linguistics," in *General and Amerindian Ethnolinguistics: In Remembrance of Stanley Newman*, ed. Mary Ritchie Key and Henry Hoenigswald, 71–88 (Berlin: Mouton de Gruyter, 1989).

References

American Psychiatric Association Committee on Relations with the Social Sciences. 1928. *Proceedings of the First Colloquium on Personality Investigation.* Baltimore: Lord Baltimore Press.

———. 1930. *Second Colloquium on Personality Investigation.* Baltimore: Johns Hopkins.

Cowan, William, Michael Foster, and Konrad Koerner, eds. 1986. *New Perspectives in Language, Culture and Personality: Proceedings of the Edward Sapir Centenary Conference.* Amsterdam: John Benjamins.

Darnell, Regna. 1986. "Personality and Culture: The Fate of the Sapirian Alternative." In *Malinowski, Rivers, Benedict and Others: Essays on Culture and Personality,* edited by George W. Stocking, 156–83. Madison: University of Wisconsin Press.

———. (1990) 2010. *Edward Sapir: Linguist, Anthropologist, Humanist.* Berkeley: University of California Press.

Eggan, Fred. 1974. "Among the Anthropologists." *Annual Review of Anthropology* 3:1–19.

Gayton, Anna, and Stanley Newman. 1940. *Yokuts and Western Mono Myths.* Anthropological Records 5. Berkeley: University of California Press.

Harris, Zellig. (1951) 1984. Review of *Selected Writings of Edward Sapir in Language, Culture and Personality*, by Edward Sapir, edited by David G. Mandelbaum. *Language* 27:288–333. Reprinted in Koerner 1984:69–114.

Hoijer, Harry, ed. 1946. *Linguistic Structures of Native America.* Viking Fund Publications in Anthropology 6. New York: Viking Fund.

Hymes, Dell. 1983. "Morris Swadesh: From the First Yale School to World Prehistory." In *Essays in the History of Linguistic Anthropology*, 273–330. Amsterdam: John Benjamins.

Irvine, Judith T., ed. 1994. *The Psychology of Culture: A Course of Lectures.* [Reconstructed from class notes of Edward Sapir] Berlin: Mouton de Gruyter.

Koerner, Konrad, ed. 1984. *Edward Sapir: Appraisals of His Life and Work.* Amsterdam: John Benjamins.

Leeds-Hurwitz, Wendy. 1985. "The Committee on Research in Native American Languages." *Proceedings of the American Philosophical Society* 129:129–60.

McQuown, Norman A. 1957. "Linguistic Transcription and Specification of Psychiatric Interview Materials." *Psychiatry* 20:79–86.

Murray, Stephen O. 1986. "Edward Sapir and the Chicago School of Sociology." In Cowan, Foster, and Koerner 1986:241–92.

Newman, Stanley. 1939. "Personal Symbolism in Language Patterns." *Psychiatry* 2:177–82.

———. 1941. "Behavior Patterns in Linguistic Structure: A Case Study." In Spier, Newman, and Hallowell 1941:94–111.

———. 1944. *The Yokuts Language of California.* Viking Fund Publications in Anthropology 2. New York: Viking Fund.

———. (1951) 1984. Review of *Selected Writings of Edward Sapir in Language, Culture and Personality*, by Edward Sapir, edited by David G. Mandelbaum. *International Journal of American Linguistics* 17:180–86. Reprinted in Koerner 1984:59–65.

———. 1986. "The Development of Sapir's Psychology of Human Behavior." In Cowan, Foster, and Koerner 1986:405–31.

Newman, Stanley, and Vera G. Mather. 1938. "Analysis of Spoken Languages of Patients with Affective Disorders." *American Journal of Psychiatry* 94:912–47.

Sapir, Edward. 1925. "Sound Patterns in Language." *Language* 1:37–51.

———. 1927. "Speech as a Personality Trait." *American Journal of Sociology* 32:892–905.

———. 1929. "A Study in Phonetic Symbolism." *Journal of Experimental Psychology* 12:225–39.

———. (1933) 1949. "La realité psychologique des phonemes." *Journal de Psychologie Normale et Pathologique* 30:247–65. Reprinted English translation as "The Psychological Reality of Phonemes" in Sapir 1949:46–60.

———. 1949. *Selected Writings of Edward Sapir.* Edited by David G. Mandelbaum. Berkeley: University of California Press.

Spier, Leslie, Stanley Newman, and A. Irving Hallowell, eds. 1941. *Language, Culture and Personality: Essays in Memory of Edward Sapir.* Menasha WI: Sapir Memorial Publication Fund.

16

Hallowell's "Bear Ceremonialism" and the Emergence of Boasian Anthropology

The Americanist tradition that grew up around Franz Boas and his early students, especially the emphasis on extensive fieldwork in particular cultures, evolved its intellectual dominance only gradually, coalescing around 1920 when theoretical syntheses of the collective approach began to appear (Darnell 1969).[1] By this time Boas had already completed what would be an exceptional scholarly career for most scholars (Stocking 1974). Boas had produced a group of students with rigorous training in anthropology as he conceived it, descriptive data had been amassed for many American Indian [*sic*] groups, and it was time to take stock. A. Irving "Pete" Hallowell began his long career in anthropology in the early 1920s during this transitional period. His dissertation on bear ceremonialism is an unmistakably Boasian product. It is the last of the major distributional studies of its era and presents an explicit defense of the Boasian strategy for cross-cultural comparison. Simultaneously, it offers a harbinger of the future, in which cultural integration, described on the basis of both extensive and intensive fieldwork, a good portion of it by Hallowell himself, would be the central theme. Hallowell's Ojibwa [Anishinaabeg] fieldwork began somewhat later. Even in this early literature-based distributional study, however, his concern with the psychological integration of particular cultures in relation to their environment is already explicit, albeit in a programmatic manner. Hallowell, along with Boasian anthropology generally, realized this was the direction in which the discipline must move.

Hallowell received his PhD from the University of Pennsylvania and acquired his focus on northeastern Indians [*sic*] from Frank

Speck, but he was also a product of the Boasian tradition centered at Columbia. He commuted to New York to take courses from Boas and collaborated in New York with Alexander Goldenweiser (Hallowell 1964, 1967). His dissertation topic, bear ceremonialism in the Northern Hemisphere, interested Boas on several counts.

After the Jesup North Pacific Expedition began in 1898, Boas's attempt to extend the geographical scope of American anthropology beyond the continent was explicit. He wrote to Zelia Nuttall (May 16, 1901: APS): "The Jesup Expedition gave me the first foothold outside of our continent. This is now being followed out by our Chinese enterprises, and plans have been laid for the successive steps also, although they have not matured yet." Although the optimism of this letter was modified after Boas's break with the American Museum of Natural History in 1905, his drive to escape restriction to North America remained despite the practical necessity of many field workers continuing to study the American Indian [*sic*]. In addition to preparing a comprehensive review of the North American Indian [*sic*] literature on bear ceremonialism, Hallowell's dissertation encompassed the entire circumpolar region. Moreover, its distributional methodology was characteristic of Boasian output at that time. Publication of a 175-page dissertation in the Boasian-dominated *American Anthropologist* in 1926 indicates the seriousness with which this distributional study was received. Yet Hallowell, along with most other Boasians, turned to other kinds of problems in the 1930s and thereafter.

This chapter examines the crystallization of Boasian anthropology in the early 1920s, then turns to its articulation in Hallowell's discussion of bear ceremonialism to summarize the characteristic concerns of the period. Boas and his students recognized themselves as a group within the discipline at an early period and were so perceived by the older establishment centered in the BAE around the turn of the century. Melville Herskovits (1953:65) summarized Boas's influence this way:

> The four decades of the tenure of [Boas's] professorship at Columbia gave a continuity to his teaching that permitted him to develop students who eventually made up the greater part of the significant professional core of American anthropology,

and who came to man and direct most of the major departments of anthropology in the United States. In their turn, they have trained the students who . . . have continued in the tradition in which their teachers were trained.

Although Boas's students shared a disciplinary culture, each utilized the common assumptions and perspectives in a unique manner. From outside the emerging paradigm, the Boasians appeared to present a united front; in their own view, however, diversity was more salient, and no single individual could be taken as typical. Robert H. Lowie (1963:412) noted:

His students have often differed from their teacher and from each other. Kroeber, Sapir, and Radin have repeatedly expressed their dissent from cardinal "Boasian" views, and even I have uttered misgivings on certain points.

Lowie contrasted his own "pedestrian" intellectual approach to that of the "American superintelligentsia—[Alexander] Goldenweiser, [Paul] Radin, [Ruth] Benedict, [Edward] Sapir" (1959:133). Especially after the mid-1920s, the majority of Boasian intellectual dialogue was internal to the group. Hallowell, because of his involvement with the Pennsylvania tradition (Darnell 1970, chapter 4, this volume), was in some senses Boasian, but in others was able to interact with the Columbia core group from a distance. This ambiguous position forced him to be explicit in formulating his version of the Boasian program and his professional affiliation.

Each Boas student had a slightly different theoretical focus. Sapir worked with language; Clark Wissler was primarily museum based; Lowie studied social organization; Alfred Kroeber concentrated on California ethnology. All of these subjects, however, were encompassed by Boas's broad conception of anthropology. Boas himself contributed to all of the subdisciplines, although his archaeological work was more organizational than substantive. In both physical anthropology and archaeology, his major focus was on delineating problems that cultural anthropology could not ignore. None of his students were as diversified as their teacher (Spier 1943:111):

Boas had to concern himself with the whole field of anthropology in a way that may never be forced on another man [*sic*]. . . . Where some of the later students seem to be more systematic because they stayed with one topic, one cannot but feel that this was the result of rather narrow interests, of too limited a conception of anthropology.

Because Boas believed as a matter of principle that the scope of anthropology was broader than any single scholar could encompass, he depended on his students to fill in the details of the paradigm (1908:5, 8). His own statements remained self-consciously programmatic.

What was at stake was the nature of the generalizations that anthropology could make. Method and theory were not separable for Boas, and adequate methods were rarely available for rigorous study of the most interesting theoretical questions. Many Boasians were less optimistic than Boas himself about the possibility of defining laws of human cultural development. Lowie, for example, thought that "fruitful correlations" might prove to be the final result of research (1963:13). Boas himself foresaw "laws governing the growth of culture" (1898:2), although his later formulations were more cautious, stressing that preceding evolutionary theories had been premature but that a different methodology might now shed light on them (1906:642):

As we have penetrated more deeply into these problems we have observed that the general laws for which we have been searching prove elusive, that the forms of primitive [*sic*] culture are infinitely more complex than had been supposed, that a clear understanding of the individual problem can not be reached without taking into consideration its historical and geographical relations.

Boas's own methods for studying the history of particular peoples were developed in the course of his fieldwork on the distribution of Northwest Coast folklore elements. Comparison of contemporary forms was the only direct evidence for past history and enabled legitimate inference about element combination and adaptation (1891:13). Evolutionary theory had assumed that myths originated in contemplation of nature or some other set cause, but Boas demonstrated that the actual myths of a given people developed by more proximate causes as a result of borrowing and culture contact. Moreover, he believed that original causes were subordinated and lost to contemporary memory because myths also had social causes. They were constantly being reinterpreted after borrowing to fit with the culture in which they were told ([1898] 1940:423). Cultural use, then, was the most direct determinant of mythological form.

Although Boas thought the ultimate questions of anthropology were psychological—why particular elements were selected by particular cultures (Mead 1958:36)—in practice he tended to attain methodological rigor by discussing distribution of the elements in a statistical, and therefore presumably objective, manner. The method was not historical in the sense that elements were to be traced through time; rather, at a single time level, inferences could be projected backward in time on the basis of present geographical distribution (Darnell 1974). This early Boasian formulation of the distributional problem has much in common with Hallowell's treatment of bear ceremonialism.

Fieldwork during the formative Boasian period rarely permitted detailed generalizations about the psychological integration of cultures. Boas himself had been forced into survey ethnography under the auspices of the British Association for the Advancement of Science (Gruber 1967). Similar frustrations plagued his students. Lowie's Plains fieldwork for the American Museum was focused on collecting specimens to the detriment of cultural context (Lowie 1959). Distributional studies were feasible in this context; psychological conclusions were not, however much researchers might wish to move in this direction.

Boasian distribution studies were designed to provide an empirical database for a critique of the evolutionary theory that had predominated up to that time in American anthropology. A series of Boas-inspired historical critiques cumulatively illustrated that a unilinear sequence did not exist, that the parts of a given culture advanced at different rates, and that the patterning in culture was to be found within single cultures. Boas praised Goldenweiser's critique of the concept of "totemism" as supporting his position, because it could be applied "in regard to practically all ethnological phenomena" (1910:393). That is, the patterning in cultures was not a function of the distribution of elements as complexes but because of their synchronic cultural integration. Labels such as totemism were inappropriate because they represented whole clusters of traits and attitudes that were not necessarily found together.

Lowie, in a passage that has been consistently misinterpreted, stated the matter:

> Cultures develop mainly through the borrowings due to chance contact. Our own civilization is even more largely than the rest a complex of borrowed traits. . . . To that planless hodgepodge, that thing of shreds and patches called civilization, its historian can no longer yield superstitious reverence. ([1920] 1960:441–42)

Although the traits of a culture are arbitrary in origin, at any given moment they are integrated within a particular culture.

Benedict's study of the vision quest in North America in 1923 demonstrated that the meaning of this complex was specific to each participating culture, a conclusion that led logically to *Patterns of Culture* a decade later. In her previous work, Benedict had argued that "fluid recombination of cultural elements" was characteristic of culture process in general and that psychological questions were most intriguing (1923:82). She continued:

> It is only by distributional analysis that we can get an insight into the role which the particular concept plays in different tribal settings, and the sort of relation it establishes with the tribal background. We can then arrive at some understanding of what happens in the inner life, as it were, of beliefs and practices assimilated into diverse tribal complexes, and to judge to some extent whether or not it is some fixed causality which is at work. (1923:7)

The matter could only be approached distributionally because the theory did not yet provide a reliable interpretive matrix:

> It is only when we put aside philosophical discussions and turn to the descriptive monographs that we find in spite of the theorists that there is a very fair degree of similarity in the type of facts that are discussed under the heading of "religion." (1923:6)

Spier's description of the Plains sun dance indicated that elements were acquired through intertribal borrowing but that the associated ideas and behavior were variable:

> The corollary of this is that tribal individuality has been expressed principally in pattern concepts of organization and motivation. Since there is no difference in the character of borrowed or invented traits which are incorporated in the sun dance and those which are rejected, it follows that the determinants must be sought in the conditions under which incorporation proceeds. It will be shown that the character of individual contributions to the ceremonial complex and the diversity in receptiveness and interest, explain in part the elaboration and individualization of the several sun dances. (1921:453)

The cumulative evidence indicated that borrowing and readaptation were general cultural processes that could be analyzed on the basis of distributional methodology.

Hallowell's bear ceremonialism follows this established strategy although its wording is couched in terms of the psychology of trait integration. His paper marks the transition from trait distribution as a critique of evolution to a psychologically oriented examination of the integration of cultural wholes. Boas himself had recognized the shift in the discipline:

> I stressed the necessity of the study of acculturation and dissemination. When I thought these *historical* methods were firmly established, I began to stress, about 1910, the problems of cultural dynamics, of integration of culture and of the interaction between the individual and society. (1936:311).

These are the roots of the culture and personality focus of Benedict, Margaret Mead, Hallowell, and others in the 1920s and 1930s. Boasians were decidedly unimpressed by what they saw as the newfangled British functionalism that developed in the wake of the publication of Bronislaw Malinowski's *Argonauts of the Western Pacific* in 1922. Although they had not used the term "functionalism," the Boasian program by that time already included substantial emphasis on psychological integration of particular cultures with diverse historical roots for the elements that were integrated. Extended field work and attention to the native point of view were already central to Boasian ethnographic practice well in advance of the advent of the so-called functionalist school of anthropology.

By around 1920 the Boasians were engaged in a sustained effort to synthesize their point of view. Enough had been accomplished that it seemed feasible to sum up the accomplishments of the previous two decades as a program for the future, with the implicit claim that Boasian anthropology had come of age. At the same time, American anthropology under the leadership of Boas was becoming increasingly academic. This professionalization and growth in magnitude beyond the face-to-face character experienced by the first generation made the need for textbooks urgent. The trend began with Boas's *The Mind of Primitive Man* and introduction to the *Handbook of American Indian Languages* in 1911. Both are programmatic in that they present a credo rather than the results of applying new methods to large bodies of descriptive data. These works were quickly followed by others, for example:

1916 Edward Sapir, *Time Perspective in Aboriginal American Culture*

1917 Robert Lowie, *Culture and Ethnology*

      Clark Wissler, *The American Indian*

1920 Robert Lowie, *Primitive Society*

      Alfred L. Kroeber and Thomas T. Waterman, *Sourcebook in Anthropology*

1921 Edward Sapir, *Language*

1922 Alexander Goldenweiser, *Early Civilization*

1923 A. L. Kroeber, *Anthropology*

      Clark Wissler, *Man and Culture*

Boas preferred to discuss "theoretical questions in connection with definite problems" but advised his students to state "opinions in a somewhat formal way, and not tie them up with detailed investigations" (Boas to Kroeber, July 24, 1917: ALK).

Once such general works were available, the emergence of Boasian particularism in the need to criticize premature generalization in the older evolutionary paradigm could be relegated to the past. After about 1925 this was no longer an issue. In the oral history of the discipline, the earlier period has faded into oblivion. Removed from its context, retrospective examination of the trait distribution era then appeared as merely unproductive particularism. I argue in contrast that the distribution studies constituted a seminal stage in the development of Boasian anthropology that necessarily preceded the pattern-integration concerns that came afterward. The students of trait distribution were eager to move on to the next stage; their concerns were theoretical even as they developed the necessary prior methodological step.

Hallowell's study of bear ceremonialism begins with a theoretical rather than a methodological statement of problem. He is concerned with the basic fact of how human groups are related to their environment. Natural phenomena provide a means to understanding "magico-religious beliefs." Adjustment to the environment is not exclusively utilitarian but involves "factors of a socio-psychological order" (1926:2–3). One can legitimately study utilitarian explanations about animals, but "man's relation to the animals of his environment as he himself [*sic*] views it; that is to say, in its psychological aspect" is of greater interest (1926: 3). Hallowell claims that the two aspects grew up together historically in each culture, with culture-specific variation in different areas (1926:4–5).

The average individual in a hunting or fishing culture has much greater practical knowledge about the animal world than in our own rational, practical culture. The difference is that, for the hunter, explanation is inseparably interwoven with folklore or magico-religious beliefs. The basic premise is that animals "are believed to have essentially the same sort of animating agency which man[-kind] possesses" (1926:7). The categories of rational thought are different in different societies, and "we must rebuild the specific content of these categories upon the foundation of *their* beliefs, not ours" (1926:9–10). To the individual hunter, the "subjective" aspects of hunting are more salient than the practical, which can be taken for granted. What is problematic for the individual whose thought is guided by his "cultural milieu" is how to explain success or failure in the hunt. Although the definition of psychological factors is still framed in early Boasian terms, the concern for cultural patterning of individual behavior is consistent with Hallowell's later ethnographic work. Yet it occurs in the context of introducing a library-based distributional study. Already in 1926, the important point for Hallowell was that the two were not discrete or unrelated questions.

Bear ceremonialism was necessarily a work based in the established theory of the time. Therefore, Hallowell began with a Boasian critique of evolutionary method. The older theory assumed that so-called primitive attitudes toward animals were common to the entire human species and "entirely divorced from antecedent cultural determination" (1926:12). These theoreticians take animal worship as a unilinear stage in the evolution of religion. The whole notion of bear worship, however, is untenable in the light of ethnographic facts as cataloged by Hallowell. The "seriousness" of rites performed to the dead bear, for example, indicates a purpose that is "magico-religious in character, being directed toward the successful capture of game in the future" (1926:65).

> The bear was believed to represent, or was under the spiritual control of[,] some supernatural being or power which governed either the potential supply of certain game animals or the bear species alone. It is the propitiation of this supernatural agent which is actually desired, and not the animal itself, conceived simply as a terrestrial creature. (1926:145)

Postmortem ceremonies indicate that conciliatory spirit is the focus of rites showing respect for the bear. Where ethnographic data are sufficiently detailed to record "motivation," the reports are "consistent" with such an interpretation (1926:145). Again, the psychological questions interest Hallowell, but information in the existing literature was rarely adequate to draw such conclusions or to define his dissertation topic in terms of them.

The evolutionary theorists have erred most importantly in turning descriptive generalizations into explanations. What explanation is seen as appropriate has depended more on the a priori theory of the writer than on the ethnographic documentation. Animism, fear, and animal worship are all framed in this manner:

> Such descriptive categories soon turn into ready-made catch-alls, into which customs and attitudes are hastily thrust without a previous study of their integration in the cultural patterns

from which they have been taken. . . . Furthermore, a classification on the basis of similarity generally causes differences in customs and beliefs to be ignored, minimized or glossed over. (Hallowell 1926:17)

Evolutionary theory has no conceptual tools to deal with psychological integration, and Hallowell is interested in going beyond established anthropological theory by extending the explanatory scope rather than by rejecting the problems as formulated in Boasian anthropology up to that time.

Hallowell defends the Boasian call for detailed historical study of particular cultures. "Each culture exhibits its own peculiar combination of features which cannot be deduced from any general principles of association" (1926:18). Studies are needed of "specific cultures in terms of their own range of values and concrete expressions. . . . Only in this setting do qualitative terms . . . have any real force as descriptions of subjective attitudes" (18). Detailed analysis of particular cases will "describe or explain" cultural differences. This particularist position does not require Hallowell to distinguish description and explanation: the explanation is that evolutionary generalization does not constitute an explanation. Hallowell bases this conclusion on the limited availability of adequate ethnographic description and emphasizes the need for further survey ethnography and comparative analysis. Boasian anthropology was not yet situated to do intensive fieldwork in single cultures because the general state of knowledge was not yet such as to put particular ethnographic facts into an appropriate cross-cultural context. This priority precluded tackling the potentially most interesting questions directly or immediately.

Hallowell clarifies his attitude toward the relationship of psychology and culture. Psychology within anthropology cannot be individual psychology; rather, individuals interpret their experience of natural phenomena in terms of cultural traditions. "The source of their beliefs and practices is, therefore, the historic tradition [i.e., culture], and the history of particular customs and beliefs must be pursued at the cultural, not the psychological, level" (1926:19). The continuity to Hallowell's later work in culture and personality is unmistakable.

Two possible methodological approaches to the relation of humankind to the animal world present themselves: First, one may choose to study the point of view of a particular culture in depth; this has rarely been done. Alternatively, one may choose a comparative framework that will "bring out the similarities and differences that characterize the use of related species in different cultures" (1926:20). If the cultures are continuous in their geographic distribution, the further possibility exists of demonstrating probable historical connections.

With regard to bear ceremonialism, Hallowell acknowledges that the data, taken singly, are rather superficial. "Collectively, however, these observations serve to draw attention to the very significant fact that many of the native tribes of North America, Asia, and Europe do exhibit toward the bear an attitude which . . . is more or less unique in character" (1926:22). Indeed, given the present state of our ethnographic knowledge, trait distribution is a more objective and reliable method than psychology. It provides data that can be analyzed and compared without falling prey to undue subjectivity of the reporters (23):

> Fortunately, we do not have to depend on mere statements of attitude toward the bear, suggestive as these may be. A much more tangible basis of approach to the fundamental problems involved is afforded by the complex of customs of which bears are the object among the peoples who inhabit the regions already mentioned.

For example, there is a "rough correlation" between the belief that bears suck their paws for nourishment during hibernation with the distribution of bear ceremonialism (1926:30). This trait is not found everywhere that bears are hunted. Here Hallowell relies heavily on Boas-trained anthropologists for his data and therefore is confident of their quality. His own training gave him access to the field workers themselves, not just to their published reports, which might fail to mention data of interest to Hallowell. Because bear ceremonialism is less widely distributed than hibernation, limited diffusion is the only descriptively reasonable explanation for the presence of bear ceremonialism as "an ancient notion which is associated with other customs connected with bears in both the Old World and the New" (31). A conclusion about particular history, then, is more valid than earlier generalizations based on an amorphous "psychic unity of mankind." There seems to be "an ancient hunting complex" associated with "conservative" customs in many tribes (33). The northern tribes that have bear ceremonialism are "more specifically those peoples who do not practice agriculture or at least have their cultural roots in a hunting economy" (43).

Historical inference from these distributional facts is fairly straightforward. Conclusions about the psychological status or meaning of the customs are more difficult because there is so little information. In many tribes, for example, Hallowell finds that euphemistic or honorific terms are used for the bear. If more information were available, the case might prove to be more complex: "This is, however, a psychological generalization which it would be hazardous to insist upon, in view of the many cultures in which the practice appears and considering the absence of detailed information in so many of them" (1926:43).

On the basis of trait distributions, no animal except the bear is given so much prominence and has such a large series of customs associated with it over such a wide area. Generalized explanations of the distribution based on psychology or economic use are inadequate. The so-called humanness of the bear cannot be seen as a cause of its veneration, given that bears are found over a wider area than bear ceremonialism. Further, veneration is not correlated with the complexity of the customs or their number in particular societies (1926:150–51). Economic use fails as an explanation because it is wider in distribution than the ceremonialism, and no special rites exist for animals that are economically more significant than the bear (152). The only plausible explanation is historico-geographical.

Bear ceremonialism characterizes northern boreal hunting peoples on both continents. It is absent on the Arctic coast to the north or among more southern tribes. Northern and northeastern Algonquian peoples are more similar to Eurasia than to the tribes of western America. The following traits appear consistently over the area (Hallowell 1926:154):

postmortem rites

standardized method of disposal of the skull

varied synonymy for the bear, usually with a taboo on the
generic term

animal felt to suck paws for hibernation nutrition

hunting with thrusting and striking weapons at close range

bear under guidance of some sort of spiritual controller.

Only the last of these traits is psychological.

It would be too much of an accident for these traits to occur together over a wide area and not in other areas unless particular historical processes of diffusion were at work. In fact, bear ceremonialism seems to have diffused along with other, even more basic traits: the distribution of this complex is similar to others of "considerable antiquity on both continents" (Hallowell 1926:156). Hallowell concludes that the economically important caribou was the diffuser of these traits (157). He goes on to note that this is a different culture stratum than the similarities of the Northwest Coast to Eurasia, well known through the work of Boas and the Jesup North Pacific Expedition. Cultural influences moved in both directions across the Bering Strait (160–61). Such an "intercontinental perspective" is crucial to understanding American culture history (163), again a Boasian conclusion.

The explanation on the basis of an ancient boreal hunting culture is useful in understanding present variations in the practices of bear ceremonialism as well. The original traits of the complex were diffused widely along with the caribou until the distribution became intercontinental. Over time, the original traits were "radically modified." At the present time, simple rites and an attitude of veneration are found everywhere bear ceremonialism occurs, but the overlying complexity or degree of detail differs drastically (Hallowell 1926:162). Other boreal traits seem to operate similarly, for example, in an analysis of moccasin types. The distributional facts shed light on the history of bear ceremonialism.

Hallowell's conclusion on the evidence of distribution is a significant one. He uses some of the terminology of the German diffusionist school, particularly "culture stratum," but does not accept the premise of the *Kulturkreislehre* (culture circle) that a complex of traits is necessarily linked and diffused as a unit. Hallowell (1966) noted in retrospect that the scholars of this school drew heavily on his work because it fit Fritz Graebner's idea of a northern culture circle. But this was not the trajectory of his own thinking. Rather, Hallowell's conclusion was the converse of Alexander Goldenweiser's demolition of the artificial concept of totemism: he established that "bear ceremonialism" was an analytical construct that grew organically out of the ethnographic facts and therefore was an appropriate representation of the native view of the matter. Moreover, Hallowell's final remarks in the bear ceremonialism paper return to the question of psychological integration in particular cultures that remains to be explained in terms of developments internal to particular cultures. In this framework the obvious next step is to study bear ceremonialism in limited ethnographic context. Hallowell's own study provides a baseline for interpretation of such culture-specific data in light of bear ceremonialism as a general phenomenon.

After 1926 Hallowell's work gradually moved away from trait distribution as a mode of formulating theoretical problems, the major exception being his comparative work on kinship and cross-cousin marriage. He retained, however, a concern with the methodological problems of overgeneralization, for example, writing in 1951 (1955:357):

> Finally, I should like to emphasize the fact that the psychological consequences of acculturation among the Ojibwa [Anishinaabeg] that I have described must not be generalized to include all American Indians [*sic*] or aboriginal peoples elsewhere that have come in contact with Western civilization. While we do not have any precisely comparable data from other groups I can think of peoples where the contrary situation may exist.

This caution in extending inference is a product of the Boasian critique of evolution and remains one of its major contributions to method in anthropology. Hallowell never lost his commitment to this portion of the Boasian heritage.

When Hallowell selected his major papers for *Culture and Experience* in 1955, he did not mention or include parts of this early work.

In terms of his later work it is indeed dated, precisely because the period of trait distribution studies in Boasian anthropology had attained its goals and moved on. Revisiting the question of bear ceremonialism once more in a paper read to the American Association for the Advancement of Science in 1966, Hallowell noted the constraints under which his original study had proceeded:

> I realized that there was a local setting for bear ceremonialism everywhere involving mythology, world view, the hunting of other animals etc. but I chose to be selective here in favor of a broad distributional study of traits and a general culture-historical setting. (1966:1)

Most of this paper is devoted to the kind of questions that he raised but could not answer in 1926:

> One obvious kind of reexamination would be to look at the attitudes towards, and treatment of, the bear in the framework of the world view of a people. In other words, how are the relations of man and animal conceived in general? How is this conceptualization expressed in relations with them? to hunting and its rituals etc. In this perspective the bear, instead of being selected out for independent treatment, would fall into place in the total picture of the animal world and man's relation to it. (1966:2)

In sum, Hallowell moves from problems of distribution to those of how members of a culture see their own world:

> Not only bear ceremonialism is boreal in its scope. What we have to consider is a generalized conception of the nature of the animal world in relation to man[kind]. At the root of this relationship there appears to lie a generalized belief that animals by their essential nature are not so different from human beings and that animals are sent to hunters by controlling "spirit masters." This is a conception common among the peoples of Eurasia and America. My conclusion is that bear ceremonialism was only an introduction to a much wider range of problems. Man[kind] and animals instead of being separate categories of being are deeply rooted in a world of nature that is unified. Perhaps the approach of ethnoscience or ethnosemantics can help us here. (1966:12)

With this statement, Hallowell has come full circle. He has discovered new methods of approaching the psychological integration of bear ceremonialism, methods that developed at least partially out of the insights of his later work in culture and personality. At the same time, he retains the concern with the historical implications and cross-cultural context that his original distributional methods were able to explicate. Both have their place in the Boasian tradition, and it is part of Hallowell's strength as an anthropologist is that he balanced diverse but equally legitimate concerns despite giving them different weights at different points in his career.

Notes

1. Originally published as "Hallowell's 'Bear Ceremonialism' and the Emergence of Boasian Anthropology," *Ethos* 5 (1977): 13–30.

References

Benedict, Ruth. 1923. *The Concept of the Guardian Spirit in North America.* American Anthropological Association Memoir 29. Menasha WI: George Banta.

———. 1934. *Patterns of Culture.* Boston: Houghton Mifflin.

Boas, Franz. 1891. "Dissemination of Tales among the Natives of North America." *Journal of American Folklore* 4:13–20.

———. 1898. Introduction to *The Traditions of the Thompson Indians of British Columbia,* by James Teit, 1–18. Memoirs of the American Folklore Society 6. Published for the American Folklore Society. Boston: Houghton, Mifflin.

———. 1906. "Some Philological Aspects of Anthropological Research." *Science* 23:641–45.

———. 1908. *Anthropology.* New York: Columbia University Press.

———. 1911a. Introduction to *Handbook of American Indian Languages.* Bureau of American Ethnology Bulletin 40. Washington DC: Government Printing Office.

———. 1911b. *The Mind of Primitive Man.* New York: Macmillan.

———. 1936. "History and Science in Anthropology: A Reply." In Boas 1940:305–11.

———. 1940 *Race, Language and Culture.* New York: Free Press.

Darnell, Regna. 1969. "The Development of American Anthropology, 1880–1920: From the Bureau of American Ethnology to Franz Boas." PhD diss., University of Pennsylvania.

———. 1970. "The Emergence of Academic Anthropology at the University of Pennsylvania." *Journal of the History of the Behavioral Sciences* 6:81–92.

———. 1974. "From Lore to Linguistics in American Anthropology." Paper presented at the annual meeting of the American Anthropological Association, Mexico City.

Goldenweiser, Alexander. 1910. "Totemism, An Analytical Study." *Journal of American Folklore* 23:179–294.

Gruber, Jacob. 1967. "Horatio Hale and the Development Anthropology." *Proceedings of the American Philosophical Society* 111:5–37.

Hallowell, A. Irving. 1926. "Bear Ceremonialism in the Northern Hemisphere." *American Anthropologist* 28:1–175.

———. 1955. *Culture and Experience.* Philadelphia: University of Pennsylvania Press.

———. 1964. "Anthropology at the University of Pennsylvania." *Philadelphia Anthropological Society Bulletin.*

———. 1966. "Bear Ceremonialism in the Northern Hemisphere." Paper presented at the annual meeting of the American Association for the Advancement of Science.

———. 1967. "Anthropology in Philadelphia." In *The Philadelphia Anthropological Society*, edited by Jacob Gruber, 1–31. New York: Columbia University Press.

Herskovits, Melville. 1953. *Franz Boas: The Science of Man in the Making.* New York: Charles Scribner's Sons.

Lowie, Robert H. (1920) 1961. *Primitive Society.* New York: Boni and Liveright. Reprint, New York: Harper.

———. 1959. *Robert H. Lowie, Ethnologist: A Personal Record.* Berkeley: University of California Press.

———. 1963. *Collected Writings of Robert H. Lowie.* Edited by Cora DuBois. Berkeley: University of California Press.

Malinowski, Bronislaw. 1922. *Argonauts of the Western Pacific.* New York: E. P. Dutton.

Mead, Margaret. 1959. "Apprenticeship under Boas." In *The Anthropology of Franz Boas: Essays on the Centennial of His Birth*, edited by Walter Goldschmidt, 29–45. American Anthropological Association Memoir 89. Menasha WI: American Anthropological Association.

Spier, Leslie. 1921. *The Sun Dance of the Plains Indians: Its Development and Diffusion.* Anthropological Papers, American Museum of Natural History 16. New York: American Museum of Natural History.

———. 1943. "Franz Boas and Some of His Views." *Sobretiro de Acta Americana* 1:108–27.

Stocking, George W., Jr., ed. 1974. *The Shaping of American Anthropology, 1883–1911.* New York: Basic Books.

17

Franz Boas and the Development of Physical
Anthropology in North America

Early twentieth-century anthropology in North America was dominated to a large extent by the single figure of Franz Boas.[1] Certain inaccuracies of historical retrospect have, however, had the cumulative effect of minimizing Boas's work before about 1920 and obscuring the considerable significance of his researches in physical anthropology for the discipline as a whole. I have argued elsewhere (Darnell 1969, 1971) that although Boas began to teach at Columbia University in New York City in 1899, it was approximately 1920 before "Boasian anthropology" could be recognized as the clearly dominant paradigm of American anthropology. Moreover, Boas's work prior to 1911 was sufficiently prolific and broadly distributed across the scope of the discipline to ensure his importance even if he had not continued to publish until his death in 1942 (Stocking 1974). Any career that spans sixty-odd years is bound to show changes of focus and modifications of theoretical claims. Because of Boas's significance in determining the course of development of North American anthropology, it is crucial to reexamine the early work in order to place his total contribution in accurate historical perspective.

Although Boas has been remembered primarily as a cultural anthropologist, folklorist, and linguist, he is also credited with establishing the characteristic four-subdiscipline emphasis of North American anthropology. The context of its emergence is complex. Boas's early fieldwork on the Northwest Coast was constrained by an urgent need for basic mapping of ethnic units, stressing the acquisition of physical, cultural, and linguistic information through survey methodology (Darnell 1969, 1971; Gruber, 1967).

It was not entirely by personal choice that much of Boas's early field research ranged widely in topic and aimed toward rudimentary classification of groups. Then, as now, availability of funding was a major determinant of what research could actually be carried out. Despite Boas's conviction that the scope of American anthropology must be wide-ranging and interdisciplinary, he did not contribute equally to the four subdisciplines. His archaeological work was largely organizational, and most American archaeologists were trained at Harvard rather than Columbia during the early twentieth century. His researches in physical anthropology concentrated on the question of racial classification and its implications for society. He did not participate actively in the increasing specialization of physical anthropology and did not seriously concern himself with questions of human evolution or primatology that became central later. Stocking concluded:

> His immediate influence on physical anthropology was limited. He had few students in this field, and the fruitfulness of his own work was curtailed by the fact that it was carried out in essentially Galtonian terms before the union of biometry and Mendelism in modern population genetics. By and large, physical anthropology developed for the next several decades in terms of traditional assumptions and methods. But when a "new" physical anthropology emerged around 1950, it bore marked, if only analogical, similarities to Boas' thinking. (1968:188–89)

Boas's contributions to physical anthropology were a product of his times and their direct influence restricted to that era. His enduring significance lies more in his insistence that physical anthropology was part of the holistic discipline of anthropology than in his research reports. Whatever the original reasons for including physical anthropology, this traditional disciplinary boundary has been long enshrined in the self-identification of North American physical anthropologists (although this has broken down in recent years).

Within physical anthropology, Boas is best remembered for his demonstration that head-form of immigrants was subject to rapid change, thereby calling into question traditional concepts of racial type. Retrospective evaluation of the merit of that work had been varied. T. K. Penniman notes:

The question arises whether the various characters employed in racial classification are constant racially, or subject to rapid modification. Franz Boas is of the opinion that various round- and long-headed immigrants to the United States tend to change their head-shape within a period of about ten years, and to approach a uniform type, but his conclusions have not generally been accepted. (1935:209–10)

In the same volume assessing the state of the art in physical anthropology, Joseph S. Weiner refers to Boas's "pioneering investigations of the alterations in the bodily features of the descendants of immigrants" on the basis of "more convincingly presented" follow-up studies by Gabriel Lasker and Harry Shapiro (Weiner 1935:286). The report focuses on eugenics and fascism but does not cite Boas on the social and political implications of race research. This may be attributable to the British focus of the volume. As a more recent example of how Boas was left behind by the increasingly specialized character of professionalization within physical anthropology, Sherwood Washburn notes:

> Since in anthropology there has been extreme reliance on typological thinking, orthogenesis, irreversibility, and the importance of non-adaptive characters, the synthetic theory devastated most of the structure of traditional anthropological thought. This can be seen most clearly in the study of human races. The majority of physical anthropologists had been busy dividing populations into types, and then manipulating the types in order to reconstitute racial history. . . . Substitution of the variable Mendelian population for the type (composed of phenotypically similar individuals) simply destroyed the theoretical basis for the vast majority of [previous] anthropological thought. (1968:100)

The relationship of Boas to "modern" physical anthropology is somewhat ambiguous. He was virtually unique among early physical anthropologists in insisting that racial types were arbitrary. On the other hand, his explanation of the plasticity of observed changes in head-form was couched in premodern terms. The paradox is that he contributed significantly to impending theoretical change but never himself became part of the new physical anthropology.

The selection and ordering of papers for *Race, Language and Culture* (RLC) in 1940 attests to the critical role that physical anthropology played in Boas's assessment of his own work as the underpinning of his entire oeuvre. The tripartite title emphasizes his contention that race, language, and culture are the three major classificatory variables applicable to human societies. Of the sixty-three essays included, twenty deal with race, five with language, thirty-five with culture and folklore, and five are miscellaneous. Race was the foundation of how he defined anthropology as a discipline. Boas did not arrange his selected writings chronologically; changes in his thinking over time were less significant to him than the internal organization and logical connection of the topics treated.

Physical anthropology was changing rapidly during the years spanned by these papers, but Boas saw his own concerns as internally consistent, focusing on methodological points and their social implications. Encroaching Nazi racism in his native Germany lent poignancy and relevance to issues of race that already had preoccupied Boas in much the same terms for at least five decades.

Different types of publication are included in the *Race* section of RLC. Boas made at least three major statements of his stance on the subject of race from an anthropological standpoint: as president of the American Association for the Advancement of Science in 1931 (the lead article in the volume), to the International Congress of Americanists in 1915, and for the inaugural volume of the new series of the *American Anthropologist* as a journal of putatively national scope in 1899 (1899b). Other chapters were originally directed to an audience of concerned and intelligent laypersons: the Insurance Medical Directors in 1935 (1935a), the International Congress on Hygiene and Demography in 1912, the *American Physical Education Review* in 1902, *Popular Science Monthly* in 1894, and a quarterly publication of the American Statistical Association in 1922 (1922a). Boas retained his concern for the implications of race study to society in general and his conviction that physical anthropology had a significant message to offer in this regard. Indeed, Boas ([1931] 1940:3) argued: "If we wish to reach a reasonable attitude, it is necessary to separate clearly the biological and psychological aspects from the social and economic implications of this problem."

Legislation, in this instance on the intermixture of racial types, was an issue to be resolved by scientific experiment, and its implication transcended immanent political issues. Race studies could not help but have inevitable political implications. Boas accepted the eugenicist argument that social problems could be solved by biological means, a position Stocking (1968:179) characterizes as "oddly archaic." Boas further believed that immigration policies should be constrained by the results of physical anthropology. His head-form studies were done for the Immigration Department, and he hoped they would settle the question of the relative importance of heredity and environment once and for all; his data proved that the relationship was far more complex and variable across populations than he had initially assumed.

On the subject of racial mixture, Boas ([1915] 1940:20) noted that "half-breed" offspring were often physically improved, citing his own studies of half-blood [North American] Indians [*sic*] in 1892 and Puerto Ricans in 1915. "If racial antipathy were based on innate human traits this would be expressed in interracial sexual aversion"; therefore, there could be no biological basis for racial prejudice ([1931] 1940:15). Racial struggle was, purely and simply, a product of social stratification along racial lines (17).

Boas saw no evidence that modern races were degenerating, arguing rather that modern conditions required more physical and mental energy to excel because life was more complex and more individuals were in competition ([1922b] 1940:44). Eugenics, the dominant early twentieth-century solution to racial problems, "cannot have any possible meaning with regard to whole races. It can have a meaning only with regard to strains" (45). One of Boas's major contributions to physical anthropology was to distinguish between variable populations characterized as races and individual family lines in which heredity could be treated as real. His data demonstrated that family lines within a race varied more than populations as a whole ([1931] 1940:5). By his own estimate, his studies of head-form in descendants of immigrants proved that natural selection could not be an adequate explanatory variable because he had compared children with their own parents; natural selection would apply only if it could distinguish between different family lines ([1912] 1940:70). Further, Boas was concerned that eugenics did not in principle conform to the natural development of the human species ([1915] 1940:27). In spite of the motive of eliminating human suffering, the natural development of the species seemed to require uncontrolled development. Science could not expect to provide a simple route to evolutionary viability.

Several papers on race appeared in German sources, two in 1913 and one in 1932. Boas was introduced to physical anthropology through Rudolph Virchow during his training in physics in Germany. During his self-professionalization as an anthropologist in the late 1880s and early 1890s, Virchow's influence was crucial to the development of his thinking about race. Virchow had moved from anatomy to cellular pathology and discussed biological process in terms of environment, history, and anti-Darwinian science, even allowing for environmental influences on head-form (Stocking 1968:166). Boas's idea of science included from the start the possibility of research into the plasticity of human racial types. Throughout his career he continued to publish in Germany and recognized the continuity and compatibility of his anthropology with the German science of his training.

The remainder of Boas's publication outlets are unremarkable for an anthropologist. Three book reviews in *Science* reflect his position as book review editor, and two through the National Academy of Sciences in 1916 and 1935 reach out to speak to a larger audience beyond his own discipline. One further paper in the *American Anthropologist* reported on the immigrant head-form study carried out between 1910 and 1913. A final paper in a volume honoring Alfred L. Kroeber dealt with the relationship between physical and social anthropology. The range of audiences for Boas's physical anthropology papers and the time span over which they appeared are at least as significant as the range of topics.

> The problem of physical anthropology is as definite as that of the other branches of anthropology. It is the determination and explanation of the occurrence of different types of man[kind] in different countries. The fact that individuals cannot be classified as belonging to a certain type shows that physical anthropology cannot possibly lead to a classification of mankind as detailed as does the classification based on language. The sta-

tistical study of types will, however, lead to an understanding of the blood-relationship between different types. It is probable that it will also lead to the establishment of a number of good types which have remained permanent through long periods. ([1936] 1940: n.p.).

The later papers in RLC suggest that the original empirical question of the priority of biology over culture had been resolved for the discipline as a whole so that it was possible to stress one classificatory variable for analytical purposes without that provisional reductionism destroying the overall perspectives on types and variability of mankind. Boas argued ([1931] 1940:13) that ethnological evidence documents that hereditary racial traits are far less important than cultural conditions, and that ethnologists therefore tend to ignore questions of race in order to focus on variations in cultural form. He further noted ([1936] 1940:172) that physical and social anthropology had drifted apart in recent decades and that it was probably no longer possible for a single individual to deal in depth with both. On the other hand, he saw it as crucial that the borderline area between the two not be neglected. To understand the history of society, one must first understand the history and origin of each racial type. The physical anthropologist must employ ethnic data in order to interpret his statistical results. Therefore, the two remain analytically interdependent, although each continues to use his [sic] own methods: "While the physical anthropologist is likely to look at functional phenomena as expressions of structure, the ethnologist will bear in mind the varying conditions influencing functions" (172). By implication, the anthropologist needs both perspectives.

As specialization continued apace, the significance of headform as an anthropometric measurement became the paramount issue for his colleagues in assessing Boas's contribution to physical anthropology. Boas initially accepted the conventional position that cephalic index was useful for classifying the types of mankind as a permanent racial characteristic, not subject to environmental modification. Boas was surprised by the initial results of his 1908 studies of New York Russian Jewish boys indicating unsuspected changes in cephalic index and consequently expanded his research design to demonstrate that economic advantage was an insufficient explanation for the results. Wide changes took place for immigrants from all populations in the American context, although not all were in the same direction and not all were beneficial; Boas realized these research results were radical and self-consciously argued for the plasticity of the human type, even with regard to the presumably stable trait of head-form (Stocking 1968:176–77).

Between 1908 and 1910, Boas carried out extensive investigations of head-form for the United States Immigration Commission. Although he refers ([1912] 1940:60) to "a work entrusted to me" by the commission, Boas in fact solicited the assignment and welcomed its funding for his researches; the commission was concerned to restrict immigration and accepted Boas's contribution largely because he defined his research in social as well as physical terms (Stocking 1968:175–76).

Boas summarized the major conclusions of the study:

1. American-born descendants of immigrants differ in type from their foreign born parents. These differences are not all the same for different ethnic groups. They develop early and persist throughout life.

2. The influence of the American environment becomes stronger in direct relationship to the time elapsed between the arrival of the mother and the birth of the child.

3. Variability is increased in direct proportion to the dissimilarity of the parents.

4. Head as well as body bulk measurements accelerate in the period before puberty.

5. The average stature of children decreases with family size.

6. The data necessitate comparison of groups which have immigrated at different times. Correlations still hold, however, when individuals born in Europe in the same year are compared.

7. The difference between immigrants and their European-born children is less than between them and their American-born children.

8. American-born children of immigrants have a narrower facial width, presumably a cumulative effect of the American urban environment, although the matter is complicated by the fact that the face width of immigrants is also declining.

9. Studies of Hebrew boys at different stages of puberty demonstrate that retardation of growth tempo will not explain the variation.

10. Numerical values can be obtained for pigmentation which provide another dimension to the analysis. ([1912] 1940:60–67)

Differences in ancestry cannot explain the differences in head-form because parents are being compared to their own children. Explanations based on a selection factor favoring urban populations are inadequate because the same differences occur in children of immigrants. Plasticity of form must be acknowledged even though it cannot be explained. Thus, Boas eschews explanation on methodological grounds:

> It will, therefore, be seen that my position is that I find myself unable to find an explanation of the phenomena, and that all I can try to do is to prove that certain explanations are impossible. I think this position is not surprising, since what happens here happens in every purely statistical investigation. The resultant figures are merely descriptions of facts which in most cases cannot be discovered by any other means. These observations, however, merely set us a biological problem that can be solved only by biological methods. ([1912] 1940:70)

It is possible to place far too much emphasis on arbitrary types:

> If we establish a number of arbitrary types, it is always possible to analyze a series of observations accordingly, but this analysis does not prove the correctness of our subjective classification and the existence of the selected forms as types, but is due merely to the fact that the distribution of observations can be made according to any fitting theory; but the correctness or incorrectness of the theory can be proved only in exceptional cases. The greater the number of types that are to be segregated, the more arbi-

trary becomes the method, and almost any analysis according to a sufficient number of types can be made. ([1912] 1940:73)

A genuine type must be described in terms of its average, its variability, and its relative frequency.

Boas's concept of the importance of head-form was substantially modified by his experimental work. He suggested ([1899b] 1940:158) that the cephalic index was one means of describing racial types but not the only one. Measurements should be selected according to observed differences, not decided in advance. After the immigration studies, Boas no longer argued that head-form was useful for classifying racial groups. Rather, he felt that physiological change occurred in a new environment and that genetic factors could not be responsible ([1916] 1940:80). Soon he was arguing ([1899b] 1940:159) that his evidence for environmental influence was "entirely incontrovertible," although the causes of the changes remained "entirely obscure." He referred vaguely to animal experiments dealing with "chemical change under new environmental conditions," but clearly an effective causal mechanism was not yet available in the theoretical toolkit of physical anthropology. The old notion of natural selection had been "overestimated" ([1931] 1940:8) because changes were necessarily limited by the range of variation in the original population. Boas toyed with the idea of neo-Lamarckian direct environmentalism but was not satisfied with this either (Stocking 1968:184).

The immigrant head-form studies were more effective at posing questions than at answering them. Boas stated the basic issues of studying the population of the United States in remarkably succinct form ([1922b] 1940:48):

1. degree of population homogeneity

2. hereditary characteristics of existing lines

3. influences of environment

4. influence of selection

Despite of his initial optimism that physical anthropology would ultimately answer the pressing problems of American immigration policy, real explanations were not, and perhaps could not be, forthcoming at the time.

Much of Boas's emphasis on the importance of physical anthropology arose from his fieldwork. Rohner (1966:205–7) catalogs the subjects Boas studied during his various expeditions. Anthropometric measurements, photographs, and skeletal collections appeared in 1886, 1888, 1890, 1894, 1897, 1900, and 1914 and were absent only in 1889 and 1891. After 1914 physical anthropology played no further role in Boas's fieldwork. His fieldwork reflected the need for basic classification in the early twentieth century and moved on when that was accomplished. The institutions that sponsored Boas's fieldwork, primarily the British Association for the Advancement of Science and the Bureau of American Ethnology, were not yet prepared to support intensive fieldwork on particular topics in particular societies. Boas's letters and diaries clarify his thinking on the value of anthropometric measurements (or ethnic classification in general): In 1888, he complained (Rohner 1969:88): "It is most unpleasant work to steal bones from a grave, but what is the use, someone has to do it. . . . I hope to get a great deal of anthropometric material here." In 1890 he noted (122–23) that his measurements gave clear evidence of a migration from the east to the Columbia River. He was particularly elated by this conclusion because John Wesley Powell, director of the Bureau of American Ethnology, which sponsored the work, did not recognize the utility of racial classification for reconstructing culture history. Boas believed that his data would prove to Powell the significance of such sources of inference; there is no evidence whether Powell responded. In 1894 (Rohner 1966:157) he was delighted at locating a group of Indians [*sic*] representing "a completely new type" that had the characteristics of the tribes found further to the north. By implication, Boas expected this to aid in reconstructing the culture history of the Northwest Coast.

These results are at variance with Boas's later research on immigrant head-form in which he demonstrated to his own satisfaction that basic anthropometric measurements were subject to rapid change and therefore had no utility for the reconstruction of culture history. As Boas became less concerned with the classification of Indian [*sic*] tribes on an anthropometric basis, he turned increasingly to ethnological research for that purpose. In 1897 he noted (Rohner 1969:225): "Although I should like to get some

Physical Anthropology   337

more measurements, I think that the ethnological work is more important, and so I cannot use much time for measurements." The Northwest Coast fieldwork was quite traditional and conservative in its use of the tools of physical anthropology. Only in his later studies, particularly of immigrant head-form, did Boas break new theoretical ground. This is why he is legitimately remembered as a physical anthropologist, but it also masks the early importance of the anthropometric markers that he applied alongside folk-lore elements when tracing migrations and culture contacts in the absence of written records.

Boas was appointed as docent in the psychology department at Clark University in 1889. In his subsequent association with its president, psychologist G. Stanley Hall, Boas began to study child development and the effects of environment on growth and was "shocked by the formalism" of studies of racial type; he came to believe that particular measurements might well be subject to influence of the environment and that historical inference must await explanation of observed phenomena (Stocking 1968:165–66). Boas's studies of Worcester, Massachusetts, schoolchildren, begun in 1891, pioneered in longitudinal methods and were supplemented by cross-sectional data from Oakland, California, and Toronto, Ontario, carried out in conjunction with the World's Columbian Exposition in Chicago (Stocking 1968:171). Boas was also a pioneer in discussing tempo of growth, noting, for example, that boys and girls developed at different rates. In reference to implications of growth studies for racial classification, he emphasized the most generalized forms, those of women and children (Boas [1897] 1940:154). Given the small size of the body at birth, environment had to influence development. "Proof" for this assertion came from the correlation of European stature increase over the last half-century with improving economic conditions ([1922b] 1940:36). Boas therefore argued that hereditary differences had to be distinguished from those due to acceleration or retardation of growth (53). Types should be based on the adult male because female forms have developed faster, and younger forms showed less evidence of racial type (48). Progressive differentiation, differently manifested in different parts of the population by age and sex, was the necessary basis of any meaningful classification.

In spite of Boas's contributions to the early study of growth, however, his conclusions were framed in terms of the basis of the racial classification that was always the crux of his physical anthropology.

The analytic distinction between race, language, and culture is one of the most characteristic tenets of Boas's anthropological theory. His best-known expositions of the interdependence of these three variables came in the introduction to the *Handbook of American Indian Languages* (1911a) and in *The Mind of Primitive Man* (1911b). In the former he began by claiming independence of linguistic classification from that by physical type or customs and elaborated on ethnographic and historical examples that the three were not necessarily connected. A single, adequate classification was not possible:

> We recognize thus that every classification of mankind must be more or less artificial, according to the point of view selected, and here, even more than in the domain of biology, we find that classification can only be a substitute for the genesis and history of the now existing types. (1911a:10)

In other words, the real questions could not yet be answered, and any single classificatory variable could provide only a partial picture of ethnic history.

Boas's notions of the independence of race, language, and culture were established long before this formal statement in 1911. His review of William Z. Ripley ([1899a] 1940:159) praised the author for recognizing this point:

> We most heartily concur with the author's emphatic demand for treating physical, ethnographic, and linguistic methods separately. . . . The three methods may be used, each in its particular domain, for reconstructing part of the history of mankind, and each may be used, to a limited extent, as a check on the two others.

An 1897 review of Ehrenreich praised the combination of somatological, ethnological, and linguistic methods, generalizing that the three variables provided answers to different questions because they did not refer to the same class of facts ([1897] 1940:153): "In our investigations on the early history of mankind, three methods are available, each directed to a certain species of phenomena—physical type, language, customs. These are not transmitted and do not develop in the same manner."

In the new series of the *American Anthropologist*, Boas stressed that physical anthropology must not abrogate the search for meaningful types in spite of classification problems ([1899b] 1940:171). The reality, or lack of reality, of racial types continued to be Boas's particular hobbyhorse. He asserted that racial differences were quantitative, showing greater variability within than between types, such that postulation of idealized types obscured real variation. Man[kind] was, however, a typologizing animal ([1931] 1940:4): "We are apt to construct ideal local types which are based on our everyday experience, abstracted from a combination of forms that are most frequently seen in a given locality."

Boas went so far as to claim that homogeneous populations existed nowhere in the world ([1922b] 1940:38), which entails that ideal types could not exist either. In order for a population to sustain stable heredity, each generation would have to have the same distribution of forms; this was quite a different matter from the individual heredity of bodily form and function (33). Moreover, the head-form studies had indicated considerable "environmental influence within lines of descent. There is no necessary reason to assume that racial mixture will always produce increased variability or that variability cannot occur within pure lines of descent" (55). Because this variability is so extensive, and cannot be tidily explained, racial types become useless for reconstruction of culture history. It remains, therefore, an empirical question what changes take place in particular groups under particular environmental conditions.

Once environmental influence could be demonstrated, a genetic type could never be said to exist in stable form; rather, every genetic type had to be specified in terms of the variable environmental conditions under which it might appear; the classification of European races could not be taken as proving genetic differentiation because variation within the type was as extensive as the variation between types (1916 1940:77). Boas did not consider the American case, from which his own data came, to be intrinsically different from the European one:

> The differences are due to the large number of individuals
> involved in the whole process, in its rapidity, in its extension
> over rural communities, and in the forms of cohesion between
> members of the same group which are dependent upon the
> mode of settlement of the country. ([1922b] 1940:31)

The processes, whatever their explanation, were characteristic of
all human populations; they did not operate differently in the case
of relatively isolated portions of humankind.

Much of the absence of explanation in these data and their
analysis arises from the state of theory in physical anthropology at
the time. Mendel's laws of inheritance were rediscovered in 1900,
but the implications for modern genetics were not fully clarified
until the 1930s (Washburn 1968:99). In the period before 1900,
the pressing question was simply to demonstrate the existence of
evolution (Penniman 1935:182; Washburn 1968:99). Boas partici-
pated minimally in both of these paradigms of physical anthropology. His critique of the evolution of culture precluded the one, and
his lack of involvement in emerging genetic researches obscured
the importance of the other. The issue for Boas was the conflict
between Galton's notion of new intermediate types and the Mendelian concept of unit characters of parents that are segregated
in a mixed population. He felt that some traits illustrated both
phenomena: "It is hardly possible at the present time to answer
this important problem with any degree of definiteness, although
in regard to a number of traits sufficient evidence is available."
In the instance of head-form, there is considerable variability in
the offspring of diverse parents, but also a tendency to revert to
the parental types ([1915] 1940:23): "Whether or not the classical
ratios of Mendelian inheritance prevail is a question that is quite
impossible to answer. On the whole, it seems much more likely
that we have varying types of alternating inheritance rather than
true Mendelian forms."

Boas believed that answers would be forthcoming:

> Unfortunately, the laws of heredity in man are not clearly known,
> and it is not yet possible without overstepping the bounds of
> sound, critical, scientific method to apply them to the study of
> the characteristics of a population. A considerable amount of

work must be done before we can proceed to the explanation of special complex phenomena. ([1922b] 1940:34)

Boas was correct that future developments in genetics would clarify these issues, but he himself made no contribution to that process. If nothing else his skepticism about the generalizations of genetics prevented him from devoting further attention to the matter:

> It is obvious that all phenomena of such complexity as length of body and tempo of development must be governed by many hereditary factors and that we are dealing with a phenomenon of general organization of the body and that a search for genes would not be advisable. Is there not some danger anyway, that the number of genes will depend rather on the number of investigators than on their actual existence? ([1935] 1940:88)

This rather querulous comment confirms that Boas did not understand the work being done in the new genetics and that his own thinking remained mired in the earlier conflict between the models of Galton and Mendel for explaining racial variability.

Boas's methodological observations, however, are more substantial. In all of his scientific work, Boas stressed that classification was in danger of being arbitrary unless causes were definitely and empirically delimited. The cephalic index was a convenient measure, but there was no evidence that it was biologically significant. Any anthropometric measurement was an artifact of multiple causes that could rarely be specified. Boas further believed that such measurements were not independent ([1902] 1940:136). "As a matter of fact, there are hardly two measurements that do not influence each other to a certain extent." It was not, then, scientifically valid to treat measurements as biological realities. Despite the difficulties in using measurements, it was crucial to seek non-arbitrary measurements:

> A number of investigators object to the metric method of anthropology, and desire to bring about a substitution of description for measurements. The necessity of making measurements developed when it was found that the local varieties of mankind were very much alike—so much so that a verbal description failed to make their characteristics sufficiently clear. The process by

means of which measurements have been selected has been a purely empirical one. It has been found that certain measurements differ considerably in various races and are for this reason good classificatory criteria. The function of measurements is therefore solely that of giving greater accuracy to the vague verbal description. It is true that in the course of time a tendency has developed of considering as the sole available criteria of race the measurements which by experience have been found to be useful. This is true particularly of the so-called cephalic index. . . . Anthropologists who limit their work to the mechanical application of measurements, particularly of single measurements, and who try to trace the relationships of races by such means, do not apply the metric method in a correct way. . . . I believe the tendency of developing a cast-iron system of measurements, to be applied to all problems of physical anthropology, is a movement in the wrong direction. Measurements must be selected in accordance with the problem that we are trying to investigate. . . . Measurements should always have biological significance. As soon as they lose their significance they also lose their descriptive values. ([1899] 1940:168–69)

Biological significance was an issue that deeply concerned Boas. Because of his emphasis on the functional role of metric measurements, his theory of human physical development and variability must be characterized as a dynamic one. Boas believed that the form of the body was less important than its functioning ([1931] 1940:8) and that behavioral differences could never be explained solely by anatomy; every human organism has the capacity to adjust to a wide range of environmental conditions, and racial groups in the same conditions generally react similarly (9).

Boas extended this argument to the question of racial distribution of intelligence, asserting that intelligence was socially determined and correlated with experience, economic conditions, and other cultural variables. His examination of human history convinced him that major changes in mental behavior occurred frequently among peoples with the same genetic heritage; the complexity of human cultural constructs makes it unlikely that the biological basis for behavior could ever be isolated ([1931]

1940:11): "I strongly suspect . . . that it will be found impossible to construct any test in which this element of experience is so completely eliminated that we could consider the results as an expression of purely biologically determined factors."

In summarizing Boas's position as a physical anthropologist, we may recognize his insistence that the physical variability of mankind is not particularly important, and that biological problems in the study of mankind lead inevitably to cultural questions. Boas's physical anthropology was always part of his anthropology in the broader sense beyond anatomical study. Questions of race had to take priority because they were limiting factors on cultural expression; but the shift in priority from race to language to culture was theoretically significant and consistent throughout Boas's long career.

His influence cannot, however, be understood solely in terms of his ideas. Institutional factors are equally crucial in the development of a discipline, even of an intellectual paradigm. Boas aspired in the first two decades of the twentieth century to organize anthropological research in America, and to organize it under his control. Established gatekeepers did not fall under his dominance, and the emergence of Boasian anthropology (Darnell 1969, 1971) was a gradual process that even Boas himself at times considered problematical. On the one hand, it involved professionalization around academic departments of anthropology, leaving government and museum anthropology largely within the older establishment. Boasian anthropology became, simply because of these conditions, increasingly focused around cultural anthropology. The dual centers for physical anthropology and archaeology in North America during the first two decades of the century were the BAE and Harvard. Opposition to the emerging Boasian hegemony was focused in these camps.

Stocking (1968) has taken Boas's censure by the American Anthropological Association in 1919 (only incidentally precipitated by his strong stand against spying activities of scientists during wartime) as a microcosm of the inherent tensions dividing the discipline at that time. It was, in retrospect, the death throes of the older establishment dominance of anthropology. For present purposes, it is significant that the physical anthropologists allied themselves with the archaeologists and voted for censure. Boas was also forced to resign from the NRC Committee on Anthropology, again an issue that raised questions of who would control the focus of the discipline (through funding and prestige) as it moved toward professionalization. Henry Holmes and Aleš Hrdlička agreed to serve, alongside amateurs with racialist tendencies such as Charles Davenport and Madison Grant. Superpatriotism was in vogue, as was eugenics, and many of the moving forces behind the NRC were nonprofessionals. Stocking (1968:289) refers to the "scientific reaction against cultural anthropology," but stresses that professionalism was well established within anthropology as a whole and those who supported the excesses of the NRC eventually suffered for it professionally. Stocking (289) further suggests that the scientific legitimacy of anthropology was questioned because it subordinated biology to culture. As long as anthropology focused on problems of human biology within an evolutionary framework, it was acceptable as a science and seemed to offer potential solutions to serious social problems that could be redefined as biological problems. Boas's critique of evolution made it more difficult for non-anthropologists in the academy and the general public alike to comprehend the nature of the generalizations that might be expected to emerge from anthropology. The interdisciplinary NRC Committee was critical of anthropology because of its perceived myopic focus on the American Indian [sic] and because it devoted so little attention to the question of races in America (Stocking 1968:297). Paradoxically, these were issues that Boas had addressed. But because he saw the scope of anthropology as being far wider, he found himself increasingly pigeonholed, at least outside the discipline, as a cultural anthropologist.

The retrospective evaluation of Boas's contribution to the history of physical anthropology cannot be made in simple terms. His early research stressed plasticity and variability in the study of race; he pioneered in studies of growth and development. Many of his statements are surprisingly modern; other are very much of a bygone era. Regardless, there is little continuity from Boas to modern physical anthropology. His work has effectively faded into oblivion, perhaps to be rediscovered by later generations to the extent that his observations have stood the test of time. This paradox is explained partly in Boas's failure to grapple successfully with explanation of the phenomena he described. His lack of understanding of genetics led him in a direction counter to that of the emerging physical anthropology.

Boas played a crucial role in influencing public opinion on questions of race and the social implications of research in physical anthropology. He took on this spokesperson role self-consciously and was consistently concerned to point out the lack of scientific basis for stereotypes, prejudices, and racial strife. Twentieth-century politics have rendered these issues particularly acute in determining the future history of mankind, particularly in North America. Many of Boas's basic claims about the nature of racial and individual variability and the influence of environment on both physical and mental development have become so widely accepted in our society generally that they no longer appear innovative or even very interesting.

Finally, there is the issue of what Boas contributed to the institutional development of physical anthropology in North America. After about 1920, physical anthropology became increasingly specialized and decreasingly Boasian. His students and close associates tended to work in cultural anthropology or linguistics. Nonetheless, there is one sense in which Boas's influence on the institutional development of physical anthropology is undeniable: he insisted on a broad definition of the scope of anthropology that integrated physical, cultural. and linguistic anthropology, as well as archaeology. In spite of its specialization, therefore, physical anthropology remains, to a considerable degree, a social or biocultural science rather than solely a biological one, at least with regard to questions it asks and the kind of explanatory variables that are legitimately proposed for empirical examination.[2]

Notes

1. Originally published as "Franz Boas and the Development of Physical Anthropology in North America," *Canadian Journal of Anthropology* 3 (1982): 101–12.

2. Other discussions of Boasian physical anthropology not cited in this paper include Cole (1931), Goldstein (1948, 1981), Herskovits (1943), Hyatt (1979), Slater (1975), and Tanner (1959).

References

Boas, Franz. (1894) 1940. "The Half-Blood Indian." *Popular Science Monthly (October)*. RLC: 138–48.

———. (1897) 1940. "Review of Dr. Paul Ehrenreich, 'Anthropoligische Studien ueber die Urechwohner Brasiliens.'" *Science* 6:880–83. RLC: 149–54.

———. (1899a) 1940. "Review of William Z. Ripley, 'The Races of Europe.'" *Science*. RLC: 155–59.

———. (1899b) 1940. "Some Recent Criticism of Physical Anthropology." *American Anthropologist* 1. RLC: 165–71.

———. (1902) 1940. "Statistical Study of Anthropometry." *American Physical Education Review*. RLC: 131–37.

———. (1910–13) 1940. "Changes in Bodily Form of Descendants of Immigrants." *American Anthropologist*. RLC: 60–75.

———. 1911a. Introduction to *Handbook of American Indian Languages. Bureau of American Ethnology Bulletin* 40:1–83. Washington DC: Government Printing Office.

———. 1911b. *The Mind of Primitive Man*. New York: Macmillan.

———. (1912) 1940. "Remarks on the Anthropological Study of Children." International Congress on Hygiene and Demography. RLC: 94–102.

———. (1913) 1940. "Influence of Heredity and Environment upon Growth." *Zeitschrift für Ethnologie*. RLC: 82–85.

———. (1915) 1940. "Modern Populations of America." Nineteenth International Congress of Americanists. RLC: 18–27.

———. (1916) 1940. "New Evidence in Regard to the Instability of Human Types." National Academy of Sciences. RLC: 76–78.

———. (1922a) 1940. "The Measurement of Differences between Variable Quantities." *Quarterly Publication of the American Statistical Union*. RLC: 181–90.

———. (1922b) 1940. "Report on an Anthropometric Investigation of the Population of the United States." RLC: 28–59.

———. (1931) 1940. "Race and Progress." American Association for the Advancement of Science, Presidential Address. RLC: 3–17.

———. (1932) 1940. "Race and Character." *Anthropologischer Anzeiger*. RLC: 191–95.

———. (1935a) 1940. "Conditions Controlling the Tempo of Development and Decay." Association of Life Insurance Medical Directors of America. RLC: 89–93.

———. (1935b) 1940. "The Tempo of Growth of Fraternities." National Academy of Sciences. RLC: 86–88.

———. (1936) 1940. "The Relations between Physical and Social Anthropology." *Essays for A. L. Kroeber*. Analysis of Anthropometrical Series, 1913, Archiv fiir Rassen-und Gesellschafts Biologie. RLC: 172–75.

———. 1940. *Race, Language and Culture*. New York: Free Press. (All papers cited to their original date of publication, in RLC)

Cole, Fay-Cooper. 1931. "The Concept of Race in the Light of Franz Boas' Studies of Head Form among Immigrants." In *Methods in Social Science*, edited by Stuart A. Rice, 582–85. Chicago: University of Chicago Press.

Darnell, Regna. 1969. "The Development of American Anthropology, 1879–1920: From the Bureau of American Ethnology to Franz Boas." PhD diss., University of Pennsylvania.

———. 1971. "The Professionalization of American Anthropology: A Case Study in the Sociology of Knowledge." *Social Science Information* 10:83–103.

Goldstein, M. 1948. "Franz Boas' Contributions to Physical Anthropology." *American Journal of Physical Anthropology* 6:145–61.

———. 1981. "Franz Boas, 1858–1942." *American Journal of Physical Anthropology* 5:491–93.

Gruber, Jacob W. 1967. "Horatio Hale and the Development of American Anthropology." *Proceedings of the American Philosophical Society* 111:5–37.

Herskovits, Melville J. 1943. "Franz Boas as Physical Anthropologist." *American Anthropologist* 45:39–51.

Hyatt, Marshall. 1979. "The Emergence of a Discipline: Franz Boas and the Study of Man." PhD diss., University of Delaware.

Penniman, T. K. 1935. *A Hundred Years of Anthropology*. London: Gerald Duckworth.

Rohner, Ronald P. 1966. "Franz Boas: Ethnographer on the Northwest Coast." In *Pioneers of American Anthropology*, edited by June Helm, 149–212. Seattle: University of Washington Press.

———, ed. 1969. *The Ethnography of Franz Boas: Letters and Diaries of Franz Boas Written on the Northwest Coast from 1886 to 1931*. Chicago: University of Chicago Press.

Slater, P. G. 1975. "Franz Boas and the American Physical Character." *History of Anthropology Newsletter* 2:11–13.

Stocking, George W., Jr. 1968. *Race, Culture and Evolution: Essays in the History of Anthropology*. New York: Free Press.

———, ed. 1974. *The Shaping of American Anthropology, 1883–1911: A Franz Boas Reader*. New York: Basic Books.

Tanner, J. M. 1959. "Boas's Contributions to Knowledge of Human Growth and Form." In *The Anthropology of Franz Boas*, edited by Walter Goldschmidt, 76–111. Washington DC: American Anthropological Association.

Washburn, Sherwood. 1968. "Biosocial Anthropology." In *One Hundred Years of Anthropology*, edited by John O. Brew, 97–118. Cambridge MA: Harvard University Press.

Weiner, Joseph S. 1935. "Physical Anthropology: A Survey of Development." In *A Hundred Years of Anthropology*, edited by T. K. Penniman, 285–320. London: Gerald Duckworth.

INDEX

Page locators in italics refer to illustrations.

Franklin, Benjamin, 24, 97–98, 111
Franz Boas Papers (FBP): editorial decisions and selections for thematic editions, 102
freedom: standards of (Benedict), 243, 248; as value (Boas), 31
functionalism, British, 315. *See also* Institute of Human Relations (IHR)
funding for research, 290, 299, 328; during Depression, 260; in Haas field report, 282–83; for language psychology, 306; in Philadelphia, 75; for Sapir at Yale, 212; during World War I cutbacks in Ottawa, 174

Gallatin, Albert, 98, 192–93
Galton, Sir Francis, on intermediate types, 341
Gatschet, Albert: as APS cohort, 10; on authorship of linguistic classification, 191–94
Geertz, Clifford, 79. *See also* Malinowski, Bronislaw: impact of diaries
—Works: *Works and Lives*, 79–80, 83, 236, 239, 250
gender inclusivity, xxiv
General Education Board, New York City, 301, 304
general law, 17
general laws as premature, 312; for growth of culture, 312; for human cultural development, 312
general public: as audience for science, 13, 18; evaluating generalizations in science, 345
"genius," 4; Sapir as, 154–55, 263; Whorf as, 264
geology (Powell), 24
German scholarship: as American model, 29; and German university system, 30
Gestalt psychology, 296. *See also* Jung, Carl
Gifford, Edward, 170–71
Gillin, John, 227, 231
Gleach, Frederic W., ix
Goddard, Ives: on Ritwan, 203
Goddard, Pliny Earle: on Indo-European, 162, 196
Goldenweiser, Alexander, 7, 10 , 89, 157,

310; artificial character of, 323; on totemism, 239, 313–14
Gordon, George: as director of Penn Museum, 69–75
"gossip," 86, 92, 182
government service: linguists in, post–World War II, 284
Graebner, Fritz: and northern culture circle, 323
grammar, dictionary, and texts as necessary to describe a language, 8, 138, 150, 196, 282
Grant, Madison: racialist tendencies of, 345. *See also* eugenics
"Great Man" Theory of History, 16, 292

Haas, Mary, xvi, 275–85, 276; divorce from Swadesh, 279, 282; ethnological task as linguist, 280; interview with Stephen O. Murray, 277; as mentor, 277; need for job placement after divorce, 279; on responsibility to language, 277; Tunica in *Handbook of American Indian Languages*, 283
Haile, Father Berard, 147–49
Hall, G. Stanley, 338
Hallowell, A. Irving "Pete," xvii, 2–3, 231, 239; anthropology as an anthropological problem, 84, 104, 309–25
—Works: *Culture and Experience*, 323
Harrington, John P., 88; idiosyncratic orthography, 277; on philology, 196
Harris, Marvin, 235
—Works: *The Rise of Anthropological Theory*, 14
Hatoum, Rainer: and Boas's shorthand Kwakiutl (Kwakwala) fieldnotes, 107
head-form: in family lines for anthropometric measurement, 333; for Immigration Commission, major conclusions of, 99, 334–35; as stable trait, 334
Henry, Joseph, 26. *See also* institutions: Smithsonian Institution
Henshaw, H. W.: on authorship of Powell classification, 191–94, 195–96
Herskovits, Melville, 125, 127; as second-generation Boasian student of race, 130. *See also* historiography
Herzog, George: as ethnomusicologist

and linguist, 284; and first and second Yale schools of linguistics, 285; on Yale courses, 215. *See also* Swadesh, Morris; Voegelin, Carl

Hilprecht, Herman: as archaeologist at Penn Museum, 60, 62, 67

historical particularism, 99, 118, 146, 158, 271, 316–17

historiography, 1, 190, 203

history, definition of, 25

history of anthropology: definition of, as anthropological problem (Hallowell), 2; as narrative (H. White), 3

Hockett, Charles: on Indo-European sound change, 201; on Kickapoo and Pottawatomi, 218; on principles of comparative method in Bloomfield's Algonquian, 200–201

Hoenigswald, Henry: on Indo-European, 189

Hoijer, Harry, 230; as editor of Whorf, 263

Holmes, Henry: at National Research Council, 345

hormonal gene expression, epigenetic, 106

Hrdlička, Aleš, 84; at National Research Council, 345. *See also* eugenics

Hull, Clark: behaviorism of, 227, 303. *See also* Institute of Human Relations (IHR); May, Mark; Murdock, George Peter

immigrant head-form, 99, 104–5, 332, 336–38

Immigration Commission, U.S. *See* cephalic index

immigration policy, political implications of, 331

Indian [*sic*] tribes: Alabama, 282; Aymara (Peru), 275–76; Aztec, 244; Bella Coola, 299–300, 304; Canadian Blackfoot, 248; Choctaw, 282; Creek (Muskogee), 283, 289; Hitchiti, 280, 282, 283; Hopi, 264, 281; Kickapoo, 218; Koasati, 282; Kwakiutl (Kwakwala), 241, 244; Natchez, 279, 283; Navajo, 229, 278; Ojibwe (Anishinaabeg), 245, 309; Plains Cree, xxvi, viii, 8, 275; Pottawatomi, 218, 245; San Blas (Pueblo), 281; Serano, 141, 243; Takelma, 278–79; Tsimshian, 144;

Wyandot, 27; Yana, 143, 180; Yokuts, 290–91, 299–300; Zuni, 244

Indigenous consultants: Albert "Chic" Sandoval (Navajo), 144, 147; Alex Thomas (Nootka), 184; Charley Mack (Ute), 143; Ernest Naquayouma (Hopi), 259; George Hunt (Kwakiutl [Kwakwala]), 144; Ishi (Yahi), 143, 180, 185; Tony Tillohash (Southern Paiute), 143, 148, 184–85

Indigenous protocols: governed by stewardship, 110; and visit to communities and territories, 111

Indo-European methodology, 189–203

Institute of Human Relations (IHR), 207–8, 211, 214, 226, 302. *See also* May, Mark

institutions: American Anthropological Association (AAA), Centennial Commission, ix; American Association for the Advancement of Science (AAAS), 40, 44–48, 65, 68, 89, 123, 330; American Philosophical Society (APS), ix, xii, 24, 39, 59, 97–112; American Statistical Association, 330; Anthropological Society of Washington (ASW), 25, 40, 44–46, 48; British Association for the Advancement of Science, 69, 313, 337; Bureau of [American] Ethnology (BAE), 23, 25–30, 337; Bureau of Indian Affairs (BIA), 20, 21; Canadian Association of Physical Anthropologists, xvii; Center for Urban Ethnography, x; Congress (United States), 26, 27, 29; Geological Survey of Canada, 46, 71, 91, 139; Geological Survey of the Rocky Mountain Region, 25, 26; Institute of Human Relations (IHR), 6, 207–8, 211, 226; and intertextual construction of academic arguments over time, xx; National Academy of Sciences, 332; National Research Council, subcommittee on training fellowships, 167, 183, 291–92; Research Contemporary Cultures (RCC), 250–51; Rockefeller Foundation, 5, 148, 207–8, 211, 251, 290; Smithsonian Institution, 26–27, 40; U.S. government, 26; U.S. National Museum, 51, 64, 84, 172, 194

intellectual property: not covered by copyright, 199
intelligence as socially determined, 343
interdisciplinary social science, 289. *See also* Sullivan, Harry Stack
Irvine, Judith T., ix, xi, xiii, xv

Jackson, Jean: anthropological defensiveness about fieldnotes, 80
Jastrow, Morris, 60, 62. *See also* Brinton, Daniel Garrison
Jefferson, Thomas: APS cohort, 97; collected vocabularies, 98; Lewis and Clark Expedition, 28, 192–98. *See also* learned societies
Jenness, Diamond, 10, *87*, 140
Jessup North Pacific Expedition, 310
Joseph, John: "magic key" view of language, 270. *See also* Indo-European methodology
Jung, Carl, 179–80. *See also* Gestalt psychology

Kardiner, Abram, 243, 249, 306
Keesing, Roger, xvi
Keller, Albert, 21, 212, 228
key term, standpoint as, 9
King, Charles, xxiv–xxv
kinship and cross-cousin marriage: comparative work on (Hallowell), 323
kinship systems, 170–71
knowledge: Indigenous, 9; transportable, 26
Koerner, Konrad: as editor, 3, 111, 189
Kroeber, Alfred L.: on California language myth and diversity, 54, 56, 142; California research mandate, 140, 154; concept of superorganic, 144, 146; on culture, genuine and spurious, 181–82; as editor, 22; on native speaker intuitions, 186; on *Time Perspective*, 157
Kuhn, Thomas: "normal science," 18–19, 154; "paradigm," 19; "paradigm statement," 156; "pre-paradigmatic," 19; "scientific revolution," 6, 19
—Works: *The Structure of Scientific Revolutions*, xxv, 18–19

La Barre, Weston, 229, 278

language families: Algonquian, 189–90; Algonquian-Ritwan, 167; Athabascan, 161, 245; Indo-Chinese, 167–68; Iroquoian, 245; Muskogean, 279, 281; Nadene, 160, 167–68, 194; Penutian, 276; Pottawatomi, 245; Pueblo, 245; Siouan, 167, 281; "Standard Average European (SAE)" (Whorf), 262; Tanoan, 281, 282; Uto-Aztecan, 162, 264, 281
languages: Aymara, 275; Beothuk, 170, 194; Carrier, 184; Chippewyan, 200; Eskimo (Inuktitut), 99, 196; Haida, 162; Hebrew, 266; Hupa, 200; Kootenay, 194; Kwakiutl (Kwakwala), 142; Mayan, 266; Milpe Aztec, 264; Nahuatl, 200, 266; Navajo, 160, 200, 229; Nootka, 180; Odawa, 245; Ojibwe (Anishanaabeg), 245, 309; Ritwan, 109, 303; Southern Paiute, 184–85; Swampy Cree, 199; Takelma, 141; Thai, 275; Tlingit, 162; Tocharian, 160; Ute, 185; Wailatpuan-Lutuami-Sahaptin, 170; Wishram, 139; Wiyot, 161, 167, 199; Yana/Yahi, 143, 180, 185; Yurok, 161, 167, 199, 200; Zuni, 170, 194
Lasswell, Harold, 5, 146. *See also* Sapir, Edward; Sullivan, Harry Stack
Laufer, Berthold, 168
learned societies, 24; cohort at APS, 98, 192; in Philadelphia, 50
Levinson, Stephen C., 268–70
life history, as method, 7, 146, 227, 305
lineage, scholarly, 4
linguist, anthropologist, humanist, 4
Linton, Ralph, 231, 306
longitudinal methods, 338
Lounsbury, Floyd, 230
Lowie, Robert H., 220; on kin terms, 170; Plains collecting, for American Museum, 138, 220, 313; "shreds and patches," 239, 314; on *Time Perspective*, 138
—Works: *The History of Ethnological Theory*, 14, 22, 221
Lucy, John, 270
Lynd, Robert S. and Mary M., 245

Malinowski, Bronislaw, 224–25, 231,

Rockefeller Foundation, 5, 148, 207–8, 211
Rohner, Ronald, 337
roots of culture and personality (Boas): in Benedict, 246; in Hallowell, 319; in Newman, 306
Rouse, Irving, 229–30

salvage anthropology, 106, 111, 144, 196, 299
Sapir, Edward: concept of phoneme, 183–86; on culture genuine and spurious, 184–85; death of, 210, 285–86, 290, 296; as mentor, 305; at Penn, 71; on poetry and the aesthetic, 155; and superorganic, 146. *See also* Bloomfield, Leonard: and second Yale school of linguistics
—Works: "The Blind Old Indian and his Names," 176; collected works, xiii; "The Concept of the Phoneme," 243, 295; "Culture, Genuine and Spurious," 6; "The Psychological Reality of the Phoneme," 143, 184; "Speech as a Personality Trait," 298; "A Study in Phonetic Symbolism," 297–98; *Time Perspective in Aboriginal American Culture*, 154–55, 157–60, 196
Sapir, Florence (neé Delson), 172–73, 174, 179
Sapir, Philip: as editor, xvii
Sapir Centenary Conference (Ottawa), xiii, xvi, 189, 297
Sapirian synthesis (Darnell), 207, 211, 219
Sapir-Whorf Hypothesis, 262
"schools," xxviii; Boasian, 35, 131; Chicago School of Sociology, 5, 16, 86, 198, 207, 244; Yale linguistics, xvi
science: as a civilizational value (Boas), 100; as group product, 18
"scientific reaction against cultural anthropology," 345. *See also* Stocking, George W., Jr.
scientific societies: American Anthropological Association, 285; American Association for the Advancement of Science, 337; Linguistic Society of America, Summer Institute, 275; NAAHOLS, 189; World Congress of Sociology, x

Scott, Duncan Campbell, 176
self-concept, in history of human sciences, 18
Silverman, Sydel, xi
Small, Albion, 16–17
Smith, Harlan, 10, 174
Smith, Joshua, 106
socialization, professional, 23
Social Science Research Council: and Newman training fellowship, 292
Social Sciences and Humanities Research Council of Canada (SSHRC), xii, xiv, 101–2
society vs. culture, 5, 41. *See also* Ogburn, William Fielding; Sapir, Edward
sociology of knowledge, 13, 15
sound correspondences, xiv, 163, 189–203
specializations of early Boas students, 311
Speck, Frank: at Penn, 71–75; as Sapir cohort, 10, 161–62, 165
speech community, 7, 272
Spier, Leslie: employment of Yale students, 219; on sun dance, 239; at Yale, 222, 265. *See also* distributional studies
standardization of linguistic format for grammars, 138, 141
standpoint, 28; of Sapir, 5
statistical analysis: Sapir skeptical about, 292
statistical results: ethnic data for evaluation of, 333
Stevenson, Mrs. Sara, 61–64
Steward, Julian: *The Theory of Culture Change: The Methodology of Multicultural Evolution*, 235
Stocking, George W., Jr.: at Chicago, 24; as gatekeeper, editor, and reviewer, xxiv–xxvi; and historicism, 15; and history of anthropology, 14; as mentor, xi; pillars of divergence from (Darnell), xxiv, xxv; presentism and historicism, 1, 103
—Works: *Race, Culture and Evolution: Essays in the History of Anthropology*, 1, 15, 35, 74–75, 103, 120–21, 332–38, 345
Sturtevant, Edgar, 209, 223
subdisciplines, xxviii, xix, 311, 327–28

In the Critical Studies in the History of Anthropology series

To order or obtain more information on these or other University of Nebraska Press titles, visit nebraskapress.unl.edu.